"Patrick Regan provides a valuable study that will be an essential tool for academic research, pastoral practice, and liturgical planning. He demonstrates the organic development of the *Missale Romanum* 1970 in continuity not only with *Missale Romanum* 1962 but also with all that preceded it, and in so doing he presents the close relationship between the 'Ordinary' and the 'Extraordinary' forms of the Roman Rite. Regan's research sheds new light on the purpose and meaning of the liturgical seasons and feasts of the Roman calendar."

— Msgr. Richard B. Hilgartner
Executive Director, USCCB Secretariat of Divine Worship

"Abbot Patrick has produced a gem here. It is necessary and timely reading for anyone seeking to understand the current shape, contents, theology, and spirituality of the liturgical year, especially in the Roman Catholic Church, but ecumenically as well, given the adaptations of the *Ordo Lectionum Missae* in the New Common Lectionary used by many churches as well as common principles governing the calendar of the Church's feasts and seasons. Highly recommended."

— Maxwell E. Johnson
University of Notre Dame

"Patrick Regan's *Advent to Pentecost* is destined to become a classic in the fields of liturgiology and pastoral theology. His analysis is both meticulous and pastoral. He provides the reader with a scholarly historical orientation that is far more spiritual than it is pedantic. Throughout he offers excellent pastoral suggestions that pastors and preachers will want as a regular reference. For those of us who were shaped by the 1962 Missal, this analysis enables us to see how richer our lives and spirituality are following the reforms of the Second Vatican Council. For many it will clear away the cobwebs of nostalgia and the illusion that the 1962 Missal was inherently more reverent as Fr. Regan ably makes up for what was lacking in liturgical formation forty years ago."

— Julia Upton, RSM
St. John's University, Jamaica, New York

"What a marvelous piece of scholarship! Abbot Regan has gifted us with a novel, insightful, and fresh approach to the festal seasons. Rich theological insight, practical pastoral critique, carefully researched textual development, invaluable ritual and scriptural analysis, and a pervasive liturgical spirituality mark this book. Its content is thoroughly grounded in the paschal mystery. Its methodology is, in effect, a contemporary mystagogy. This book would quicken anyone's heart to celebrate more eagerly the readings and chants, prayers and other texts of the Eucharistic liturgy during the festal seasons."

— Joyce Ann Zimmerman, CPPS
Director, Institute for Liturgical Mi

D0148906

Patrick Regan, OSB

Foreword by Rev. Msgr. Kevin W. Irwin

Advent to Pentecost

*Comparing the Seasons
in the Ordinary and Extraordinary Forms
of the Roman Rite*

A PUEBLO BOOK

Liturgical Press   Collegeville, Minnesota

www.litpress.org

A Pueblo Book published by Liturgical Press

Cover design by David Manahan, OSB. Illustration by Frank Kacmarcik, OblSB.

© 2012 Patrick Regan

1	2	3	4	5	6	7	8

Library of Congress Cataloging-in-Publication Data

Regan, Patrick, 1938–
    Advent to Pentecost : comparing the seasons in the ordinary and extraordinary forms of the Roman rite / Patrick Regan.
        p.   cm.
    "A Pueblo book."
    Includes index.
    ISBN 978-0-8146-6241-0 — ISBN 978-0-8146-6279-3 (ebook)
    1. Church year meditations.   2. Catholic Church. Missale Romanum (1970)   I. Title.
    BX2170.C55R423   2012
    264'.02—dc23   2012022331

To Abbot David Melancon, OSB,

third abbot of Saint Joseph Abbey,

who in September of 1962

sent me to Collegeville for studies

Contents

Foreword

Since the publication of Pope Benedict XVI's apostolic letter *Summorum Pontificum* on the possibility of extending the celebration of the Mass as revised after the Council of Trent, the terms "ordinary form" and "extraordinary form" of the Roman Rite have become commonplace in church circles. What is also commonplace are debates about the desirability of expanding the opportunities to celebrate the extraordinary rite beyond those already established in the preexisting documents: *Quattuor abhinc annos* from the Sacred Congregation for Divine Worship (1984); *Ecclesia Dei*, the *motu proprio* of Pope John Paul II (1988); and the subsequent *motu proprio* on the application of *Summorum Pontificum* (2011). What is also commonplace, in my judgment, is that such debates are often characterized more by emotion than by reasoned arguments. Some might say they generate more heat than light.

What *Advent to Pentecost: Comparing the Seasons in the Ordinary and Extraordinary Forms of the Roman Rite* offers is a guide for how to evaluate these two forms of the Mass as they were and are celebrated. Fr. Patrick Regan's background and unquestioned competence as an eminent liturgical scholar and student of the liturgy shines forth on every page.

He admits candidly in the preface that the purpose of the book "is to show the excellence and superiority of the reformed liturgy over the previous one . . . the ordinary form over the extraordinary one." He argues this thesis by setting forth the data from all of the (very many) liturgical sources at work here: the Missal of 1570 (in light of the range of preceding sacramentaries, lectionaries, pontificals, rituals, etc.), the Missal of 1962, and the Missal of 1970 and its subsequent revisions through the (Latin) edition of 2008 and the English translation in 2011. Fr. Regan's knowledge of and engagement with these liturgical texts along with patristic and medieval authors and the Sacred Scriptures themselves reflect a man steeped in the church *lex orandi* by way of academic study, theological reflection, *lectio divina*, and personal prayer. Again and again I found myself musing about his turns of phrase, mild-mannered judgments, and keen insights into the church's prayer, especially texts and rites.

After close to forty years of praying with the Missal revised after Vatican II, one can tend to take for granted much of its richness, its theological center in the paschal mystery, and its breadth in terms of how it expands far beyond what the Missal from Trent has to offer. The amazing sea change in terms of appreciating the proclaimed Word of God from the revised Lectionary is a case in point, underscored again and again by Fr. Regan in the way he relates the readings with the Missal's texts and rites and vice versa.

What makes this book truly remarkable and truly a model for liturgical writing in general is the way he assesses both the ordinary and extraordinary forms of the Mass. While revering both forms of the Mass and indicating the theological superiority of the ordinary form, he is nonetheless very willing to critique the Missal as revised after Vatican II where necessary.

He is willing to take on "hot-button" issues, such as the translation of *pro multis* as "for many" (citing references from the Servant Songs of Isaiah and Synoptic Gospel texts to indicate where this usage came from) while at the same time noting that the literal "for many" does, in fact, mean that Christ's salvation is offered to all. He critiques the "clericalization" of the present Chrism Mass, preferring to underscore its more traditional emphases on the paschal mystery through the celebration of sacraments whose oils are consecrated and blessed at this Mass.

This very important book can be read by a number of audiences and in a number of ways. Those trained in liturgical studies will want to read it page after page and study it thoroughly. Priests and pastoral ministers will want to read it section by section as they prepare the liturgies for a given season because of the depth of historical data and theological insight it offers. Those looking for a summary of the issues involved in the "ordinary"/"extraordinary" debate will find in the final chapter an excellent and succinct summary of the issues.

This is the work of a trained and seasoned liturgical theologian. It is clear that what he writes about is what he has prayed in and through the liturgy for many years as a Benedictine monk. If "moderation" can be said to characterize the Rule of St. Benedict, "moderation" can certainly be used to characterize the style, tone, and message of this very important book. In it the author reflects the best of liturgical scholarship and wisdom gleaned from the liturgy. We are the richer for all of his efforts to write about and invite us into the prayers and rites of the liturgical seasons.

It is my hope that, given the present debates about the Mass and liturgy in general, this book will generate much light (not heat) in those debates at a time when in some quarters' shadows have tended to eclipse the breadth, depth, and profundity of the post–Vatican II reformed liturgy. This book suggests on every page why there had to be a reform and how rich it is.

Rev. Msgr. Kevin W. Irwin
Walter J. Schmitz Chair in Liturgical Studies
School of Theology and Religious Studies
The Catholic University of America
Washington, DC

Abbreviations

AAS	*Acta Apostolicae Sedis*, 103 vols. (Città del Vaticano: Libreria Editrice Vaticana, 1909 to present)
ACW	Ancient Christian Writers, 58 vols. (Westminster, MD, then New York: The Newman Press, 1949 to present)
Alc	André Wilmart, OSB, ed., *Le Lectionnaire d'Alcuin*, Biblioteca Ephemerides Liturgicae 2 (Roma: Ephemerides Liturgicae, 1937)
AMS	René-Jean Hesbert, ed., *Antiphonale Missarum Sextuplex* (Bruxelles: Vromant & Co., 1935)
ANF	The Ante-Nicene Fathers, 10 vols. (Grand Rapids, MI: Wm. B. Eerdmans Publishing Company, 1989–93, reprint)
B	Angelo Paredi and Giuseppe Fassi, eds., *Sacramentarium Bergomense*, Monumenta Bergomense VI (Bergamo: Edizioni Monumenta Bergomensia, 1962)
Bruylants	Placide Bruylants, OSB, ed., *Les oraisons du Missel Romain*, 2 vols. (Louvain: Abbaye du Mont César, 1952)
Church	Aimé Georges Martimort et al., eds., *The Church at Prayer*, trans. Matthew J. O'Connell, new ed., 4 vols. (Collegeville, MN: Liturgical Press, 1987)
CCC	*Catechism of the Catholic Church*, 2nd ed. (Washington, DC: United States Catholic Conference, 1994)
CCL	Corpus Christianorum, Series Latina, 176 vols. (Turnhout: Brepols Publishers, 1954 to present)
CSEL	Corpus Scriptorum Ecclesiasticorum Latinorum, 97 vols. (Wien: Carolus Gerold, then Osterreichischen Akademie der Wissenschaften, 1866 to present)

DACL	*Dictionnaire d'archéologie Chrétienne e de liturgie*, 15 tomes, each in 2 parts (Paris: Letouzey et Ané, 1907–53)
DOL	International Commission on English in the Liturgy, *Documents on the Liturgy 1963–1979: Conciliar, Papal, and Curial Texts* (Collegeville, MN: Liturgical Press, 1982)
EL	Ephemerides Liturgicae, 125 vols. (Roma: Centro Liturgico Vincenziano-Edizioni Liturgiche, 1887 to present)
EpW	Germain Morin, ed., "Le plus ancien *COMES* ou lectionnaire de l'Eglise romaine," *Revue Bénédictine* 27 (1910) 41–74
EvW	Germain Morin, ed., "Liturgie et basiliques de Rome au milieu du VIIe siècle d'après les listes d'evangiles de Würzburg," *Revue Bénédictine* 28 (1911) 296–330
FC	The Fathers of the Church, 122 vols. (Washington, DC: The Catholic University of America Press, 1962 to present)
G	Antoine Dumas, OSB, ed., *Liber Sacramentorum Gellonensis*, CCL 159 (1981)
GeV	Leo Cunibert Mohlberg, OSB, ed., *Liber Sacramentorum Romanae Aeclesiae Ordinis Anni Circuli (Cod. Vat. Reg. Lat. 316 / Paris Bibl. Nat. 7193, 41/56) (Sacramenarium Gelasianum)* Rerum Ecclesiasticarum Documenta, Series Maior, Fontes IV (Roma: Casa Editrice Herder, 1960)
Go	Els Rose, ed., *Missale Gothicum*, CCL 159 D (2005)
H	Jean Deshusses, ed., "*Hadrianum ex Authentico*," in *Le Sacramentaire Grégorien. Ses principales formes d'après les plus anciens manuscrits*, 2nd ed., Spicilegium Friburgense 16 (Fribourg: Editions Universitaires, 1979), nos. 2–1018
ICEL	International Commission on English in the Liturgy
JBC	Raymond E. Brown, SS, Joseph A. Fitzmyer, SJ, and Roland E. Murphy, OCarm, eds., *The Jerome Biblical Commentary*, 2 vols. in one (London: Geoffrey Chapman, 1970)

LMS	Marius Férotin, OSB, ed., *Le Liber Mozarabicus Sacramentorum*, reprint of 1912 ed., prepared by Anthony Ward, SM, and Cuthbert Johnson, OSB, Biblioteca Subsidia 78 (Roma: CLV-Edizioni Liturgiche, 1995)
M	André Wilmart, ed., "Le *COMES* de Murbach," *Revue Bénédictine* 30 (1913) 25–69
MP	Cuthbert Johnson and Anthony Ward, eds., *Missale Parisiense 1738*, Biblioteca Ephemerides Liturgicae, Subsidia, Instrumenta Liturgica Quarreriensia, Supplementa 1 (Roma: CLV-Edizioni Liturgiche, 1993)
MR 1570	Manlio Sodi and Achille Maria Triacca, eds., *Missale Romanum: Editio Princeps (1570)*, Monumenta Liturgica Concilii Tridentini 2 (Città del Vaticano: Libreria Editrice Vaticana, 1998)
MR 1962	Manlio Sodi and Alessandro Toniolo, eds., *Missale Romanum ex Decreto SS. Concilii Tridentini Restitutum Summorum Pontificum Cura Recognitum, Editio Typica, 1962*, Monumenta Liturgica Piana 1 (Città del Vaticano: Libreria Editrice Vaticana, 2007)
MR 1970	*Missale Romanum ex Decreto Sacrosancti Oecumenici Concilii Vaticani II Instauratum Auctoritate Pauli PP. VI Promulgatum, Editio Typica* (Roma: Typis Polyglottis Vaticanis, 1970)
MR 1975	*Missale Romanum ex Decreto Sacrosancti Oecumenici Concilii Vaticani II Instauratum Auctoritate Pauli PP. VI Promulgatum, Editio Typica Altera* (Città del Vaticano: Libreria Editrice Vaticana, 1975)
MR 2002	*Missale Romanum ex Decreto Sacrosancti Oecumenici Concilii Vaticani II Instauratum Auctoritate Pauli PP. VI Promulgatum Ioannis Pauli PP. II Cura Recognitum, Editio Typica Tertia* (Roma: Typis Polyglottis Vaticanis 2002)
MR 2008	*Missale Romanum ex Decreto Sacrosancti Oecumenici Concilii Vaticani II Instauratum Auctoritate Pauli PP. VI Promulgatum Ioannis Pauli PP. II Cura Recognitum, Editio Typica Tertia (emendata)* (Roma: Typis Polyglottis Vaticanis 2008)

NCE	*New Catholic Encyclopedia*, 17 vols. (New York: Mc-Graw-Hill Book Company, 1967)
NPNF	Nicene and Post-Nicene Fathers, 2nd series, 14 vols. (Grand Rapids, MI: Wm. B. Eerdmans Publishing Company, 1988–91 reprint)
NRSV	New Revised Standard Version
OHS	*Ordo Hebdomadae Sanctae Instauratus, Editio Typica* (Roma: Typis Polyglottis Vaticanis, 1956)
OLM 1981	*Missale Romanum ex Decreto Sacrosancti Oecumenici Concilii Vaticani II Instauratum Auctoritate Pauli PP. VI Promulgatum: Ordo Lectionum Missae, Editio Typica Altera* (Città del Vaticano: Libreria Editrice Vaticana, 1981)
OR	Michel Andrieu, ed., *Les Ordines Romani du haut moyen age*, 5 vols., Spicilegium Sacrum Lovaniense 11, 23, 24, 28, 29 (Louvain: Spicilegium Sacrum Lovaniense Administration, 1931–61)
PG	*Patrologiae Cursus Completus, Series Graeca*, compiled by J. P. Migne, 161 vols. (Paris, 1857–66)
PL	*Patrologiae Cursus Completus, Series Latina*, compiled by J. P. Migne, 221 vols. (Paris, 1844–64)
PR 1962	Manlio Sodi and Alessandro Tonilio, eds., *Pontificale Romanum, Editio Typica, 1961–62*, Monumenta Liturgica Piana 3 (Città del Vaticano: Libreria Editrice Vaticana, 2008)
PRG	Cyrille Vogel and Reinhard Elze, eds., *Le Pontifical Romano-Germanique du dixième siècle*, 3 vols., Studi e Testi 226, 227, and 269 (Città del Vaticano: Biblioteca Apostolica Vaticana, 1963, 1972)
PRMA	Michel Andrieu, ed., *Le Pontifical Romain au moyen-âge*, 4 vols., Studi e Testi 86–89 (Città del Vaticano: Biblioteca Apostolica Vaticana, 1938–41)
Rites	*The Roman Ritual Revised by Decree of the Second Vatican Ecumenical Council and Published by Authority of Pope Paul VI: The Rites of the Catholic Church*, study ed., 2 vols. (New York: Pueblo Publishing Company, 1990)

Rot	*Rotulus* of Ravenna, in Leo Cunibert Mohlberg, OSB, ed., *Sacramentarium Veronense (Cod. Bibl. Capit. Veron. LXXXV [80])*, Rerum Ecclesiasticarum Documenta, Series Maior, Fontes I (Roma: Casa Editrice Herder, 1956), nos. 1332–71.
RCIA	Rite of Christian Initiation of Adults, in *The Rites of the Catholic Church*, study ed., vol. 1 (New York: Pueblo Publishing Company, 1990), pp. 1–336
RM 1962	*The Daily Missal and Liturgical Manual with Vespers for Sundays and Feasts from the Editio Typica of the Roman Missal and Breviary, 1962*, Summorum Pontificum edition (London: Baronius Press, 2008)
RM 1974	*The Roman Missal Revised by Decree of the Second Vatican Ecumenical Council and Published by Authority of Pope Paul VI: The Sacramentary* (Collegeville, MN: Liturgical Press, 1974)
RM 1985	*The Roman Missal Revised by Decree of the Second Vatican Ecumenical Council and Published by Authority of Pope Paul VI: The Sacramentary* (Collegeville, MN: Liturgical Press, 1985)
RM 2011	*The Roman Missal Renewed by Decree of the Most Holy Second Ecumenical Council of the Vatican, Promulgated by Authority of Pope Paul VI and Revised at the Direction of Pope John Paul II*, third typical edition (Collegeville, MN: Liturgical Press, 2011)
RML 1981	*The Roman Missal Revised by Decree of the Second Vatican Council and Published by Authority of Pope Paul VI: Lectionary*, 3 vols. (London: Geoffrey Chapman, 1981)
Sup	Jean Deshusses, ed., *"Hadrianum Revisum Anianense cum Supplemento,"* in *Le Sacramentaire Grégorien. Ses principales formes d'après les plus anciens manuscrits*, 2nd ed., Spicilegium Friburgense 16 (Fribourg: Editions Universitaires, 1979), nos. 1019a–1805
V	Leo Cunibert Mohlberg, OSB, ed., *Sacramentarium Veronense (Cod. Bibl.Capit. Veron. LXXXV [80])*, Rerum Ecclesiasticarum Documenta, Series Maior, Fontes I (Roma: Casa Editrice Herder, 1956), nos. 1–1331

Preface

This book began in early January of 2009 with an invitation by Sister Joyce Ann Zimmerman, CPPS, then editor of *Liturgical Ministry*, to write an article about Lent for a future issue of that magazine. I agreed to do so and started to think about what I might say. In the previous year, 2008, the third typical edition of the *Missale Romanum* of Paul VI, published in 2002, had appeared in emended form. I was curious to find out how it compared with the 2002 version as well as with the first typical edition of 1970 and the second one in 1975. I was also curious about how it compared with the Missal used before 1970—one issued in 1962 under Pope John XXIII, incorporating the simplification of rubrics begun in the mid-fifties by his predecessor, Pope Pius XII, and the restored liturgies of Holy Week. I decided to write about the readings, prayers, prefaces, and chants of Lent in the most recent edition of the postconciliar Missal and how they compared with those in the last edition of the preconciliar one.[1]

This turned out to be a most rewarding exploration. I was immediately impressed at how thoughtfully the readings were selected and at how well they went together—much more so than those in the old Missal—and at how improved was the content of the new prayers and prefaces, especially in light of changed discipline concerning fast and abstinence. During the Easter holidays of 2009, as I was typing the article for *Liturgical Ministry*, the idea came of doing for the other liturgical seasons what I had just done for Lent and of doing it not in a series of articles but in a book. Liturgical Press accepted the proposal and here it is: a comparative study of the readings and rubrics, prefaces and prayers, antiphons and chants of the third edition of the Missal of Paul VI, translated into English and in use since the First Sunday of Advent 2011, with their counterparts in the 1962 Missal of John XXIII, the latest update of the so-called Tridentine Missal, first

---

[1] I am, of course, well aware that readings are not in any of the three editions of the postconciliar Missal but in the Lectionary.

published under Pope Pius V in 1570. Pope Benedict XVI in a *motu proprio* of July 7, 2007, titled *Summorum Pontificum* recognized the postconciliar Missal as the ordinary form of Mass in the Roman Rite but permitted the 1962 Missal to be used as an extraordinary form under conditions that he immediately spelled out.

It is fitting that the book appears at the present moment. This year, 2012, is the fiftieth anniversary of the 1962 Missal, and next year, 2013, will be the fiftieth anniversary of the Constitution on the Sacred Liturgy, approved by Paul VI on December 4, 1963, laying down the principles for the reform of the 1962 Missal and other service books in subsequent years. The purpose of this volume is to show the excellence and superiority of the reformed liturgy over the previous one, or, in the terminology of *Summorum Pontificum*, of the ordinary form over the extraordinary one. It is limited to the liturgical seasons—more precisely, to the temporal cycle, now called the Proper of Time. Ordinary Time, solemnities of the Lord during Ordinary Time, and feasts of saints are not included and, except for Advent and Lent, neither are weekdays. There was simply not enough time to do the research that including them would have involved. Nor was there space to print it. Being limited to the major seasons and feasts, the book does not touch the *Ordo Missae*, or Order of Mass, and contains only as much about origins and history as is necessary to explain how the Proper of Time got to be the way it is and why it is better now than it used to be.

The organization of the book is eminently simple. It treats the seasons in the order in which they occur in the 2011 translation, beginning with the First Sunday of Advent and ending with Pentecost Sunday. Since this is a comparison of two missals, depending on how similar or different they are, sometimes one is presented after the other, sometimes they are presented alongside each other, sometimes they are presented topically or thematically. In each chapter I rely as much as possible on official documents: the general rubrics of the 1962 Missal, the 1969 Universal Norms on the Liturgical Year and the Calendar, the introduction to the 1981 revised Order of Readings for Mass, which is also the introduction to the Lectionary, and, of course, texts from the missals, the Lectionary, and at times other liturgical books. More than a mere description of externals, however, this work seeks to identify and call attention to underlying theological shifts as it moves from the preconciliar Missal to the ones after Vatican II. Indeed, the originality and greatest value of the book may lie precisely here. I also point out the sources of the prayers and prefaces in the two missals, showing how each draws upon different streams of older tradition, both Roman.

During the months leading up to implementation of the new English translation of the 2008 Missal last November, many lamented the inadequacy of catechesis on the Missal when it first appeared in the early seventies. The Lectionary may have fared better. In any case, large numbers of the faithful do not yet sufficiently appreciate the astounding spiritual profundity of the reformed Missal, while others, attracted by the theocentricity and apparent reverence of the preconciliar Mass, are unaware of the deficiencies of the 1962 Missal, of how outdated is its calendar, of how weak is its repertoire of readings, prefaces, and prayers, and hence of why extensive revision was deemed desirable. This book seeks to make up for what was not done some forty years ago, while also explaining the significance of more recent developments. In this way it aims to help Catholics get beyond present tensions and make progress in realizing the hopes of the Second Vatican Council.

In concluding this introduction, I express thanks to my colleagues and confrères in Rome and at home for their interest in this project throughout the three years of research and writing, especially to Father Jeremy Driscoll, OSB, my next-door neighbor at Sant' Anselmo, who read the manuscript in the various stages of its production, made suggestions, and encouraged me to keep going.

April 1, 2012
Collegio Sant' Anselmo
Rome

Chapter 1

Advent

A. THE WORD AND ITS MEANING

1. Classical Latin

The Latin word *adventus*, from the verb *advenire*, means coming, arrival, or the fact of having arrived and so of being present. The prepositional prefix *ad* expresses movement toward and suggests arrival from afar or after a journey. In classical Latin the visit of a sovereign to a city or province in his realm, especially a first visit, is designated as an *adventus* and is frequently commemorated by a public monument or a coin bearing an inscription such as *Adventus Augusti*, "The Advent of Augustus," followed by the name of the place and date.[1] Such appearances usually involve elaborate ceremonial displays. Like papal visits in our own day, they require extensive preparation and generate enthusiastic expectation.

Adventus is also applied to the annual visit of divinities to shrines and temples in which they are thought to dwell for the duration of festivals. Reflecting the belief that emperors were deified, a Roman calendar copied in 354 refers to Constantine's accession to the throne as *Adventus Divi*, "Advent of God."[2] Early Christian mosaics sometimes show an empty throne awaiting the arrival of Christ in glory. Already we glimpse some of the resonances that the word will assume when used as the name of the season that precedes Christmas and prepares for its celebration. Absolutely essential to the meaning of the term, however, is its use in the New Testament.

[1] See Aegidius Forcellinus, ed., "Adventus," *Totius Latinitatis Lexicon*, 6 vols. (Prati: Typis Aldinianis, 1858–60) I, 110; P. G. W. Glare, ed., "Aduentus," *Oxford Latin Dictionary* (Oxford: The Clarendon Press, 1997) 55–56; Charlton T. Lewis and Charles Short, eds., "Adventus," *A Latin Dictionary* (Oxford: The Clarendon Press, 1879, reprinted in 1995) 48.

[2] Pierre Jounel, *Church* IV, 91.

2. New Testament

In the Vulgate New Testament *adventus* translates the Greek words *parousia* and *epiphaneia*. The basic meaning of *parousia* is presence, coming, advent.[3] We find it with the meaning of "presence" in 1 Corinthians 16:17 where Paul rejoices "at the coming [*parousia*] of Stephanas and Fortunatus and Achaicus."[4] Here *parousia* is rendered in Latin not as *adventus* but as *presentia*. In Philippians 2:12 Paul contrasts his presence, *parousia*, with his absence, *apousia*, writing, "You have always obeyed me, not only in my presence, but much more now in my absence." Here again the Latin counterpart of *parousia* is *presentia*. *Parousia* is also translated by *presentia* in 2 Peter 1:16.

Besides this general meaning of presence, however, *parousia* became a technical term to designate two different but closely related events. "On the one hand the word served as a cult expression for the coming of a hidden divinity, who makes his presence felt by a revelation of his power or whose presence is celebrated in the cult" and is frequently accompanied by miracles and other extraordinary phenomena. "On the other hand *parousia* became the official term for a visit of a person of high rank, especially kings and emperors visiting a province."[5] In this sense *parousia* is synonymous with the Latin *adventus* already discussed.

These two technical uses of the term "can approach each other closely in meaning, can shade off into one another or even coincide." This is seen in the New Testament when authors use *parousia* to refer to the advent or coming of Christ "and nearly always of his Messianic Advent in glory to judge the world at the end of this age."[6] In the Latin version of such passages *parousia* is *adventus*. In Matthew 24:3, for example, the disciples ask Jesus, "What will be the sign of your coming [*parousia, adventus*] and of the end of the age?" He answers that "as the

---

[3] William F. Arndt and F. Wilbur Gingrich, eds., *"parousia," A Greek-English Lexicon of the New Testament* (Chicago: The University of Chicago Press, 1957) 635.

[4] The English translation of the Bible used throughout is the *New Revised Standard Version Bible: Catholic Edition* (Nashville: Thomas Nelson Publishers, 1993). The Greek and Latin texts of the New Testament are from Eberhard Nestle, ed., *Novum Testamentum Graece et Latine* (Stuttgart: Württembergischen Bibelanstalt, 1964).

[5] Arndt-Gingrich, *"parousia,"* 635.

[6] Ibid., 635.

lightning comes from the east and flashes as far as the west, so will be the coming [*parousia, adventus*] of the Son of Man" (Matt 24:27).

In Saint Paul's two letters to the Thessalonians *adventus* translates *parousia* several times. In 1 Thessalonians 2:19 the apostle declares that the faith of Christians in Thessalonica is reason for "boasting before our Lord Jesus at his coming [*parousia, adventus*]." He prays that they be found blameless "at the coming [*parousia, adventus*] of our Lord Jesus Christ with all his saints" (3:13) and cautions that the living will have no advantage over the dead at "the coming [*parousia, adventus*] of the Lord" (4:15). Near the end of the letter he again prays that God keep the Thessalonians blameless "at the coming [*parousia, adventus*] of the Lord" (5:23). In 2 Thessalonians 2:1 Paul returns to the theme of "the coming [*parousia, adventus*] of the Lord Jesus Christ," linking it with "the day of the Lord" in 2:2 and urging his readers not to be alarmed.[7]

Except for 1 Thessalonians 2:19, the other four passages just cited all contain the expression *adventus Domini*, or "advent of the Lord." The Letter of James contains it twice: "Be patient, therefore, beloved, until the coming [*parousia, adventus*] of the Lord. . . . Strengthen your hearts, for the coming [*parousia, adventus*] of the Lord is near (Jas 5:7-8). As we will see shortly, the same expression, *adventus Domini*, will appear innumerable times in patristic and liturgical texts and for centuries will be the name of the season of Advent.

On the other hand, the Pastoral Epistles never use the word *parousia*. In them *adventus* translates *epiphaneia*, which means "appearing, appearance." Like *parousia* it likewise is a religious technical term. It refers to "a visible manifestation of a hidden divinity, either in the form of a personal appearance or by some deed of power by which its presence is made known."[8] It too refers to the final coming of Christ. Here, however, the contrast is not between presence and absence but between manifest and hidden, revealed and concealed, visible and invisible. Hence light, splendor, and glory usually surround an epiphany.

In 1 Timothy 6:14, 16, Paul charges Timothy to persevere "until the manifestation [*epiphaneia, adventus*] of our Lord Jesus Christ. . . . It is he alone who has immortality and dwells in approachable light, whom no one has ever seen or can see." The Second Letter of Paul to

---

[7] Second Peter 3:4-13 further elaborates on the connection between the Parousia, the Day of Judgment, and the Day of the Lord.

[8] Arndt-Gingrich, "*epiphaneia*," 304.

Timothy places the Lord's manifestation in the context of judgment. "In the presence of God and of Christ Jesus, who is to judge the living and the dead, and in view of his appearing [*epiphaneia, adventus*] and his kingdom" (2 Tim 4:1), it urges the recipient to continue proclaiming the message despite opposition. As a reward for such fidelity, the apostle is confident of receiving "the crown of righteousness, which the Lord, the righteous judge, will give me on that day, and not only to me but also to all who have longed for his appearance [*epiphaneia, adventus*] (2 Tim 4:8). The Letter of Paul to Titus 2:13 states that "we wait for the blessed hope and the manifestation [*epiphaneia, adventus*] of the glory of our great God and Savior, Jesus Christ."

Although the letters of Paul as well as those of James and Peter use the word *parousia* to designate the final advent of Christ, whereas the Pastoral Letters use *epiphaneia* for the same event, 2 Thessalonians 2:8 puts the two words together, declaring that the Lord Jesus will destroy the lawless one "by the manifestation [*epiphaneia, illuminatio*] of his coming [*parousia, adventus*]," or literally "by the epiphany of his parousia," which of course "is pleonastic, since both words have the same technical sense."[9]

Only once in the New Testament does the Greek word *epiphaneia* designate the appearance of Jesus in the flesh. It is in 2 Timothy 1:10, which declares that the purpose and grace of God has now been revealed "through the appearing [*epiphaneia*] of our Savior Jesus Christ, who abolished death and brought life and immortality to light through the gospel." But here, as in 2 Thessalonians 2:8, *epiphaneia* is translated by *illuminatio*, not *adventus*. In the Latin New Testament, therefore, the term *adventus*, whether translating *parousia* or *epiphaneia*, always refers to the advent of the Lord in glory as judge at the end of the ages and never to his coming in the flesh. Early in the history of the church, however, this changes.

3. Greek Fathers

Already in the opening years of the second century, Ignatius, bishop of Antioch, tells Christians in Philadelphia that what distinguishes the Gospel from the old dispensation is that it "contains the coming [*parousia*] of the Savior, our Lord Jesus Christ, his passion, his

---

[9] Ibid.

resurrection."[10] This may be the first passage in which *parousia* refers not to the advent of the Lord as judge at the close of history but to his appearance on earth as incarnate Word.

In the mid-second century Justin Martyr, writing in Greek to the emperor Antoninus Pius, for the first time mentions two comings, two *parousias*—one in the past, the other in the future. "The prophets," he asserts, "have foretold two comings [*duo parousias*] of Christ: the one, which already took place, was that of a dishonored and suffering man; the other coming will take place, as it is predicted, when he shall gloriously come from heaven with his angelic army, when he shall also raise to life the bodies of all the men that ever were, shall cloak the worthy with immortality and shall relegate the wicked, subject to sensible pain for all eternity, into the eternal fire together with the evil demons."[11]

In the *Dialogue with Trypho* Justin several times contrasts the characteristics of the two advents as found in the prophets. Some passages "refer to the first coming [*parousia*] of Christ, in which he is described as coming in disgrace, obscurity and mortality; other passages allude to his second coming [*parousia*] when he shall appear from the clouds in glory."[12] Elsewhere he asserts that Scripture "predicted that there would be two advents [*parousias*] of Christ—one in which he will appear in suffering and without honor or beauty, and the other in which he will return in glory to judge all men." He adds that "Elias will be the forerunner of the great and terrible day, namely, of his second advent [*parousia*]."[13] Later he writes that Christ at his first advent [*parousia*] was "without honor or comeliness" and "was scorned," but that "at his coming [*parousia*] in glory" he will "completely destroy all who hated him and maliciously turned their backs on him, while

---

[10] Ignatius of Antioch, *To the Philadelphians* 9, trans. Gerald G. Walsh, in FC 1, 117. Greek text in PG 5, 705.

[11] Justin Martyr, *First Apology* 52, 3, trans. Thomas B. Falls, in FC 6, 89. Greek text in PG 6, 404–5.

[12] Justin Martyr, *Trypho* 14, 8, in FC 6, 170. Greek text of this work is in PG 6, 471–800. See also *Trypho* 32, 2, in FC 6, 195.

[13] Justin Martyr, *Trypho* 49, 2, in FC 6, 221. Along similar lines in *Trypho* 40, 4, in FC 6, 209, he relates that the two goats required for Jewish sacrifice—nowhere mentioned in the Bible—"were an announcement of the two advents [*parousias*] of Christ."

bestowing upon his faithful followers rest and every other blessing they expected."[14]

Perhaps the most eloquent and extensive treatment of the difference between the two advents of Christ is that of Cyril of Jerusalem in the third quarter of the fourth century. In a Lenten catechesis based on Daniel 7:9, 13, he declares that "we preach not one coming [*parousia*] of Christ, but a second as well, far more glorious than the first. The first gave us a spectacle of his patience; the second will bring with it the crown of the kingdom of God." After contrasting Christ's two births— one of the Father and the other of Mary—he remarks that "in his first coming [*parousia*] he was wrapped in swaddling clothes in the manger; in his second he will be 'robed in light as with a cloak' (Ps 103:2). In his first coming [*parousia*] he 'endured a cross, despising shame' (Heb 12: 2); in his second he will come in glory, attended by a host of angels. We do not rest, therefore, in his first coming [*parousia*], but we look also for his second." The bishop adds that "of these two comings [*parousias*] the prophet Malachia says, 'And suddenly there will come to the temple the Lord whom you seek'; that is one coming [*parousia*]. Of the second coming [*parousia*] he says: 'And the messenger of the covenant whom you desire. Yes, he is coming, says the Lord of hosts' (Mal 3:1-3)."[15] In the Liturgy of the Hours this catechesis of Cyril is the second reading at the Office of Readings on the First Sunday of Advent and sets the tone for the whole season.

4. Latin Fathers

Evolution of the meaning of the Latin term *adventus* proceeds in much the same way as did the Greek *parousia*. Tertullian, writing in North Africa at the beginning of the third century, declares that after *Pascha*, the period of Pentecost is the most appropriate time for baptism because then was "the grace of the Holy Spirit first given and the hope of our Lord's coming [*adventus Domini*] made evident."[16] Here, of course, *adventus Domini* has its New Testament meaning of the Lord's coming in glory. In his treatise *Against Marcian*, however, Tertullian

---

[14] Justin Martyr, *Trypho* 121, 3, in FC 6, 335–36. See also the whole of *Trypho* 52, in FC 6, 226–27.

[15] Cyril of Jerusalem, *Catechesis* XV, 1–2, trans. Leo P. McCauley, SJ, and Anthony A. Stephenson, in FC 64, 53–54. Greek text in PG 33, 870–72.

[16] Tertullian, *On Baptism* 19, in Ernest Evans, ed. and trans., *Tertullian's Homily on Baptism* (London: SPCK, 1964) 41.

provides a lengthy list of quotations from the Old Testament to show that there would be two advents of Christ: the first in lowliness, the second in majesty; the one obscured by insults inflicted, the other glorious and "altogether worthy of God."[17]

Ambrose (339–97) too understands the advent of the Lord to be his coming on the clouds of heaven (Matt 24: 30) when his presence will fill the whole world, both human and natural, as it fills the heart of each believer.[18] But he also uses *adventus Domini* for the coming to earth of the Savior in his incarnation, as was prophesied.[19] For the bishop of Milan, then, there are two advents. Both are redemptive: a first for forgiving sins, *propter redimenda peccata*, and a second for curbing transgressions, *propter reprimenda delicta*.[20] Slightly later Jerome (347–419 or 420) likewise writes that the prophets and gospels teach that there are two advents of the Lord: the first when he came in humility and after that when he would come in glory.[21]

Augustine (354–430) too speaks of a first and second coming of Christ, criticizing those who failed to recognize "the time of his first coming, so that they might believe in him and so await his second coming by watching for him whenever that coming should be." He adds, "Whoever does not recognize the first coming of the Lord cannot prepare himself for the second" (*Qui enim aduentum Domini non cognouerit primum, preparare se non poterit ad secundum*).[22] The first coming is the time of Jesus' redemptive mission on earth. The second is his appearance as judge at the end of the world. In sum, the bishop of Hippo, like the other Latin fathers, maintains that "we believe in two advents of the Lord [*duos adventus Domini credimus*], one in the past, another in the future."[23]

All the authors examined thus far, both Greek and Latin, understand the Lord's first coming in the broad sense of his entire earthly

---

[17] Tertullian, *The Five Books against Marcian* 111, VII, trans. Peter Holmes, in ANF III, 326–27. Latin text in CSEL 47, 386–87.

[18] Ambrose, *Expositio evangelii secundum Lucan* X, 39, in CSEL 32, 4, 469–70. Unless otherwise noted, translations from CSEL are mine.

[19] Ambrose, *Explanatio psalmi XXXV*, 22, in CSEL 64, 65.

[20] Ambrose, *Expositio evangelii secundum Lucan* X, 17, in CSEL 32, 4, 462.

[21] Jerome, *Epistula* 121, 11, in CSEL 56, 51–52.

[22] Augustine, *Epistula* 199, 6, trans. Sister Wilfrid Parsons, SND, in FC 30, 362. Latin text in CSEL 57, 250.

[23] Augustine, *In Psalmum IX enarratio* 1, trans. mine from CCL 38, 58.

ministry marked by humility, lowliness, and obscurity and culminating in his being rejected, condemned, and crucified. A decisive change takes place in the early fifth century with John Cassian, who identifies the *adventus Domini* with his *nativitas*, thereby narrowing down the first advent to the Lord's birth. In his *Seven Books on the Incarnation of the Lord, against Nestorius*, written between 429 and 430 "at the request of the then–Roman deacon, later Pope Leo I,"[24] Cassian twice cites Baruch 3:36-38, erroneously thought to be from Jeremiah: "He was seen upon earth and conversed with men." After the second citation he comments, "You see how plainly this points to the advent and nativity of the Lord [*adventus Domini ac nativitas*]. For surely the Father . . . was not seen upon earth, nor born in the flesh."[25] Elsewhere in the same treatise he calls the words spoken to Mary by the angel Gabriel in Luke 1:31 "the announcement of a sacred advent," *sacri adventus nuntio*.[26] Insisting that the incarnation is beyond the power of any human to effect and is due entirely to God's initiative, he states that "the nativity [of Christ] could not come about except by way of an advent" (*natiuitas agenda non erat nisi per aduentum*).[27]

To conclude, the phrase *adventus Domini* is dynamic in meaning. It is an act, it has the person of Christ as its subject, and it has strong eschatological resonances, especially when referring to the Lord's advent in glory. But even when applied to his birth it emphasizes that this event is no mere physiological occurrence. It is theophanic and salvific. It is the dawn in time of the fullness of time, the entrance into history of the goal of history, the appearance in one man of the ultimate future of all. Despite the contrasts that the fathers never tire of expounding, the birth of the Lord on earth and his coming from heaven are both advents—are both parousias and epiphanies—the first inaugurating what the second will perfect, the second completing what the first began. In the Word made flesh, divinity shows itself in human form, permanently binding itself to humanity and reconciling creation with its Creator. The mystery of the incarnation is already the paschal mystery, and Christmas is a feast of redemption.

[24] Berthold Altaner, *Patrology* (Freiburg: Herder, 1960), 538.
[25] John Cassian, *Seven Books on the Incarnation of the Lord, against Nestorius* IV, 9, trans. Edgar C. S. Gibson, in NPNF 11, 578. Latin text in CSEL 17, 296.
[26] *Against Nestorius* II, 2. My translation of the Latin in CSEL 17, 248.
[27] Ibid.

B. A SEASON OF FOUR SUNDAYS

1. Name

The Old Gelasian Sacramentary—*Gelasianum vetus* in Latin—uses the New Testament phrase *adventus Domini* in its title *Orationes de adventum Domini*, "Orations for the Advent of the Lord."[28] Consistent with this, many of its orations and prefaces, besides referring to Christ's coming in the flesh, also refer to his coming in glory and give voice to the church's eschatological hope. This sacramentary dates from the seventh century and was used in the neighborhood churches of Rome, known as titular churches, or *tituli*, served by presbyters.[29] It is the oldest of the Roman sacramentaries, preceded only by an unofficial collection of papal Masses preserved in a manuscript in Verona.[30]

The New Testament expression is also found in other liturgical books. Although the earliest Roman lectionary, the Epistolary of Würzburg, dating from the mid-sixth century, omits a general heading, it places *de adventu Domini* in front of the pericope for each week.[31]

The eighth-century Lectionary of Murbach, from which readings in the Roman Missal of 1570 generally derive, introduces its Advent material with the words *Incipiunt lectiones de adventu Domini*, "Here begin the readings for the advent of the Lord."[32] Four of the six oldest Roman antiphonals likewise use *adventus Domini* in their titles, at least for the first Sunday.[33]

By way of contrast, the sacramentary that Pope Hadrian (772–95) sent to Charlemagne between 784 and 791 omits the word *Domini* from its title, retaining only *adventus*. Here the term has lost its connection with the New Testament, with the person of Christ, and with the act that will bring salvation history to its climax. "Advent" has become simply a period of time before Christmas. Consistent with eliminating *Domini* from the name of the season and consequently all the

---

[28] GeV, title LXXX.

[29] On the titular churches, see John F. Baldovin, SJ, *The Urban Character of Christian Worship*, Orientalia Christiana Analecta 228 (Roma: Pontificium Institutum Studiorum Orientalium, 1987) 108, 112–15.

[30] For information about this collection as well as the other liturgical sources used here, see the pertinent sections of Cyrille Vogel, *Medieval Liturgy: An Introduction to the Sources* (Washington, DC: The Pastoral Press, 1986).

[31] EpW CLXX–CLXXIIII.

[32] M CXLVII.

[33] AMS 1a.

eschatological overtones that *adventus Domini* has in the gospels and Pauline letters, this sacramentary also excludes all the prayers that refer to the advent of Christ in glory and keeps only those that refer to his coming in the flesh—in other words, to the *adventus* understood to be his birth.

Though one of the four forms of the Gregorian Sacramentary, this Mass book is not a work of Pope Gregory the Great (590–604). Scholars call it the *Hadrianum*. The oldest sections may go back to Pope Honorius (625–38). It contains the prayers of Masses celebrated by the pope at the Lateran or at stational churches.[34] If the *Gelasianum vetus* hands on the presbyteral form of Roman liturgy, the *Hadrianum* transmits the papal one. These two sacramentaries, therefore, are of capital importance and will be cited frequently, for they attest the simultaneous coexistence of two types of liturgy in early medieval Rome. Of the two, the papal form eventually prevailed and is enshrined in the *Missale Romanum* of 1570 and its successors, the latest being that of 1962. Reform of the Missal after the Second Vatican Council draws heavily on the presbyteral tradition preserved in the Old Gelasian.

The name of the four weeks preceding Christmas in the 1962 Missal as well as in the three typical editions of the Missal of Paul VI is *tempus Adventus*, "season of Advent," derived of course from the Sacramentary of Pope Hadrian. Redactors of the postconciliar Missal availed themselves of many prayers from the Old Gelasian in order to recover the eschatological aspect of the season but unfortunately stopped short of restoring *Domini* to the title as found in that sacramentary as well as in the lectionaries of Würzburg and Murbach and four of the early antiphonals.

2. From Six Sundays to Four

Besides the name of the season, another difference between the Advent of the Old Gelasian and that of the *Hadrianum* is its length.[35]

---

[34] On the stational churches and stational liturgy of Rome, see Baldovin, *Urban Character*, 143–166.

[35] On this see Antoine Chavasse, *Le Sacramentaire Gélasien (Vaticanus Reginensis 316): Sacramentaire presbytéral en usage dans les titres romains au VII siècle* (Tournai: Desclée & Co., 1958) 412–26. An excellent exposition in English of the origins and early history of Advent is Martin J. Connell, "The Origins and Evolution of Advent in the West," in Maxwell E. Johnson, ed., *Between Memory and Hope* (Collegeville, MN: Liturgical Press, 2000) 349–71. More recent is Paul

In the former as well as in the Epistolary of Würzburg, Advent is six weeks—as it was in Gaul and Spain, and still is in Milan. In the Sacramentary of Pope Hadrian, the Lectionary of Murbach, and five of the six ancient antiphonals, however, it is only four weeks. It is thought that Pope Gregory the Great is the one responsible for shortening the season and that his motive was to clearly differentiate Advent from Lent and make it generally coincide with the month of December. Reduction of the weeks, however, affected mainly the papal liturgy at the Lateran and not that of the neighborhood churches where presbyters used some form of the Gelasian Sacramentary. An Advent of two different lengths at Rome lasted until well into the seventh century when the papal practice eventually triumphed.

The general rubrics of the Roman Missal of 1962 specify that "the time of sacred Advent [*tempus sacri Adventus*] runs from First Vespers of the First Sunday of Advent until None of the Vigil of the Nativity of the Lord inclusive" (no. 71).[36] The Universal Norms on the Liturgical Year and the Calendar, published on March 21, 1969,[37] describes the season a bit differently. No. 40 states that "Advent [*tempus Adventus*] begins with First Vespers (Evening Prayer I) of the Sunday that falls on or closest to November 30 and it ends before First Vespers (Evening Prayer I) of Christmas." The reason for changing the end of Advent from None of the Vigil of the Nativity to Evening Prayer I of Christmas is probably because the office of None, meant to be prayed at the ninth hour, or 3:00 p.m., has been replaced, for those not bound by particular law, by the daytime hour that can be prayed at the most appropriate time between morning and evening.[38]

F. Bradshaw and Maxwell E. Johnson, "Advent," in their *The Origins of Feasts, Fasts and Seasons in Early Christianity*, Alcuin Club Collections 86 (Collegeville, MN: Liturgical Press, 2011), 158–68.

[36] The translation is mine throughout this work. These rubrics were first published by Pope John XXIII in a *motu proprio* of July 25, 1960, and can be found in *Rubrics of the Roman Breviary and Missal* (Collegeville, MN: Liturgical Press, 1960).

[37] These are newly translated at the beginning of the 2011 Roman Missal. The previous translation, with many inaccuracies, is in DOL doc. 442, nos. 3767–827. The Latin text is in the front of the third typical edition of the *Missale Romanum*, published in 2008.

[38] See General Instruction of the Liturgy of the Hours, nos. 74–78, in DOL doc. 426, nos. 3504–8.

The season of Advent, then, as it has come down in both of our missals, consists of four Sundays before Christmas and a variable number of weekdays, depending on which day of the week Christmas falls. When Christmas falls on a Sunday, there are four full weeks, or twenty-eight days, in Advent. When it falls on a Monday, however, there are only three full weeks in Advent, plus the fourth Sunday on December 24, making a total of twenty-two days.

3. Ember Days

A major difference in the two missals is the presence in RM 1962 of Ember Days on Wednesday, Friday, and Saturday of the third week. Ember days were unique to Rome and unknown elsewhere. Always Wednesday, Friday, and Saturday—they are primarily fast days rooted in ancient agricultural society. Roughly coinciding with the change of seasons, they occur four times a year—during the first week of Lent in spring, the octave of Pentecost in summer, the week after September 14 in autumn,[39] and the third week of Advent in winter. The Latin name for these days is *Quatuor Temporum*, meaning "the four seasons." The English word "ember" is said to derive from *temporum* "via the German *Quatember*," remarks Thomas Talley.[40] The generic designation *Quatuor Temporum*, however, is not ancient. It makes its appearance only in the first printed edition of the Roman Missal at Milan in 1474.[41]

These days eventually gave rise to a very distinctive set of eucharistic celebrations. Pierre Jounel writes that "an ember week included not only fasting but stational liturgical assemblies on Wednesday and Friday and again during the night between Saturday and Sunday. These assemblies were held successively at the churches of St. Mary Major and of the Holy Apostles and the Basilica of St. Peter."[42] Conse-

---

[39] In RM 1962 the formularies for these days are found between the seventeenth and eighteenth Sundays after Pentecost.

[40] Thomas Talley, *The Origins of the Liturgical Year*, 2nd ed. (Collegeville, MN: Liturgical Press, 1986) 148.

[41] See the lists of titles in Bruylants, I, nos. 5, 6, and 7. In no. 5 inclusion of *in quatuor tempora* in the title of Wednesday of the third week seems to be a mistake. In the edition of this manuscript by Giovanni Bosco Shin-Ho Chang, *Vetus Missale Romanum Monasticum Lateranensis* (Città del Vaticano: Libreria Editrice Vaticana, 2002) 1373, is found only *Feria IIII*. This *Vetus Missale* is commonly called the Lateran Missal.

[42] *Church* IV, 28–29.

quently, each day has proper Mass texts, unlike the other weekdays of Advent on which the Sunday Mass is repeated. The Mass formularies of these days display archaic characteristics. Ember Wednesday always has two lessons before the gospel. A gradual is sung after each one, and an oration follows the first. Both lessons are taken from the Old Testament except during the octave of Pentecost when they are from the Acts of the Apostles.

Ember Saturdays have five Old Testament lessons before the epistle, for a total of six readings before the gospel. Because these were once done in Latin and Greek, the sacramentaries assign these Saturdays the title of *Sabbato in XII Lectiones*, "Saturday of the Twelve Lessons." The last Old Testament lesson is always Daniel 3:47-51. Each Old Testament lesson is followed by a gradual and an oration, and a tract replaces the Alleluia before the gospel. In the centuries when these Saturday liturgies were nocturnal vigils culminating in a eucharistic celebration in the early hours of the Lord's Day and so fulfilling the object of Saturday's fast, there was no Mass later in the day. Ancient documents indicate the absence of a Mass on Sunday by the expression *Dominica vacat*. In the formularies that have come down in the 1962 Missal these ancient fast days, once autonomous, have been annexed by Advent and in fact are the clearest expression of what the season is commonly taken to be: preparation for the birth of Jesus.

As for the origin of Ember Days, Jounel states that they "may go back to Pope Siricius at the end of the fourth century. St. Leo the Great already regarded them as traditional." He adds that "ordinations soon came to be connected with the three stations: the names of the candidates were announced on Wednesday; the men themselves were presented to the people on Friday; and they were ordained during the Saturday night vigil."[43]

The revised Roman Calendar of 1969 eliminated Ember Days from the universal calendar and did so for a number of reasons. For centuries the all-night vigil from Saturday to Sunday, like the Paschal Vigil, had moved up to Saturday morning. The successive steps of ordination rites were no longer tied to these days. After Paul VI in 1966 lifted the obligation of fasting from all days except Ash Wednesday and Good Friday,[44] Ember Days ceased being obligatory fast days, which

---

[43] *Church* IV, 28–29. The texts he cites on p. 28 in note 51 are particularly valuable.

[44] See his apostolic constitution *Paenitemini* III, II, 3, in DOL doc. 358, no. 3022.

was one of their essential characteristics. Moreover, these days, except for the ones in September, had long ago forfeited their distinctively agricultural character and had been thoroughly absorbed by Advent, Lent, and the octave of Pentecost. Finally, in many parts of the world into which the church spread in recent centuries, the *Quatuor Temporum* or four seasons does not coincide with the times presumed by the liturgical texts. No. 45 of the Universal Norms on the Liturgical Year and the Calendar stipulates that the purpose of Ember Days is "to entreat the Lord for the various needs of humanity, especially for the fruits of the earth and for human labor, and to give thanks to him publicly." Then nos. 46–47 decree that the duration and frequency of these days should be determined by conferences of bishops and that texts be taken from votive Masses for various occasions.

4. Counting the Sundays

The 1969 Universal Norms on the Liturgical Year and the Calendar, no. 41, declares that "the Sundays of this time of year are named the First, Second, Third, and Fourth Sundays of Advent," which is how they are designated in both of our missals. Though this seems obvious to us, it took centuries to come about and become standard.

Early documents show a surprising amount of diversity in this matter. The Old Gelasian contains the general heading *Orationes de aduentum Domini* but does not number the formularies. Each of those following the first one is simply designated as another Mass, *Item alia Missa*. At the other extreme the Epistolary of Würzburg has no general heading but places the phrase *de aduentu Domini* in front of each of its pericopes, without numbering them and without connecting them to either Sundays after Pentecost or Sundays before Christmas as other books sometimes do.

The Sacramentary of Gellone covers all possibilities. It contains the general title "Here Begin Orations for the Advent of the Lord," then lists Masses for the Sundays, numbering them in two ways—as Sundays of weeks after Pentecost, as well as in reverse numerical order as Sundays before Christmas, except for the last, which it labels *Dominica vacat*. But it does not include the word Advent in the titles of any of the Sundays.[45] Other eighth-century Gelasians, after a general title referring to Advent, count the Sundays only in reverse order before Christmas, eliminating references to weeks after Pentecost and omit-

---

[45] G titles 277, 281, 288, 290, 294.

ting Advent from the names of individual Sundays. The Lectionary of Alcuin does the same but, strangely, does not place a general heading above any of the pericopes. Hence the word Advent appears nowhere in the titles of these four sets of readings *ante natale Domini*.[46]

The Sacramentary of Pope Hadrian comes closest to current nomenclature—but only partially. It lists the first three Sundays in ascending numerical order as the first, second, and third Sundays but refers to the fourth as *Dominica vacat* and does not include the word Advent in any of them. The general title "Orations for Advent" was sufficient to indicate their purpose. The first Missal to employ exactly the terminology found in the 1962 Missal and the three editions of the Missal of Paul VI is the second typical edition of the Roman Missal by Clement VIII in 1604.[47]

5. From End to Beginning

The ancient Roman sacramentaries and lectionaries all start the yearly cycle with the Vigil of the Nativity of the Lord. Although the nativity was being celebrated at Rome as early as 336, Advent does not emerge there until the middle of the sixth century.[48] By that time the annual round of prayers and readings, starting with the Lord's birth, continuing with Lent, culminating with the Easter season, and concluding with the long series of Sundays after Pentecost together with Ember Days and commemorations of martyrs and other saints, was well established. Formularies for Advent, therefore, represent relatively late additions to a liturgical calendar already shaped by some two centuries of tradition.

Maintaining the birth of the Lord as the beginning of the year—a practice that could receive ample theological justification—the early sacramentaries and lectionaries insert their Advent material at the end of the Sundays after Pentecost. This tends to accentuate the eschatological content of the season, especially when it is called *Adventus Domini*. Since the Ember Days and feasts of saints were in the calendar long before Advent got started, their presence determined the precise place where the new material would be located. The Old Gelasian inserts its "Orations for the Advent of the Lord" before the three Ember Days of December, the generic title of which is "Orations and Prayers for the Tenth Month" (GeV 1157–77). The *Hadrianum* integrates Masses

---

[46] Alc CXCVII, CXCVIII, CXCVIIII, CCVIII.

[47] See Bruylants I, nos. 1, 3, 4, 6.

[48] The earliest evidence is the list of pericopes in the Epistolary of Würzburg.

for the first three Sundays with memorials of saints but places that of the fourth Sunday after the three Ember Days (H 790–804).

Early Roman antiphonals, on the other hand, like Gallican and Hispanic liturgical books, begin with Advent, thus creating the awkward situation of chants for the Mass being found in the front of books and prayers and readings near the end. Only in twelfth- and thirteenth-century plenary missals do the Advent Masses start to appear before Christmas.[49] Consequently, the First Sunday of Advent is commonly taken to be the beginning of the liturgical year. Though not stated in any magisterial document, the claim receives some justification by the placement in the 1969 calendar of the solemnity of Christ, King of the Universe, on the previous Sunday, the last Sunday of Ordinary Time, which therefore is taken to be the last Sunday of the liturgical year. Additionally, in the postconciliar Lectionary the cycle of readings at Sunday Mass changes each year on the First Sunday of Advent. This, more than anything else, suggests that a new liturgical year is beginning on that day. On the other hand, the Constitution on the Sacred Liturgy, no. 102, reflects the older view of Advent coming at the end of the year and being mainly eschatological. It says that "within the course of the year," Holy Mother Church "unfolds the whole mystery of Christ, from the incarnation and nativity to the ascension, to Pentecost, and the expectation of the blessed hope of the coming of the Lord."[50] The concluding words are an adaptation of Titus 2:13 and in Latin end with the phrase *adventus Domini*.

6. Purple and Penitential

In both the ordinary and the extraordinary forms of eucharistic celebration purple vestments are worn during Advent, and the Gloria is omitted. In RM 1962 the Alleluia is likewise omitted on weekdays but not on Sundays. These are sometimes taken as signs of penance, and, in fact, Pope Pius XII in his famous encyclical on the liturgy, *Mediator Dei*, written in 1947, presents the season in strongly penitential terms: "In the period of Advent," he writes, "the Church arouses in us the

[49] See, for example, the Lateran Missal edited by Chang, referred to in note 41. In this Missal from the mid-thirteenth century, by the way, the phrase *in adventu Domini* is still in the title of the first Sunday.

[50] Throughout this work the translation of council documents is from Austin Flannery, OP, ed., *Vatican Council II, vol. 1, The Conciliar and Post Conciliar Documents*, new rev. ed. (Northport, NY: Costello Publishing Co., 1996).

consciousness of the sins we have had the misfortune to commit, and urges us, by restraining our desires and practicing voluntary mortification of the body, to recollect ourselves in meditation, and experience a longing desire to return to God who alone can free us by His grace from the stain of sin and from its evil consequences."[51]

Historically, this view is relatively recent. At first, Advent was exclusively liturgical, not ascetical, both at Rome and at Ravenna. In the eighth and ninth centuries, when the liturgy of the city of Rome spread north of the Alps where fasting and abstinence had for centuries formed part of preparing for Christmas or Epiphany,[52] people in those places interpreted the season in the way familiar to them. Though this had no effect on the texts of the Masses, in the twelfth century it led to the wearing of purple vestments, omission of the Gloria, and, on weekdays, omission of the Alleluia.[53]

To summarize, the foregoing review of variations in the name, content, length, and placement of Advent texts in service books shows that this most recent of liturgical seasons was still evolving well into the thirteenth century, and, as we saw, the way of identifying the Sundays was not fixed until 1604. Stripped of most of its eschatological content, shorn of its title *Adventus Domini* with its New Testament evocations, reduced from six Sundays to four, placed immediately before the Nativity of the Lord, and assigned purple vestments, *tempus Adventus* in the Roman Rite, until the postconciliar reforms, was partially penitential and aimed only at preparing the faithful to celebrate Christmas. So it remains in the extraordinary form. Since the season is quite different in the ordinary form, we will present one after the other, beginning with the Missal of 1962.

C. THE ROMAN MISSAL OF 1962

1. Sundays

Orations. In RM 1962 the three presidential prayers, called oration, secret, and post-Communion, all derive from the Sacramentary of Pope

---

[51] No. 154 in Pamela Jackson, *An Abundance of Graces* (Chicago: Liturgy Training Publications, 2004) 160–61.

[52] See Connell, "The Origins and Evolution of Advent," 349–71.

[53] Adolf Adam, *The Liturgical Year* (Collegeville, MN: Liturgical Press, 1979) 131.

Hadrian.[54] No mention is made in any of these prayers of Christ's coming in glory, of his return as judge, of the end of the world, or of any other eschatological events. Three of them make explicit reference to preparation for Christmas. The post-Communion of the first Sunday asks that "we may prepare with due honor for the approaching feast of our redemption," that of the third Sunday asks that "these divine helps may . . . prepare us for the approaching feast," and the collect for Wednesday of the third week, the first of the three Ember Days, begs "that the coming solemnity of our redemption may both confer upon us assistance in this present life and bestow the rewards of everlasting blessedness."[55]

This shows that the seventh- or eighth-century papal Advent preserved in RM 1962 is a period of time dedicated not to preparing the faithful to meet the Lord at his Parousia but to preparing them for the liturgical celebration of his birth, understood broadly and dogmatically as a feast of redemption. The collect for the second Sunday expresses this most clearly. Alluding to the gospel of the day, Matthew 11:2-10, which presents John the Baptist as the one sent to prepare the way of the Lord, the prayer asks, "Stir up our hearts, O Lord, to prepare the ways of thine only-begotten Son: that through his coming [*per ejus adventum*] we may deserve to serve thee with purified minds."

The first words of this prayer, "Stir up," which translate the Latin *Excita*, are the opening entreaty of three of the four Sunday collects— the first, the second, and the fourth. In that of the second Sunday, God is asked to "stir up our hearts." In that of the first and fourth Sundays, he is asked to stir up his power and come. That bold petition, *Excita, quaesumus, Domine, potentiam tuam et veni*, is from Psalm 79:3 and is chanted as the gradual and Alleluia of the third Sunday. Recurrence of this petition in the prayers and chants of Advent is one of the elements that make this season so unique.

Readings. In the Tridentine Mass there are only two biblical readings for each Sunday, called the epistle and the gospel. They are read by the priest at the right- and left-hand sides of the altar, respectively, and are found not in a separate book, the Lectionary, but in the Missal itself, as are the chants appointed for the day. A missal, then, contains all the

---

[54] Instead of oration, we designate the first prayer as the collect.

[55] Unless otherwise indicated, translations of the prayers and chants of the 1962 Roman Missal are from *The Daily Missal and Liturgical Manual*, 3rd ed. (London: Baronius Press, 2008).

texts a priest needs to celebrate Mass. Though usually assisted by one or two servers, he reads all the prayers, readings, and chants himself. When at a solemn high Mass a subdeacon chants the epistle, a deacon chants the gospel, and a choir chants the proper, the priest is still required to read all of them silently or in a low voice. The Tridentine Mass, then, is organized in function of a single priest offering Mass alone. When the choir and congregation sing the *Kyrie*, Gloria, *Credo*, *Sanctus*, and *Agnus Dei*, or when other ministers discharge functions pertaining to them, the priest is not affected. He does what he would do even in their absence.

For the four Sundays of Advent there are a total of eight readings in RM 1962—four epistles and four gospels. Except for the gospel of the fourth Sunday, all eight are found in the Lectionary of Murbach,[56] though not in the same order and usually with epistles and gospels paired differently. For example, the account of the Son of Man coming on a cloud in Luke 21:25-33, prescribed for the first Sunday in RM 1962, is reserved for the third Sunday in the Lectionary of Murbach. With it is read Romans 15:4-13, read in RM 1962 on the second Sunday with Matthew 11:2-10.

We see, then, that in the early sources the same readings occupy different positions. The arrangement of the gospels in the Tridentine Missal of 1570 and hence in RM 1962 might be the most logical: on the first Sunday the coming of the Son of Man with great power and majesty (Luke 21:25-33), and on the next three Sundays John the Baptist—the testimony of Jesus about him (Matt 11:2-10) on the second Sunday, John's self-effacement before Jesus (John 1:19-28) on the third, and the solemn inauguration of the precursor's preaching (Luke 3:1-6) on the fourth, which is a repetition of the gospel of the previous day, ember Saturday. But the epistles of these Sundays have no intrinsic connection with the gospels.

Cyrille Vogel explains that in the Epistolary and Evangelary of Würzburg the lists of epistles and gospels "are Roman and done by the same scribe but they come from different eras and do not correspond to one another."[57] He continues, "Churches used books of readings that came from different periods and belonged to different types. The fact that a Roman lectionary, or rather a Romano-Frankish

---

[56] M CXLVII, CL, CLI, CLII, CLVI. For lists of readings in the ancient lectionaries and the Missal of 1570, see Adrian Nocent, OSB, *The Liturgical Year*, 4 vols. (Collegeville, MN: Liturgical Press, 1977) I, 168–71.

[57] Vogel, *Medieval Liturgy*, 339.

lectionary like the *Comes* of Murbach, finally prevailed in the West is an accidental result of the Romanization of worship brought about by the Carolingian reformers. Nowhere is there to be found a systematic attempt at organizing a system of readings."[58] That, we might add, comes only after the Second Vatican Council.

Chants. All the sung texts for the first three Sundays of Advent in RM 1962 are already found in the six oldest manuscripts of the Roman Antiphonal, dating from the eighth and ninth centuries. This unanimity, especially with regard to the Alleluia verses, prompts René-Jean Hesbert, editor of the *Antiphonale Missarum Sextuplex*, to remark that "we are in the presence of a primitive organization."[59] For reasons to be explained below, choice of chants for the fourth Sunday diverges slightly in the manuscripts, three of which list no chants at all because of the lack of a Sunday Mass after the vigil on Saturday night. RM 1962 reproduces the manuscript in which the chants for the fourth Sunday are taken from ember Wednesday.

Texts for the first Sunday reflect an unusual unity and coherence. Three of the five are drawn from Psalm 24. The introit antiphon is Psalm 24:1-3: "To thee have I lifted up my soul. . . . None of them that trust in thee shall be confounded." The second half of the antiphon serves as the gradual: "All them that wait on thee shall not be confounded." The complete antiphon of the introit returns verbatim at the offertory: "To thee have I lifted up my soul. Let me not be ashamed. None of them that wait for thee shall be confounded." More than any other texts, these verses of Psalm 24 show Advent to be a time of expectation, hope, and waiting coupled with confidence of not being disappointed by a God attentive to the needs of his people.

The Alleluia verse on the first Sunday uses the familiar words of Psalm 84:8, "Show us, O Lord, thy mercy and grant us thy salvation." The same verse is used as the offertory of the second Sunday, preceded by verse 7 of the same psalm, "Thou wilt turn, O God, and bring us to life and thy people shall rejoice in thee." Psalm 84:13, "The Lord will give goodness and our earth shall yield her fruit," is the communion chant of the first Sunday, and the opening words of the psalm, "Lord,

---

[58] Ibid., 349.

[59] AMS xxxvii. On the chants of the Roman Missal, especially those of Advent, see the marvelous study of James McKinnon, *The Advent Project* (Berkeley: University of California Press, 2000).

thou has blessed thy land," are heard in both the introit and the offertory of the third Sunday.

As was already pointed out, Psalm 79:3b, "Stir up your power and come," besides being the opening petition of several orations, is the Alleluia verse of the third Sunday. Psalm 79:2, 3, 6 is the gradual of that Sunday: "Thou, O Lord, that sitteth upon the Cherubim, stir up thy might and come. Give ear, O thou that rulest Israel, that leadest Joseph like a sheep." Thus, the first few verses of the same psalm comprise both the gradual and the Alleluia of the third Sunday. From all this it is clear that Psalms 24, 79, and 84 stand out as the preferred Advent psalms.

Chants for the second Sunday are connected by the theme of Sion or Jerusalem and three of the six most ancient manuscripts of the Roman Antiphonal indicate that the stational church of the day is the Basilica of the Holy Cross in Jerusalem.[60] The introit antiphon announces, "People of Sion, behold the Lord shall come to save the nations" (Isa 30:30). The gradual declares, "Out of Sion the loveliness of his beauty. God shall come manifestly" (Ps 49:2-3, 5). Immediately thereafter the Alleluia sings, "I rejoiced at the things that were said to me. We shall go unto the house of the Lord" (Ps 121:4). The communion exclaims, "Arise, O Jerusalem, and stand on high, and behold the joy that cometh to thee from thy God" (Bar 5:5; 4:36). Only the offertory, *Deus, tu*, fails to include any reference to Jerusalem or Sion, and Hesbert strongly suspects that this is due to a scribal error.[61]

Be that as it may, it is surprising to note that the theme of Sion or Jerusalem is limited to the chants and is not found in the readings or prayers. Such is not the case on the third Sunday. On that day the rather lengthy introit antiphon *Gaudete in Domino semper*, "Rejoice in the Lord always," is the first half of the epistle, Philippians 4:4-7. Because of the first word of the antiphon, this Sunday is popularly known as Gaudete Sunday and is the Advent counterpart of Laetare Sunday during Lent. Rose vestments are worn on each.

2. Ember Days

In RM 1962 the prayers of these three days, like those of Sundays, are from the Sacramentary of Pope Hadrian (H 790–804). By the time ember Wednesday is reached, what the church has been preparing

---

[60] AMS 2.
[61] AMS xxxvii–xxxviii.

for, waiting for, and longing for is much closer than it was on the first Sunday. When Christmas falls on a Monday, ember Saturday can be the day before Christmas Eve. The imminent fulfillment of the Advent hope is expressed in the second gradual of Wednesday, *Prope est Dominus*, "The Lord is nigh unto them that call upon him" (Ps 144:18). The introit on Friday addresses God in similar words, *Prope es tu, Domine*, "You are near, O Lord, and all thy ways are truth" (Ps 118:151).

On these days prayers become more intense, more urgent. Three times is heard the plea of Psalm 79:3, *Excita potentiam tuam et veni*, "Stir up thy might, we beseech thee, O Lord, and come." The first is in the collect of Friday, which adds, "that those who trust in thy loving kindness may be the more speedily freed from all adversity." The other two are in chants on Saturday. The gradual following the third lesson on that day sings, "O Lord God of hosts, convert us and show thy face, and we shall be saved. Stir up thy might, O Lord, and come to save us." Before the gospel the tract asks, "Give ear, O thou that rulest Israel, thou that leadest Joseph like a sheep. Thou that sittest upon the Cherubim, shine forth before Ephraim, Benjamin and Manasses. Stir up thy might, O Lord, and come and save us." As if growing short on patience, the second oration of Wednesday, possibly alluding to Habakkuk 2:3 and Hebrews 10:37, begs, "Hasten, we beseech thee, O Lord, tarry not." In the words of Psalm 79:2, 4, the introit on Saturday cries out, "Come, O Lord, and show us thy face, thou that sittest upon the Cherubim, and we shall be saved."

Another feature of the Ember Days is the frequency with which readings and chants are taken from the prophet Isaiah.[62] On Wednesday the introit antiphon is *Rorate, coeli*, the well-known plea of Isaiah 45:8, "Drop down dew, ye heavens, from above and let the clouds rain down the Just. Let the earth open and bud forth a Saviour." Both lessons before the gospel are from Isaiah. The first, Isaiah 2:2-5, is the eschatological vision of the nations streaming to the house of the God of Jacob, prepared on the highest of mountains. The second, Isaiah 7:10-15, tells that "a virgin shall conceive and bear a son and his name shall be called Emmanuel." The gospel, Luke 1:26-38, without citing this passage, as does Matthew 1:23, announces its fulfillment when the Virgin Mary gives her consent to the divine plan disclosed by the angel

---

[62] Until now only two chants have come from Isaiah: the introit on the second Sunday (Isa 30:30) already cited, and the communion on the third Sunday (Isa 35:4).

Gabriel. The offertory is Isaiah 35:4, "Take courage and fear not, for behold our God will bring judgment. He himself will come and will save us." The communion repeats Isaiah 7:14, "Behold, a virgin shall conceive and bear a son," heard in the first lesson. The Mass of ember Wednesday, then, is exceptionally coherent.

Friday has only one lesson before the gospel, and it is Isaiah 11:1-5, depicted countless times in manuscript illuminations, murals, and stained-glass windows: "There shall come forth a rod out of the root of Jesse and a flower shall rise up out of his root. And the spirit of the Lord shall rest upon him." On ember Saturday, or Saturday of the Twelve Lessons, four of the five Old Testament readings are from Isaiah, the fifth being, as always, Daniel 3:47-51, issuing onto the canticle of the three young men in the fiery furnace in Daniel 3:52-56. The gospels of these three days recount key episodes leading to the birth of Jesus—on Wednesday the annunciation (Luke 1:26-38), on Friday the visitation (Luke 1:37-47), and on Saturday the cry of John, son of Zachary, in the desert to prepare the way of the Lord, "as it was written," the evangelist points out, "in the book of the sayings of Isaiah the prophet." Since these passages are all drawn from the Gospel of Luke, the three Ember Days of Advent receive additional unity and direction.

The Mass formulary for the fourth Sunday is later than those of the first three because originally the only Eucharist on this day was the one concluding the all-night vigil on Saturday. When a formulary for the fourth Sunday was assembled, several texts were taken from the preceding Ember Days, making it a composite. The gospel, the mission of John the Baptist in Luke 3:1-6, is taken from ember Saturday. The introit, *Rorate coeli*, the gradual, *Prope est Dominus*, and the communion, *Ecce virgo concipiet*, are all from ember Wednesday.

3. *Vigil of the Nativity*

The title of the Mass formulary for this day has remained practically the same throughout its history: Vigil of the Nativity of the Lord. The hour of its celebration, however, has changed. The early sacramentaries add to the title *ad nonam*, or "at the ninth hour,"[63] indicating that the Mass was celebrated at roughly three in the afternoon. As such, it inaugurated the Christmas feasts. For this reason the formulary is found at the very beginning of the ancient sacramentaries, just before

---

[63] Bruylants I, no. 9.

the three Christmas Masses—Advent material, as we have seen, being inserted in various ways at the end of the temporal cycle, following the Sundays after Pentecost. Contrary to its original time and purpose, in RM 1962 the Eucharist for the Vigil of the Nativity is celebrated on the morning of December 24. No longer the inaugural Mass of Christmas, it has become the last Mass of Advent.

The chants are superb. Looking forward on this day to the next day's wonder, the introit and the gradual announce, "This day you shall know that the Lord will come and save us, and in the morning you shall see his glory." In Exodus 16:6-7 these are the words of Moses and Aaron making known the Lord's promise to rain down bread from heaven for the people he just led out of Egypt but who are now murmuring in the desert. Besides evoking the Bread of Life discourse in John 6: 28-58 and the heavenly origin of Jesus, whose earthly birth is about to be celebrated, this announcement places the entire Christmas liturgy in the context of exodus, that is to say, in the context of redemption—begun at Passover and completed in Christ.

The collect, a masterful composition from H 36, also found in GeV 1156, identifies Christ as "our Redeemer" and his birth as "our redemption." It prays, "O God, who dost gladden us by the yearly expectation of our redemption, grant that we, who now joyfully receive thine only-begotten Son as our Redeemer, may also without fear behold him coming as our judge." This is the only mention of the Second Coming in the Advent prayers of the extraordinary form.

The Alleluia verse, unfortunately sung only on Sundays, contributes further to the redemptive character of Christmas. Taken from 4 Esdras 16:53, it declares, "Tomorrow shall the iniquity of the earth be abolished and the Savior of the world shall reign over us." The phrase "Savior of the world" recalls the invitatory during the unveiling of the cross on Good Friday as translated in RM 1962, "Behold the wood of the cross on which hung the savior of the world," and the ancient gloss on Psalm 98, "The Lord reigns *from the wood*" (emphasis mine).

The epistle, Romans 1:1-16, looks forward not only to Christmas but to Easter as well, or rather looks forward to Christmas in the light of Easter, setting forth the person of Christ as the seed of David according to the flesh but Son of God by the resurrection from the dead. In the gospel (Matt 1:18-21) the angel of the Lord addresses Joseph as "son of David," telling him that it is by the Holy Spirit that his spouse has conceived and that he is to name the child Jesus, "for he shall save his people from their sins." Jesus traces his Davidic and, hence,

24

messianic lineage through Joseph, not Mary, and through his saving deeds—his earthly ministry culminating in his death and glorification—actualizes the meaning of his name.

4. Concluding Comments

Reflecting on the material enshrined in the 1962 Missal, one is first of all astounded at its antiquity and durability. Readings, prayers, and chants all go back to some of the earliest written sources of the Roman liturgy and have remained unchanged through the centuries. Recurrence of the cry *Excita* from Psalm 79:3 connects the weeks and binds together texts of diverse genres, thereby imparting continuity to the season. A limited number of verses from Psalm 24 and Psalm 84 instill familiarity. Words and melodies of the chants are splendid and remain so even when sung throughout the week. The Ember Days of the third week with their proper formulas and distinctive structures are a welcome contrast to the previous two weeks. Having passed from the vision of the Last Judgment in the gospel of the first Sunday through the Baptist's call to conversion in the next two, the readings from Isaiah on the Ember Days and the gospel accounts of the annunciation and visitation lead the faithful steadily to the threshold of the Christmas mystery and instill in them childlike wonder.

But RM 1962 also has shortcomings. It has no proper prefaces and no proper Masses for weekdays besides those of the Ember Days. It contains the prayers of only one of the two liturgical zones of the city of Rome: the papal, stational one, represented by the Gregorian Sacramentary sent to Charlemagne by Pope Hadrian in which Advent comprises only four weeks. Many of the prayers of the other liturgical zone, the presbyteral one, preserved in the Old Gelasian Sacramentary in which Advent consists of six weeks, have not been transmitted. The formulary for the fourth Sunday is an artificial construct assembled of pieces taken from previous days. The Lectionary is particularly weak. Epistles and gospels are randomly selected and not well paired. Gospels about John the Baptist on three of the four Sundays might be too much, given the wealth of other available material. Readings are abundant and rich on the Ember Days but unfortunately are heard only by the relatively small number of faithful who attend weekday Mass. Without readings from Isaiah and other prophets and books of the Old Testament on Sundays, the place of the birth of Christ in the larger sweep of salvation history is not presented to the majority of churchgoers, and the hopes of Israel and the nations that the incarnation fulfills are not articulated. Finally, although references to the Second Coming are heard in the epistles of the first and fourth Sundays as well as ember Saturday, they are absent from the gospels after the first Sunday and from all the prayers except the collect of Christmas Eve. These are defects that the Order of Readings for Mass, first published in 1969, then revised in 1981, and the three editions of the Missal of Paul VI admirably redress.

D. THE MISSAL OF PAUL VI

1. *Sundays*

The 1969 Universal Norms on the Liturgical Year and the Calendar, no. 39, declares that "Advent has a twofold character, for it is a time of preparation for the Solemnities of Christmas, in which the First Coming of the Son of God to humanity is remembered, and likewise a time when, by remembrance of this, minds and hearts are led to look forward to Christ's Second Coming at the end of time." Immediately, we notice a major difference between our two missals. Whereas RM 1962 focuses primarily if not exclusively on the first coming, the reformed Missal broadens the view to include the second as well. This may be one of many liturgical echoes of the Second Vatican Council's effort to recover and integrate eschatology into Catholic thought, notably the teaching on the eschatological nature of the pilgrim church in chapter 7 of the Dogmatic Constitution on the Church, *Lumen Gentium*. The Universal Norms, no. 39, adds that "Advent is a period of devout and expectant delight"—a refreshingly positive outlook in contrast to the gloomy assessment of Pius XII we saw in *Mediator Dei*.

Readings. Here we must recall that in keeping with *Sacrosanctum Concilium* nos. 35 and 51, the Mass of Paul VI has three readings on Sunday distributed over a three-year period, making nine readings for each of the four Sundays of Advent and a total of thirty-six for the season in contrast to the eight in RM 1962. Furthermore, except during Easter Time, the first reading is from the Old Testament. Readings are contained no longer in the Missal but in other books, the Lectionary and Gospel Book, and read no longer at the altar—now reserved for the eucharistic offerings—but from a lectern or ambo. The first two readings are done from the Lectionary by lectors, preferably two of them, one for each reading, and the gospel from the Book of the Gospels by a deacon or, if there is no deacon, by the priest himself. While each minister is proclaiming the Word of the Lord, the others listen, as does the entire congregation. No one should read the text silently to himself or herself. After the first reading a soloist chants the responsorial psalm, and the assembly repeats the refrain. Unlike the graduals of RM 1962, which were just one or two verses of a psalm and usually generic in content, the responsorial psalms are much longer and carefully chosen to echo the specific content of the reading they follow.[64]

In sum, the Liturgy of the Word, like the rest of the eucharistic liturgy, is now a corporate undertaking, an ecclesial act, in which each participant has his or her distinct role. This is reflected in the different types of liturgical books corresponding to different ministries.

In the current Mass, biblical readings are not only more numerous than in the past but chosen with greater discrimination and systematically arranged in accord with clearly enunciated principles. Beginning with the gospels, the 1981 introduction to the Lectionary,[65] no. 93, explains that on the Sundays of Advent "each Gospel reading has a distinctive theme: the Lord's coming at the end of time (First Sunday of Advent), John the Baptist (Second and Third Sunday), and the events that prepared immediately for the Lord's birth (Fourth Sunday)." This defines the fundamental structure of the Advent thematic. Other readings are chosen in function of the gospel, and on occasion prayers reflect the content of the readings. The theme of the fourth Sunday, events immediately preceding the birth of Christ, is new—found on the Ember Days in RM 1962 but not on Sunday. The theme of the first Sunday, the Second Coming, and that of the second and third Sundays, John the Baptist, are roughly the same as before. The difference is that these themes, though the same for each week, over a three-year cycle are now articulated by different evangelists, each having his own viewpoint and accents, outlook, and emphases.

On the first Sunday in Year A Jesus urges readiness and watchfulness in Matthew 24:37-44 because the Son of Man will come as suddenly and unexpectedly as the flood in Noah's day or as a thief in the night. In the parallel passage from Mark 13:33-37 in Year B Jesus likewise enjoins vigilance lest, returning without warning like the master of a household

[64] Unfortunately, limits of space do not permit us to comment on these psalms and their link with the reading that precedes them.

[65] The introduction to the Lectionary, found in RML 1981, pp. xvi–xlvi, is a translation of the *praenotanda*, or general introduction, to the OLM 1981, or Order of Readings for Mass. The translation in DOL, nos. 1843–69, is that of the 1969 version and hence is outdated.

who went on a journey, he find us not discharging the duties entrusted to us, but sleeping. In the first part of the gospel in Year C, Luke 21:25-28, which is the same as in RM 1962, Jesus presents the apocalyptic upheaval and distress of the end time as the prelude to the dawn of redemption. To this the Lectionary appends verses 34-36, not in RM 1962, a characteristically Lukan exhortation to prayer that in the midst of cosmic dissolution believers may encounter the approaching Son of Man.

The next two Sundays set before us the person of John the Baptist. On the second Sunday all three years portray him as the voice crying in the wilderness (Isa 40:3) and stress his summons to conversion. In Year A Matthew 3:1-12 relates that he preached repentance and baptized in view of impending judgment. In Year B Mark 1:1-8, with no reference to judgment, coordinates the two activities of the Baptist, saying that he preached a baptism of repentance, adding that it was for the forgiveness of sins, not mentioned by Matthew. In Year C Luke 3:1-6 opens with a grand introduction, placing John in historical context, then, with no description of his unconventional dress and foods, declares, like Mark, that he proclaimed a baptism of repentance for forgiveness of sins. In RM 1962 this is the gospel for ember Saturday, repeated on the fourth Sunday.

On the third Sunday the gospel readings of all three years are again about the precursor but do not line up with each other as neatly as do those of the previous Sunday. In Year A Jesus recounts in Matthew 11:2-11 the actions that should suffice for him to be recognized as the Messiah, then praises John as a prophet—and more than a prophet— sent to prepare his way.

In Year B John confesses in John 1:6-8, 19-28 that not he but one coming after him and as yet unknown is the Messiah, the straps of whose sandals he is not worthy to untie. The gospel of the third Sunday in Year C, Luke 3:10-18, continues that of the previous week, Luke 3:1-6. On this Sunday, however, John tells the crowds how to bear fruits worthy of repentance and so escape the coming divine wrath.

The fourth Sunday, says the introduction to the Lectionary, no. 93, is devoted to "the events that prepared immediately for the Lord's birth." In Year A Matthew 1:18-24 narrates how an angel discloses to Joseph that his wife, Mary, would conceive and bear a son whom he would name Jesus. The evangelist adds that this fulfills Isaiah 7:14, heard in the first reading. In Year B Luke 1:26-38 recounts the annunciation to Mary, followed in Year C by Luke 1:39-48, Mary's visit to her cousin Elizabeth. We notice that the gospel on all four Sundays of

Advent in Year A are taken from Matthew, as they are for the rest of the year, and that in Year C all four gospels are from Luke, as they are for the other Sundays of that year. In Year B the gospels are normally taken from Mark, and in Advent this is true for the first two Sundays. But since Mark is shorter than the others and has no infancy narratives, the gospel on the third Sunday in that year is from John, and that on the fourth Sunday is from Luke.

Turning now to the first reading, from the Old Testament, the introduction to the Lectionary, no. 93, states that these "are prophecies about the Messiah and the Messianic age, especially from the Book of Isaiah." In Year A the readings are from the first part of Isaiah, chapters 1–39, generally about God's offer of unlimited pardon to all who seek him. On the first Sunday Isaiah 2:1-5 sketches the vision of a glorious future in which all nations stream to the mountain of the Lord. On the second Sunday Isaiah 11:1-10 foresees a branch sprouting from the root of Jesse on which the Spirit of the Lord rests. On the third Sunday Isaiah 35:1-6a, 8a-10 describes the redeemed returning to Zion—the lame, the feeble, the blind, and the deaf. On the fourth Sunday is read Isaiah 7:10-14 from the so-called book of Emmanuel. It tells of a virgin conceiving and bearing a son whom she shall call Emmanuel. The gospel of that day, Matthew 1:28-24, cites these words and declares them fulfilled in Mary.[66]

In Year B the selection on the second Sunday, Isaiah 40:1-5, 9-11, the beginning of the Book of Consolation, is noteworthy because it contains the well-known passage about the voice crying in the wilderness that will be cited in various ways and applied to John the Baptist in the gospels of all three years on that Sunday and in Year B on the third Sunday as well. On the first Sunday of Year B is read Isaiah 63:16b-17; 64:1-3b, 8, and on the third Sunday is read Isaiah 61:1-2a, 10-11—all from the third part of Isaiah, chapters 56–66. The readings from Isaiah finish on the third Sunday of Year B. On the fourth Sunday of that year the first reading, 2 Samuel 7:1-5, 8-12, 16, though from a historical book and not a prophetic one, is prophetic in content—Nathan's words about the Lord's determination to build David a house, words fulfilled beyond all imagining in the gospel of that day, Luke 1: 26-38, Mary's conception of a son who would rule on David's throne forever.

[66] In RM 1962 Isa 2:2-5, Isa 7:10-15, and Luke 1:26-38 are read on ember Wednesday and Isa 11:1-5 on ember Friday.

In Year C the first reading is not from Isaiah but from four other prophets: Jeremiah (33:14-16) on the first Sunday, Baruch (5:1-9) on the second, and Zephaniah (3:14-18a) on the third, all of which express the joy and gladness of Jerusalem. On the fourth Sunday is Micah 5:2-5a with its reference to Bethlehem and "to the mother of the Messiah."[67]

As for the second reading, the introduction to the Lectionary, no. 93, states that "the readings from an Apostle serve as exhortations and proclamations, in keeping with the different themes of Advent." Those on the first Sunday are about how Christians should comport themselves while awaiting the return of the Lord and accord well with the eschatological character of that day as found in the gospels and Old Testament readings. Those on the fourth Sunday relate rather explicitly with events recounted in the gospels and foretold by the prophets. Those on the second and third Sundays are more generic in content and pertain more to the season than to an individual day.

Prayers. The Missal of Paul VI replaces the four Sunday collects of RM 1962 with others drawn from ancient sources that better express the themes of the season as defined in the introduction to the Lectionary, no. 93, thereby producing more coherent and unified formularies in which prayers, readings, and at times chants are connected to each other.[68] It substitutes for *Aurem tuam* on the third Sunday a prayer very similar in wording from GeV 1137 and moves the three collects beginning with *Excita* to weekdays.

The one formerly on the first Sunday, *Excita, quaesumus, Domine, potentiam tuam et veni*, is now on Friday of the first week.[69] Its replacement is taken from one of the Advent Masses in the Old Gelasian Sacramentary, where it was a post-Communion (GeV 1139). It asks God for

---

[67] Note to Mic 5:3 in *The Jerusalem Bible* (Garden City: Doubleday & Company, 1966).

[68] For the liturgical sources of the prayers of Advent and the Christmas season together with possible biblical and patristic allusions, see Cuthbert Johnson, OSB, and Anthony Ward, SM, *The Sources of the Roman Missal (1975) I: Advent, Christmas* (Rome, 1986), a reprint of articles in *Notitiae* 22 (1986) nos. 240–42. See also the six articles of Antoine Dumas, OSB, "Les sources du Missel Romain," *Notitiae* 7 (1971), which indicate, season by season, the sources of all the prayers in the 1970 *Missale Romanum*.

[69] It was unrecognizable in the 1975 translation, "Jesus, our Lord, save us from our sins. Come, protect us from all dangers."

the resolve to run forth to meet your Christ
with righteous deeds at his coming,
so that, gathered at his right hand,
they may be worthy to possess the heavenly Kingdom.

Being gathered at Christ's right hand in the kingdom is an allusion to the Last Judgment scene in Matthew 25:34-36 in which the king invites those at his right side to come and take possession of the kingdom prepared for them. The petition accords perfectly with the eschatological content of the readings of the first Sunday.

The collect of the second Sunday in RM 1962 is another *Excita* oration, "Stir up our hearts, O Lord, to prepare the ways of thine only-begotten Son." It has been moved to Thursday of the second week.[70] In its place is another prayer from the Old Gelasian (GeV 1153):

Almighty and merciful God,
may no earthly undertaking hinder those
who set out in haste to meet your Son.

Here too we note an eschatological overtone missed in the previous translation. The petitioners are portrayed as *in occursum festinantes*, "hastening to meet" or to encounter Christ—like the bridesmaids in Matthew 25:6 being told at midnight that the bridegroom whom they await has come, and they go out to meet him. Thus the collects on each of the first two Sundays make reference to the Lord's Parousia.

While the collects of the first two Sundays refer to the Lord's glorious return, that of the third Sunday, taken from the *Rotulus* of Ravenna (Rot 25 = V 1356),[71] focuses on the other half of the Advent thematic, preparation for the celebration of his birth.[72] It prays,

[70] It too was unrecognizable when translated as "Almighty Father, give us the joy of your love to prepare the way for Christ our Lord."

[71] This is a scroll containing forty-two orations dealing with themes characteristic of Advent and Christmas. Most of the prayers are included in the reformed Roman and Ambrosian missals. See Anthony Ward, SM, "The Rotulus of Ravenna as a Source in the 2000 'Missale Romanum,'" EL 121 (2007) 129–76. Latin texts of the prayers are printed in Mohlberg's edition of the *Veronensis*, here abbreviated V, pp. 173–78. They are identified by their number in the *Rotulus* and by their number in the Mohlberg edition.

[72] The prayer after Communion does likewise. Retained from MR 1962, it asks that "this divine sustenance / may cleanse us of our faults / and prepare us for the coming feasts."

31

O God, who see how your people
faithfully await the feast of the Lord's Nativity,
enable us, we pray,
to attain the joys of so great a salvation
and to celebrate them always
with solemn worship and glad rejoicing.

Mention of "the joys of salvation" and "glad rejoicing" echoes the traditional entrance chant of the third Sunday, *Gaudete in Domino semper*, "Rejoice in the Lord always." The biblical passage from which this exhortation is taken, Philippians 4:4-5, is read in Year C. The first reading in that year, Zechariah 3:14-18a, several times calls daughter Zion to rejoice at the presence of the king of Israel, the Lord, in her midst. In Year B both readings before the gospel, Isaiah 61:1-2a, 10-11 and 1 Thessalonians 5:16-24, contain many references to rejoicing, as does the first reading in Year A, Isaiah 35:1-6a, 8a, 10. Expressions of joy and gladness, rejoicing and exultation, then, bind together the introit, collect, and readings of the third Sunday in all three years.

On the fourth Sunday in the 1962 Missal is the third of the *Excita* collects, crying out to the Lord, "Stir up thy power and come, and with great might succour us." The Missal of Paul VI shifts it to Thursday of the first week,[73] replacing it with the familiar prayer after the Angelus, rendered in RM 2011 as

Pour forth, we beseech you, O Lord,
your grace into our hearts,
that we, to whom the Incarnation of Christ your Son
was made known by the message of an Angel,
may by his Passion and Cross
be brought to the glory of his Resurrection.

The previous translation was a lot looser: "Lord, fill our hearts with your love, and as you revealed to us by an angel the coming of your Son as man, so lead us through his suffering and death to the glory of his resurrection." In the *Hadrianum* this is the post-Communion of the feast of the Annunciation on March 25 (H 142), but it functions perfectly as the collect of the fourth Sunday because of its mention of the incarnation, which is at the center of all the readings on this Sunday and, as we will see below, is even referred to in the prayer over

---

[73] RM 1975 translated it lamely as "Father, we need your help."

the offerings. However, it quickly passes from the incarnation to the paschal events and concludes with the petition that we be granted a share in the glory of the resurrection, which, of course, is reserved for the eschatological future. The prayer, then, admirably binds together the two advents of Christ and in the final petition connects the last Sunday of the season with the first two on which we prayed to be at Christ's side in his kingdom and to be admitted to his company in heaven.

This section would not be complete without a few words about the two other presidential prayers, the prayer over the offerings, and the prayer after Communion. On the first Sunday the prayer over the offerings is taken from the *Veronensis* (V 575). It asks that what we celebrate here below may "gain for us the prize of eternal redemption." In the gospel of Year C Jesus declares that "your redemption is near at hand" (Luke 21:28). The post-Communion of the first Sunday in RM 1962 is now on December 18. Its replacement is a combination of two texts from the collection in Verona—V 1053 and V 175—asking that "as we walk amid passing things" God teach us "to love the things of heaven." Both of these prayers fit well with the eschatological character of the first Sunday and probably for this reason were chosen to replace the secret and post-Communion of RM 1962.

On the second and third Sundays the prayer over the offerings and the prayer after Communion are the same in both missals. Those of the fourth Sunday, leaning toward the coming celebration of Christ's birth, are different. The prayer over the offerings is from the Sacramentary of Bergamo (B 84). Echoing the gospel of Year A when Mary is "found to be with child from the Holy Spirit" (Matt 1:18) and Year B when the angel Gabriel assures her that "the Holy Spirit will come upon you" (Luke 1:35), it prays:

> May the Holy Spirit, O Lord,
> sanctify these gifts laid upon your altar,
> just as he filled with his power
>   the womb of the Blessed Virgin Mary.

The prayer after Communion, the first words of which are from V 741 and the rest a modification of a Lenten preface,[74] looks entirely toward Christmas, calling it "the feast day of our salvation" and asking that

---

[74] See Johnson-Ward, *Sources*, 495.

at its approach "we may press forward all the more eagerly/to the worthy celebration of the mystery of your Son's Nativity." As we will see shortly, the prayers over the offerings and the prayers after Communion of the first three Sundays are repeated on weekdays through the third Friday.

Following the prayer after Communion on every Sunday during the seasons of Advent, Christmas, and Easter, the current Missal indicates that "a formula of solemn blessing may be used." These formulas are found after the Order of Mass. They are introduced by an invitation of the deacon or priest—bow down for the blessing—and consist of three parts after each of which the faithful respond, "Amen." The first and third parts of the solemn blessing for Advent refer to both comings of Christ. The first part prays,

> May the almighty and merciful God,
> by whose grace you have placed your faith
> in the First Coming of his Only Begotten Son
> and yearn for his coming again,
> sanctify you by the radiance of Christ's Advent
> and enrich you with his blessing.

The third part adds,

> So that, rejoicing now with devotion
> at the Redeemer's coming in the flesh,
> you may be endowed with the rich reward of eternal life
> when he comes again in majesty.

2. Weekdays through December 16

In the Lectionary and Missal of Paul VI there are two series of weekday Masses. Both are new and have no counterparts in RM 1962. The first series is for days of the week: from Monday of the first week through Friday of the third week. The second series is for days of the month: December 17 through December 24. This series takes precedence over the first one, except for Sundays, and can begin as early as the second Saturday when Christmas falls on a Monday.

Readings. As the introduction to the Lectionary, no. 94, explains, in the first series "there are readings from the Book of Isaiah, distributed in accord with the sequence of the book itself and including the more important texts that are also read on the Sundays." This holds at least up to Thursday of the second week. Until then the first reading is a semicontinuous reading of Isaiah 1–40. The gospels are an assortment of passages from Matthew and Luke for the choice of which "the first reading has been taken into consideration," declares the introduction to the Lectionary, no. 94. In those early days, though, the accent is on Isaiah.

This changes on Thursday of the second week when the emphasis shifts to the gospels. Beginning on that day and extending through Friday of the third week are passages from the gospels pertaining to John the Baptist. These are taken from Matthew and Luke except on the last day when John 5:33-36 is chosen. On these days, says the introduction to the Lectionary, no. 94, "the first reading is either a continuation of Isaiah or a text chosen in view of the Gospel." Actually, there are only three readings during that period that are not from Isaiah: Sirach 48:1-3, 9-11 on the second Saturday, the praise of Elijah to whom Jesus in the gospel likens John the Baptist; Numbers 24:2-7, 15-17a on Monday of the third week, the oracle of Balaam; and Zephaniah 3:1-2, 9-13 on Tuesday of the third week, the promise of salvation to a faithful remnant in Jerusalem.

Prayers. Of the seventeen collects of these Masses six are from the Old Gelasian,[75] six are from the *Rotulus* of Ravenna,[76] and five are from RM 1962—the three *Excita* collects of the first, second, and fourth Sundays transferred to Friday of the first week, Thursday of the second week, and Thursday of the first week, respectively, and two from ember Saturday, the third transferred to Thursday of the third week and the fourth to Wednesday of the third week.

Some of these prayers, especially those from the Old Gelasian, look to the Parousia. That of the first Monday, for example, asks God to

> Keep us alert . . .
> as we await the advent of Christ your Son,
> so that, when he comes and knocks,
> he may find us watchful in prayer
> and exultant in his praise.

---

[75] M 1 = GeV 1128; W 1 = GeV 1131; F 2 = GeV 1136; M 3 = GeV 1137; Tu 3 = GeV 49; F 3 = GeV 1126.

[76] Tu 1 = Rot 3 (V 1334); Sa 1 = Rot 7 (V 1338); M 2 = Rot 13 (V 1344); Tu 2 = Rot 14 (V 1345); W 2 = Rot 6 (V 1337); Sa 2 = Rot 19 (V 1350).

That of the first Wednesday prays that

> at the coming of Christ your Son
> we may be found worthy of the banquet of eternal life
> and merit to receive heavenly nourishment from his hands.

That of the second Friday requests that

> as the author of our salvation himself has taught us,
> we may hasten, alert and with lighted lamps,
> to meet him when he comes.

All three of these prayers are based on Luke 12:35-37: "Have your lamps lit; be like those who are waiting for their master to return from the wedding banquet, so that they may open the door for him as soon as he comes and knocks. . . . He will . . . have them sit down to eat, and he will come and serve them."

Other prayers are concerned with preparation for Christmas. That of the second Monday asks that

> with purity unblemished,
> we, your servants, may come . . .
> to celebrate the great mystery
> of the Incarnation.

That of the second Tuesday prays that "we may look forward in joy / to the glorious Nativity of Christ." That of the first Saturday includes both comings. After recalling that God sent his "Only Begotten Son into this world / to free the human race from its ancient enslavement," it entreats him to "bestow on those who devoutly await him / the grace of your compassion from on high."

The prayers over the offerings and prayers after Communion on weekdays through the third Friday are not proper but, as was pointed out above, taken from the first three Sundays. Those of the first Sunday are repeated every Monday and Thursday, those of the second Sunday are repeated every Tuesday and Friday, and those of the third Sunday are repeated every Wednesday and on Saturday of the first two weeks but not the third. The third Saturday already forms part of the second series of weekday Masses, those meant for days of the month—that is, December 17 through December 24. For over a thousand years the "O" antiphons[77] have been chanted with the Magnificat during this period, and Morning Prayer has had proper antiphons for each day. In 384 the Council of Saragossa decreed that starting on December 17, the faithful should gather in church daily until Epiphany.[78]

3. Weekdays from December 17 through December 24

Readings. The introduction to the Lectionary, no. 94, states, "In the last week before Christmas the events that immediately prepared for the Lord's birth are presented from the Gospels of Matthew (chapter 1) and Luke (chapter 1)." The readings from Matthew are on December 17 and 18—the opening genealogy in 1:1-17, followed by the annunciation to Joseph in 1:18-24. On December 19–24 is continuous reading of the first chapter of Luke—on December 19 the appearance of the angel Gabriel to Zechariah in the temple, announcing the conception of John (1:5-25); on December 20 the annunciation to Mary (1:26-38); on December 21 the visitation (1:39-45); on December 22 Mary's Magnificat; on December 23 the birth and naming of John (1:57-66); and on December 24 the prophecy of Zechariah, or *Benedictus* (1:67-79). "The texts in the first reading," the introduction to the Lectionary, no. 94, adds, "chosen in view of the Gospel reading, are from different Old Testament books and include important Messianic prophecies." The content of this second series of weekday Masses, then, is basically the same as that of the Ember Days in RM 1962, only much fuller.

An innovation of the Lectionary of Paul VI is that the Alleluia verses at these Masses are the "O" antiphons.

Prayers. Like the collects of the first series of weekday Masses, those of December 17–24 derive from a variety of sources. Two are from RM 1962: that of December 18 is the second oration of ember Saturday. That of December 24 is the collect of ember Wednesday. Of the six others, four are from the *Rotulus* of Ravenna—those of December 17, 19,

---

[77] For short reflections on these, including indications of biblical allusions, see Nocent, *Liturgical Year* I, 162–67.

[78] See Connell, "The Origins and Evolution of Advent," 363–65.

20, and 23.[79] These prayers do not so much prepare for Christmas as anticipate it.[80] The one for December 17 may be the richest doctrinally:

> O God, Creator and Redeemer of human nature,
> who willed that your Word should take flesh
> in an ever-virgin womb,
> look with favor on our prayers,
> that your Only Begotten Son,
> having taken to himself our humanity,
> may be pleased to grant us a share in his divinity.

On December 20, when the first reading relates the Lord's sign to Ahaz in Isaiah 7:10-14 and the gospel recounts the annunciation to Mary from Luke 1:26-38, the collect is entirely Marian in content:

> O God, eternal majesty, whose ineffable Word
> the immaculate Virgin received through the message of an Angel
> and so became the dwelling-place of divinity,
> filled with the light of the Holy Spirit,
> grant, we pray, that by her example
> we may in humility hold fast to your will.

On December 21 both comings of Christ are included in the request

> that those who rejoice
> at the coming of your Only Begotten Son in our flesh
> may, when at last he comes in glory,
> gain the reward of eternal life.

Reference to Christ's coming "in our flesh" and his future coming "in glory" recalls the contrast many of the fathers made between the two advents of the Lord.

Unlike the first series of weekday Masses, each day from December 17 through December 24 has its own prayer over the offerings and prayer after Communion. On December 18 the post-Communion of the first Sunday in RM 1962 is used. The others are taken from a broad

---

[79] They are Rot 31 (= V 1362), Rot 2 (= V 1333), Rot 30 (= V 1361), and Rot 24 (= V 1355), respectively.

[80] Preface II of Advent declares this explicitly: "It is by his [Christ's] gift that already we rejoice / at the mystery of his Nativity."

range of ancient sources, sometimes with modifications. Several take note of the approach of Christmas. The prayer over the offerings on December 23 asks "that we may celebrate with minds made pure / the Nativity of our Redeemer." The prayer after Communion of December 19 asks that "we may welcome the Nativity of our Savior." Other prayers mention the Second Coming. The one after Communion on December 17 prays that "aflame with your Spirit, / we may shine like bright torches before your Christ when he comes." That of December 22 asks "that we may go out to meet our Savior / with worthy deeds when he comes"—another allusion to the bridesmaids of Matthew 25:6, first heard in the collect of the second Sunday. On December 24 both comings of Christ are mentioned but in different prayers. The prayer over the offerings refers to the Parousia, asking to be cleansed of sins in order "to stand ready with pure hearts / for the coming in glory of your Son." The prayer after Communion acknowledges that "we prepare to celebrate in adoration / the festivities of your Son's Nativity," then adds a petition eschatological in character, praying that "we may possess in gladness / his everlasting rewards."

4. Two New Prefaces

The third typical edition of the Missal of Paul VI contains some ninety-two prefaces, two of which are for Advent.[81] The first is used through December 16; the second from December 17 to 24. Both have the same structure: recollection of divine munificence in past salvation history, a brief mention of present activity, and a longer expression of future hope. The subtitle of the first preface is "The two comings of Christ." It begins by recalling that Christ

> assumed at his first coming
> the lowliness of human flesh,
> and so fulfilled the design you formed long ago,
> and opened for us the way to eternal salvation.

At present, it says, "we watch" and "we dare to hope." The object of our hope is that "when he comes again in glory and majesty / and

---

[81] The 1975 Roman Missal contained eighty-two prefaces. For their liturgical sources as well as possible biblical and patristic allusions, see Anthony Ward, SM, and Cuthbert Johnson, OSB, *The Prefaces of the Roman Missal* (Rome: Tipografia Poliglotta Vaticana, 1989).

all is at last made manifest," we "may inherit the great promise." The preface gives daily expression to the theme that dominates the readings and prayers of the first part of the season and tells how what Christ did for us in the past makes us confident of receiving what he promised to do for us in the future.[82] In other words, thanksgiving for the first coming generates longing for the second—and should, we might add, dispel inordinate fears of divine punishment. The contrast between the two comings—the humility of the first and the glory of the second—expounded by the fathers and mentioned in several prayers is also highlighted here.

The first section of the second preface singles out the persons who figure so prominently in the readings of the last eight days of Advent: the prophets, the virgin mother, the baptizer. It recalls that

> the oracles of the prophets foretold him [Christ],
> the Virgin Mother longed for him
> with love beyond all telling,
> John the Baptist sang of his coming
> and proclaimed his presence when he came.

In the last week of this season, it confesses that "already we rejoice / at the mystery of his Nativity." Our hope is that when this mystery is finally celebrated at the arrival of Christmas, "he may find us watchful in prayer / and exultant in his praise." The subtitle of this preface is "The twofold expectation of Christ." The first preface spoke of the two comings of Christ. The second speaks of only one coming but of two groups waiting for it. The first group is the prophets, the virgin mother, and the baptizer. The second group is us. They awaited it in the past. We do so in the present. Theirs was historical. Ours is liturgical.

5. Conclusion

The Missal of Paul VI makes expectation of the second coming of Christ as integral a part of Advent as recollection of his first coming. It provides Mass formularies for all the weekdays of the season. Those

---

[82] This corresponds exactly to the description of the season in Universal Norms, no. 39: a time "in which the First Coming of the Son of God to humanity is remembered, and likewise a time when, by remembrance of this, minds and hearts are led to look forward to Christ's Second Coming at the end of time."

on December 17–24 prepare for Christmas in an explicit way and are far more comprehensive in content than the Ember Days of RM 1962. Since many of the new prayers are taken from the Old Gelasian Sacramentary, Advent in the Missal of Paul VI gives wonderful expression, perhaps for the first time, to the full liturgical heritage of the church of Rome, presbyteral as well as papal. Prayers taken from the *Rotulus* of Ravenna disclose the profound doctrinal content of the season. The two new prefaces exemplify the best of what contemporary creative skill, rooted in tradition, can produce.

Whereas readings in the 1962 Missal are few and often randomly arranged, the postconciliar Lectionary is marvelous in structure and content. It includes virtually all the messianic prophecies of the Old Testament, especially those of Isaiah, all the texts about the mission of John the Baptist, and all the material in the gospels leading up to the birth of Jesus. Presidential prayers are frequently aligned with the readings.

Chapter 2

Christmas Time

Preliminaries. The general rubrics of the Roman Missal of 1962 state in no. 72 that "the Christmas season [*tempus Natalicium*] runs from First Vespers of the Nativity of the Lord through January 13 inclusive." The same number adds that this season encompasses two periods: (a) the time of the Nativity (*tempus Nativitatis*) and (b) the time of Epiphany (*tempus Epiphaniae*). The first extends "from First Vespers of the Nativity of the Lord through None of January 5 inclusive," and the second "from First Vespers of the Epiphany through January 13 inclusive." On January 13 the Missal provides a Mass commemorating the baptism of the Lord, unless this day falls on a Sunday, in which case the feast of the Holy Family is celebrated.

The 1969 Universal Norms on the Liturgical Year and the Calendar is noticeably different. They begin by setting forth the importance of the Christmas season and what it now includes. "After the annual celebration of the Paschal Mystery," states no. 32, "the Church has no more ancient custom than celebrating the memorial of the Nativity of the Lord and of his first manifestations, and this takes place in Christmas Time [*tempus Nativitatis*]." The season, then, is second in importance to the Triduum and the fifty days of Easter, and it is no longer divided into two periods as it is in RM 1962 but forms a single whole celebrating both the birth of Christ and his early manifestations.

The Universal Norms then specifies the temporal boundaries of this liturgical period. According to no. 33, "Christmas Time [*tempus Nativitatis*] runs from First Vespers (Evening Prayer I) of the Nativity of the Lord up to and including the Sunday after Epiphany or after 6 January." The beginning of the season is the same as in RM 1962, but its end is extended until the Sunday after Epiphany or after January 6, on which day the baptism of the Lord is celebrated, as stipulated in nos. 37 and 38. *Tempus Nativitatis*, then, has been broadened to include not only the Nativity but also what RM 1962 calls *tempus Epiphaniae*, the Epiphany and baptism of the Lord. In other words, it is "the memorial of the Nativity of the Lord and of his first manifestations," as no. 32 of the Universal Norms declares.

43

The feast of the Nativity originated at Rome, as is known from a calendar included in the so-called Chronograph of 354, copied by Furius Dionysius Philocalus, friend and admirer of Pope Damasus (366–84). The calendar, bearing the title *Depositio martyrum* and compiled in 336, contains the names and burial places of Roman martyrs as well as the dates of their birth to eternal life. At the head of the list is written, *VIII kal. Ian. Natus Christus in Betleem Iudeae*, "On the eighth of the calends of January [that is, December 25] Christ is born in Bethlehem of Judea." Since the purpose of the calendar is practical, to provide information about when and where the anniversaries of the martyrs were being celebrated so that the faithful could attend, we may conclude that at Rome December 25 was being observed liturgically as the feast of Christ's earthly birth.[1]

It may seem strange that the first notice of a celebration of the nativity should show up in a list of martyrs. We should observe how the list is organized. At the time it was compiled, December was the tenth month of the civil year, which began in March. But in the *Depositio martyrum* it is the first month, and the birth of Christ, though not celebrated until the twenty-fifth day, is the first entry on that month. The compiler is obviously not organizing his material chronologically, either according to the months of the civil year or according to the days of the month, but highlighting the birth of Christ by putting it at the top of his list and making it the beginning of the year as arranged by him. His intention may have been to emphasize the primacy of Christ when the enormous popularity of devotion to martyrs threatened to eclipse him.[2]

Significantly, the *Veronensis*, which has much in common with the *Depositio martyrum* in the Philocalian Calendar, likewise couples the birth of Christ with that of martyrs. Above its nine sets of Christmas Masses it places the title *VIII kalendas Ianuarias. Natale Domini et martyrum pastoris Basilei et Iouiani et Uictorini et Eugeniae et Felicitatis et Anastasiae*, "On the eighth of the calends of January. The birth of the Lord and of the martyrs bishop Basil and Jovian and Victorinus and

---

[1] On the notice of Christ's birth on December 25 in the Philocalian Calendar and reasons for the choice of this date, see Susan K. Roll, "The Origins of Christmas: The State of the Question," in Maxwell E. Johnson, ed., *Between Memory and Hope* (Collegeville, MN: Liturgical Press, 2000) 273–90, and more recently Bradshaw-Johnson, "25 December: Two Competing Theories," in their *Origins of Feasts*, 123–30. They provide an English translation of the *Depositio martyrum* on p. 176.

[2] See Bradshaw-Johnson, *Origins of Feasts*, 173.

Eugenia and Felicity and Anastasia." Just as the list of martyrs in the Calendar of 354 begins with notice of the birth of Christ, so does the title of Masses meant for celebrating the Lord's *natale* on December 25 disclose the names of that day's martyrs—even though no Mass texts are provided for them. The point is that December 25 is the *natale* of both the Lord and these six martyrs. All were born on the same day, though not in the same way. He was born to earthly life, they to heavenly life.[3] But his made theirs possible, and theirs is the full realization of the purpose of his. Remembrance of his *natale*, therefore, is inseparable from recollection of theirs.

We notice, then, that these two Roman documents—the *Depositio martyrum* and the *Veronensis*—situate celebration of the birth of Christ, Roman in origin, within the context of another characteristically Roman practice: celebration of the birthdays of martyrs. From this perspective Christmas in early Christian Rome may have been understood primarily as celebrating the earthly birth of him to whom the martyrs by their heavenly birth bore witness and apart from whom the shedding of their blood is worthless. This would explain why liturgical texts generated by the feast show so little interest in details surrounding the birth of Jesus as portrayed in Luke 2:1-14—the manger, the shepherds, the angels—and focus instead almost exclusively on the marvelous consequences of that event for the regeneration of a human race fallen but destined for glory.[4] Nor can we forget that on the day immediately following celebration of the nativity of Christ on earth is celebrated the birth in heaven of the protomartyr, Stephen.[5]

---

[3] On December 25 the first Roman Martyrology, published in 1584, notes that in Nicomedia on this day a multitude had convened in church to celebrate the birth of Christ, and the emperor Diocletian ordered the doors locked and set the building on fire, thus burning them alive. The entry concludes by saying that these martyrs "merited to be born in heaven on the same day on which Christ was once born on earth for the salvation of the world" (trans. mine). Latin text in Manlio Sodi and Roberto Fusco, eds., *Martyrologium Romanum: Editio Princeps*, Monumenta Liturgica Concilii Tridentini 6 (Città del Vaticano: Libreria Editrice Vaticana, 2005) no. 2833.

[4] Dogmatic acquisitions of the fourth and fifth centuries also had enormous impact. But these too were grounded in the event of salvation. The fundamental conviction is that Christ could not reconcile sinful humanity to God without himself being both fully divine and fully human.

[5] The post-Communion for the Mass of Saint Stephen in the Old Gelasian, GeV 34, recalls both the nativity of Christ and the martyrdom of Stephen.

The Universal Norms, no. 34, indicates that "on the day of the Nativity of the Lord, following ancient Roman tradition, Mass may be celebrated three times, that is, in the night, at dawn and during the day."[6] Both of our missals have formularies for these Masses. The oldest of the three is the third, celebrated in the early fourth century by the pope and Christian populace at Saint Peter's around 9:00 a.m. The one during the night was probably introduced by Sixtus III (432–40) after the Council of Ephesus in 431 defended the divine maternity of Mary and the legitimacy of calling her *Theotokos*, or "Bearer of God." It was celebrated at Saint Mary Major in a chapel that Sixtus had constructed there in imitation of the grotto in Bethlehem where Jesus was born. The second Mass, celebrated at Saint Anastasia on the southwest tip of the Palatine Hill at dawn, began in the second half of the sixth century. Anastasia of Sirmium, highly venerated at Constantinople, was martyred on December 25. She is the last of the six martyrs mentioned in the title of the Christmas Masses in the *Veronensis*. It seems that Pope John III (561–74), on his way from Saint Mary Major after the night Mass to Saint Peter's for the day Mass, began the practice of celebrating a Eucharist with the Byzantine court and the Greek community at Saint Anastasia. Righetti maintains that this Mass originally was in honor of the martyr, had nothing to do with the nativity, and that only when Byzantine domination waned in the eighth century did it become a Christmas Mass with only a commemoration of Anastasia.[7] If correct, this would show yet again how at Rome, even on Christmas Day, liturgical activity was divided between two births: that of Christ and that of a martyr.

Before mentioning the custom of the three Christmas Masses, the Universal Norms, no. 34, declares that "the Vigil Mass of the Nativity is used on the evening of 24 December, either before or after First Vespers (Evening Prayer I)." It is here that our discussion of the Mass formularies begins.

Incorporated into the postconciliar Missal, it reads, "[W]e give thanks to you, O Lord, / who save us through the Nativity of your Son / and gladden us with the celebration of the blessed Martyr Stephen."

[6] On the origin and history of these three Masses, see Mario Righetti, *Manuale di storia liturgica*, 3rd ed., 4 vols. (Milano: Editirce Ancora, 1969) II, 72–80; Jounel, *Church* IV, 83–84; and Adam, *Liturgical Year*, 125–26.

[7] Righetti, *Manuale* II, 76.

A. THE NATIVITY OF THE LORD

1. Vigil Mass

As we have seen, in the 1962 Missal this is the last Mass of Advent, celebrated on the morning of December 24. The Missal of Paul VI provides a different formulary for that occasion and restores the vigil to its original position in the early evening where once again it ushers in the Christmas season. The magnificent entrance antiphon, Alleluia verse, and communion antiphon are still in place, as are the collect and prayer after Communion. A new prayer over the offerings from V 1254 and GeV 3 replaces the one in RM 1962, probably because the latter declares that at this Eucharist "we anticipate the adorable birthday of thy Son." Since 1970, however, the vigil is already Christmas, not an anticipation of it. The new prayer also picks up the redemption theme of the collect, declaring that the solemnity being celebrated is the *principium nostrae redemptionis*, "the beginning of our redemption."

The introduction to the Lectionary, no. 95, informs us that "for the Vigil and the three Masses of Christmas both the prophetic readings and the others have been chosen from the Roman tradition," by which it probably means the Lectionary of Murbach because, except for the second reading at the vigil, the readings in that lectionary are exactly the same as those in the postconciliar one, including the four selections from Isaiah. Readings at the Christmas Masses are the same on all three years.

The Old Testament reading at the vigil, Isaiah 62:1-5, of course, is not found in RM 1962 but taken from the Lectionary of Murbach (M I). It is the second poem about the glorious restoration of Jerusalem, the first, Isaiah 61, being saved until Epiphany. In liturgical context it brings out the profoundly spousal dimension of the incarnation. "For the Lord delights in you, and your land shall be married. For as a young man marries a young woman, so shall your builder marry you, and as the bridegroom rejoices over the bride, so shall your God rejoice over you."

The gospel of the vigil, Matthew 1:1-25, incorporates that of RM 1962, the annunciation to Joseph in Matthew 1:18-21, but adds the last four verses of that chapter which, after relating that Mary's virginal conception fulfills the prophecy of Isaiah 7:14, tell how Joseph took Mary as his wife and named the child Jesus. More important, this narrative is prefaced by the genealogy in Matthew 1:1-16, connecting Jesus to David and Abraham, thereby making him the one toward whom all of salvation history is directed and in whom all the promises are fulfilled.[8]

To complement this addition and reinforce its message, the Lectionary replaces the epistle of RM 1962 with Saint Paul's inaugural discourse in the synagogue at Antioch in Pisidia (Acts 13:16-17, 22-25), recalling key episodes in Israel's history—the exodus, the choice of David, and the exhortation of John the Baptist to look for one coming after him—to show that in Jesus, raised from the dead, everything God intended for his people from the beginning has at last been realized, though not recognized. Inclusion in this passage of John's preaching a baptism of repentance neatly binds this opening Eucharist of Christmas to many of the Advent readings and makes a smooth transition between the two seasons. Nor must we forget that for Cassian the nativity too is an advent.

2. Mass during the Night

Unlike popular parlance, liturgical sources never identify this eucharistic celebration as Midnight Mass but always the Mass *in nocte*, "during the night."[9] The texts in both missals are practically the same. The gospel recounts the birth of the Savior and the announcement of this "good news of great joy" to the shepherds. The passage brings to mind many details of the burial and resurrection narratives. The infant wrapped in swaddling bands and lying in a manger (Luke 2:7, 16) anticipates his being wrapped in a linen cloth and laid in the tomb (Luke 23:53). The shepherds "keeping watch by night" in Luke 2:8 evoke the women at the foot of the cross "watching these things" in Luke 23:49 after darkness had fallen (Luke 23:44), as well as Joseph of Arimathea "waiting expectantly for the kingdom of God" in Luke 23:51. The terror of the shepherds at seeing the angel and the glory of the Lord in Luke 2:9 parallels that of the women seeing "two men in dazzling clothes" at the empty tomb (Luke 24:5) and that of the Eleven and other disciples at the sight of the risen Jesus (Luke 24:37), whose greeting of "Peace" in Luke 24:36 echoes the song of the angelic throng at his birth (Luke 2:14). Finally, at the conclusion of the pericope—not read until the Mass at dawn—the shepherds' "glorifying and praising God for all that they had heard and seen" in Luke 2:20 foretells the

---

[8] The shorter form of the gospel omits the genealogy.

[9] See titles in Bruylants I, no. 10.

journey of faith of all who later will hear and see Christ risen from the dead. Glimpses of the Savior's saving work are already evident at his birth.

The epistle of RM 1962, Titus 2:11-15, is the second reading in the postconciliar Mass but without the last verse. It presents Christian life as unfolding between two epiphanies—the appearance of divine grace in the earthly ministry of Christ and the manifestation of future glory awaited as a blessed hope. Inclusion of the statement that Christ "gave himself for us that he might redeem us from all iniquity and purify for himself a people of his own who are zealous for good deeds" (Titus 2:14) is one of the biblical foundations for all the references to redemption in the Christmas liturgy. We have already called attention to three of them in two orations of the vigil. The prayer after Communion on this night contains another. It calls Christmas "the feast of our Redeemer's Nativity."

The first reading in the Lectionary, not in RM 1962, is Isaiah 9:1-3, 5-6. It tells that a "child has been born for us" and a "son given to us," then discloses four names to be conferred upon him: "Wonderful Counselor, Mighty God, Everlasting Father, Prince of Peace." In biblical context this is the child whom a virgin, probably a young wife of the king, would conceive and name Emmanuel (Isa 7:14), thereby perpetuating a threatened dynasty and providing assurance of God's continued favor—the "sign" of Isaiah 7:11, 14. Since Matthew 1:22-23 identifies the child in question as Jesus, it is legitimate to see the "child born" and the "son given" as likewise applying to him. It is his birth that prompts the rejoicing and exultation foreseen in Isaiah 9:2, his resurrection that makes David's throne eternal (Acts 2:22-36) and establishes the everlasting peace of Isaiah 9:7.

The introit in RM 1962, *Dominus dixit ad me*, is Psalm 2:7, "The Lord hath said to me: thou art my Son, this day have I begotten thee," repeated in the Alleluia verse. The gradual is Psalm 109:3, "from the womb before the day star I begot thee," words heard again in the communion. These texts as well as Psalm 88:26-27 make known the Old Testament belief, found in Nathan's message to David in 2 Samuel 7:14 and 2 Chronicles 17:13, that God adopts or begets the reigning monarch as his son. In the context of the Mass *in nocte* these passages give liturgical expression to the doctrine that the son of Mary born in Bethlehem is also the Son of God, begotten by the Father from all eternity.

The Missal of Paul VI retains the introit of RM 1962 but also provides an alternate, "Let us all rejoice in the Lord, for our Savior has been born to the world. / Today true peace has come down to us from heaven." It changes the Alleluia verse from Psalm 109:3 to the message of the heavenly host in Luke 2:10-11, about to be heard in the gospel, "I bring you news of great joy: today a savior has been born to us, Christ the Lord." For the communion antiphon it replaces Psalm 109:3 with John 1:14: "The Word became flesh and we have seen his glory," from the gospel of the Mass during the day. These changes seem aimed at obtaining greater correspondence between the chants and the biblical readings. But the elimination of Psalms 2 and 109 is unfortunate. In the past the doctrinal punch came from the juxtaposition of these psalms with the gospel story. Unless Psalm 2:7 is sung at the entrance, it now comes from the juxtaposition of the communion antiphon with the birth narrative.

The three presidential orations, taken from H 36, 37, and 40, are the same in both missals, except that the postconciliar one changes the first word of the Latin version of the prayer over the offerings from *Accepta* to *Grata*, based on V 1249, and "nativity of our Lord Jesus Christ" in the prayer after Communion to "our Redeemer's Nativity," thereby strengthening the redemption theme. As translated in RM 2011, mention in the collect of God making "this most sacred night radiant with the splendor of the true light" is certainly appropriate for the time at which this Mass is celebrated. The secret, or prayer over the offerings, on the other hand, is more dogmatic. It calls the Eucharist a *sacrosanctum commercium*, a "sacred interchange" in RM 1962 or "most holy exchange" in RM 2011, and it asks that through it we may be conformed to him in whom our human nature is one with God. The prayer, then, is making a parallel between two communions—Christ's communion in our humanity through the incarnation and our communion with him through the Eucharist.

3. *Mass at Dawn*

At the second Christmas Mass the current Lectionary repeats the epistle and gospel of RM 1962. Both of these continue the readings begun at the night Mass. The gospel, Luke 2:15-20, besides describing the visit of the shepherds to Bethlehem, adds that "Mary treasured all these words and pondered them in her heart" (Luke 2:19). The epistle, or reading from the apostle, Titus 3:4-7, again presents salvation as an epiphany, this time of divine goodness and mercy, specifying that the redemption and purification mentioned in 2:14 at the night Mass reach us through "the water of rebirth" and include "renewal by the

Holy Spirit" (3:5). The first reading, Isaiah 62:11-12, added in the 1969 Order of Readings, resumes that of the vigil Mass (Isa 62:1-5), calling the exiles whom the Lord delivers and espouses "holy" and his "redeemed"—a condition fully realized in "the waters of rebirth" and "renewal by the Holy Spirit" mentioned in the second reading.

The collect, from H 41, is common to both missals. Like the one during the night, it too makes use of light imagery. In the 2011 translation it asks that

> as we are bathed in the new radiance of your incarnate Word,
> the light of faith, which illumines our minds,
> may also shine through in our deeds.

The prayer over the offerings is also the same, except that the 2011 version omits the petition in the 1962 Missal that the gifts "ever shed forth peace upon us," not found in H 44 or GeV 7. Like the *Super oblata* of the night Mass, this one too draws a parallel between the incarnation and the Eucharist, praying that "just as Christ was born a man and also shone forth as God, / so these earthly gifts may confer on us what is divine." The post-Communion in RM 1962 is a profound and tightly constructed formula from H 48, asking that the Eucharist renew the communicants as the birth of Christ renews the whole human race: "Let the newness of this sacrament, O Lord, ever restore us on the birthday of him whose birth revived mankind grown old." The reformed Missal replaces it with part of a Visigothic one[10] that prays,

> Grant us, Lord, as we honor with joyful devotion
> the Nativity of your Son,
> that we may come to know with fullness of faith
> the hidden depths of this mystery
> and to love them ever more and more.

Strangely, neither this nor the prayers after Communion of the two other Christmas Masses mention receiving Holy Communion.

The entrance antiphon in both missals, *Lux fulgebit*, is based on Isaiah 9:2, 6, read at the night Mass. "Today a light will shine upon us," it sings in RM 2011, "for the Lord is born to us"—eminently appropriate for a eucharistic celebration at dawn. The antiphon then mentions the

---

[10] See Johnson-Ward, *Sources*, 615.

four symbolic names conferred upon the newborn Lord, though the phraseology and order of these in the introit is slightly different from that of the Vulgate.[11] To the names it attaches words from Luke 1:33. In the latest translation they are "and his reign will be without end." The communion antiphon, taken from Zechariah 9:9, is likewise common to both missals. Matthew 21:5 and John 12:15 cite phrases from this passage and apply them to Jesus' entrance into Jerusalem on the back of a donkey. Significantly, Zechariah 9:9 describes the king who comes as "triumphant and victorious." The antiphon changes this to *sanctus et salvator mundi*, though two of the ancient antiphonals in AMS 10 read, *justus et salvator mundi*. In the 2011 translation the full text is "Rejoice, O Daughter Sion; lift up praise, Daughter Jerusalem: / Behold, your King will come, the Holy One and Savior of the world."[12]

The gradual in RM 1962 is taken from the great paschal psalm, Psalm 117:26, 27, 23, no doubt because of verse 27, "The Lord is God and he hath shone upon us." The rather generic Alleluia verse in RM 1962, Psalm 92:1, is replaced in the Lectionary by a more explicitly Christmas text, the song of the angelic chorus in Luke 2:14, the closing words of the gospel of the night Mass. In this way the gospel about to be heard at dawn is connected to the one already heard during the night.

The 1962 Missal requires a commemoration of Saint Anastasia after each of the presidential prayers. In 1970 the first typical edition of the reformed Missal eliminated them.

4. *Mass during the Day*

The gospel in RM 1962 is the prologue to the Gospel of John, ending at 1:14 with the declaration that "the Word was made flesh and dwelt

[11] As printed in the Vulgate, the names are *Admirabilis consiliarius, Deus fortis, Pater futuri saeculi,* and *Princeps pacis.* The introit changes them to *Admirabilis, Deus, Princeps pacis,* and *Pater futuri saeculi,* and does so already in the ancient antiphonals (see AMS 10). The 1962 Missal translates them exactly as "Wonderful, God, Prince of Peace, the Father of the World to Come." Although the Latin text of the introit in the 2008 *Missale Romanum* is the same as the 1962 Missal, the English version of 2011 reduces the names to three and translates them "Wondrous God, Prince of Peace, Father of Future Ages." Except for *Pater aeternitatis* instead of *Pater futuri saeculi,* the Neo-Vulgate is the same as the Vulgate.

[12] RM 1962 has "Rejoice greatly, O daughter of Sion, shout for joy, O daughter of Jerusalem: behold thy King comes, holy, the Savior of the world."

among us." The Lectionary retains the prologue but adds verses 15-18, the testimony of John the Baptist and the contrast between Moses and Christ, thus providing all three parts of this magnificent hymn about the divine Word—his eternal existence with God, his incarnation as only-begotten Son, and his earthly mission of making known the Father. The beginning of the Letter to the Hebrews, similar in content to the prologue to the Fourth Gospel, is the epistle in RM 1962 and the reading from the apostle in the postconciliar Lectionary. Both contain the dense doctrinal message of the Son's relationship to the Father and his expiation of sins, subsequent exaltation, and superiority to the angels (Heb 1:1-6). In the Lectionary the reading ends here. RM 1962 continues the comparison between Christ and the angels to verse 12. The Old Testament reading, proper to the Mass of Paul VI, is Isaiah 52:7-10, telling of the redemption of Jerusalem and a new era in which not a merely earthly king but the Lord himself would reign, and not only over Israel but to the ends of the earth—a glorious vision realized in Christ.

The collect of RM 1962, from H 49, is mainly moral, praying that the new birth of Christ "may set us free, who are held by the old bondage under the yoke of sin." The reformed Missal shifts this prayer to December 30 and replaces it on Christmas Day with a more dogmatic one, first found with a slight verbal variant in V 1239. After marveling at how God wonderfully created human beings and even more wonderfully re-created them, it asks that "we may share in the divinity of Christ, who humbled himself to share in our humanity"—another expression of the divine-human exchange effected by the incarnation.[13]

The Missal of Paul VI also replaces the secret of the 1962 Missal, from H 50, with a theologically richer one from GeV 19, asking that God make acceptable

> our oblation on this solemn day,
> when you manifested the reconciliation
> that makes us wholly pleasing in your sight
> and inaugurated for us the fullness of divine worship.

The prayer after Communion, from H 53, is the same in both missals. In the latest translation it asks

---

[13] In the extraordinary form the priest recites another version of this prayer at the offertory when blessing and pouring water into the chalice.

that, just as the Savior of the world, born this day,
is the author of divine generation for us,
so he may be the giver even of immortality.

Noteworthy is the phrase "Savior of the world," already encountered several times in the Christmas liturgy, most recently in the communion antiphon of the Mass at dawn. Here it is followed by the words "born this day." Given the inseparability of person and work, being and acting, in the case of Christ,[14] salvation is not just something the Savior does but the reality that he is. Salvation, in other words, is identical with the person of the Savior. To assert that "the Savior of the world" is "born this day" is to affirm not only the entrance into the world of the Savior but also the presence and availability in him of salvation. The same phrase appears in the proper *communicantes* of the Roman Canon, taken from H 39 and 52. In the 2011 translation it asserts that we are

[c]elebrating the most sacred night (day)
on which blessed Mary the immaculate Virgin
brought forth the Savior for this world.

Christmas, then, is not a mere mental recall of the birth of Jesus in past history but the annual ecclesial making present in word and sacrament of the always-actual salvation subsisting in his person and thereby appropriating it.

All the chants of the 1962 Missal are retained in the new one. The introit, *Puer natus est nobis*, is drawn from Isaiah 9:6, as is that of the dawn Mass. Here, however, the "child born to us" is called by only one name, *magni consilii angelus*, translated "Angel of great counsel" in RM 1962 and "Messenger of great counsel" in RM 2011. In the Vulgate the first name is *Admirabilis consiliarius*, "Wonderful Counselor." The introit of the dawn Mass omits the noun, retaining only the adjective "Wonderful" as the first of the four names. The introit of the Mass during the day, for its part, omits "Wonderful," adds *angelus*, and, changing "Counselor" to "of great counsel," produces the name "Angel of great counsel" or "Messenger of great counsel."

---

[14] Joseph Ratzinger, *Introduction to Christianity* (New York: Herder and Herder, 1973), 148–51.

The communion antiphon in RM 1962 is Psalm 97:3, "All the ends of the earth have seen the salvation of our God," a text also used in the gradual with two other verses of that psalm. The Missal of Paul VI retains Psalm 97:3 as the communion antiphon and adopts Psalm 97 as the responsorial psalm, using verse 3 as the congregational refrain. The content of these chants is enhanced in the postconciliar Mass by the choice of Isaiah 52:7-10 as the first reading, the conclusion of which is the same as Psalm 97:3 except for the verb being in the future: "All the ends of the earth shall see the salvation of our God." The salvation that for Isaiah still lay in the future is made present in Christ and acclaimed as such in the refrain of the responsorial psalm, "All the ends of the earth have seen the salvation of our God."

The Alleluia verse, common to both missals and reaching back to the earliest antiphonals,[15] splendidly expresses the universality of salvation. As found in the RML 1981, it sings, "A hallowed day has dawned upon us. Come, you nations, worship the Lord, for today a great light has shown down upon the earth."[16] The invitation issued to the nations at this third Mass of Christmas is a preview of what will be celebrated more fully at Epiphany. Interestingly, neither Psalm 2:7 nor Psalm 109:3, both prominent at the night Mass, are sung at the one during the day. The prologue to the Gospel of John read at this Mass suffices to make known that the one whose nativity is being celebrated is the Word of God, who "was in the beginning with God" (John 1:2) and who "became flesh" (John 1:14).

Prefaces. In the 1962 Missal there is a proper preface of the Nativity used at the three Christmas Masses and throughout the octave. It is from the Sacramentary of Pope Hadrian (H 38). Addressed to the Father, the motive of thanksgiving is that "through the mystery of the Word made flesh, new radiance from thy glory hath so shone on the eye of the soul that the recognition of our God made visible draweth us to love what is invisible." This is the first of three prefaces of the Nativity in the Missal of Paul VI. The contrast between the visible and the invisible unfortunately was blunted in the 1975 translation, declaring that in Christ "we see our God made visible and so are caught up in love of the God we cannot see." The sharpness of the contrast is

---

[15] AMS 11b.

[16] RM 1962 has, "A sanctified day hath shone upon us. Come ye Gentiles and adore the Lord, for this day a great light hath descended upon the earth."

restored in the 2011 version: "as we recognize in him God made visible, / we may be caught up through him in love of things invisible."

Preface II of the Nativity of the Lord in the 2011 Missal likewise accentuates the contrast between the visible and the invisible. It begins by affirming that

> on the feast of this awe-filled mystery,
> though invisible in his own divine nature,
> he [Christ] has appeared visibly in ours.

The Latin is quite poetic: *Invisibilis in suis, visibilis in nostris apparuit.* The 1975 rendering of this line was a true statement but hardly a translation: "No eye can see his glory as our God, yet now he is seen as one like us." The preface then makes another contrast, this one between eternity and time. "Begotten before all ages," it declares, alluding to Psalm 109:3, "he has begun to exist in time." This part of the preface is heavily dependent on a section of Pope Leo the Great's second Christmas sermon, asserting that Christ "was brought forth in an unusual manner because, though invisible in his own nature, he has been made visible in ours; because, though incomprehensible, he willed to be comprehended; because, though already existing before time, he came into being at a certain point in time."[17] Incorporating phrases from various biblical, patristic, and liturgical sources,[18] the preface explains that the purpose of Christ's existence in time is

> so that, raising up in himself all that was cast down,
> he might restore unity to all creation [Eph 1:9-10]
> and call straying humanity back to the heavenly Kingdom.

Here the incarnation of the Word and the salvation of the world are one and the same. This is the most profound of the three prefaces of the Nativity.

The third preface of the Nativity, loosely inspired by a Christmas preface in the *Veronensis* (V 1260), opens with the declaration that through Christ "the holy exchange that restores our life / has shone forth today in splendor." We saw that the prayer over the offerings

---

[17] Leo the Great, *Sermon* 22, 2, trans. Jane Patricia Freeland, CSJB, and Agnes Josephine Conway, SSJ, in FC 93, 81.

[18] See Ward-Johnson, *Prefaces*, 76–80.

at the night Mass of the Nativity likewise mentions "this most holy exchange."[19] The prayer over the offerings on the fifth day within the octave does the same but understands it more with reference to the Eucharist than to the person of Christ. It asks,

> receive our oblation, O Lord,
> by which is brought about a glorious exchange,
> that, by offering what you have given,
> we may merit to receive your very self.

The preface goes on to set forth two astounding effects of the assumption of our frailty by the Word of God: "[N]ot only does human mortality receive unending honor / but by this wondrous union we, too, are made eternal."

Solemn blessing. The first of the three invocations articulates yet again the light theme heard in the collects of all three Christmas Masses:

> May the God of infinite goodness,
> who by the Incarnation of his Son has driven darkness from the world
> and by that glorious Birth has illumined this most holy night (day),
> drive far from you the darkness of vice
> and illumine your hearts with the light of virtue.

The third invocation gives expression to the exchange theme of Preface III and several orations, broadening it to include communion between the liturgical assembly on earth and the church in heaven:

> May God, who by the Incarnation
> brought together the earthly and heavenly realm,
> fill you with the gift of his peace and favor
> and make you sharers with the Church in heaven.

---

[19] At least two other prayers express the reality of the exchange without using the term. The prayer over the offerings at the dawn Mass asks that "just as Christ was born a man and also shone forth as God, / so these earthly gifts may confer on us what is divine." The collect of the Mass during the day prays that "we may share in the divinity of Christ, / who humbled himself to share in our humanity."

The second invocation is the most unique, original, and untypical not only of the three invocations of the solemn blessing but of all the prayers and prefaces of the Christmas Masses, those of the solemnity, and those of weekdays. The reason is because it mentions that the angel announced the birth of Christ to shepherds:

> May God, who willed that the great joy
> of his Son's saving Birth
> be announced to shepherds by the Angel,
> fill your minds with the gladness he gives
> and make you heralds of his Gospel.

No other euchological text even alludes to the gospel of the night Mass, the birth of Jesus as recounted in Luke 2:1-14. No mention is made anywhere of the census, Bethlehem, swaddling clothes, the manger, shepherds, the angel, or the heavenly host and their song of praise. On the contrary, prayers of the Christmas Masses are not narrative but doctrinal in content. Inspired by John 1:1-18 read at the day Mass and from fourth- and fifth-century dogmatic pronouncements about the person and natures of the Word made flesh, they are endlessly fresh reflections on the inexhaustible mystery of the incarnation and its salvific import for human beings and for the whole of creation.

5. Solemnity of Mary, the Holy Mother of God

In all the early sacramentaries January 1 bears the title *Octava Domini*, "Octave of the Lord." The first printed edition of the Roman Missal in 1474 supplies reference to the nativity, expanding the title to "Octave of the Nativity of the Lord." Only in 1570 does the first typical edition of the Missal of Pius V, or Tridentine Missal, place *In die Circumcisione* in front of the existing title.[20] The 1962 Missal, however, removes this phrase, leaving only "Octave of the Nativity of the Lord."

The Mass formulary in RM 1962 is a composite one. The gospel, Luke 2:21, though only one verse, is the obvious choice because it recounts the circumcision and naming of Jesus eight days after his birth, that is, on the octave day. But the epistle is taken from the night Mass of Christmas, four of the five chants are from the day Mass,[21] and the preface is that of the Nativity—repetitions consistent with the day

---

[20] See the titles in Bruylants I, no. 22.

[21] The only proper chant is the Alleluia verse, taken from Heb 1:1-2.

being the octave of the Nativity. Two of the three presidential prayers, on the other hand, mention Mary by name and seek her intercession. The collect, taken from H 82, recalls her "fruitful virginity," and the post-Communion, from H 84, designates her "Mother of God," the phrase sanctioned at the Council of Ephesus in 431 that triggered an explosion of Marian feasts and devotion[22] and, as we saw, was influential in the origin of the night Mass of Christmas. The Mass of the octave, then, represents two streams of tradition: a Marian one in these two prayers and a Christmas one in the other texts.

Of these the Marian stream is the more ancient. As Dom Bernard Botte has demonstrated, January 1 was originally set aside at Rome to honor the Mother of God and in fact for a long time was the only feast of Mary. In the course of the seventh century the Roman church adopted other Marian feasts that had originated elsewhere—Assumption, Nativity, Annunciation, and Purification. These had great popular appeal and quickly gained ascendancy over the older generic festival of the Virgin Mother, allowing it to be eclipsed by the octave of Christmas except for mention of Mary in the collect and post-Communion, but not in the secret.[23]

The reformed calendar of 1969, while not abandoning the term "octave day," reclaimed January 1 for our Lady, thereby restoring a precious link with primitive tradition, until then largely unknown. It also slipped in something new: the naming of Jesus. The Universal Norms on the Liturgical Year and the Calendar, no. 35f, stipulate that "1 January, the Octave Day of the Nativity of the Lord, is the Solemnity of Mary, the Holy Mother of God, and also the commemoration of the conferral of the Most Holy Name of Jesus." Because the naming of Jesus is included on this day, the feast of the Holy Name of Jesus, instituted for the universal church by Innocent XIII in 1721, was abolished. Consequently, it does not appear in the first two editions of the Missal of Paul VI. The third typical edition of this Missal in 2002, however, restores it as an optional memorial on January 3. In RM 1962 it is

---

[22] See Ignazio M. Calabuig, OSM, "The Liturgical Cult of Mary in the East and West," in Anscar J. Chupungco, OSB, ed., *Handbook for Liturgical Studies*, 5 vols. (Collegeville, MN: Liturgical Press, 2000) V, 244–55.

[23] Bernard Botte, OSB, "La première fête mariale de la liturgie romaine," EL 47 (1933) 425–30. The antiphons for Lauds and Vespers on this day are entirely Marian in content.

observed on the Sunday after the octave day of the Nativity or, if this Sunday falls on January 1, 6, or 7, on January 2.

Most of the texts for the Mass in the Missal of Paul VI are new and reflect the changed content of the day as defined by no. 35f of the Universal Norms just cited: the motherhood of Mary and the naming of Jesus. The title of the formulary in the 2011 translation is Solemnity of Mary, the Holy Mother of God. Above that in small print is "The Octave Day of the Nativity of the Lord." There may be a few nods to the new year, but these are quite veiled and indirect until the solemn blessing. In retrospect, the decision to combine the motherhood of Mary with the naming of Jesus and the octave of Christmas in a Mass celebrated on New Year's Day may have produced a thematic overload with consequent insufficient development of some aspects, as well as imbalance and shifting focus.

The celebration opens with the entrance antiphon *Salve, sancta Parens*, placing the Virgin Mother and her divine child in the foreground: "Hail, holy Mother, who gave birth to the King / who rules heaven and earth forever." An alternative introit is that of the dawn Mass of Christmas, *Lux fulgebit*. It may have been preferred to the *Puer natus est* of RM 1962, taken from the day Mass, because it mentions that the child shall be called "Prince of peace," which would connect with the naming part of the feast and also might be thought appropriate for New Year's Day. By way of contrast, the new communion antiphon, "Jesus Christ is the same yesterday, today and for ever" (Heb 13:8), has nothing to do with Mary's divine motherhood. The antiphon begins with "Jesus," the name given to the child. This may have contributed to the choice of this text. But there is another factor. In the Missal of Paul VI under the heading of "Masses and Prayers for Various Needs," no. 25 is a Mass for the Beginning of the Civil Year, the communion antiphon of which is Heb 13:8. The communion antiphon for the Solemnity of Mary, the Holy Mother of God, celebrated on the first day of the year, seems to have been lifted from that Mass. Incidentally, a notice under the title of the Mass for the Beginning of the Civil Year forbids its being celebrated on January 1, the Solemnity of Mary, the Holy Mother of God.[24] This is

---

[24] Adolf Adam writes in his *Liturgical Year*, p. 141, that "behind this statement lies an anxious fidelity to the general rubrical principle that no votive Masses may be celebrated on solemnities." Yet for decades the Holy Father has been celebrating a votive Mass for peace at Saint Peter's on January 1.

puzzling. If the Mass for the Beginning of the Civil Year cannot be used on January 1, when is it ever celebrated, and why is it in the Missal?

The introduction to the Lectionary, no. 95, states much the same as the Universal Norms, no. 35f: "On the Octave Day of Christmas, Solemnity of the Blessed Virgin Mary, the Mother of God, the readings are about the Virgin Mother of God and the giving of the holy Name of Jesus." The Lectionary expands the gospel from Luke 2:21 in the preconciliar Missal to Luke 2:16-21, thereby including the five verses before the circumcision and naming of Jesus that twice refer to Mary. The Alleluia verse before the gospel, Hebrews 1:1-2, is the same as in RM 1962, where it is the only proper chant on the octave day. It seems out of place in this Mass, however, unless the contrast it makes between "various times in the past" and "our own time, the last days," is thought to make it suitable for the first day of the year. The epistle of the 1962 Missal simply repeats that of the night Mass of the Nativity, Titus 2:11-15. The Mass of Paul VI replaces it with Galatians 4:4-7, probably because of its declaration in verse 4 that "when the fullness of time had come, God sent his Son, born of a woman." But the purpose of this sending in the following verse should not be missed: "to redeem those who were under the law."

The Lectionary prescribes the Aaronic blessing in Numbers 6:22-27 as the Old Testament reading. Consisting of a threefold invocation of the divine name, Lord, which consequently is said to be "put" (NRSV) upon the Israelites, this passage can be connected to the naming of Jesus in the gospel. Divine blessing is sought in the responsorial psalm after the first reading, Psalm 66. In RML 1981, the refrain is "O God, be gracious and bless us." The psalm begins, "O God, be gracious and bless us, and let your face shed its light upon us" and concludes, "May God still give us his blessing that all the ends of the earth may revere him." Repeated requests for God's blessing, especially his gift of peace, are particularly welcome at the beginning of a new year.

As for the prayers, the Missal of Paul VI keeps the collect of its predecessor but replaces the other two presidential prayers. The prayer over the offerings, from V 1006, may have been selected because its invocation of God as the one who begins all good things and brings them to fulfillment was considered fitting for the start of a new year. The description of the petitioners as those "who find joy in the Solemnity of the holy Mother of God" is an interpolation. The new prayer after Communion is a recasting of GeV 1262. To "the blessed ever-Virgin Mary / Mother of your Son" in the original is added "and

Mother of the Church." With these retouches all three sacerdotal orations now mention Mary by name or as Mother of God. Instead of the preface of the Nativity, required by the 1962 Missal, the reformed Missal prescribes the first preface of the Blessed Virgin Mary. With the insertion proper to the day, it glorifies God

> on the Solemnity of the Motherhood
> of the Blessed ever-Virgin Mary.
> For by the overshadowing of the Holy Spirit
> she conceived your Only Begotten Son.

After Communion at this Mass the solemn blessing for the beginning of the year may be used. The first invocation asks,

> May God, the source and origin of all blessing,
> grant you grace,
> pour out his blessing in abundance,
> and keep you safe from harm throughout the year.

As revised after the Second Vatican Council, the formulary for the eucharistic celebration on January 1 is unassailable from a historical and theological viewpoint and is an advance over its predecessor, which repeated much of the Christmas Masses. Its shortcoming is that apart from the invocation just cited and a few allusions and hints elsewhere, it fails to express openly and directly that this is New Year's. The initial remarks of the priest and the prayer of the faithful may do so. But many will find the official texts of this solemnity insufficiently related to the real reason they are at Mass that day.

B. THE EPIPHANY OF THE LORD

1. Introduction

Unlike the Nativity of the Lord on December 25, the solemnity of the Epiphany on January 6 originated not at Rome but in the Christian East, possibly Egypt but more probably Syria. It is also older than Christmas. In most Oriental churches it celebrates the baptism of Jesus by John in the Jordan. Already near the end of the second century or the beginning of the third century, Clement of Alexandria writes that "the followers of Basilides hold the day of his baptism as a festival, spending the night in readings." Basilides was a Syrian who moved to Alexandria and founded one of the innumerable Gnostic sects of that time.[25] Clement adds that some say the baptism of Jesus was "the fifteenth day of the month Tubi; and some that it was the eleventh of the same month."[26] The dates 15 Tubi and 11 Tubi in the Egyptian calendar correspond to January 10 and 6. The latter is the date that prevailed for the feast.[27]

In this early period, especially in Syria, those celebrating the baptism of Jesus on January 6 understood and spoke of it as his birth—not his physical birth, but his birth in the Spirit as Son of God. They also took it as the model of Christian baptism, by which sinful humans receive the Spirit and are born again as children of God in accord with John 3:5. Hence, the conferral of baptism was an integral part of the day's celebration. The Christology underlying the feast at its inception, however, was clearly adoptionist and was fiercely attacked by orthodox theologians who together with ecumenical councils in the fourth and fifth centuries insisted that the child born of Mary in Bethlehem was already the Son of God and that at the Jordan his divine sonship did not come into being but was only made manifest.

This theological development precipitated a number of changes in the liturgical observance of January 6. These vary from place to place. One was to eliminate the baptism of Jesus from the feast and replace it with his birth in Bethlehem.[28] Another was to join celebration of his birth in Bethlehem to the celebration on January 6 of his baptism. A third was to retain January 6 as the celebration of the Lord's baptism but preface it with celebration of his birth in Bethlehem on December 25 as at Rome. This latter development of course leads to the spread of Christmas just about everywhere in the East. The aim of all these alterations is identical: to assure that anything pertaining to the birth of Jesus is linked to the Bethlehem event and that the Jordan episode is limited to being purely revelatory or epiphanic.[29] Thus does Theophany or Epiphany become the name of the feast.

[25] See G. W. Mac Rae, "Basilides," NCE 2, 160.

[26] Clement of Alexandria, Stromata I, XXI, trans. A. Cleveland Coxe, in ANF II, 333.

[27] For the reasons why this date was chosen, see Bradshaw-Johnson, Origins of Feasts, 131–37.

[28] This is what may have happened in Jerusalem. See Bradshaw-Johnson, Origins of Feasts, 146–47.

[29] For the evidence and details, see Bradshaw-Johnson, Origins of Feasts, 141–51.

A fourth possibility is to avoid the baptism of Jesus altogether. This is the course chosen at Rome. Its celebration on January 6 centers entirely on the adoration of the magi. Between 441 and 453 Pope Leo the Great preached eight sermons on January 6.[30] All are about the manifestation of salvation to the nations in the person of the magi. None mention the baptism of Jesus.[31] In two Christmas sermons Leo speaks of baptism. In one he asserts that "the water of baptism is an image of the Virgin's womb—as the same Holy Spirit fills the font who also filled the Virgin."[32] In the other he declares that the Lord Jesus "placed in the font of baptism that very origin which he had assumed in the Virgin's womb. He gave to the water what he had given to his mother. For, the same 'power of the Most High' and 'overshadowing' of the Holy Spirit that caused Mary to bear the Savior makes the water regenerate the believer."[33]

To summarize, the primitive adoptionist Epiphany in Egypt and Syria celebrated the baptism of Jesus in the Jordan as his birth to divine sonship in the Spirit and as the foundation of baptismal rebirth. In the mid-fifth-century Roman Epiphany of Pope Leo the baptism of Jesus has been completely eliminated from January 6, and his being conceived by the Holy Spirit and born of the Virgin's womb is held up as the model of Christian rebirth. Thus both the feast and the sacrament are purged of any link with the Jordan event. Seen from this point of view, the entire Christmas season is orthodox belief become public prayer.

In retrospect these doctrinal currents may shed light on the use of Psalm 2:7 and Psalm 109:3 in practically all the chants of the night Mass of Christmas at Rome. In several manuscripts the voice from

---

[30] They are *Sermons* 31–38, trans. Jane Patricia Freeland, CSJB, and Agnes Josephine Conway, SSJ, in FC 93, 132–65.

[31] Epiphany in Gaul was more diversified. Bradshaw and Johnson write in *Origins of Feasts*, 153, that "6 January in Gaul included the visit of the Magi, the baptism of Jesus and the wedding at Cana. In fact, various prayers assigned to Epiphany in the extant Gallican Missals of the eighth century, most notably the *Missale Gallicanum vetus* and the *Missale Gothicum*, contain abundant references to what will come to be called the *tria miracula*, the 'three miracles' of the Magi, Jesus' baptism and his changing water into wine at Cana." The *Benedictus* and *Magnificat* antiphons in the Roman Breviary that mention these three events, therefore, must come from Gaul, not Rome.

[32] Leo the Great, *Sermon* 24, 3, in FC 93, 95.

[33] Leo the Great, *Sermon* 25, 5, in FC 93, 103.

heaven in Luke 3:22 addresses the words of Psalm 2:7 to Jesus while he was at prayer after his baptism. This of course provided support for the adoptionist claim that Jesus was born as Son of God in the Spirit at the Jordan. By using these same words as the introit and Alleluia verse and Psalm 109:3 as the gradual and communion antiphon, the ancient Roman Mass for Christmas night may be emphasizing that the child whose birth in Bethlehem is recounted in the gospel is not only son of Mary but the one of whom the Lord said, "You are my son" (Ps 2:7), begotten by him not at the Jordan but *ante luciferum*, "before the day-star" (Ps 109:3). By surrounding the gospel story with these statements of the psalms, the Mass may be affirming that what is being celebrated on this night is nothing less than the birth on earth of the eternally existing Son of God.

In the Old Gelasian Sacramentary, the Frankish Gelasians, and the ancient lectionaries, January 6 is *Theophania*. In the Sacramentary of Pope Hadrian, in most of the antiphonals, and in later missals it is *Epiphania*, to which *Domini* has been added since 1474 to make "Epiphany of the Lord."[34] Both terms, of course, are Greek and reflect the non-Roman origin of the feast. We recall that according to no.70 of the general rubrics of the 1962 Missal, First Vespers of Epiphany marks the start of the second half of Christmas Time, called *tempus Epiphaniae*, the season of Epiphany, which runs through January 13. The postconciliar Universal Norms, on the contrary, makes "the early manifestations" of Christ part of *tempus Nativitatis* (no. 32). Christmas Time, therefore, is an undivided unit running from First Vespers of the Nativity "up to and including the Sunday after Epiphany or after 6 January." No. 37 adds that in places where Epiphany is not a holy day of obligation, "it has been assigned to the Sunday occurring between 2 and 8 January (cf. no. 7)." This is the case in the dioceses in the United States.

The 1570 Missal of Pius V, like the Old Gelasian, some other sacramentaries, and early missals, provides a Mass *In vigila Epiphaniae* for the morning of January 5. The *Hadrianum* does not.[35] The 1962 Missal eliminated the vigil Mass, leaving only the one for January 6. Similarly, the first two editions of the Missal of Paul VI contain but one Mass. If a Mass were celebrated on the previous evening, texts of the solemnity

[34] For a list of the titles in sacramentaries and missals, see Bruylants I, no. 29.
[35] For the list, see Bruylants I, no. 27. The prayers of this Mass are the same as those of Sunday within the octave of the Nativity.

would be used. The third typical edition of 2002 changes this by providing another formulary for the vigil. Consequently, although the extraordinary form has but one Mass for Epiphany, the ordinary form now has two: one *in vigilia* and the other *in die*. We begin with the vigil.

2. Vigil Mass

The vigil Mass has no proper readings.[36] All three readings are taken from the Mass during the day. The collect is from the Vigil of Theophany in the Old Gelasian (GeV 57). In the first and second editions of the *Missale Romanum* of Paul VI it was the collect for the Monday after Epiphany. The third typical edition of 2002 transferred it to the newly fashioned vigil Mass. Anticipating Isaiah 60:2, 5, about to be heard in the first reading—"darkness shall cover the earth, and thick darkness the peoples; but the LORD will arise upon you, and his glory will appear over you" and "your heart shall thrill and rejoice"—it prays,

> May the splendor of your majesty, O Lord, we pray,
> shed its light upon our hearts,
> that we may pass through the shadows of this world
> and reach the brightness of our eternal home.

In place of this collect on the Monday after Epiphany in the 2002 Missal is an adaptation of a prayer from the *Rotulus* of Ravenna (Rot 37 = V 1368).

The other two presidential orations of the vigil Mass make specific reference to the mystery of the day. Based on a phrase in an Epiphany sermon of Saint Augustine,[37] the *Super oblata* implores God to accept our offerings "in honor of the appearing of your Only Begotten Son / and the first fruits of the nations." The beautifully balanced purpose clause asking that "to you praise may be rendered / and eternal salvation be ours" comes from the *Rotulus* of Ravenna (Rot 38 = V 1369). In the Latin text the word for "praise," *laudatio*, and the word for "salvation," *salvatio*, rhyme.

---

[36] Angelo Lameri has expressed disappointment at this and has proposed three readings, a responsorial psalm, and a gospel acclamation for a possible future Liturgy of the Word at the vigil Mass. See his "Tempo di Avvento e di Natale," *Rivista Liturgica* 90 (2003) 593–94.

[37] Augustine, *Sermon* 104, 2, in PL 38, 1038.

The touching request in the prayer after Communion is from the collect of the feast of Theophany in the Old Gelasian (GeV 61). It not only mentions the star, as does the collect of the Mass of the day, but also refers to the treasure chests that the gospel about to be read says the magi opened at the feet of the Christ Child (Matt 2:11). It prays that "the star of your justice may shine always bright in our minds and that our true treasure may ever consist in our confession of you." It is a pity that place was not found for the whole of this oration, which is quite lovely. It reads, "Almighty eternal God, who pointed out the incarnation of your Son by the witness of a brilliant star, seeing which the magi adore your majesty by offering gifts, grant that the star of your justice may always shine in our minds and that praising you may be our treasure" (trans. mine).

The first reading, from Isaiah 60:1-6, summons Jerusalem to welcome back her scattered sons and daughters as well as foreign nations: "Arise, shine; for your light has come, and the glory of the LORD has risen upon you."[38] The entrance antiphon of the vigil, from Baruch 5:5, expresses the same summons: "Arise, Jerusalem, and look to the east and see your children gathered from the rising to the setting of the sun." This final chapter of Baruch, like the whole of Isaiah's Book of Consolation (40:1–55:13), portrays the return of exiles from Babylonia to Jerusalem as a new exodus. The communion antiphon, from Revelation 21:23, is well chosen: "The brightness of God illuminated the holy city Jerusalem, / and the nations will walk by its light." Insertion of the name of the holy city, not in the biblical text, produces a parallel between this concluding chant and the *Surge, Jerusalem* of the introit. Both the entrance antiphon and the communion antiphon of this Mass *in vigilia* are taken from the Mass for the Vigil of Epiphany in the Paris Missal of 1738 (MP 323 and 333).

3. Mass during the Day

This Mass in the reformed Missal is almost the same as that of 1962. There are only two new elements. The first is the addition of Ephesians 3:2-3, 5-6 as the second reading, in keeping with no. 95 of the introduction to the Lectionary, which states that "on the Epiphany of the Lord, the Old Testament reading and the Gospel continue the Roman

---

[38] In RM 1962 the epistle begins, *Surge, illuminare, Jerusalem*. The same text is used in the gradual. But the word "Jerusalem" is an insertion, not found in either the Vulgate or the Neo-Vulgate.

tradition; the text for the reading from the Letters of the Apostles is about the calling of the nations to salvation." Ordinarily, the Lectionary has to supply a first reading from the Old Testament. But since the first reading in RM 1962 is Isaiah 60:1-6, Epiphany is a rare occasion on which the reading from the apostle is the new one. The passage selected discloses a truth that is at the center of this celebration, that "the Gentiles have become fellow heirs, members of the same body, and sharers in the promise in Christ Jesus through the gospel" (Eph 3:6). The Gentiles are, of course, personified in the magi who, as the gospel of the day, Matthew 2:1-2, recounts, are led by a star to adore and offer gifts to the "king of the Jews," an expression that will return several times in the passion narrative, specifically in Matthew 27:11, 29, 37, alerting us in advance that just as Herod's scheme to eliminate the "king of the Jews" as an infant failed, so will that of other potentates later.

The second new element is the prayer after Communion. The post-Communion in RM 1962, from H 91, is completely generic. It asks that "we may grasp the meaning of what with solemn rite we celebrate" but gives not even a hint of what is being celebrated. The Missal of Paul VI replaces it with *Caelesti lumine*, first found in the Mass for this day in the Old Gelasian (GeV 67) but used in RM 1962 on January 13, the octave of Epiphany and the commemoration of the baptism of Jesus. Its request that the Lord "go before us with heavenly light always and everywhere" is a splendid sequel to the words of the magi cited in the communion antiphon, "We have seen his star in the East / and have come with gifts to adore the Lord" (Matt 2:2). In effect the prayer is asking that God now lead us "with heavenly light" as he once led the magi by a star "that we may perceive with clear sight / and revere with true affection" the mystery in which he "willed us to participate."

The other two presidential prayers, common to both missals, are from the *Hadrianum*. Like the new post-Communion just mentioned, each is a masterpiece. The collect, from H 87, begins by summing up the meaning of the feast as the day on which God revealed his only-begotten Son to the nations, adding "by the guidance of a star"—a rare reference to the gospel of the day. It asks that "we, who know you already by faith, / may be brought to behold the beauty of your sublime glory." The contrast between faith and vision, the already and the yet to come, is striking. With another direct reference to the gospel of the day, the prayer over the offerings, from H 88, affirms that the eucharistic gifts of the church were prefigured in those of the magi but far surpass them.[39] It states that no longer are gold, frankincense, and myrrh offered, "but," in the rendering of the 1962 Missal, "he who by these same gifts was signified, is sacrificed and received." The 2011 translation interprets the Latin differently, stating that gold, frankincense, and myrrh are not offered now, "but he who by them is proclaimed, / sacrificed and received."

The chants are the same in both missals and, except for the entrance antiphon, are taken from the reading from Isaiah, the gospel, or Psalm 71, resulting in a very coherent and unified formulary. The introit, *Ecce advenit dominator Dominus*, "Behold, the Lord, the Mighty One, has come," is taken from Malachi 3:1 and 1 Chronicles 29:12. The second word, *advenit*, is the verbal form of *adventus*. When we recall that in the New Testament *epiphaneia* is one of the two Greek words translated into Latin as *adventus*—the other being *parousia*—we see the fundamental continuity between Advent, Christmas, and Epiphany. Each celebrates in its own way the *adventus Domini*.

Preface. In the 1962 Missal, Epiphany has a proper preface. Taken from H 89, it asserts that "when thine only-begotten Son was manifested in the substance of our mortal flesh, with the new light of his own immortality he restored us." This is yet another formulation of the holy exchange theme already noted in several Christmas prayers. The point here is that Christ, in taking unto himself our mortality, gave us in return his immortality. The preface in the Missal of Paul VI is in two parts. The first part is new. It sums up the content of the feast with a declaration taken from a Christmas preface in the *Veronensis* (V 1247) that today God

> revealed the mystery
> of our salvation in Christ
> as a light for the nations.

The phrase "light for the nations," *lumen gentium*, is from Isaiah 42:6, the first Servant Song, and Luke 2:32, the Canticle of Simeon, which acclaims Christ as "a light for revelation to the Gentiles" and the glory of God's people Israel. The second half of the postconciliar preface is

---

[39] For the symbolic meaning of the gifts, see my "The Mystical Gifts of the Magi," *Assembly* 35 (2009) 8–11.

the preconciliar one with a change. In the 2011 translation it says that when Christ "appeared in our mortal nature, / you made us new by the glory of his immortal nature." To be noticed here is the change of persons or acting subjects. In the original it is Christ who "restored us [*reparavit*]." In the modified one it is the person to whom the prayer is addressed, the Father, who does so: "you made us new [*reparasti*]."

Epiphany also has a proper *communicantes* to be used with the Roman Canon. Derived from H 90, it is a succinct doctrinal statement and is the same in both missals. In the 2011 translation, it affirms that we are

> [c]elebrating the most sacred day
> on which your Only Begotten Son,
> eternal with you in glory,
> appeared in a human body, truly sharing our flesh.

Solemn blessing. In a way similar to the preface in RM 2011, which calls Christ a "light for the nations," the second invocation of the solemn blessing, alluding to John 1:5, refers to him "who today appeared in the world / as a light shining in darkness." The third invocation brings the eucharistic celebration to a close by praying that the assembled faithful, at the end of their pilgrimage on earth, may "come to him whom the Magi sought as they followed the star / and whom they found with great joy, the Light from Light." The concluding words, of course, are from the Creed that authoritatively defined the relationship of strict equality between the Son and the Father and so dismissed as heretical the adoptionist Christology that lay at the origins of this day's feast.

C. THE BAPTISM OF THE LORD

1. *Commemoration in the 1962 Missal*

The Roman Missal of 1962 designates January 13 as the Commemoration of the Baptism of the Lord, introduced into the calendar in 1960. The Tridentine Missal of 1570 called it the octave of Epiphany. But this is neither ancient nor Roman. Absent from both the Old Gelasian and the Sacramentary of Pope Hadrian, an octave day appears for the first time only in some of the Frankish Gelasians of the eighth century.[40]

---

[40] See titles in Bruylants I, no. 32.

Although RM 1962 eliminated *In Octava Epiphaniae* as the name of the day and replaced it with "Commemoration of the Baptism of the Lord," it changed nothing in the content of the formulary, which, consequently, remains as it was in the 1570 Missal when the day was simply the octave of Epiphany.

Consistent with its being an octave day, the chants of this Mass as well as the epistle and the preface are all taken from Epiphany. The three presidential prayers come from the Old Gelasian's feast of Theophany. As might be expected on that occasion, the collect (GeV 62) recalls the appearance of God's Son "in the substance of our flesh," the secret (GeV 64) remembers the "manifestation of thy Son born for us," and the post-Communion (GeV 67) asks that God's "heavenly light go before us always and everywhere." As was explained earlier, the third typical edition of the Missal of Paul VI uses this post-Communion in its new formulary for the Vigil of Epiphany.

The point to notice, however, is that none of these prayers say anything about Jesus' baptism. Passing reference to this event is found in the gospel, John 1:25-34, which, like the three presidential prayers and chants, was part of the formulary for centuries when it was simply the octave of Epiphany. Although this pericope provides some justification for the change of the day's title in RM 1962, it does not describe the baptism of Jesus as do the three Synoptics but merely records John the Baptist's testimony of having seen the Spirit descend on Jesus like a dove and remain on him (John 1:32), without disclosing when or where, and without citing the declaration of the Father. Consequently, it cannot be read in an adoptionist sense.[41]

In sum, January 13 in the preconciliar Missal is a commemoration of the Lord's baptism in name only. The Mass formulary remains in every respect that of the octave of Epiphany. This said, it can be wondered what prompted redactors of the 1960 calendar to change

---

[41] Citing Theodore Klauser's *Das römische Capitulare Evangeliorum*, p. 14, Bradshaw and Johnson write in *Origins of Feasts*, 154, that at Rome "according to the earliest lectionary evidence, the Johannine version of Jesus' 'baptism' (John 1:29-34) is assigned to the third day after 'Theophany' (*Feria III post theophania*)." This is a mistake. It is assigned to *Feria IIII post theophania*, which means Wednesday after Theophany. The late eighth-century *Comes* of Murbach assigns Matt 3:13-17, the baptism of Jesus, to Wednesday after Theophany and the testimony of the Baptist in John 1:29-34 to the octave of Theophany, where it is in RM 1962.

the name of the day. The baptism of Jesus had never before been celebrated in the Roman Rite. The new title in RM 1962, therefore, is a
breakthrough—timid though it be.

2. *Feast in the Missal of Paul VI*

The 1969 Universal Norms on the Liturgical Year and the Calendar,
nos. 6b and 38, elevate the baptism of the Lord to the rank of a feast
and fix its celebration on the Sunday after January 6. Between the title
and the entrance antiphon, the 2011 Missal states that "where the Solemnity of the Epiphany is transferred to Sunday, if this Sunday occurs
on January 7 or 8, the Feast of the Baptism of the Lord is celebrated on
the following Monday." This feast marks the last of the "first manifestations" of Christ that the Universal Norms, no. 32, states now form
part of Christmastide and so brings this season to a close, as determined by no. 33 of those same norms.

The introduction to the Lectionary for Mass, no. 95, declares that
"on the Feast of the Baptism of the Lord, the texts chosen are about
this mystery." Unlike Christmas and Epiphany, however, the gospels
for this Mass are on the familiar three-year rotation. The oldest and
most succinct account of Jesus' baptism is heard in Year B when Mark
1:7-11 is read. With no infancy narratives, this is virtually the opening scene of that gospel, which makes it susceptible to an adoptionist
interpretation. In Year A the text of Matthew 3:13-17 follows Mark's
report closely but inserts a preliminary dialogue between John and
Jesus. Luke's version in Year C (Luke 3:15-16, 21-22) is very different
from that of the other two Synoptics. First of all, John the Baptist is not
present. Verses 19-20, omitted from the Lectionary, explain that Herod
the tetrarch had him put in prison. Further, although Luke mentions
the baptism of Jesus, he does not describe it and omits reference to the
Jordan. What is important for him comes later. "When all the people
were baptized, and when Jesus himself had been baptized *and was
praying* [emphasis mine]," Luke relates, "the heaven was opened, and
the Holy Spirit descended upon him in bodily form like a dove" (Luke
3:21-22). Thus Luke presents the descent of the Spirit upon Jesus not
while he is in the water but after that, while at prayer. In the larger
context of the gospels and Acts, this is the prelude to a more spectacular descent of the same Spirit upon the praying apostles at Pentecost
(Acts 2:1-4).

For the Old Testament reading in all three years the Lectionary provides Isaiah 42:1-4, 6-7, the first of the four songs about the servant of

the Lord. The other three are Isaiah 49:1-6; 50:4-11; and 52:13–53:12. This one begins with God declaring, "Here is my servant, whom I uphold, my chosen, in whom my soul delights. I have put my spirit upon him" (Isa 42:1). The Synoptic authors no doubt have this text in mind when they recount the voice from heaven and the descent of the Spirit upon Jesus at or, in the case of Luke, after his baptism. In this way they identify Christ at the very beginning of his public ministry as the servant of the Lord foretold by Isaiah—"a light to the nations" sent "to open the eyes that are blind, to bring out the prisoners from the dungeon, from the prison those who sit in darkness" (Isa 42:6-7).

The second reading in all three years is Acts 10:34-38, in which Peter makes known to Cornelius, a Roman centurion and Gentile, that God's message of peace began with the people of Israel "in Galilee after the baptism that John announced: how God anointed Jesus of Nazareth with the Holy Spirit and with power; how he went about doing good and healing all who were oppressed by the devil" (Acts 10:37-38). Peter's main point, however, is that Jesus Christ, in virtue of his resurrection, is "Lord of all" (Acts 10:36) and that "God shows no partiality, but in every nation anyone who fears him and does what is right is acceptable to him" (Acts 10:35). As Servant of God and light to the nations, therefore, the mission of Jesus is universal.

As the first and second readings in Year B the Lectionary permits Isaiah 55:1-11 and 1 John 5:1-5. In Year C it permits Isaiah 40:1-5, 9-11 and Titus 2:11-14; 3:4-7. These selections are not nearly as appropriate as the first Servant Song in Isaiah 42:1-4, 6-7 and Peter's discourse in Acts 10:34-38. Where the alternative readings in Years B and C are used, these latter readings are listed under Year A.

All three presidential prayers are new compositions for which Johnson and Ward can find no liturgical antecedents.[42] This is rare but not surprising, because a feast of the Lord's baptism did not exist prior to the Missal of Paul VI. The prayers contain explicit references to the biblical readings and hence to the event being celebrated. The collect recalls that God declared Christ to be his beloved Son when he "had been baptized in the River Jordan / and as the Holy Spirit descended

---

[42] They do point out that the last few words of the prayer after Communion about our being God's children "in name and in truth" also occur in the collect of the Mass of Saint Jerome Aemilian on July 20 in RM 1962. See their *Sources* I, 679.

upon him." It asks that God's "children by adoption, / reborn of water and the Holy Spirit," always remain well-pleasing to him. The prayer is drawing a parallel between the condition of Jesus at his baptism and that of the faithful at theirs. Reborn of water and the Spirit (John 3:5), the faithful become by adoption what Jesus is by nature, and as the Father declared himself well-pleased with his beloved Son at the waters of the Jordan, the prayer asks that he be well pleased with those whom he adopts in the water of baptism. The Missal of Paul VI retains the collect of RM 1962 as an alternate, which is strange because, as was pointed out earlier, appearing for the first time in the Old Gelasian's feast of Theophany (GeV 62), the prayer says nothing about the baptism of Jesus.

The dignity of the baptized as children of God returns in the prayer after Communion, which asks that "faithfully listening to your Only Begotten Son, / we may be your children in name and in truth." The reference to "listening" may be taken from the Father's declaration about his beloved Son at the transfiguration, which, in all three Synoptic Gospels, ends with the command "Listen to him" (Matt 17:5; Mark 9:8; Luke 9:35). The prayer seems to be joining this command on the mount of transfiguration with the declaration of the voice from heaven at the Jordan. Being God's children "in name and in truth" may be alluding to 1 John 3:1, which marvels "that we should be called children of God; and that is what we are." The prayer over the offerings looks to the definitive purification from sin effected by the cross of Christ, whom John the Baptist, perhaps still "across the Jordan where [he] was baptizing" (John 1:28), identified as "the Lamb of God who takes away the sin of the world" (John 1:29). It prays that

> the oblation of your faithful
> may be transformed into the sacrifice of him
> who willed in his compassion
> to wash away the sins of the world.

The preface, likewise a new composition,[43] recalls externals of Jesus' baptism to bring out the inner meaning of the event. Very carefully constructed, it gives thanks to God for the "signs and wonders" at the Jordan that reveal a new washing, a *novum lavacrum*, translated as "a

[43] Ward-Johnson, *Prefaces*, 94–97, list several texts that they think may have inspired redaction of the preface, but literary dependence seems nonexistent.

new Baptism." It then specifies what they are. One is the voice from heaven; the other is the descent of the dove. The Father is expressed in the one, the Spirit in the other. Both point to Christ. The voice of the Father enables him to be recognized in faith as the Word of God "dwelling among us"; the descent of the Spirit enables him to be seen as the Servant of God "anointed with the oil of gladness / and sent to bring the good news to the poor." The eucharistic celebration calls to mind and actualizes the entire redemptive mission of Christ, Word and Servant of God, culminating in his resurrection from the dead, which, according to Paul (Rom 1:4), manifests his identity as Son of the Father.

The new entrance antiphon, a bit long, sums up the mystery of the day.

> After the Lord was baptized, the heavens were opened
> and the Spirit descended upon him like a dove,
> and the voice of the Father thundered:
> This is my beloved Son, with whom I am well pleased.

The communion antiphon, the statement of the Baptist in John 1:32, 34, "I have seen and testified that this is the Son of God," is all that remains of the gospel in the 1962 Missal.

Chapter 3

Lent

A. SEPTUAGESIMA

The first difference between the 1962 Missal and that of Paul VI is the presence in the former of three Sundays before Ash Wednesday called, respectively, Septuagesima, Sexagesima, and Quinquagesima. Together they comprise the season of Septuagesima. According to no. 73 of the general rubrics of RM 1962, it "runs from First Vespers of Septuagesima Sunday until after Compline on Tuesday of Quinquagesima week." During this time purple vestments are worn, the Gloria is omitted, and the Alleluia is replaced by the tract. Liturgically, then, these days are already penitential in tone and anticipate the characteristic features of Lent. Septuagesima Sunday can fall as early as January 18, in which case there is only one Sunday between it and Epiphany.

This season developed from the early sixth to the early seventh centuries as the result of monks extending the forty-day prepaschal fast for progressively longer periods. In doing so they may have been imitating Oriental churches that had to begin their time of penance at least eight weeks before Easter, since they fasted only five days a week, excluding Saturdays as well as Sundays. If Holy Week was not considered part of Lent, then the Lenten fast had to begin nine weeks before Easter, on the day that coincides with the Roman Septuagesima Sunday. Efforts to make the weeks of fasting in Rome match those of the East would have been supported by several seventh-century popes who were Orientals. Another reason for lengthening the fast at this time is that "repeated Gothic and Lombard invasions caused people to be predisposed to supplementary practices of prayer and penance."[1] By the time of Pope Gregory the Great (590–604), the three Sundays before the beginning of Lent had acquired special Masses, the texts of which are found in the ancient sacramentaries.

---

[1] Matias Augé, "The Liturgical Year in the Roman Rite," in *Handbook for Liturgical Studies*, ed. Anscar J. Chupungco, 5 vols. (Collegeville, MN: Liturgical Press, 2000) V, 184. On this season, see also Thomas J. Talley, *The Origins of the Liturgical Year* (Collegeville, MN: Liturgical Press, 1986) 219–20, and Jounel, *Church* IV, 69.

The revised Roman Calendar of 1969 and the Universal Norms on the Liturgical Year and Calendar make no mention of this season. The commentary accompanying them explains that "Septuagesima time, an anticipation of Lent, is suppressed. . . . This revision returns Lent to its original unity and significance. The season of Septuagesima is abolished since it had no meaning of its own. . . . It was difficult to explain this season to the people, and even the names of its Sundays were obscure. Most of all, it took away from the 'newness' of the penance theme, proper to the liturgy of Lent."[2] Since 1970, therefore, the Missal of Paul VI contains no Septuagesima, Sexagesima, or Quinquagesima Sunday. These are now Sundays in Ordinary Time.

B. THE BEGINNING AND END OF LENT

As stated in the 1962 general rubrics, "The season of Lent runs from Matins of Ash Wednesday until the Mass of the Paschal Vigil exclusive." The first part of the vigil, therefore, takes place during Lent, the *Kyrie* and Gloria marking the transition from Lent to Easter. In this calculation Lent is understood to be forty fast days before Easter Sunday, beginning on Ash Wednesday. Because fasting is forbidden on Sundays, these are not considered as belonging to Lent. The Triduum, designated "Sacred Triduum" in no. 75 of the general rubrics, consists of Holy Thursday, Good Friday, and Holy Saturday, the last three days of Holy Week. Here Lent and Triduum overlap, and the Triduum is taken to be the climax of Lent.

This is quite a different arrangement than that which prevailed in the early centuries. At the time of Pope Leo the Great (440–61), for example, Lent was not forty fast days but forty consecutive days before Good Friday. Not part of Lent, Good Friday and Holy Saturday were days of strict fast leading up to the great vigil on the night from Saturday to Sunday. The fast and the feast were two inseparable parts of one paschal celebration. Hence the fast is known as the paschal fast and the vigil as the Paschal Vigil. In a way all three days—Friday, Saturday, and Sunday—comprised a paschal Triduum. Though none of the ancients used that term,[3] it helps us to understand better that in Leo's time the forty days of Lent and the three days of *Pascha* were

---

[2] *Roman Calendar: Text and Commentary* (Washington, DC: United States Catholic Conference, 1976) 21.

[3] See Harald Buchinger, "Was There Ever a Liturgical Triduum in Antiquity? Theological Idea and Liturgical Reality," *Ecclesia Orans* 27 (2010) 257–70.

two distinct periods, and the purpose of the former was to prepare for the latter. Sundays, though not fast days, were days of Lent because Lent was not yet synonymous with fasting. The last day of Lent was the day before what we call the Triduum, our Holy Thursday. The first day was forty calendar days before Good Friday—namely, the sixth Sunday before Easter, called *Quadragesima*, "the fortieth day." The First Sunday of Lent, therefore, was the first *day* of Lent, which it still is in the Ambrosian Rite, and was commonly identified as *caput Quadragesimae*, that is, the beginning of Lent.[4]

The 1969 Universal Norms, no. 28, determined that Lent would once again end where it did in the fifth century, on Holy Thursday evening. Where it would begin was ultimately the decision of Pope Paul VI. At stake was the status of Ash Wednesday. Annibale Bugnini quotes the pope as saying of the first four days of Lent that "it would admittedly be difficult, and even questionable, to introduce them for the first time in our day; but now that they have been accepted by all the peoples who follow the Roman Rite, it is not a good idea to suppress them, especially if the rite of imposition of ashes is to be observed on the Wednesday before the first Sunday, as is now the case."[5] Accordingly, no. 28 of the Universal Norms determines that "the forty days of Lent run from Ash Wednesday up to but excluding the Mass of the Lord's Supper exclusive." The translation is inaccurate. What is rendered as "the forty days of Lent" is in the Latin text *tempus Quadragesimae*, "the season of Lent." In fact, Lent is no longer forty days but forty-*four* days. This is the price paid for retaining—for sound pastoral reasons— the Wednesday before the first Sunday as the beginning of Lent. As stated in no. 29 of the Universal Norms, "On Ash Wednesday, the beginning of Lent, which is observed everywhere as a fast day, ashes are distributed." Having seen how the *caput Quadragesimae*, or beginning

[4] See the groundbreaking exposition of Camillus Callewaert, "La durée et le caractère du Carême ancien dans l'Eglise latine," *Sacris Erudiri* (Steenbrugis: Abbatia S. Petri, 1940) 449–506, a series of articles published between 1913 and 1920.

[5] Annibale Bugnini, *The Reform of the Liturgy, 1948–1975* (Collegeville, MN: Liturgical Press, 1990) 310–11, n. 15. For a more detailed explanation of the two ways in which Lent and Triduum were calculated, see my "The Three Days and the Forty Days," *Worship* 54 (1980) 2–18, reprinted in Maxwell E. Johnson, ed., *Between Memory and Hope* (Collegeville, MN: Liturgical Press, 2000) 125–41.

of Lent, shifted from the first Sunday to the preceding Wednesday, we now investigate why on that Wednesday "ashes are distributed."

C. BLESSING AND DISTRIBUTION OF ASHES

The oldest description of ceremonies for Wednesday of Quinquagesima week at Rome is *Ordo* XXII, compiled between 795 and 800 in Frankish territory by someone using Roman documents to promote the spread of Roman usages there.[6] It begins by stating that "at the beginning of Lent," *initium Quadragesimae*, everyone gathers at the Church of Saint Anastasia at the foot of the Palatine Hill. This is one of the earliest references to this day, not the first Sunday, being the beginning of Lent, and it comes from outside Rome. The *ordo* continues by saying that after a prayer by the pope, all walk in procession to an unnamed church, known from other sources to be Saint Sabina, where Mass is celebrated. There is as yet no blessing and distribution of ashes. But the early Roman antiphonals list as one of three antiphons sung during the procession *Immutemur habitu* (AMS 37a), still in the 1962 and 2011 missals. In the latter it reads, "Let us change our garments to sackcloth and ashes." Here the word "ashes" is used in a figurative sense. In the Rhineland a century and a half after *Ordo* XXII was written, this changes.

The Romano-Germanic Pontifical, compiled around 950 at Mainz, contains a description of this day's liturgy.[7] When compared with *Ordo* XXII, important advances are noticeable. First of all, the service begins with the blessing of ashes. Four orations are provided for this purpose, the same four in the 1962 Missal. Once blessed, the ashes are applied to the heads of the faithful. As justification for doing so, the Pontifical invokes the antiphon *Immutemur habitu*, "Let us change our garments to sackcloth and ashes." Obviously, the imposition of ashes is the acting out of the antiphon. "In the Rhenish countries," writes Jounel, "there was a desire to give the liturgical text a corresponding visible expression and so the rite of imposition of ashes was instituted."[8] This is what gives rise to the name Ash Wednesday. A still-later development is the formula of distribution, "Remember, man, that you are dust and to dust you shall return" (Gen 3:19), taken from the Lord's rebuke of Adam after the Fall and still found in all

[6] *Ordo* XXII, 1–12, in Andrieu, OR III, 254–55. Text on pp. 259–60.
[7] PRG XCIX, 74–80, in Vogel-Elze II, 21–23.
[8] Jounel, *Church* IV, 69.

missals. The Roman Pontifical of the Twelfth Century instructs the priest to say these words during the imposition of ashes before the Mass on this Wednesday.[9] But the formula existed long before that. A lengthy rite of private penance intended for this day and preserved in the Romano-Germanic Pontifical ends with the statement "Here ashes are to be placed upon the head of the penitent, saying, 'Remember, man, that you are dust and to dust you shall return.'"[10] After being covered with sackcloth, the penitent is ejected from the church as the first man and woman were banished from the Garden of Eden. In origin, then, the formula is part of what amounts to a liturgical drama, the enactment of the expulsion from Paradise and the first steps of the long journey of reconciliation with God.

The 1962 Missal prescribes that the dish containing the ashes be placed upon the altar before the service. After an opening antiphon the priest blesses the ashes at the epistle side with his back to the people, then distributes them as antiphons are sung, among them *Immutemur habitu*. Distribution concludes with the oration that the Sacramentary of Pope Hadrian appoints for the preliminary gathering at Saint Anastasia (H 153). Mass follows, beginning with the introit, as in the Romano-Germanic Pontifical. In this arrangement the ash rite precedes the Mass but is not part of it. The two are merely juxtaposed. Either could be done without the other. The Missal of Paul VI changes this by shifting the blessing and imposition of ashes to after the homily, thereby integrating them within the eucharistic celebration and allowing the priest to explain their meaning before performing them. A rubric following the prayer over the people allows ashes to be blessed and distributed outside Mass. "In this case," explains RM 2011, "the rite is preceded by a Liturgy of the Word, with the Entrance Antiphon, the Collect, and the readings with their chants as at Mass. Then there follow the Homily and the blessing and distribution of ashes. The rite is concluded with the Universal Prayer, the Blessing, and the Dismissal of the Faithful." In other words, the postconciliar ash rite, even when it takes place outside Mass, includes everything in the Mass except the eucharistic meal.

---

[9] Roman Pontifical of the Twelfth Century XXVIII, 5, in Andrieu, PRMA I, 210.

[10] PRG XCIX, 71, in Vogel-Elze II, 21.

The reformed Missal replaces the four prayers for blessing the ashes in RM 1962 with two new formulas, from which one is chosen.[11] Although after the homily the priest enjoins the faithful to ask God "to bless with the abundance of his grace these ashes," the first prayer, a modification of the third one in RM 1962, asks him to bless not the ashes but those marked with them.[12] The second formula is preferable because, expressed far more clearly in the 2011 translation than in the previous one, it asks that the ashes be blessed, mentions that they are to be placed upon our heads, and alludes to the traditional words of imposition by acknowledging that we are dust and destined to return to dust. "O God," it begins,

> who desire not the death of sinners,
> but their conversion,
> mercifully hear our prayers
> and in your kindness be pleased to bless ✚ these ashes,
> which we intend to receive upon our heads,
> that we, who acknowledge we are but ashes
> and shall return to dust,
> may, through a steadfast observance of Lent,
> gain pardon for sins and newness of life
> after the likeness of your Risen Son.

Both prayers in RM 2011 end on a paschal note, lacking in all four of the previous ones, thus reflecting the position of the Constitution on the Sacred Liturgy, no. 109, that Lent "prepares the faithful for the celebration of Easter."

The postconciliar Missal, while eliminating "man" from the traditional formula of imposition, also introduces an alternate: "Repent, and believe the Gospel," from Mark 1:15. This is a moral exhortation

[11] For the sources of these two formulas as well as the prayers of the Mass together with possible biblical and patristic allusions, see Anthony Ward, SM, "The Orations for Ash Wednesday in the Present Roman Missal," *Notitiae* 43 (2007) 45–64.

[12] The formula is "O God, who are moved by acts of humility / and respond with forgiveness to works of penance, / lend your merciful ear to our prayers / and in your kindness pour out the grace of your ✚ blessing / on your servants who are marked with these ashes, / that, as they follow the Lenten observances, / they may be worthy to come with minds made pure / to celebrate the Paschal Mystery of your Son."

appropriate for the beginning of Lent but with no necessary connection with the ash rite. The older one from Genesis 3:19 is more congruent with the ritual action it accompanies. It historicizes the meaning of the gesture by connecting it with the Fall, consciousness of mortality, and expulsion from the garden, thereby recalling the beginning of the salvation history that will climax with the mysteries celebrated at the Triduum.

D. FROM FORTY DAYS TO FORTY FAST DAYS

As originally calculated, Lent at Rome contained only thirty-four fast days because there was no fasting on the six Sundays. This was of no concern because fasting, although important, was not the defining practice of the season but one of numerous disciplines aimed at internal purification and subjecting human needs, drives, and appetites to the control of grace. Most of all, Lent was the annual symbolic period for the Christian community through ascesis and sacraments to appropriate anew the divine gifts lavishly dispensed during events of salvation history lasting forty days or forty years. Among these are the Great Flood (Exod 7:12, 17; 8:6), the dwelling of Moses with God on the mountain (Exod 24: 18), the desert wanderings of Israel (Num 14:33-34; 32:13; Ps 94:10), the journey of Elijah to Horeb (1 Kgs 19:8), the preaching of Jonah to the Ninevites (Jonah 3:4), and the temptations of Jesus (Mark 1:13; Matt 4:2; Luke 4:2).[13]

All these episodes are threshold events—passages from one place, condition, or situation to another. Like all liminal experiences, they are characterized by separation, transition, and reaggregation. Participants emerge from them tested and transformed, renewed in their resolve to serve the divine purpose. Although this spiritual combat and confrontation with conflicting pulls within the self is incumbent upon all the faithful, in the foreground during these forty days before the Triduum are catechumens entering the Christian community and penitents returning to it. The most eloquent expositions of Lent understood in this

---

[13] The commentary published with the revised calendar recognizes this. It states that Lent, "as the Latin name Quadragesima implies, lasts for forty days. The biblical significance was the greatest factor in determining this number of days in which Christians would prepare themselves for the feast of the Lord's Passover." *Roman Calendar* 21.

way are the twelve sermons that Pope Leo the Great preached on the first Sunday.[14]

As for the forty-day fast, it is obviously inspired by Jesus' fast in the desert after his baptism by John (Matt 4:2), the episode recounted in the gospel of the First Sunday of Lent. But when and how it came to be practiced in the various churches is far from clear. In the face of widespread criticism directed against the elaborate hypothesis of Thomas Talley,[15] Nicholas Russo has proposed an alternative. It could be, he argues, that third-century adoptionists who on January 6 celebrated the baptism of Jesus as his birth to divine sonship and accorded rebirth to converts on the same day also imitated the Lord's postbaptismal fast, and that the forty-day prepaschal fast ending with baptism at the great vigil was an orthodox reaction in the aftermath of the Council of Nicea.[16]

Be that as it may, since fasting was forbidden on Sundays, in order to arrive at forty fast days before Easter at Rome, Good Friday and Holy Saturday, already fast days but belonging to the Triduum, not Lent, have to be included,[17] and fasting must begin on the Wednesday before the first Sunday.[18] This Wednesday is commonly designated *caput ieiunii*, "the beginning of the fast," as in five of the six ancient antiphonals in AMS 37a. The antiphonals also show that starting on Wednesday and Friday of Quinquagesima week and extending through Friday of the fifth week of Lent, communion antiphons on weekdays are all taken from the first twenty-six psalms in numerical order, except for Thursdays, which acquired eucharistic celebrations only under Pope Gregory II (715–31). So do they remain in RM 1962. These twenty-six days are thereby bound together into a consciously designed unit in which those preceding the first Sunday are on the

[14] These are *Sermons* 39–50, translated by Freeland and Conway in FC 93, 166–217, published in 1996. NPNF XII, 152–62, contains only five of these sermons, 39, 40, 42, 46, and 49, translated by Charles Lett Feltoe in 1894.

[15] Talley expounds his views in *Origins*, 168–74, 194–203, 214–25. See also his "The Origins of Lent at Alexandria," in Johnson, ed., *Between Memory and Hope*, 183–206.

[16] For a summary of Talley's views, critiques of it, and Russo's alternative explanation, see Bradshaw-Johnson, "The Development of Lent," *Origins of Feasts*, 99–108.

[17] This blurs and eventually eliminates the distinction between the older paschal fast and the Lenten fast.

[18] According to Jounel in *Church* IV, 68, this took place "at the beginning of the sixth century."

same footing as those following it. As far as the Eucharist is concerned, therefore, the Lenten season effectively begins on the Wednesday before *Quadragesima*, the same day on which the forty-day fast begins.

In the previous section we saw that the late eighth-century Frankish *Ordo* XXII considers this Wednesday to be the *initium Quadragesimae*, "the beginning of Lent," thus bringing to light an ambivalence between the older view of Lent as a period of forty consecutive days beginning on the first Sunday and a more recent view of Lent as a period of forty *fast* days beginning on Ash Wednesday. This ambivalence was resolved only in the revised rubrics of 1960, no. 74, which determined that Lent begins on Ash Wednesday, in effect accepting the view that Lent is a period of forty fast days. This, however, was short-lived.

On February 17, 1966, Pope Paul VI in his apostolic constitution *Paenitemini*, lifted the obligation of fasting from all days except Ash Wednesday and Good Friday.[19] Insofar as the sacred season had been identified with the forty fast days, for many this took the starch out of Lent. A further modification came in 1969 when no. 28 of the Universal Norms on the Liturgical Year, while maintaining Ash Wednesday as the beginning of Lent, determined that the season would end on the evening of Holy Thursday. Consequently, the postconciliar *Quadragesima* is neither forty consecutive days nor forty fast days but forty-four calendar days, on only one of which the faithful are obliged to fast—namely, the first.

Although ambivalence concerning the beginning of Lent was resolved in the 1960 revised rubrics, repeated in the 1962 Missal and 1969 Universal Norms, it perdures in three prayers of the postconciliar Missal. On Ash Wednesday the collect, from H 153, prays that "we may begin with holy fasting / this campaign of Christian service," and the prayer over the offerings, from H 167 and GeV 106, declares that "we solemnly offer / the annual sacrifice for the beginning of Lent." According to these two prayers, Ash Wednesday is the beginning of Lent. This is to be expected. On the other hand, the prayer over the offerings on the first Sunday, from H 155 and GeV 91, asks for the right dispositions "to make these offerings, / for with them we celebrate the beginning / of this venerable and sacred time." For this prayer the beginning of Lent is still the first Sunday. The January 16, 1988, circular letter of the Congregation for Divine Worship, *Paschalis Sollemnitatis*, On Preparing and Celebrating the Paschal Feasts, referring to this prayer in note 25, declares in no. 23 that "the First Sunday of Lent

[19] Apostolic constitution *Paenitemini*, III, II, 3, in DOL doc. 358, no. 3022.

marks the beginning of the annual Lenten observance."[20] We see, then, that the prayers for these two days reflect a lingering discrepancy as to when Lent begins, a discrepancy inadvertently reinforced by the circular letter. The proper preface for the first Sunday, for its part, continues to regard Lent as a period of forty fast days. Pieced together from various words and phrases in ancient texts,[21] it declares that

> [b]y abstaining forty long days from earthly food,
> he [Christ] consecrated through his fast
> the pattern of our Lenten observance.

But when fasting is required on only one day, Christ's abstinence for "forty long days from earthly food" can hardly be "the pattern of our Lenten observance."

E. EMBER DAYS

In the Missal of 1962, Wednesday, Friday, and Saturday of the first week are Ember Days. Wednesday has one Old Testament reading before the epistle, and Saturday has five Old Testament readings before the epistle. Silent prayer on bended knee and an oration follow each of them, except the fifth reading on Saturday. Apart from this, the Ember Days are indistinguishable from other days of the season because, in virtue of being days of Lent, they are already fast days—or at least they were until *Paenitemini* in 1966. All the prayers on these days derive from the Sacramentary of Pope Hadrian. The Missal of Paul VI does not have Ember Days because, as was pointed out in the chapter on Advent, no. 46 of the Universal Norms of 1969 entrusts the time and manner of observing them to conferences of bishops.

F. WEEK FOUR: A TURNING POINT

The Fourth Sunday of Lent is popularly known as Laetare Sunday, after the opening word of the introit in both missals, *Laetare,*

---

[20] This letter synthesizes postconciliar legislation on Lent, Holy Week, and Triduum and brings it to bear on pastoral practice. It is very handy and can be found with introductory comments by John F. Baldovin, SJ, in *The Liturgy Documents: A Parish Resource*, vol. 2 (Chicago: Liturgy Training Publications, 1999) 52–80. There, however, the Latin title is mistakenly given as *Paschale Solemnitatis.*

[21] See Ward-Johnson, *Prefaces*, 123–25.

Jerusalem, "Rejoice, Jerusalem!" (Isa 66:10-11). A rubric under the title in RM 2011, not in the first two typical editions of the Missal of Paul VI, points out that "[i]n this Mass, the color violet or rose is used. Instrumental music is permitted, and the altar may be decorated with flowers."[22] Although this Sunday now marks the halfway point in the church's preparation for celebrating the Triduum, in all likelihood it was originally the beginning of such preparation. This is to say that, at first, preparation for *Pascha* lasted not six but three weeks. This is persuasively demonstrated by Antoine Chavasse in a series of articles, summarized briefly by Talley and at greater length by Maxwell Johnson, who adds a contribution of his own.[23] Evidence for this is the following: (1) the Greek historian Socrates (ca. 380–ca. 450) wrote that Christians at Rome fasted three consecutive weeks before Easter; (2) early Roman lectionaries attest continuous readings from the Gospel of John during these weeks—a practice still found in RM 1962 and the postconciliar Lectionary; (3) the early lectionaries designate the present fifth Sunday as *Mediana*, "Middle Sunday," implying that it was in the middle of two others; and (4) the scrutiny of candidates for baptism took place on these Sundays before being shifted to the third, fourth, and fifth Sundays after Lent was established as a forty-day period.

To this Johnson adds that in several other ancient Christian centers three weeks of preparation seem to have preceded baptism, no matter what time of year the sacrament was celebrated. "If correct," he writes, "this would go a long way towards explaining how Lent itself may have developed. When Easter finally became the preferred time for baptism, this 'free-floating' three-week period would have naturally become attached to it as the final period of catechetical instruction and preparation now in a pre-paschal context. Then, after Nicea, and

[22] This rubric is the counterpart of no. 4 of an instruction preceding the Mass of Ash Wednesday, likewise missing from the first two typical editions. It says, "During Lent, it is not permitted to decorate the altar with flowers, and the use of musical instruments is allowed only so as to support the singing. Nevertheless, Laetare Sunday (the Fourth Sunday of Lent), Solemnities, and Feasts are exceptions to this rule."

[23] Talley, *Origins*, 165–67; Johnson, "From Three Weeks to Forty Days: Baptismal Preparation and the Origins of Lent," in *Living Water, Sealing Spirit*, ed. Maxwell E. Johnson (Collegeville, MN: Liturgical Press, 1995) 118–36. See also Bradshaw-Johnson, "Three Weeks and Forty Days," in *Origins of Feasts*, 92–98.

under the influence of the Alexandrian forty-day post-Epiphany fast, Lent itself came to be created in various ways on the basis of this 'core' resulting in the differing lengths calculated in the various traditions." He concludes that "the forty days of Lent represent a synthesis of two traditions, both of which are baptismal in their origins and orientation: the forty-day Alexandrian post-Epiphany fast, and a three-week baptismal preparation period elsewhere. In its origins, therefore, 'Lent' has nothing to do with Easter at all but everything to do with the final training of candidates for baptism."[24]

G. PASSIONTIDE

In the Roman Missal of 1962 the Fifth Sunday of Lent is called the First Sunday of the Passion and is the beginning of Passion Week. The following Sunday is the Second Sunday of the Passion, or Palm Sunday, and is the beginning of Holy Week. Taken together these two weeks constitute a subdivision of Lent called *tempus Passionis*, or season of the Passion, as defined in the general rubrics, nos. 74b and 75. During it, as a rubric after the Mass of the fourth Saturday directs, crucifixes and statues throughout the church are covered, usually with purple cloth.

Recollection of the Lord's passion at first was limited to the Triduum, then to the Sunday and four weekdays preceding it, that is, Holy Week. By the end of the seventh century, however, it had spilled into the fifth week as well, declares Mario Righetti,[25] because of the decline of catechumenal rites and spread of devotion to the true cross. Along similar lines Maxwell Johnson asserts that when infant baptism replaced that of adults and canonical penance was abandoned, the forty days "take on the sole character of preparation of the faithful for the events of Holy Week and the celebration of Easter. Such a focus— extremely penitential and oriented in character and piety toward 'the passion of Jesus,' with little attention given to the period's baptismal and catechumenal origins—has tended to shape the interpretation and practice of the 'forty days' of Lent until the present day."[26]

[24] Johnson, "From Three Weeks," 135–36. See also his "Preparation for Pascha? Lent in Christian Antiquity," in *Between Memory and Hope*, 207–22.

[25] Righetti, *Manuale II*, 137.

[26] Johnson, "Preparation for Pascha?" 221. He adds on p. 221, note 47, that Stations of the Cross and other such devotions "can tend to turn Lent into a forty-day Passion Sunday or Good Friday."

The 1969 Universal Norms on the Liturgical Year and the Calendar says nothing about Passiontide, but the commentary on the revised calendar declares that "Passiontide has been suppressed to preserve the unity of Lent. The first Sunday of Passiontide will now be called the Fifth Sunday of Lent."[27] Instead of a series of prepaschal periods—Septuagesima for three weeks, Lent for four, and Passiontide for two, with Passiontide being subdivided into Passion Week and Holy Week—the new calendar prescribes a single season, Lent, with no anticipation and sustained until the commencement of the Triduum on Holy Thursday evening. While striving to maintain the integrity of the Lenten season, no. 31 of the Universal Norms concedes that "Holy Week is ordered to the commemoration of Christ's Passion, beginning with his Messianic entry into Jerusalem." But we should avoid speaking of Lent and Holy Week as if they were distinct liturgical times. If a distinction is to be made, it is between Lent and Triduum.

A residue of Passiontide remains in the Missal of Paul VI in the requirement that Preface I of the Passion be used on weekdays of the fifth week of Lent and that Preface II of the Passion be used from Monday through Wednesday of the sixth week, just as the preface of the Holy Cross is required throughout the last two weeks in RM 1962. Preface I of the Passion, based on an exclamation of Pope Leo the Great in a sermon preached on Wednesday of Holy Week in 444, declares that

> through the saving Passion of your Son
> the whole world has received a heart
> to confess the infinite power of your majesty,
> since by the wondrous power of the Cross
> your judgment on the world is now revealed
> and the authority of Christ crucified.[28]

Another vestige of Passiontide is the rubric under the title of the Fifth Sunday of Lent in RM 2011, saying that "[i]n the Dioceses of the United States, the practice of covering crosses and images throughout

[27] *Roman Calendar* 21.

[28] The words of Leo are in his *Sermon* 59, 7. In the translation of Freeland and Conway in FC 93, 258, it reads, "O wondrous power of the Cross! O indescribable glory of the Passion! In this is the tribunal of the Lord, and the judgment of the world, and the power of the Crucified." Through it "all the world received the understanding to confess your majesty."

the church from this Sunday may be observed." This practice is a powerful nonverbal statement, but what it means is far from clear. If it is what remains of the custom, already attested north of the Alps in the ninth century, of hanging a curtain between the nave and the sanctuary throughout Lent, it would be better to begin it on Ash Wednesday. If, on the other hand, it is associated with the Lord's passion, as it is in RM 1962, it should be done during Holy Week.[29] But inaugurating it on the Fifth Sunday of Lent has no foundation in the current understanding of the season and is explicable only as a leftover from a liturgical period now abolished.

H. STATIONAL CHURCHES, STATIONAL LITURGY

For the faithful, Lent initially was an ascetical period, not a liturgical one. Only in stages and over centuries did the forty days all become eucharistic. Not until the early eighth century, under Pope Gregory II (715–31), did Thursdays acquire Masses.[30] Starting on Septuagesima Sunday and continuing through the octave day of Easter, the Latin edition of RM 1962 indicates the name of the stational church in Rome where in former times the pope, surrounded by his court and the Christian populace, celebrated that particular Mass.[31] With some frequency the texts of these Masses allude to the place of celebration. For example, on Saturday of the third week, when the epistle from Daniel 13 tells of the two naughty men peeking at the fair Susanna while she was bathing, the stational church is Saint Susanna. Clearly, many of

---

[29] Herbert Thurston, SJ, maintains that since the faithful by receiving ashes had publicly declared themselves to be penitents, the "Lenten Veil" originally was meant to separate all of them from the place where the sacred mysteries were celebrated, just as in former times public penitents were excluded from the Eucharist until they were reconciled on Holy Thursday. Later centuries restricted it to Passiontide because of the concluding words of the gospel of the fifth Sunday, "Jesus hid himself and went out of the temple" (John 8:59). Eventually, the curtain veiling the entire sanctuary gave way to veils over crucifixes and statues. See his *Lent and Holy Week* (London: Longmans, Green and Co., 1904) 99–105. Righetti accepts this opinion in his *Manuale* II, 175–76.

[30] For details, see Jounel, *Church* IV, 67.

[31] These are missing from the English translation we are using here, which was published by Baronius Press in 2008, but well-known to users of *The Saint Andrew Daily Missal* before Vatican II.

these Mass formularies were compiled in view of the specific places where they were to be used.[32]

With rare exceptions the stational churches as well as all the prayers in RM 1962 correspond exactly to those in the sacramentary sent by Pope Hadrian (772–95) to Charlemagne sometime between 785 and 791. This is to say that the Missal preserves intact the papal stational liturgy as it existed in the last quarter of the eighth century. And since Lent and the octave days of Easter were the only times when the papal stational liturgy was celebrated daily, they are the only periods in the preconciliar Missal to have a proper Mass every day. During the rest of the year the Sunday Mass is repeated throughout the week except on feasts of saints.

One of the features of these Lenten Masses is inclusion on weekdays of an *oratio super populum*, or prayer over the people, introduced by the admonition *Humiliate capita vestra Deo*, "Bow down your heads before God."[33] The first two Latin editions of the Missal of Paul VI omit these prayers from the weekdays of Lent, but English translations provide a solemn blessing or prayer over the people for optional use on Sundays. The third typical edition of 2002 eliminates the solemn blessings and includes a prayer over the people every day—obligatory on Sundays but optional on weekdays. Another feature proper to the Lenten Masses in RM 1962 is the tract following the gradual on Sundays, Mondays, Wednesdays, and Fridays. Added north of the Alps in the early Middle Ages, the text is invariable on weekdays and is a combination of Psalm 102:10 and Psalm 78:8-9. The final part, from Psalm 78:9, is read or chanted while kneeling. It cries, *Adjuva nos, Deus salutaris noster*, "Help us, O God, our Saviour: and for the glory of thy name, O Lord, deliver us: and forgive us our sins for thy name's sake." The postconciliar liturgy replaces the gradual and tract with the responsorial psalm, chosen in function of the first reading and containing a congregational refrain.

[32] A comprehensive and authoritative treatment of Roman stational liturgy is that of Baldovin, *Urban Character*, 105–66.

[33] For more about this prayer, see Joseph A. Jungmann, SJ, *The Mass of the Roman Rite*, 2 vols. (New York: Benziger Brothers, Inc., 1951 and 1955) II, 427–32. More recent opinions can be found in Vincenzo Raffa, *Liturgia eucaristica* (Roma: CLV-Edizioni liturgiche, 2003) 579–85, and especially Antonella Meneghetti, "Tempo di Quaresima e di Pasqua," *Rivista liturgica* 90 (2003) 596–99.

The Missal of Paul VI contains no indication of stational churches, probably because it is intended to be used throughout the world, where the names of these churches have little meaning. Furthermore, nowadays the pope no longer celebrates Mass in any of them during Lent, except Saint Sabina on Ash Wednesday. So stational churches have lost their link with the pontiff's Lenten Masses. Finally, the revised Roman Rite is no longer the papal liturgy of the Eternal City transported elsewhere but a liturgy specially composed for the universal church. Recalling the ancient Roman custom, however, an instruction after the title page and before the Mass of Ash Wednesday in RM 2011 encourages the chief pastor of the diocese to celebrate the Eucharist with the faithful in selected churches of the city during this season. "It is strongly recommended," no. 1 of the instruction says, "that the tradition of gathering the local Church after the fashion of the Roman 'stations' be kept and promoted, especially during Lent and at least in larger towns and cities, in a way best suited to individual places."

I. PREFACE AND PRAYERS IN THE 1962 MISSAL

In the 1962 Roman Missal there is but a single preface for the season of Lent, repeated every day. It gives thanks to the almighty Father "who by this bodily fast dost curb our vices, lift our minds, strength and rewards bestow." The foundational element here is the fast. The preface expresses gratitude for its salutary effects. Nearly half of the collects in this Missal likewise mention fasting explicitly, sometimes more than once. A good number include abstinence. Others refer to mortification, self-denial, and occasionally chastisement of the flesh. Only the one on the second Thursday couples fasting with prayer, and none speak of almsgiving. Without using the word Easter, the collect of the second Friday prays that, "cleansed by this holy fast, we may arrive in the right dispositions at the holy Feast which is to come." None say anything about baptism or those preparing to receive it.

All these prayers stem from a papal Lent that does not include catechumenal rites and that centers on corporeal disciplines corporately practiced, especially fast and abstinence. All the Mass texts assume that everyone present is fasting and abstaining. Over and over the prayers beg God to make these bodily disciplines spiritually fruitful. The collect for the third Friday, for example, prays, "Bless our fasts with thy gracious favor: that as in body we abstain from food, so we may fast from sin in mind." The collect for the second Monday asks that "thy household, in mortifying the flesh by fasting from food, may follow after justice by abstaining from sin." The one for the fourth Wednesday is more penitential: "O God, who through fasting grantest to the just the reward of their merits and to sinners forgiveness: have mercy on thy clients, that confession of our guilt may enable us to obtain pardon for our sins." In sum, during the formative period of the papal Lenten liturgy, the orations of the Masses implored God for the spiritual benefits of the ascetical undertakings, specifically the fast, which is primal. Without it the preface and prayers preserved in RM 1962 ring hollow. In other words, to be authentic, the preconciliar Missal requires pre-*Paenitemini* penitential discipline.

In 1947 Pope Pius XII wrote in his highly acclaimed encyclical *Mediator Dei*, no. 157, that "during the days of Septuagesima and Lent, our Holy Mother the Church over and over again strives to make each of us seriously consider our misery, so that we may be urged to a practical emendation of our lives, detest our sins heartily and expiate them by prayer and penance."[34] No mention of Easter. No mention of baptism. This changes at the Second Vatican Council when the Constitution on the Sacred Liturgy, no. 109, declares that "the two elements which are especially characteristic of Lent—the recalling of baptism or the preparation for it, and penance—should be given greater emphasis in the liturgy and in liturgical catechesis." It then urges in no. 109a that "more use is to be made of the baptismal features which are proper to the Lenten liturgy. Some of them which were part of an earlier tradition are to be restored where opportune." The Universal Norms on the Liturgical Year and the Calendar, no. 27, summarizes this teaching and takes it further by speaking not only of the faithful but also of catechumens. It states that "Lent is ordered to preparing for the celebration of Easter, since the Lenten liturgy prepares for celebration of the Paschal Mystery both catechumens, by the various stages of Christian Initiation, and the faithful, who recall their own Baptism and do penance." These directives find clear expression in the prefaces and prayers of the reformed Missal, in the postconciliar Lectionary, and in celebration of the appropriate parts of the Rite of Christian Initiation of Adults (RCIA) at Sunday Masses during Lent.[35] Let us look at each of them in greater detail.

[34] In Jackson, *Abundance*, 161.
[35] For the sources of the various Lenten prefaces, see Ward-Johnson, *Prefaces*, 486–506. For sources of the prayers at Mass from Ash Wednesday through the fifth week, see their six articles in EL 121 (2007) and 122 (2008).

J. PREFACES AND PRAYERS IN THE MISSAL OF PAUL VI

The Missal of Paul VI contains four prefaces for Lent, meant to be used on Sundays that have no proper preface and on weekdays. The fourth is taken from the 1962 Missal and, as was pointed out, extols the value of fasting. "Through bodily fasting," it asserts, "you [God] restrain our faults, / raise up our minds, / and bestow both virtue and rewards."[36] The other three are new. Preface I of Lent from the outset clearly expresses that the season is an annual gift of God ordered toward preparing the faithful for *Pascha*:

> For by your gracious gift each year
> your faithful await the sacred paschal feasts
> with the joy of minds made pure.

The ultimate aim, however, is that "they may be led to the fullness of grace / that you bestow on your sons and daughters." They attain these goals by being

> more eagerly intent on prayer
> and on the works of charity,
> and participating in the mysteries
> by which they have been reborn.

Preface II likewise stresses God's grace. "[Y]ou have given your children a sacred time," it says, "for the renewing and purifying of their hearts." Both prefaces shift the focus of the season away from human exertions and toward God's action, suggesting that Lent is the manifestation or sacrament of divine grace at work in the church. According to Preface III, self-denial is thanksgiving for God's generosity, and feeding the poor is imitation of his own benevolence.

That the purpose of Lent is to prepare for Easter is strongly enunciated in the first prayer for blessing the ashes, which asks that the recipients "may be worthy to come with minds made pure / to celebrate the Paschal Mystery of your Son." The second formula states that the goal of "a steadfast observance of Lent" is to "gain pardon for sins and newness of life / after the likeness of your Risen Son." The prayer over the offerings on Ash Wednesday already looks well beyond "the beginning of Lent" to what lies in the future, desiring that

---

[36] The previous translation had rendered *corporali jejunio*, "bodily fasting," as "our observance of Lent."

we may turn away from harmful pleasures
and, cleansed from our sins, may become worthy
to celebrate devoutly the passion of your Son.

The collect of the fourth Sunday expresses the same idea eloquently:

O God, who through your Word
reconcile the human race to yourself in a wonderful way,
grant, we pray,
that with prompt devotion and eager faith
the Christian people may hasten
toward the solemn celebrations to come.[37]

Among the weekday prayers, the collect of Thursday of the third week asks that

as the feast of our salvation draws ever closer,
so we may press forward all the more eagerly
towards the worthy celebration of the Paschal Mystery.[38]

The following Thursday's collect does the same:

We invoke your mercy in humble prayer, O Lord,
that you may cause us, your servants,
corrected by penance and schooled by good works,
to persevere sincerely in your commands
and come safely to the paschal festivities.[39]

As might be expected on Ash Wednesday, the day of obligatory fasting, the collect mentions beginning Lent "with holy fasting," and

[37] The prayer over the offerings on the second Sunday asks that the faithful be sanctified "for the celebration of the paschal festivities."

[38] The collect of Saturday of the third week is also worth noting: "Rejoicing in this annual celebration / of our Lenten observance, / we pray, O Lord, / that, with our hearts set on the paschal mysteries, / we may be gladdened by their full effects."

[39] The collect on Tuesday of the fourth week is equally good: "May the venerable exercises of holy devotion / shape the hearts of your faithful, O Lord, / to welcome worthily the Paschal Mystery / and proclaim the praises of your salvation." On Saturday of the same week the prayer over the people asks God to look upon his people "as they draw near to the coming festivities."

the prayer after Communion asks that "our Lenten fast" be pleasing to God and a healing remedy for us. Besides these, fasting is mentioned only two other times: in the collect of the third Sunday, where it appears together with prayer and almsgiving,[40] and in the prayer over the offerings on Saturday of the fifth week, which asks that "the gifts we offer from our fasting be acceptable." Since fasting can be presumed only on Ash Wednesday and abstinence only on Fridays, the Missal of Paul VI designates the Lenten activity of the faithful with more generic expressions. "Lenten observances," "observance of Lent," and "bodily observances" are the most frequent, followed by "works of penance" or "the practice of penance," then "disciplines" or "age-old disciplines," "self-denial," and "good works."

K. THE LENTEN LECTIONARY

The introduction to the Lectionary, no. 97, states that "the first and second Sundays maintain the accounts of the Temptation and Transfiguration of the Lord"—as in RM 1962—"with readings, however, from all three Synoptics." These two Sundays go together, not only because they anticipate the Lord's victory over the prince of this world on the cross and his consequent glorification, but also because his struggle with the tempter lasted forty days and forty nights and because at the transfiguration Moses and Elijah appeared with Jesus, and each of them had undergone transformative experiences lasting forty days and forty nights (Exod 24:18; 1 Kgs 19:8). Thus the symbolic value of the number forty is in the foreground on these first two Sundays. Each of them also has a proper preface. That of the first Sunday declares that Christ,

> by overturning all the snares of the ancient serpent,
> taught us to cast out the leaven of malice,
> so that, celebrating worthily the Paschal Mystery,
> we might pass over at last to the eternal paschal feast.

The preface of the second Sunday places the transfiguration in paschal context, recounting that Christ,

[40] The prayer reads, "O God, author of every mercy and of all goodness, / who in fasting, prayer and almsgiving / have shown us a remedy for sin, / look graciously on this confession of our lowliness, / that we, who are bowed down by our conscience, / may always be lifted up by your mercy."

after he had told the disciples of his coming Death,
on the holy mountain he manifested to them his glory,
to show, even by the testimony of the law and the prophets,
that the Passion leads to the glory of the Resurrection.

On the first two Sundays, then, the themes of the gospels remain the same all three years—the temptation and transfiguration of Jesus. Only the evangelist changes. On the third, fourth, and fifth Sundays, however, the theme changes from year to year but remains constant from Sunday to Sunday. The theme of Year A is baptism, and the gospels are all from John. On the third Sunday Jesus promises to give living water to the Samaritan woman at the well (John 4:5-42), on the fourth Sunday he gives sight to the man born blind by having him wash in the pool of Siloam (John 9:1-41), and on the fifth Sunday he restores life to Lazarus (John 11:1-45). "Because these gospels are of major importance in regard to Christian initiation," states the introduction to the Lectionary in no. 97, "they may also be read in Year B and Year C, especially in places where there are catechumens."

Each of these Sundays in Year A has a proper preface reflecting the content of the gospel and applying it to the sacraments of initiation. That of the third Sunday stresses faith, saying that when Christ "asked the Samaritan woman for water to drink, / he had already created the gift of faith within her" and that "so ardently did he thirst for her faith, / that he kindled in her the fire of divine love." That of the fourth Sunday likewise mentions faith, adding to it water and connecting them explicitly with baptismal rebirth. "By the mystery of the Incarnation," it says, Christ "has led the human race that walked in darkness / into the radiance of the faith / and has brought those born in slavery to ancient sin / through the waters of regeneration" to become adopted children of the Father. That of the fifth Sunday is broadly sacramental, asserting that as Christ raised Lazarus from the tomb, "he leads us by sacred mysteries to new life."

In Year B the gospels of the third, fourth, and fifth Sundays, likewise taken from John, focus on Jesus proclaiming the life-giving character of his death. In John 2:13-25, read on the third Sunday, Jesus announces "as the Jewish Passover was near" that his body is to be a new temple raised up "in three days." In John 3:14-21 on the fourth Sunday he tells Nicodemus that "as Moses lifted up the serpent in the wilderness, so must the Son of Man be lifted up, that whoever believes in him may have eternal life." In John 12:20-33 on the fifth Sunday, again "at the feast of Passover," Jesus declares that the grain of wheat must fall into the ground and die in order to produce fruit. Then, referring to the death that is his exaltation, he adds, "I, when I am lifted up from the earth, will draw all people to myself."

The gospels of these three Sundays in Year C, two of which are from Luke, all proclaim God's mercy to repentant sinners. On the third Sunday Jesus assures his listeners in Luke 13:1-9 that despite the great destruction caused by wickedness, God is patient in awaiting the sinner's conversion. On the fourth Sunday is the story of the prodigal son and the merciful father in Luke 15:1-3, 11-32. On the fifth Sunday Jesus in John 8:1-18 does not condemn the adulterous woman but exhorts her to sin no more. We notice, then, that in any given year the gospel readings of the third, fourth, and fifth Sundays as a group are dedicated to one of the three aspects of the Lenten season as defined in the Constitution of the Liturgy, no. 109, and the Universal Norms, no. 27: baptism in Year A, preparation for *Pascha* in Year B, and penance in Year C.

The first readings, on the other hand, have a design of their own. "The Old Testament readings," relates the introduction to the Lectionary in no. 97, "are about the history of salvation, which is one of the themes proper to the catechesis of Lent. The series of texts for each Year presents the main elements of salvation history from its beginning until the promise of the New Covenant." Each week singles out a phase in God's ongoing offer of salvation, and the Old Testament reading of that week in each of the three years recounts something pertinent to that phase. The first readings of any given week, then, have a common theme, looking back to remote origins in the first week and moving forward to prophetic visions of the future in the fifth week, visions that Christians see realized in the redemptive work of Christ. While respecting this basic structure, the Old Testament readings in Year A, but not in other years, also have affinities with the gospels. Let us now turn to specifics.

On the first Sunday are narrated incidents from the prehistory of the human race or of the chosen people. Year A tells how the first parents succumbed to the tempter (Gen 2:7-9; 3:1-7) whom Christ in the gospels conquers; Year B describes the covenant with Noah following the Flood (Gen 9:8-15); Year C provides an archaic account of the origins of Israel (Deut 26:4-10). The second Sunday relates episodes involving Abraham, who stands at the head of the patriarchal period—in Year A the promise made to him (Gen 12:1-4), in Year B the renewal of the promise after the sparing of Isaac (Gen 22:1-18), and in Year C an earlier account of the promise (Gen 15:5-12, 17-18). The third Sunday recounts marvels during the desert wanderings—in Year A water from the rock (Exod 17:3-7), the prelude to Christ's revelation of himself as the source of living water to the Samaritan woman in the gospel; in Year B dictation of the commandments (Exod 20:1-17); and in Year C disclosure of the divine name (Exod 3:1-8, 13-15). The fourth Sunday presents highlights from the historical books—in Year A the choice and anointing of David (1 Sam 16:1, 6-7, 10-13),[41] in Year B the deportation to Babylon and the end of the monarchy, followed by liberation (2 Chr 36:14-17, 19-23), and in Year C entrance into the land and observance of Passover (Josh 5:9a, 10-12). The fifth Sunday offers glimpses of the eschatological future. In Year A the Lord promises to pour out his Spirit and raise his people from their graves (Ezek 37:12-14), an appropriate backdrop to the raising of Lazarus in the gospel; in Year B he foretells a new covenant (Jer 31:31-34), and in Year C he announces a new exodus with miracles far more wonderful than those of the past (Isa 43:16-21).

As for the second reading, the introduction to the Lectionary, no. 97, explains that "the readings from the Letters of the Apostles have been selected to fit the Gospel and the Old Testament readings and, to the extent possible, to provide a connection between them." The connection between the second reading and at least one of the other readings, frequently both, is usually evident, especially in Year A. Taken as a whole, then, the Lenten Lectionary is a splendid program of Bible reading, the depth and intricacy of which only increase by being studied and prayerfully pondered year after year.

L. THE LENTEN PHASE OF ADULT INITIATION RITES

As we have seen, formation of candidates for baptism had a major impact on the origin and early growth of Lent. "The traditional rite," as the 1962 Missal is sometimes called, contains only traces of this

---

[41] The link between this episode and the gospel seems to be that in John 9:11 in the Vulgate the man born blind explains that Jesus made a paste and anointed, *unxit*, his eyes with it. This is reflected in the communion antiphon, "The Lord anointed my eyes: I went, I washed, / I saw and I believed in God." Interestingly, however, in the Latin text of the antiphon what is here rendered "anointed" is not *unxit* as in John 9:11 but *linivit* as in John 9:6, meaning "he rubbed."

tradition—the gospel of the Samaritan woman on the third Friday, that of the man born blind on the fourth Wednesday, and the raising of Lazarus on the fourth Friday, as well as the introits on Wednesday and Saturday of the fourth week.[42] Scrutinies and other prebaptismal ceremonies formerly took place at these Masses. At first the three scrutinies were held on the three Sundays before Easter. With the emergence of the forty-day Lent they were moved to the third, fourth, and fifth Sundays. Texts of the scrutiny Masses are preserved in the Old Gelasian Sacramentary of the seventh century (GeV 193–99, 225–28, 254–57). When adult baptism declined and infant baptism became common, the scrutinies were increased to seven and transferred to weekdays. This is how they are presented in the late sixth- or early seventh-century *Ordo* XI,[43] roughly contemporary with the Old Gelasian Sacramentary. Eventually, the prayers and ceremonies for all these occasions were extracted from their eucharistic setting and hence also from their link to the liturgical year, combined with each other, and placed at the beginning of the baptismal rite itself. This is where they are in the Roman Ritual of 1614, the use of which is once again permitted by article 9 of *Summorum Pontificum*. At the time of the formation of the papal liturgy handed down to us in RM 1962, then, Lent had lost its connection with preparing adults for baptism and had become simply a season of penance for the faithful.

The Constitution on the Sacred Liturgy determined that "the catechumenate for adults, comprising several distinct steps, is to be restored" (no. 64) and that "more use is to be made of the baptismal features which are proper to the Lenten liturgy. Some of them which were part of an earlier tradition are to be restored" (no. 109a). This led to the publication in 1972 of the *Ordo Initiationis Christianae Adultorum*,

[42] The introit of Wednesday of the fourth week is Ezek 36:23-26. That of Saturday is Isa 55:1.

[43] Text in Andrieu, OR II, 415-47. English translations of the pertinent sections of the Old Gelasian and *Ordo* XI are in E. C. Whitaker, *Documents of the Baptismal Liturgy*, 3rd ed. (London: SPCK, 2003) 212–43 and 244–51, respectively. For valuable comments on these and other early Roman documents, see Maxwell E. Johnson, *Rites of Christian Initiation* (Collegeville, MN: Liturgical Press, 1999) 125–35, 179–89. Chapter 5 of this book, "Baptismal Preparation and the Origins of Lent" on pp. 159–76, is relevant to the present discussion, especially when read in conjunction with other essays by the author indicated in notes 22–23 above. A very succinct presentation of the Gelasian texts is in Robert Cabié, *Church* III, 30–33.

emended and printed a second time in 1974 and translated into English as the Rite of Christian Initiation of Adults, more commonly known as the RCIA.[44] The introduction states that "the rite of election or enrollment of names should as a rule be celebrated on the First Sunday of Lent" (no. 19). This begins the third phase of preparation for the sacraments of initiation, known as the period of purification or enlightenment, which coincides with the season of Lent. As was the practice formerly, "the scrutinies should take place on the Third, Fourth, and Fifth Sundays of Lent" (no. 20). The introduction insists that the faithful "should take care to participate in the rites of the scrutinies and presentations and give the elect the example of their own renewal in the spirit of penance, faith, and charity. At the Easter Vigil, they should attach great importance to renewing their own baptismal promises" (no. 9, 4). The rite of election, says the introduction, takes place during the Mass of the First Sunday of Lent (no. 128), at which the bishop presides (nos. 12 and 121). The scrutinies, however, are held at ritual Masses specially composed for this purpose and at which the readings are taken from Year A (no. 146).

Celebration of the pertinent sections of the adult initiation rites, mention in Preface I of the faithful "participating in the mysteries / by which they have been reborn," the readings in Year A, and the proper prefaces of the third, fourth, and fifth Sundays of that year all inject a strong baptismal dimension into the season of Lent, as called for by no. 109 of the Constitution on the Sacred Liturgy. A shortcoming of the postconciliar Missal, however, is that only one presidential oration takes note of baptism, and it comes on the threshold of Holy Week when the collect of the fifth Saturday recalls that God "made all those reborn in Christ / a chosen race and a royal priesthood."

M. CONCLUSION

The undeniable merit of Lent in the extraordinary form of the Roman Rite is to preserve in our own day the papal stational liturgy of late antiquity. Its preface and many of its prayers, however, are now outmoded in light of the changes in penitential discipline inaugurated

---

[44] Translation of the 1974 version is in DOL doc. 301, nos. 2328–448. A revised edition with adaptations for the United States and approved by the Holy See in 1988 is in *Rites* I, 3–213. This is the edition used here. But the arrangement of material and numeration is different from the Latin typical edition and hence from the version in DOL.

by *Paenitemini* in 1966, and its calendar has been superseded by the postconciliar one of 1969. Furthermore, its failure to make provision for rites of initiation or to express any vital connection between Lent and Easter fall short of how the Constitution on the Sacred Liturgy and other documents of the Second Vatican Council envisage the season.

On the other hand, the distinctiveness and excellence of the ordinary form—the prefaces and prayers in the Missal of Paul VI, the readings in the Lectionary, and the adult initiation rites—consist in its relentless insistence on Lent as the privileged time when God by his grace prepares the Christian people for celebrating Easter. From this the baptismal and penitential character of Lent flows because at the heart of Easter is baptism—renewed by the whole body of faithful at all Masses on Easter Sunday or received at the vigil by candidates chosen on the First Sunday of Lent and prepared throughout the rest of the season. Inseparable from baptism, of course, is repentance—turning away from sin and embracing new life in Christ, whether for the first time or after having fallen away. Hence, the penitential aspect of Lent, including the sacrament of reconciliation, necessarily accompanies the baptismal one.

But preparing to renew and especially to receive baptism at Easter imparts a sacramental dimension to the entire Lenten season, drawing it into the broader ritual complex of Christian initiation. Lent is no longer a penitential period that happens to precede Easter but could just as well be at another time. Lent and Easter are now as intrinsically connected as are catechumenate and baptism. And since sacraments are actualizations in the church of the history of salvation at the moment of its culmination in the passion and glorification of Christ, the whole of Lent is joined to this grand historical sweep and made the annual ecclesial reassimilation of all the wonders recounted in both testaments by which God reunites fallen humanity to himself.

Chapter 4

Holy Week

A. THE RESTORED ORDER OF PIUS XII

After the overwhelmingly enthusiastic welcome accorded the experimental restoration of the Paschal Vigil in 1951,[1] the Sacred Congregation of Rites on November 16, 1955, announced that, at the request of bishops throughout the world, Pope Pius XII had approved a restored order for all the days of Holy Week to be implemented in the following year, 1956. The announcement was made in a document called *Maxima Redemptionis Nostrae Mysteria*, or The Greatest Mysteries of Our Redemption, which consists of two parts, a general decree and an instruction.[2]

---

[1] In "The Night of Resurrection: The New Papal Permission," *Orate Fratres* 25 (1951) 226, Msgr. Martin Hellriegel of St. Louis reports that upon hearing of the papal decision, he exclaimed, "Thank God! For more than 25 years we have been praying for this blessed hour. The Lord heard the appeals of thousands and ten thousands the world over who, in their love for Mother Church, have labored in season and out of season towards a restoration of the most glorious, the most sacred, the most stirring service of the year, which, unfortunately, is also the most neglected." See also Godfrey Diekmann, OSB, "The Easter-Eve Celebration," *Orate Fratres* 25 (1951) 278–87. The restored Paschal Vigil was the topic of the 1952 national liturgical week. Papers are published in *The Easter Vigil: National Liturgical Week; Cleveland, Ohio, August 19–21, 1952* (Esberry, MO: The Liturgical Conference, 1953). See the review by Kilian McDonnell, OSB, in *Worship* 27 (1953) 263–64. For a recent summary of worldwide reactions to the restored vigil, see Nicola Giampietro, "'O vere beata nox': L'accoglienza dell' 'Ordo Sabbati Sancti' de 1951–1952," EL 125 (2011) 142–189.

[2] Texts of the decree and instruction are in *Acta Apostolicae Sedis* XXXVII, ser. II, vol. XXII, no. 17 (23 December 1955) 838–47. An English translation can be found in Frederick McManus, *The Rites of Holy Week* (Paterson, NJ: Saint Anthony Guild Press, 1956) 137–46. This is the translation used here. For a commentary on the document, circulated in many languages, see Josef Löw, CSSR, "The New Holy Week Liturgy: A Pastoral Opportunity," *Worship* 30 (1956) 94–113. See also Nicola Giampietro, *The Development of the Liturgical Reform*

The decree notes that "in the beginning these rites were celebrated on the same days of the week and at the same hours of the day at which the sacred mysteries took place. Thus the institution of the Most Holy Eucharist was recalled on Thursday, in the evening, at the solemn Mass of the Lord's Supper. On Friday a special liturgical service of the Lord's Passion and Death was celebrated in the afternoon hours. Finally, on the evening of Holy Saturday the solemn vigil was begun, to be concluded the following morning in the joy of the resurrection." It goes on to explain that for various reasons "the time for observing the liturgy of these days began to be anticipated to such a degree that—towards the end of the middle ages—all these liturgical solemnities were pushed back to the morning hours; certainly with detriment to the liturgy's meaning and with confusion between the Gospel accounts and the liturgical representations referring to them."[3]

A further development is that starting in the seventeenth century the days of the Triduum ceased being holy days and became workdays. This had serious pastoral consequences. "From that time," the decree points out, "the attendance of the faithful at these sacred rites necessarily decreased, especially because their celebration had long since been put back into the morning hours, when, on weekdays, schools, businesses and public affairs of all kinds were and are conducted everywhere. In fact, common and almost universal experience teaches that these liturgical services of the sacred triduum are often performed by the clergy with the body of the church nearly deserted." The restored order of Holy Week, then, bears mainly, though not exclusively, on the times at which the liturgies of this week, especially those of the Triduum, are to be celebrated. With gracious magnanimity it fulfills the wishes of countless priests and bishops who over the years requested "that the liturgical services of the sacred triduum be returned to hours after noon, as was once the custom, to the end that all the faithful might more easily assist at these rites."[4]

The liturgical book containing these restored liturgies is the *Ordo Hebdomadae Sanctae Instauratus*, or Restored Order of Holy Week,

---

as Seen by Cardinal Ferdinando Antonelli from 1948 to 1970 (Fort Collins, CO: Roman Catholic Books, 2009), 57–72.

[3] These quotations are from the second and third paragraphs of McManus, *Rites of Holy Week*, 137. The paragraphs are not numbered.

[4] Quotations taken from the second and fourth paragraphs of McManus, *Rites of Holy Week*, 138. The paragraphs are not numbered.

published in 1956 and abbreviated OHS. The Roman Missal of 1962, or extraordinary form, repeats it verbatim, changing nothing. The following pages, therefore, will not refer to it. Rather, they present the Holy Week liturgies as they existed before 1956, sometimes explaining how they developed, then describe the modifications made in Pius XII's *Ordo*, which is how they appear in the extraordinary form. Finally, they set forth further changes introduced after the Second Vatican Council in the Missal of Paul VI, the ordinary form.[5] We begin with the sixth Sunday of Lent, the Sunday before Easter, which involves not a restoration of the original time of this celebration but the first steps of the restoration of the original meaning of the procession with palms that the postconciliar reform will complete.

B. PALM SUNDAY OF THE PASSION OF THE LORD

1. Historical Background

Although the original name of this day at Rome may have been Passion Sunday,[6] for most of its history it has been Palm Sunday.[7] Pius XII's 1956 *Ordo* changed it to *Dominica II Passionis seu in Palmis*,[8] "Second Passion Sunday or Palm Sunday"—the previous Sunday being First Passion Sunday. This is repeated in the Roman Missal of 1962. The Latin text of the 1969 Universal Norms on the Liturgical Year and the Calendar, no. 30, changes it to *Dominica in Palmis de Passione Domini*, a conflation of two Latin names taken from the Old Gelasian (GeV 329). The 1975 English translation of the norms published in DOL doc. 442, nos. 3768–827, renders the phrase as "Passion Sunday (Palm Sunday)." By placing "Palm Sunday" between parentheses, it intends to highlight "Passion Sunday" as the principal name of the day. This is what appears in English translations of the Lectionary and the first two editions of the Missal of Paul VI. The 2011 Roman Missal, however, has "Palm Sunday of the Passion of the Lord," the first literal

---

[5] For an informed and perceptive exposition of the liturgies of Holy Week in the third typical edition of the Missal of Paul VI with references to earlier books and legislation, see Paul Turner, *Glory in the Cross: Holy Week in the Third Edition of* The Roman Missal (Collegeville, MN: Liturgical Press, 2011).

[6] Chavasse, *Gélasien*, 234–35; Righetti, *Manuale* II, 184; Jounel, *Church* IV, 70.

[7] See Bruylants I, no. 83.

[8] The phrase is found already in the November 16, 1955, document, general decree II, 4, and instruction II, b.

translation of the title that goes back to the Old Gelasian of the seventh century, retrieved in the Universal Norms of 1969.

The liturgy of this first day of Holy Week is a composite one, as is expressed in the current title. It consists of two clearly distinguishable parts: the procession with palm branches, followed by a Mass centered on the Lord's passion. Each part originated independently of the other at roughly the same time but at different places in the ancient Christian world: the procession at Jerusalem, the Mass at Rome. They were joined together in neither of these but in Spain, Gaul, and elsewhere in northern Europe starting in the late eighth or early ninth century. The fusion was complete by the middle of the tenth century, as shown by the Romano-Germanic Pontifical, compiled in 950 at Mainz, in which the Jerusalem procession is the prelude to the Roman Mass.[9] From Germany the service was brought to Rome, where it appears in the Roman Pontifical of the Twelfth Century[10] and later in the Roman Missal of 1570. Let us now look more closely at each part.

The Jerusalem procession. Egeria, who visited Jerusalem from 381 to 384,[11] provides a vivid description of the palm procession. The community gathers atop the Mount of Olives in late afternoon. "At five o'clock," writes Egeria, "the passage is read from the Gospel about the children who met the Lord with palm branches, saying, 'Blessed is he that cometh in the name of the Lord.'" She continues, "At this the bishop and all the people rise from their places, and start off on foot down from the summit of the Mount of Olives. All the people go before him with psalms and antiphons, all the time repeating, 'Blessed is he that cometh in the name of the Lord.' The babies and the ones too young to walk are carried on their parents' shoulders. Everyone is carrying branches, either palm or olive, and they accompany the bishop in the very way the people did when once they went down with the Lord. They go on foot all down the Mount to the city, and all through the city to the Anastasis," the rotunda built over the tomb of Jesus, where evening prayer is celebrated.[12]

[9] See PRG XCIX, 162–93, in Vogel-Elze II, 40–51.

[10] See Roman Pontifical of the Twelfth Century XXIX, in Andrieu PRMA I, 210–14.

[11] This is the opinion of Paul Devos. See John Wilkinson, *Egeria's Travels to the Holy Land*, rev. ed. (Jerusalem: Ariel Publishing House, 1981) 237–39.

[12] Egeria, *Itinerarium* 31:2-4, in Wilkinson, *Egerias's Travels*, 133.

In this eyewitness account the structure of the service stands out clearly. Unconnected to the morning Eucharist, it begins with an afternoon assembly on the Mount of Olives. The gospel passage about Jesus entering the holy city from there is read. The procession immediately follows, enacting the event just proclaimed. All present take part: the bishop, clergy and laity, men and women, young and old. The multitude carries palm or olive branches and sings psalms and antiphons along the way.[13] The branches are not blessed or distributed ceremonially but are borne in procession because, according to the gospel just read, that is how Jesus was welcomed. Finally, there is not a word about the Lord's passion. In Jerusalem that is reserved until later in the week.

The Roman Mass. In ancient Rome the approach to this day was altogether different from that of Jerusalem in both content and context. The content is the passion. The context is the Mass. Pope Leo the Great (440–61) preached eight sermons on this occasion.[14] All are about the passion. Early lectionaries list as readings at Mass the primitive christological hymn about the self-emptying and consequent exaltation of Christ cited by Saint Paul in Philippians 2:5-11 and the passion according to Matthew, beginning with Matthew 26:2. The Old Gelasian (GeV 329) and the *Hadrianum* (H 312) have an identical collect, still in RM 1962 and all three editions of the Missal of Paul VI. After recalling that God had our Savior assume flesh and undergo the cross as an example to be imitated by the human race, it asks that we may have fellowship not only with his suffering but also with his resurrection. In sum, the Sunday before *Pascha* at Rome commemorates the passion of Christ at Mass with no mention of his entrance into Jerusalem. The Mass remains remarkably stable from its inception to the Missal of Paul VI. But in the Middle Ages ceremonies surrounding the procession undergo extensive amplification, some of which distort its meaning.

[13] Egeria states that people repeated "Blessed is he that cometh in the name of the Lord" from Ps 118:26. The Armenian Lectionary, no. 34, lists Ps 118 for the procession. A translation of this lectionary is in Wilkinson, *Egeria's Travels,* 262–75.

[14] They are *Sermons* 52, 54, 56, 58, 60, 62, 64, and 67—all in the 1996 English translation of the sermons of Pope Leo the Great by Freeland and Conway in FC 93. NPNF 12 contains an 1894 translation of only four of these sermons: 54, 58, 62, and 67.

Medieval developments. In medieval times, north of the Alps the community either gathers outside the city and walks in procession with branches to the main church inside the city walls for Mass or else begins the procession in one church and walks to another for Mass. In either case the place of assembly represents the Mount of Olives, and the church where the Mass is celebrated represents Jerusalem. These are legitimate adaptations of the original setting to new topographical conditions. But there are also additions.

As indicated in the Romano-Germanic Pontifical, a reading of Exodus 15:27–16:10, about the Israelites camping at Elim where there were seventy palm trees, is inserted before the gospel and is followed by a lengthy responsory—*Collegerunt pontifices*, from John 9:47-49, 50, 53, or *In Monte Oliveti*, from Matthew 26:39, 41. Then the bishop or priest may preach a sermon. Thus the reading of the gospel, which in Egeria's time provided the evangelical justification for the procession, grows into a full-blown Liturgy of the Word.

Another addition destined to have unfortunate consequences is that after the gospel or sermon the branches are blessed, sprinkled with holy water, incensed, and distributed to ministers and people. The Romano-Germanic Pontifical provides a total of twelve prayers for blessing the branches—some for palm branches, some for olive branches, some for flowers, some for all of them together. A few are exorcisms. One, titled *Prefatio*, begins, *Vere dignum*, and takes the form of a preface. All are typically Gallican in style and quite lengthy.

Besides the classic hymn *Gloria, laus, et honor*, or "All Glory, Laud, and Honor," composed by Theodulf of Orléans, one of the chief collaborators of Charlemagne, a large assortment of antiphons, some with psalm verses, are provided for singing at the start of the service, during the distribution of the branches, and especially during the procession. Most of them are still in missals used today and are quite lovely. Finally, several orations are spliced into the liturgy—at the beginning, after the branches are sprinkled and incensed, after they are distributed, and at the conclusion of the procession. Medieval rituals usually end by stating that everyone holds the palms until the end of Mass, thus connecting the procession to the eucharistic celebration.

This Germanic compilation is brought to Rome on the waves of eleventh-century reform movements and there undergoes further change. In the Roman Pontifical of the Twelfth Century the *Prefatio* used for blessing the branches is preceded by the dialogue with which a eucharistic prayer begins. After the preface the choir chants the *Sanctus*. Taken in conjunction with the two readings and the responsory, this part of the service resembles a Mass without a consecration.

The same pontifical relates that when the procession reaches the gates of the city or, if it did not begin outside the city, the front doors of the church, two chanters go inside and sing the verses of *Gloria, laus, et honor*. Clergy and faithful, still outside, sing the refrain. When this is finished, the procession passes through the gates as the responsory *Ingrediente Domino* is sung: "As our Lord entered the holy city, Hebrew children, declaring the resurrection of life with palm branches, cried out: Hosanna in the highest." This gateway ceremony may have been motivated by Psalm 117:19, "Open to me the gates of righteousness," since the acclamations "Hosanna" and "Blessed is he who comes in the name of the Lord" are from verses 25 and 26 of the same psalm.

Further modifications. Another change—and a most unfortunate one—is the shortening and eventual clericalization of the procession. The Roman Missal of 1570 states that the priest, wearing a purple cope, blesses the palms at a table in the center of the sanctuary or on the epistle side. No longer is there a gathering outside the city or at least outside the church. Consequently, the significance of the procession as an enactment of Jesus' entrance into Jerusalem from elsewhere—namely, the Mount of Olives—is lost. Henceforth, the procession begins and ends in the same place, the sanctuary.

Initially, the procession may have gone outside a short distance, then turned back to the church, because rubrics describe the chanting of *Gloria, laus, et honor* at the doors "when the procession returns."[15] In the twentieth century, however, the procession usually went from the sanctuary to the vestibule and back to the sanctuary, *Gloria, laus, et honor* being chanted at the doors between the vestibule and the body of the church.

As for the clericalization of the procession, rubrics in the 1570 Missal direct the priest to distribute palms first to the clergy, then to the laity, and indicate that in the procession are the priest, cantors, and others.[16] A missal published in 1920, on the other hand, states that the thurifer leads the procession, followed by the subdeacon carrying the cross between two acolytes with lighted candles. Then come the clergy in

---

[15] Translation mine from MR 1570, no. 1091.
[16] See MR 1570, nos. 1079 and 1091.

order, and lastly comes the celebrant with the deacon at his left. Lay people are no longer included—in striking contrast to Egeria's report centuries ago.

With the shortening and clericalization of the procession, the ritual core shifts to the long, complicated blessing and distribution of the branches, preceded by the service of the Word. As Hansjörg Auf der Maur points out, the dramatization of a decisive event in salvation history now takes second place to a ceremony aimed at producing sacred objects, the blessed palms.[17] This is what Pius XII reforms in 1956.

2. The Restored Order of 1956

Procession. The main objective of Pius XII in 1956 was to restore the procession to its former prominence and assure that the faithful see the liturgical action and participate in it. This is obvious from the pastoral instruction that follows the general decree of November 16, 1955. It declares that "the faithful are to be invited to come together in greater numbers for the solemn procession of palms, to render a public testimony of love and gratitude to Christ the King" (I, 2, a).

Interpretation of the procession as "a public testimony of love and gratitude to Christ the King" recurs in the title placed for the first time at the head of the day's celebration: "The Solemn Procession of Palms in Honor of Christ the King." The theme is sounded in many of the liturgical texts, starting with the opening antiphon from Matthew 21:9, into which "O King of Israel" is inserted: "Hosanna to the Son of David! Blessed is he that cometh in the name of the Lord. O King of Israel: Hosanna in the highest!" To accentuate the royal aspect, Pius XII stipulated that red, not purple, vestments be worn for the blessing of palms and procession.

In order to highlight the procession, the blessing of palms is rigorously pruned. The preface and six other prayers of RM 1570 are eliminated, leaving only the seventh one, which, unlike the others, is fairly succinct and forthright. Furthermore, it is given a new place immediately after the introductory antiphon just cited. Thus, the branches are no longer blessed after the reading of the gospel but blessed at the very start of the service with a single, short invocation.

---

[17] Hansjörg Auf der Maur, *Le celebrazioni nel ritmo del tempo*, vol. 1, *Feste del Signore nella settimana e nell'anno* (Leumann: Editrice Elle Di Ci, 1990) 158.

The instruction of November 16, 1955, introduced an option into the distribution of the branches, saying that "these branches, according to the various customs of different places, are either prepared by the faithful themselves and brought to church, or distributed to the faithful after the blessing has been completed" (II, b, 7). If the branches are distributed ceremonially, two antiphons beginning with *Pueri Hebraeorum* are sung—the first with verses from Psalm 23, the second with verses from Psalm 46. Psalm 23 is a processional chant celebrating the ascent of the King of Glory to his temple. The dialogue in vv. 5-7 may refer to the transfer of the ark of God from the house of Obed-edom to the Citadel of David, described in 2 Samuel 6:12-15. Psalm 46, like Psalms 92–99, is a kingship psalm summoning all peoples to clap their hands in honor of the Most High, for he is king of the entire world. These psalms were not in RM 1570 but were added in 1956 and are obviously meant to be interpreted christologically. They greatly enhance the kingship theme stressed by Pius XII's *Ordo*.

The reformed rite eliminates the reading from the book of Exodus and the responsory after it, retaining only the gospel as in Egeria's Jerusalem. The selection is Matthew 21:1-9, the only one of the Synoptics to assert that Jesus' entering Jerusalem on the back of a donkey fulfills the prophecy to the daughter of Zion in Zechariah 9:9: "Look, your king is coming to you, humble and mounted on a donkey, and on a colt, the foal of a donkey." Transferal of the blessing of palms from after the former service of the Word to the beginning of the liturgy has the happy consequence of enabling the procession to follow immediately upon the gospel, of which it is the enacted commemoration. The deacon introduces it with the admonition "Let us go forth in peace," to which all respond, "In the name of Christ. Amen."

The main shortcoming of the 1956 rite and hence of the extraordinary form is that normally the branches are still blessed in the sanctuary as in the Missal of 1570. Consequently, the procession begins and ends there too. Rubric 17 in OHS declares that nothing forbids the palms being blessed in one church and carried in procession to the principal church for Mass. Although an attractive possibility, it is hardly likely that this permission could ever be taken advantage of in a mid-twentieth-century parochial context. Furthermore, rubrics 1–16 of OHS all suppose that the blessing is taking place in the same church as the Mass. On a more positive note, rubric 17 indicates that, where possible, the procession goes outdoors. This is highly desirable, else how could the whole congregation take part in it, and how could it be a "public testimony of love and gratitude to Christ the King" as the introduction intends it to be?

As chants during the procession, Pius XII's *Ordo* provides a selection of eight antiphons, all of which feature in one form or another Psalm 117:25-26, the shouts heard from the crowd when Jesus entered Jerusalem, "Hosanna! Blessed is he who comes in the name of the Lord!" The fourth antiphon cites Luke 19:38, mentioning Christ as king. "Blessed be the king who cometh in the name of the Lord." To this is added, "Peace on earth and glory on high," which, of course, recalls the song of the angelic multitude in Luke 2:14 and so links Jesus' entrance into the holy city with his entrance into the world at Bethlehem. The seventh antiphon also acclaims Christ as king: "Hail, our King, O Son of David, O world's redeemer." The fifth antiphon is meant to be sung with Psalm 147, which begins, "Praise the Lord, O Jerusalem. Praise thy God, O Sion."

The 1956 restoration eliminates the ceremony at the doors of the church when the procession returns and lists *Gloria, laus, et honor* as one of the processional chants. A subtitle calls it a "Hymn to Christ the King." In the Latin text Christ is in fact identified as *Rex* in the congregational refrain as well as four times in the verses sung by chanters. In a similar vein rubric 20 of OHS adds that "nothing forbids the hymn *Christus vincit* or another hymn in honor of Christ the King being sung by the faithful." When the procession reenters the church, the traditional responsory *Ingrediente Domino* is sung.

When the priest reaches the altar, says rubric 22, he recites *versus populum*, "facing the people,"[18] a concluding oration not found in RM 1570. After recalling that "we have borne these palms and gone on praising thee, O Lord Jesus Christ, our King and Redeemer, with song and solemnity," it asks that "withersoever these palms are taken, there the grace of thy blessing may descend." The prayer emphasizes that the palms that the faithful take home are the ones they have carried in procession. Throughout the rest of the year the palms will remind them of the procession that the instruction of November 16, 1955, characterizes as "a public testimony of love and gratitude to Christ

---

[18] The expression *versus populum* also appears in rubric 5, which at the beginning of the service directs ministers to stand behind the table upon which the palms are placed "facing the people." Mass *versus populum* eventually became one of the most common characteristics of the postconciliar eucharistic celebration.

the King." This wonderful connection between liturgical action and private devotion was not possible in the centuries before the reform of Pius XII when blessed palms were eagerly sought and treasured by Catholics as bearers of spiritual power but with no memory of being carried by them in procession. The palms are now so much a part of the procession that a directive issued by the Sacred Congregation of Rites on February 1, 1957, forbade the blessing of palms on Palm Sunday without the procession and Mass.[19] Paul VI will make this bond even stronger.

Mass. The presidential prayers are from the Sacramentary of Pope Hadrian (H 312, 313, and 314); the preface is that of the Holy Cross, as during the whole of Passiontide; the epistle is Philippians 2:5-17; the tract is Psalm 21; and the gospel is the passion according to Matthew, beginning not at 26:2 as in the ancient lectionaries and RM 1570 but at 26:36, the prayer in Gethsemane, and ending at 26:60 instead of 26:66. Besides shortening the passion and omitting both the prayers at the foot of the altar and the last gospel, Pius XII made no changes to the Mass. After recitation of the oration that concludes the procession, the priest and other ministers change from red to purple vestments, and Mass begins with the introit as if nothing had gone before. Thus there is a sharp contrast between the procession in honor of Christ the King and the Eucharist that follows. As we shall now see, the Missal of Paul VI introduces measures aimed at connecting the two.

3. Missal of Paul VI

Preliminaries. The first part of the Palm Sunday liturgy in the Missal of Paul VI marks a major advance over that of its predecessor for three reasons: first, because it replaces the title "Solemn Procession in Honor of Christ the King" with "The Commemoration of the Lord's Entrance into Jerusalem"; second, because it requires that the commemoration be made at all Masses and not just the principal one; and third, because it provides three forms for doing so. Let us begin by reflecting on implications of the new title.

According to the instruction of November 16, 1955, the purpose of the procession is basically moral and honorific: "To render a public testimony of love and gratitude to Christ the King" (I, 2, a). The kingship

---

[19] See Directives and Declarations Concerning the Restored Order of Holy Week II, 5 in McManus, *Rites of Holy Week*, 145.

of Christ is, of course, a doctrinal assertion. Though it receives exuberant expression in the procession on Palm Sunday, it is not limited to this occasion. The church's display of love and gratitude toward her King is shown in many other ways and on other feasts, notably Epiphany, Ascension, and, above all, Christ the King.

The Missal of Paul VI shifts the christological dimension of the procession from the abstract and static notion of the kingship of Christ to a specific historical event in his redemptive ministry: his entrance into Jerusalem to carry out the Father's plan for the salvation of the human race. It thereby alters the character of the procession. When introducing the liturgy, the priest first recalls that the purpose of Christ's entrance into Jerusalem was to accomplish the paschal mystery. He then draws the consequence. "Therefore," he declares in no. 5, "let us commemorate / the Lord's entry into the city for our salvation, / following in his footsteps." The Latin is *Memoriam agentes huius salutiferi ingressus, sequamur Dominum*. A literal translation would be "Making memory of this entrance that brings salvation, let us follow the Lord." After the gospel reading the procession starts out with the exhortation in no. 8, "[L]ike the crowds who acclaimed Jesus in Jerusalem, / let us go forth in peace"—a surprisingly poor translation of *Imitemur turbas acclamantes Iesum, et procedamus in pace*. Far better would have been "Let us imitate the crowds acclaiming Jesus and go forth in peace."[20] The two key concepts here are "memorial" and "imitation," which correspond to the Greek words *anamnesis* and *mimesis*.

No longer moral and honorific, the procession has become unmistakably anamnetic and mimetic. The original event is proclaimed from the gospel, then ritually performed by the assembled faithful, with the hope that the purpose of the original, human salvation, may be realized in them now. By means of anamnetic imitation, participants in a way are made contemporaries of the Lord's own entry—or rather, the ultimate goal of his entry, our salvation, having reached eschatological plentitude through his passion and glorification, is accomplished in the liturgical act of the church.

[20] This in fact was the translation of ICEL that was submitted to the Holy See by conferences of English-speaking bishops around the world, then altered, according to reliable reports, by an official within the Congregation for Divine Worship and a few collaborators. It is one of hundreds of changes introduced unilaterally by this group, if information is correct, without consultation or even notification.

Certainly this is how the procession and all other liturgical undertakings in Jerusalem were understood in Egeria's time.[21] Commenting on the rites of baptism, for example, Cyril, bishop of Jerusalem from 350 to 387, exclaims, "O strange and inconceivable thing! We did not really die, we were not really buried, we were not really crucified and raised again; but our imitation [*mimesis* in Greek] was in a figure, and our salvation in reality. Christ was actually crucified and actually buried and actually rose again; and all these things he has freely bestowed upon us, that we, sharing his sufferings by imitation, might gain salvation in reality."[22] This way of thinking enables the Missal of Paul VI to bind together the palm procession and the Mass, which previous centuries had simply juxtaposed and Pius XII had strongly contrasted.

Rubric 3 prescribes red vestments for both the procession and the Mass, and during the procession it allows the priest and deacon to wear "the red sacred vestments as for Mass." The postconciliar Missal further connects the two parts of the service by making Christ's destination not just the city of Jerusalem but also the passion about to be undertaken there, and by broadening the understanding of the passion from narrow concentration on physical torment to its life-giving character, decisively revealed early in the morning of the first day of the week. In short, the Palm Sunday liturgy situates both the entry of Jesus into Jerusalem and his passion within the larger category of the paschal mystery and portrays his entrance into the city as being already his entrance upon the passion. This vision is succinctly expressed in the Universal Norms: "Holy Week is ordered to the commemoration of Christ's Passion, beginning with his Messianic entrance into Jerusalem" (no. 31). Rubric 1 of the Mass for Palm Sunday repeats it in other words: "On this day the Church recalls the entrance of Christ the Lord into Jerusalem to accomplish his Paschal Mystery."

Since the passion culminates in the victory of life, the liturgy considers the acclamations addressed to Christ at his entrance into Jerusalem to be an unconscious and unintended anticipation of the triumph that he will openly manifest in his appearances as the Risen One. "As the Lord entered the holy city," sings the *Ingrediente Domine* in no. 10 of

---

[21] For a recent exposition of this view based on a phrase of Egeria, see Mark M. Morozowich, "Historicism and Egeria: Implications of *in eo typo*," *Ecclesia Orans* 27 (2010) 169–82.

[22] Cyril of Jerusalem, *Lecture* XX (*Second Lecture on the Mysteries*) 5, trans. Edward Hamilton Gifford, in NPNF VII, 148.

RM 2011, "the children of the Hebrews proclaimed the resurrection of life. Waving their branches of palm, they cried: Hosanna in the Highest." The liturgy of this day, then, not only commemorates the Lord's historical entry into the earthly Jerusalem but also celebrates his glorious reign in the heavenly one, to which all human beings are called. As translated in no. 9 of RM 2011, one of the stanzas of *Gloria, laus, et honor* addresses Christ, saying that the Hebrews "offered gifts of praise to you, so near to your Passion; / see how we sing this song now to you reigning on high."[23] The prayer for hallowing the branches, no. 6, prays that "we, who follow Christ the King in exultation, / may reach the eternal Jerusalem through him." Through anamnetic imitation the palm procession enables the faithful to participate in their future destiny already now and gives them the grace eventually to do so in all reality.

All this is brilliantly articulated in the opening remarks of the priest:

> Today we gather together to herald with the whole Church
> the beginning of the celebration
> of our Lord's Paschal Mystery,
> that is to say, of his Passion and Resurrection.
> For it was to accomplish this mystery
> that he entered his own city of Jerusalem.

He continues,

> [L]et us commemorate
> the Lord's entry into the city for our salvation,
> following in his footsteps,
> so that, being made by his grace partakers of the Cross,
> we may have a share also in his Resurrection and in his life. (no. 5)

The circular letter *Paschalis Sollemnitatis* of January 16, 1988, in no. 28 declares that "the connection between both aspects of the Paschal Mystery should be shown and explained in the celebration and catechesis this day."

---

[23] The fourth stanza of the metrical version of this hymn, "All Glory, Laud, and Honor," has "To thee before thy passion / They sang their hymns of praise. / To thee now high exalted / Our melody we raise." This is the translation of John Mason Neale in Matthew Britt, OSB, *The Hymns of the Breviary and Missal* (New York: Benziger Brothers, 1922), 139.

The Missal enjoins in no. 1 that the memorial of the Lord's entrance into Jerusalem be made at all Masses, using one of three forms: the procession, the solemn entrance, or the simple entrance. The second two are clearly set forth in nos. 12–15 and 16–17 and require no further explanation here.[24] We confine our remarks to the first form, the traditional one featuring a procession with branches.

The procession. In rubric 2 we note a change of great magnitude: "At an appropriate hour, a gathering takes place at a smaller church *or other suitable place* other than inside the church to which the procession will go" (emphasis mine). In 1956 the reformed Order of Pius XII permitted this preliminary gathering only in another *church.* About a year later, on February 1, 1957, the Sacred Congregation of Rites determined that "where there is no second church, the blessing of branches may be performed in some other suitable place, in fact even in the open air . . . provided that the procession goes from that place to the church for the celebration of Mass."[25] This concession, welcomed in many places, is not included in the 1962 Missal. But its incorporation into the Missal of Paul VI's first form of commemorating the entrance of Jesus into Jerusalem means that when this form is chosen, the service never begins in the church where the Mass will be celebrated but always in another suitable place. Only with this permission does the procession finally regain its integrity as an anamnetic imitation of Jesus' entry into Jerusalem *from the Mount of Olives*—that is, his entry into a city in which he had not yet been.

Here we must recall that for the Synoptics, especially Matthew, Jesus is a Galilean. He grows up in Nazareth, spends his adult life preaching, healing, and expelling demons in various villages around the Sea of Galilee, particularly Capernaum, and, apart from the infancy narratives, goes to Jerusalem only once—where he meets his death. Luke, who will describe Jesus' ascension into heaven twice—in Luke 24:50-53 and in Acts 1:6-11—lays great emphasis on this journey from 9:51 to 18:14, solemnly introducing it in 9:51 as his "being taken up." This, then, is the biblical basis for the Missal's considering the Lord's entrance into Jerusalem as his entrance upon the paschal mystery, which, the priest explains in no. 5, is "his Passion and Resurrection."

---

[24] For comments, see Turner, *Glory,* 11–14.

[25] See Directives and Declarations Concerning the Restored Order of Holy Week II, 6, in McManus, *Rites of Holy Week,* 145.

Pius XII's ritual begins with the blessing of branches. Immediately after the opening antiphon it provides an oration under the subtitle "Blessing of Branches" that asks, "Bless, we beseech thee, O Lord, these branches of palm." The Missal of Paul VI contains no such title. Following the sign of the cross,[26] greeting, and opening instruction, rubric 6 directs the priest to say "one of the following prayers with hands extended."[27] Neither of them is called a blessing. The first asks God to "sanctify ✠ these branches with your blessing."[28] The second formula prays not for the branches but for those who carry them. Paul Turner says it "has the feel of a prayer over the people."[29] It asks,

> Increase the faith of those who place their hope in you, O God,
> and graciously hear the prayers of those who call on you,
> that we, who today hold high these branches
> to hail Christ in his triumph,
> may bear fruit for you by good works accomplished in him.

Thus the blessing of the branches that in medieval rituals and the 1570 Missal had grown to such enormous proportions has in the postconciliar reform been reduced to the strange circumlocution "sanctify ✠ these branches with your blessing" in only one of the two prayers.[30] Obviously, emphasis has shifted from blessing the branches to carrying them in procession. If the second formula is chosen, the branches are not blessed in the usual sense, though it could be argued that by being sprinkled with holy water and carried in the procession they are as hallowed as they would be if the first prayer were spoken over them.

[26] This is an addition to rubric 5 in the third typical edition.

[27] For the sources of these two prayers as well as the prayers of the Mass, see Cuthbert Johnson, OSB, and Anthony Ward, SM, "Sources of the Orations for Holy Week in the 2000 'Missale Romanum,'" EL 123 (2009) 314–27. On the prayers of the Mass alone, see Anthony Ward, SM, "The Palm Sunday Mass Formulary in the 2000 'Missale Romanum,'" *Notitiae* 46 (2009) 396–428.

[28] The previous translation was more direct. It asked God to "bless these branches and make them holy."

[29] Turner, *Glory*, 6.

[30] There is something similar on Ash Wednesday. Of the two prayers given under the title of "Blessing and Distribution of Ashes," only the second asks God to bless the ashes. The first asks him to bless those marked with the ashes.

It must be pointed out that the Missal of Paul VI is not altogether consistent in its use of terms, because, while avoiding the words "to bless" in both of the prayers and eliminating the title "Blessing of Branches" above them, when describing the second form, the solemn entrance, rubric 14 says that "[w]hile the Priest approaches the appointed place, the antiphon Hosanna or another appropriate chant is sung. Then the *blessing of branches* and the proclamation of the Gospel of the Lord's entrance into Jerusalem take place" (emphasis mine).

The main point to keep in mind here is why there are branches at all in this liturgy. The primary purpose for them is not to be blessed and brought home but, hallowed or not, to be borne in procession, imitating the crowds who welcomed Jesus in that way and praying—in the words of the priest's opening exhortation—"that, being made by his grace partakers of the Cross, / we may have a share also in his Resurrection and in his life." No. 29 of the circular letter of January 16, 1988, is clear and precise: "The palms or branches," it says, "are blessed so that they can be carried in the procession. The palms should be taken home, where they will serve as a reminder of the victory of Christ, which they celebrated in the procession." So closely are the palms connected to the procession that in describing the third form for commemorating the Lord's entrance into Jerusalem, the Simple Entrance, RM 2011 makes no mention of them in nos. 16–17 because it does not consider the priest's approach to the altar to be a procession.

Pius XII allowed the branches to be either brought by the faithful or distributed to them after being blessed. The Missal of Paul VI, having abolished the blessing of the branches in the way previously understood and practiced, likewise abolishes distribution of the branches. After indicating where the preliminary gathering takes place, rubric 2 adds, "The faithful hold branches in their hands." Ceremonial distribution is no longer an option. Chants formerly sung during the distribution are now done during the procession. Another original feature of the postconciliar rite is that the account of Jesus' entry into Jerusalem is proclaimed from one of the four gospels in alternate years. In Year A it is Matthew 21:1-11, two verses longer than it was previously, in Year B it is Mark 11:1-10 or John 12:12-16, and in Year C it is Luke 19:28-40.

John's version is particularly precious because, besides citing Zechariah 9:9 as does Matthew, he is the only evangelist to disclose the exact day on which Jesus entered Jerusalem and that the crowds met him carrying branches of palm. In 12:1 he declares, "Six days before the

Passover, Jesus came to Bethany, the home of Lazarus, whom he had raised from the dead." Then in 12:12-13 he continues, "The next day the great crowds that had come to the festival heard that Jesus was coming to Jerusalem. So they took branches of palm trees and went out to meet him." Since in this gospel Passover is a Friday, the day of Jesus' death, six days before that would be a Saturday and the next day Sunday, or in biblical nomenclature, the first day of the week. The chronological indications in John's account of the entrance, then, contain very strong evocations of both the passion on Passover and the appearances of the Risen One on the following Sunday—connections that the Missal of Paul VI is intent on emphasizing.

Centuries ago an anonymous author composed an antiphon paraphrasing John 12:1 and 12:12-13. Sung as the third antiphon during the procession in MR 1570, it was eliminated in Pius XII's reform but is now the entrance antiphon used with the third form of commemorating the Lord's entrance into Jerusalem, the simple entrance, which takes place at Masses with no procession or solemn entrance. In no. 18 of the 2011 translation it reads,

> Six days before the Passover,
> when the Lord came into the city of Jerusalem,
> the children ran to meet him;
> in their hands they carried palm branches.

Too bad the redactors of the Lectionary did not imitate the antiphon and insert John 12:1 before 12:12, which is where the pericope presently begins. Had they done so, the passage would have read, "Six days before the Passover, Jesus came to Bethany, the home of Lazarus, whom he had raised from the dead. The next day the great crowds that had come to the festival heard that Jesus was coming to Jerusalem. So they took branches of palm trees and went out to meet him." Be that as it may, in Year B when the choice is between John and Mark, the reading of John is preferable because of its mention of the day of the event and of the crowds carrying palm branches.

Rubric 8 states, "After the Gospel, a brief homily may be given." This is a high-risk option. Unless given with consummate skill, a homily at this point, however brief, can make the celebration bog down before it gets started. In principle the procession should start as soon as the gospel finishes because it is the anamnetic imitation of what has just been read—the Word performed following upon the Word proclaimed. A homily after the reading can drive a wedge between the two. Every care must be taken that the preliminary gathering outside the church does not regress to the medieval service of the Word abolished by Pius XII. For this reason, incensing the Gospel Book, permitted by rubric 7, should be avoided. The memorial of the Lord's entry into Jerusalem is not something read about, talked about, or thought about. It is something *done*. The commemorative act is the procession, the walk itself—with the branches, of course. The reading discloses the evangelical prototype of which it is the liturgical mimesis.

Of the two invitations proposed in rubric 8 to launch the procession, the second, "Let us go forth in peace," is the same as the one in the 1956 *Ordo* and prompts the congregational response, "In the name of Christ. Amen." Eliminated in MR 1970 but restored in the third typical edition of 2002, it contains nothing distinctive. The first is preferable but is not without difficulties. It reads,

> Dear brethren (brothers and sisters),
> like the crowds who acclaimed Jesus in Jerusalem,
> let us go forth in peace.

The priest already said "Dear brother and sisters" in his opening instruction (no. 5). It is not necessary to repeat that. Concision is essential in this type of formula. Further, as was already pointed out, the translation is deficient because it fails to express sufficiently the idea of imitation so obvious in the Latin verb *imitemur*. It is legitimate to entertain an alternate translation because rubric 8 says that "to begin the Procession, an invitation may be given by a Priest or a Deacon or a lay minister, in these *or similar words*" (emphasis mine). A much crisper and more accurate invitation, therefore, would be "Let us imitate the crowds acclaiming Jesus and go forth in peace." There is no congregational response to this invitation.

Following the invitation, rubric 9 is almost the same as the one from the Tridentine Missal of 1920 cited above, except that after listing the ministers who take part in the procession—thurifer, crossbearer, acolytes, deacon, priest—it adds, "and, after them, all the faithful carrying branches." It thereby puts an end to clericalization of the procession. Since ceremonial distribution of the branches has been discontinued, the same rubric prescribes that Psalms 23 and 46, chanted during the distribution in Pius XII's restored order, be sung during the procession. Recalling their content sketched earlier, this is a far better context for them. The hymn *Gloria, laus, et honor* is still listed under the title, "Hymn to Christ the King," in rubric 9. In English-language countries the metrical version of this hymn, "All Glory, Laud, and Honor," preferably with brass, should hold primacy of place.

In the *Ordo* of Pius XII and the 1962 Missal the procession ends with the priest *versus populum* addressing a prayer to Christ asking that "withersoever these palms are taken, there the grace of thy blessing may descend." As ministers return to the sanctuary after changing from red to purple vestments, the Mass begins with the chanting of the introit antiphon, followed by the *Kyrie*, at the end of which the priest recites the collect. In the Missal of Paul VI the procession concludes altogether differently. Rubric 11 in the third typical edition says, "When the Priest arrives at the altar, he venerates it and, if appropriate, incenses it. Then he goes to the chair." It continues, "Omitting the other Introductory Rites of the Mass and, if appropriate, the Kyrie (Lord, have mercy), he says the Collect of the Mass."

The possibility of not omitting the *Kyrie* along with the other introductory rites is an option introduced in the 2002 *Missale Romanum* and should be weighed carefully. The arrival of the priest at the chair brings an end to the procession and hence the anamnetic mimesis of the Lord's entrance into Jerusalem. Chanting the *Kyrie* at this point adds nothing to the commemorative act but, on the contrary, risks weakening the link between the procession and the Mass, which the postconciliar Missal is trying to strengthen. The version of this rubric in the first two editions of the Missal of Paul VI said that the priest, after going to the chair, "begins immediately the opening prayer of the Mass, which concludes the procession." This is still the better arrangement. Whereas in the 1956 *Ordo* the procession had its own concluding prayer and the Mass had its proper entrance chant and collect, in the reformed Missal the procession with branches is recognized as the entrance procession of the Mass and, preferably with nothing interposed, comes to a grand conclusion with the collect of the day.[31]

Mass. Although the restoration of 1956 modified the first part of the Palm Sunday liturgy, especially the blessing and distribution of

---

[31] On the relationship between the collect and the entrance procession generally, see my "The Collect in Context," in James G. Leachman, OSB, and Daniel P. McCarthy, OSB, eds, *Appreciating the Collect: An Irenic Methodology* (Farnborough: St. Michael's Abbey Press, 2008) 83–99, especially 96–99.

branches, it left the second part, the Mass, as it was in the Roman Missal of 1570. By way of contrast, the Missal of Paul VI not only further refines the first part but also introduces a few changes in the eucharistic section. It provides Isaiah 50:4-7, the third song of the Suffering Servant, as an Old Testament reading and uses Psalm 21, the former tract, as the responsorial psalm, the refrain of which is "My God, my God, why have you forsaken me?" the dying words of Jesus on the cross in Matthew 27:46 and Mark 15:34. It would have been a good idea to include another refrain to use in Year C when Luke is read because in that gospel the last words of Jesus are taken not from Psalm 21:1 but from Psalm 30:6: "Father, into your hands I commend my spirit." The familiar hymn of Philippians 2:6-11 is now the second reading—important for situating the passion within the broader theological framework of Christ's divine existence, kenotic descent, and consequent reception, once exalted, of the name above all names, conferred upon him by God because of his total self-emptying and obedient acceptance of the cross that reversed the pride and insubordination of the first Adam. The core of this passage, verses 8-9, is also the gospel acclamation on this Sunday.

The passion narratives of the three Synoptics are read in alternate years and are longer than they were in the 1956 *Ordo*, though, except for Mark, they are not as long as they were in the 1570 Missal. They now begin not with the prayer in the garden but much earlier. In Year A the passion of Matthew begins at 26:14 instead of 26:36, in Year B the passion of Mark begins at 14:1 instead of 14:32, and in Year C the passion of Luke begins at 22:14 instead of 22:39. The reason for the extensions is probably to include the Last Supper, of capital importance theologically because of the connection between the Cenacle and the cross in the Catholic understanding of sacrifice and hence of the Eucharist. But it can be wondered whether the lengthening of these already long readings does not exceed the attention span of most listeners, especially since the passion of John on Good Friday still begins after the supper.

As for the presidential prayers, the Missal of Paul VI keeps the collect of RM 1570 and Pius XII's *Ordo*. Found in H 312 as well as in GeV 329, it recalls that God "as an example of humility for the human race to follow / caused our Savior to take flesh and submit to the Cross." The Latin behind "an example of humility to follow" is *ad imitandum humilitatis exemplum*. A better translation would have been "an example of humility to *imitate*." The theme of imitation or mimesis, so fundamental to the palm procession, continues by means of this word in the collect and establishes yet another link between the two parts of the day's liturgy. But it was missed in the English translation. Had it not been missed, we would see clearly that the liturgy is calling us to imitate not only the Lord's entrance into Jerusalem but also the event to which that entrance was directed, the cross, and that the two are inseparable.

The secret and post-Communion of the Missal of 1570, retained by Pius XII, are taken from H 313 and 314, respectively. They make no mention of the passion and are not unique to Palm Sunday but found on other occasions as well.[32] The Missal of Paul VI replaces the secret with a prayer over the offerings from the Verona collection of papal Masses, V 628, inserting the phrase *Per Unigeniti tui passionem* in front of it so that it reads, "Through the Passion of your Only Begotten Son, O Lord, / may our reconciliation with you be near at hand" (no. 23). The replacement of the post-Communion (no. 26) is a composite made of two prayers from Palm Sunday of the Passion in the *Gelasianum vetus*. The first half is from GeV 332 and the second half, which mentions the death and rising of Christ, is from GeV 330. It asks the Father, "Just as through the death of your Son you have brought us to hope for what we believe, so by his resurrection you may lead us to where you call."

Whereas the 1570 Roman Missal and the *Ordo* of Pius XII prescribe the preface of the Holy Cross for this Sunday, as they do for all the days of Passiontide, the Missal of Paul VI offers a proper preface taken in part from one in the Carolingian supplement to the Sacramentary of Pope Hadrian (Sup 1585). It recalls that "though innocent," Christ "suffered willingly for sinners and accepted unjust condemnation to save the guilty. His death has washed away our sins and his resurrection has purchased our justification." The prayer over the people (no. 27), used on Wednesday of Holy Week in the *Hadrianum* (H 327), is still found there in RM 1570, in the 1956 OHS, and in the 1962 Missal. The third typical edition of the Missal of Paul VI moves it from Wednesday to Palm Sunday, where, as the last prayer of the Mass, it gives eloquent expression to the sovereign freedom the Lord showed in undertaking the passion and to that end, we might add, entering the holy city.

> Look, we pray, O Lord, on this your family,
> for whom our Lord Jesus Christ
> did not hesitate to be delivered into the hands of the wicked
> and submit to the agony of the Cross.

---

[32] See Bruylants II, nos. 132 and 813.

Conclusion. On the Sunday before Easter in fourth-century Jerusalem, the Christian community would gather on the Mount of Olives, then walk in procession to the Anastasis, carrying palm branches in imitation of Jesus' entrance into the city. In the medieval West this became the prelude to a Mass that had originated in Rome and at which the passion according to Matthew was read. With time, however, the blessing and distribution of palms, inserted before the procession, assumed ever-greater importance and eventually reduced the procession to a walk by the priest and ministers from the sanctuary, where the palms were blessed and distributed, to the front doors of the church and back to the sanctuary.

In 1956 Pius XII sought to restore the integrity of the procession by designating it a public display of homage to Christ the King, by encouraging the laity to take part in it, by reducing the blessing of palms to a single oration, and by not requiring them to be distributed during the service. But the procession continued to begin and end in the sanctuary, as it still does in the 1962 Missal, the extraordinary form. The Mass, celebrated in purple vestments and centered on the passion, contrasted sharply with the procession that bore public witness to the kingship of Christ and at which ministers wore red vestments.

Only in the postconciliar Missal, the ordinary form, is the goal of the 1956 restoration finally achieved. For here, for the first time, the opening action of this liturgy is correctly identified as a commemoration of the Lord's entrance into Jerusalem, a commemoration to be made at all Masses in one of three ways. The first is the procession with palms that, the Missal insists, must commence outside the church and conclude inside with recitation of the collect of the Mass. Since no. 5 of the third typical edition requires that the service start with the sign of the cross and greeting, as does every Eucharist, it could be said that the procession no longer precedes the Mass but begins it. Thus, instead of contrasting the entrance ceremony with the rest of the Mass, the Missal of Paul VI connects them. It requires red vestments for both and has the priest explain that Christ entered Jerusalem in order to lay down his life and be raised for our salvation, then pray that this purpose be accomplished in the gathered community precisely through its mimetic enactment of that original event and its celebration of the Eucharist at which the Lord's saving passion is proclaimed.

Having concluded our reflections on the first day of Holy Week, we turn our attention to the next three days.

C. MONDAY, TUESDAY, AND WEDNESDAY OF HOLY WEEK

1. *The Restored Order of Pius XII*

Readings. The most distinctive feature of Monday, Tuesday, and Wednesday of Holy Week in the 1956 *Ordo* is the reading of the passion according to Mark on Tuesday and that of Luke on Wednesday. These were the gospel selections in the Missal of 1570. The only difference is that the OHS, having considerably shortened the passion according to Matthew on Sunday, does the same with these. The passion of Mark now begins at 14:32, the prayer in Gethsemane, instead of at 14:1. The passion according to Luke likewise opens with the prayer of Jesus on the Mount of Olives in 22:39. Previously it began at 22:1. The passion according to John on Good Friday also begins in a garden after the Last Supper. Recalling that the passion according to Matthew as modified in 1956 begins in Gethsemane, we see that now all four passion narratives begin with events immediately following the supper that end with the arrest of Jesus. Except for the shortening of the two passion narratives, readings in the OHS are the same as they were in the Missal of 1570.

The gospel on Monday of Holy Week is John 12:1-9, the dinner at the house of Lazarus "six days before the Passover" where Mary anoints the feet of Jesus with fragrant ointment, a gesture Jesus interprets as an anticipation of his burial. The epistle on that day is Isaiah 50:5-10, the third song of the Suffering Servant. The epistle on Tuesday is Jeremiah 11:18-20. The prophet, in the face of those plotting to kill him, declares, "I was like a gentle lamb led to the slaughter." On Wednesday there are two readings before the gospel. The first is Isaiah 62:11–63:7 in which the Lord, bloodied from trampling on his enemies, likens himself to one treading the winepress, his garments stained crimson. The second, Isaiah 53:1-12, is the fourth song of the Suffering Servant. In it the image of the lamb, mentioned by Jeremiah on Tuesday, returns. "Like a lamb that is led to the slaughter," the passage declares, "and like a sheep that before its shearers is silent," so does the Servant "not open his mouth."

Prayers. All the prayers for these three days in the restored *Ordo* are the same as those in the 1570 Missal and derive ultimately from the Sacramentary of Pope Hadrian (H 315–27). The collects on Monday and Tuesday and all five prayers on Wednesday mention the passion, the cross, or the death of Christ. Wednesday has five prayers instead of four because, besides the collect, it has an oration after the first Old Testament reading.

Readings. As was pointed out earlier, the postconciliar Lectionary prescribes that all three Synoptic passion narratives be read in alternating years on Palm Sunday and restores them to their length prior to being shortened by Pius XII. It retains the anointing at Bethany as the gospel for Monday but replaces the passion narratives of Mark and Luke on Tuesday and Wednesday. For Tuesday it chooses John 13:21-33, 36-38 in which Jesus, at supper with the Twelve, dips a piece of bread in a dish and gives it to his betrayer, then tells Peter, "Before the cock crows you will have denied me three times." On Wednesday it appoints Matthew 26:14-25 in which Judas agrees to betray Jesus for thirty pieces of silver and the disciples make preparations for the Passover meal.

As for the first reading, the Lectionary moves the fourth Servant Song from Wednesday to Good Friday and replaces it with the third Servant Song, previously on Monday. In its place on Monday is the first Servant Song, Isaiah 42:1-7. On Tuesday is the second Servant Song, Isaiah 49:1-6. Thus all four Servant Songs are read in succession during Holy Week— the first on Monday, the second on Tuesday, the third on Wednesday, and the fourth on Friday. The third is also the Old Testament reading on Palm Sunday, though on that occasion the verses are slightly different, consisting of 50:5-10 instead of 50:4-9 as on Wednesday.

Prayers. The Missal of Paul VI keeps all the prayers in the 1956 *Ordo* that refer to the passion except the collect of Wednesday, choosing to keep the oration after the first reading instead:

> O God, who willed your Son to submit for our sake
> to the yoke of the Cross,
> so that you might drive from us the power of the enemy,
> grant us, your servants, to attain the grace of the resurrection.[33]

The secrets and post-Communions on Monday and Tuesday of Pius XII's *Ordo*, unlike the collects, include no reference to the passion and are generic in content. The postconciliar Missal replaces them with other prayers—equally generic and without reference to the passion.

---

[33] For the sources of these prayers, see Cuthbert Johnson, OSB, and Anthony Ward, SM, "Sources of the Orations for Holy Week in the 2002 'Missale Romanum,'" EL 123 (2009) 327–46.

The third typical edition also replaces the prayer over the people on Monday. It consists of a general petition from V 940 and a purpose clause from GeV 265 that, looking forward to the Triduum, asks that the faithful "may celebrate the paschal festivities / not only with bodily observance / but above all with purity of mind." The one on Tuesday is the same as that in the restored order and asks God to cleanse his people "from all seduction of former ways / and make them capable of new holiness." Since the third typical edition moved Wednesday's prayer over the people to Palm Sunday of the Passion, it puts in its place a fine formula from GeV 343 that mentions the paschal sacraments and rebirth. It reads,

> Grant your faithful, O Lord, we pray,
> to partake unceasingly of the paschal mysteries
> and to await with longing the gifts to come,
> that, persevering in the Sacraments of their rebirth,
> they may be led by Lenten works to newness of life.

Preface I of the Passion was recited during the Fifth Week of Lent. Preface II of the Passion is required on Monday, Tuesday, and Wednesday of this week. Taken from the supplement to the *Hadrianum* (Sup 1584), it declares that

> the days of his [Christ's] saving Passion
> and glorious Resurrection are approaching,
> by which the pride of the ancient foe is vanquished
> and the mystery of our redemption in Christ is celebrated.

The phrase "mystery of our redemption," *nostrae redemptionis mysterium*, recalls the title of the November 16, 1955, document announcing the reform of Holy Week, *Maxima Redemptionis Nostrae Mysteria*, The Greatest Mysteries of Our Redemption.

The splendid introit antiphon for Wednesday of Holy Week in RM 1570 and OHS goes back to five of the six most ancient manuscripts of the Roman Antiphonal (AMS 76) and is still in the Missal of Paul VI. A paraphrase of Philippians 2:10, 8, 11, in the 2011 translation it reads,

> At the name of Jesus, every knee should bend,
> of those in heaven and on the earth and under the earth,
> for the Lord became obedient to death, death on a cross:
> therefore Jesus Christ is Lord, to the glory of God the Father.

D. THURSDAY OF HOLY WEEK: CHRISM MASS AND BLESSING OF OILS

Preliminaries. In the 1956 restored order of Pius XII as well as in the Roman Missal of 1962, Holy Thursday, called *Feria V in Cena Domini*, or Thursday of the Lord's Supper, is the first day of the Sacred Triduum. In the Missal of Paul VI, in accord with no. 19 of the Universal Norms on the Liturgical Year and the Calendar, the Triduum does not begin until the evening Mass of the Lord's Supper. The part of the day preceding that belongs to Lent and is called *Feria V Hebdomadae Sanctae*, or Thursday of Holy Week. No. 31 of the norms declares that "On Thursday of Holy Week, in the morning, the bishop concelebrates Mass with his presbyterate and blesses the holy oils and consecrates the chrism." In all these documents, then, the principal liturgical event on Thursday morning is the chrism Mass at the cathedral during which the bishop, together with priests of the diocese, consecrates the chrism and blesses the oil of catechumens and the oil of the sick. White vestments are worn and the Gloria is sung.

These blessings have no necessary connection with the Last Supper or the institution of the Eucharist. The original reason for performing them on Holy Thursday was practical: to have a fresh supply of sacred chrism to use for the postbaptismal anointing and confirmation of those baptized at the Paschal Vigil. The circular letter of January 16, 1988, *Paschalis Sollemnitatis*, recognizes this in no. 35. Recalling that Thursday of Holy Week is the traditional day for the chrism Mass, it adds that "the chrism and the oil of catechumens is to be used in the celebration of the sacraments of initiation on Easter night." When it became common to administer baptism at other times of the year and the connection between the consecration of chrism on Thursday and its use at the vigil on Saturday weakened, medieval and even modern authors came up with symbolic and theological reasons for the choice of Thursday. Annibale Bugnini, for example, writes that "the sacraments in which the oils are used are the fruit of Christ's paschal mystery and give human beings a participation in that mystery."[34] This reason had some credibility as long as Thursday was part of the Triduum, as it still is in the extraordinary form. It loses much of its persuasive force, however, when as in the ordinary form the paschal Triduum does not begin until Thursday evening and the oils are blessed during Lent.

---

[34] Bugnini, *Reform*, 801.

The Old Gelasian lists three Mass formularies for what it calls Thursday of the sixth Week of Lent.[35] The first (GeV 349–51, 369–74) has no title. Into it is copied an *ordo* for reconciling penitents, probably to enable presbyters in the Roman *tituli* to reconcile penitents on their deathbeds, using the orations in the section *Reconciliatio paenitentis ad mortem* (GeV 364–68). In seventh-century Rome this was all that remained of canonical penance.[36] The third Mass (GeV 391–94) is meant to be celebrated in the evening, *ad uesperum*. Its preface (GeV 392) contrasts the actions of Judas and Jesus at the Last Supper and their respective consequences.

The second Mass (GeV 375–90) is the one that interests us here. It contains prayers that presbyters were authorized to recite for blessing the oil of the sick (GeV 381–82) and the oil of catechumens (GeV 384) for use in the titular churches. Later, probably in Gaul, a Gallican exorcism (GeV 385) and short preface (GeV 390), both intended for consecrating chrism—a rite reserved to bishops—were inserted. Still later, again probably in Gaul, a Roman preface (GeV 378) and long formula for confecting chrism were added, at which time the words *Missa chrismalis* were appended to the original Roman title, *Item in quinta feria*.[37]

Although these three formularies—all presbyteral in origin—continue to be copied in the Frankish Gelasian sacramentaries of the late eighth century, they are eventually superseded by the relentless advance of another type of Holy Thursday liturgy, the papal one. The earliest account of this liturgy is a seventh-century *ordo* for the Lateran edited by Antoine Chavasse.[38] It attests only one Mass on this day, as does the Sacramentary of Pope Hadrian (H 329–37). At this one Mass, bearing the title *Oratio in cena Domini ad missam* in the *Hadrianum*, the pope with presbyters of the city consecrates chrism and blesses the other oils. The *Ordo* of the Lateran states that this Mass begins at the sixth hour, or noon, and that following it the presbyters return to their *tituli* to celebrate another Mass—one that would correspond to the third Mass, the Mass *ad uesperum*, in the Old Gelasian (GeV 391–84).

---

[35] For a masterful analysis of their formation and use, see Chavasse, *Gélasien*, 126–39.

[36] See Bernhard Poschmann, *Penance and the Anointing of the Sick* (Freiburg: Herder, 1964) 104–9.

[37] Chavasse, *Gélasien*, 133–35.

[38] "A Rome, le Jeudi-saint, au VIIe siècle, d'après un vieil Ordo," *Revue d'histoire ecclésiastique* 50 (1955) 21–35.

The mid-tenth-century Romano-Germanic Pontifical indicates that the Mass *in cena Domini* on Thursday takes place at the third hour, or nine o'clock,[39] which is roughly the same hour at which in modern times the Holy Thursday Mass was celebrated in cathedrals, during which chrism and other oils were blessed.

Texts and rubrics for blessing the oils, though part of the *Missa chrismalis* in the Old Gelasian and the Mass *in cena Domini* in the *Hadrianum*, are extracted from later missals and incorporated into the third part of the Roman Pontifical, published in 1595–96 and reissued with no changes under Pope John XXIII in 1961–62.[40] Rubric 1 in the chrism Mass of the 1956 restored Holy Week liturgies, repeated in the 1962 Missal, indicates that oils are blessed and sacred chrism confected according to the order of the Pontifical. In the following sections we compare and contrast these ceremonies in the pontificals before and after the Second Vatican Council, then treat the formation of the 1956 chrism Mass and its replacement in the Missal of Paul VI.

1. Blessing of Oils in the Roman Pontifical of 1596

As presented in this pontifical, the blessing of oils is a most solemn and grandiose ceremony. The bishop is assisted by twelve priests, seven deacons, and seven subdeacons. The involvement of so many ministers of varying rank, observes Pierre de Puniet, "is a genuine trace of the ancient pontifical liturgy where the pope officiated surrounded by all the clergy of Rome."[41] The Pontifical calls the assisting priests *testes* and *cooperators*: "witnesses" of the bishop's action and "co-workers" with him in this ministry.[42] The expression "co-workers" led many to maintain that the bishop and twelve presbyters concelebrated the consecration of chrism.

---

[39] PRG XCIX, 252, in Vogel-Elze II, 67.

[40] Manlio Sodi and Alessandro Toniolo, eds., *Pontificale Romanum: Editio Typica 1961–1962*, Monumenta Liturgica Piana 3 (Città del Vaticano: Libreria Editrice Vaticana, 2008). Texts of the blessings are nos. 961–97. This work is subsequently referred to as PR 1962. English translations of these rites are from the English translation of RM 1962 by Baronius Press.

[41] "Concélébration liturgique," DACL III, 2, col. 2481 (trans. mine). Very informative are the etchings included in Manlio Sodi and Achille Maria Triacca, eds., *Pontificale Romanum: Editio Princeps (1595–1596)*, Monumenta Liturgica Concilii Tridentini 1 (Città del Vaticano: Libreria Editrice Vaticana, 1997) 575, 577, 580, 586.

[42] PR 1962, no. 976.

The blessings take place at a long table in the middle of the sanctuary. The faldstool of the bishop is placed in the center, facing the altar. On each side are seated six priests representing the apostles. The whole arrangement is reminiscent of the Last Supper. The oil of the sick is the first to be blessed. It takes place near the end of the Canon, after the prayer *Nobis quoque peccatoribus* and before the words *Per quem haec omnia*.[43] A rubric in the *Hadrianum* (H 333) indicates that "before the words *Per quem haec omnia* are said, the ampullas of oil that the people offered are lifted up, and the lord pope and all the presbyters bless them" (trans. mine). This is a precious reference to the ancient custom of the bishop and presbyters performing this blessing together.

The prayer, derived from GeV 382 (= H 334) opens with an epiclesis: "Send forth from heaven, we beg, O Lord, the Holy Spirit, thy Paraclete, into this juice from the olive. May all who are anointed by this unguent of heavenly healing therein find protection for mind and body, expelling every pain, every weakness, every sickness of mind and body." At the time this prayer was composed, it is obvious that the oil is meant for the sick, not the dying, as it came to be in later centuries, and that the purpose of the anointing is to bring health. Such anointings were not restricted to ordained ministers but were also performed by the faithful themselves.[44] After being blessed, the oil of the sick is brought to the sacristy, and the bishop returns to the altar to finish the Canon.

The consecration of the chrism and the blessing of the oil of catechumens take place after the ministers have received Communion.[45] The Pontifical says nothing about anyone else receiving, and Pius XII forbade it.[46] The balsam, chrism, and oil of catechumens are brought from the sacristy to the sanctuary in a solemn procession as cantors and choir sing the hymn *O Redemptor, sume carmen*. The refrain is "Accept

[43] PR 1962, nos. 966–70.

[44] A. G. Martimort writes in *Church* III, 122, that "once blessed by the bishop or his priests the oil could be given to the sick who would use it themselves as a medicine or to whom it could be applied by those caring for them; it was a liniment, an unguent, but it could also be drunk."

[45] Texts in PR 1962, nos. 972–97.

[46] Near the end of the chrism Mass in OHS, rubric 14 says, *In hac missa sacram communionem distribuere non licet*, "In this Mass it is not permitted to distribute Communion" (trans. mine).

this song, Redeemer, that we all sing to thee." One of the verses declares, "A tree rich with bountiful light produced this oil for sacring. How reverently they bear it now to the Savior of the world." The final verse prays, "King of our eternal homeland, deign to consecrate this oil as active sign against every demon's claim."

After blessing the balsam, the bishop breathes three times in the form of a cross over the mouth of the ampulla containing chrism. His twelve witnesses and co-workers do the same, one after the other. These exsufflations, exorcistic in meaning—Rabotin calls them "exorcisms in action"[47]—lead to a prayer of exorcism over the chrism. After these preliminaries comes the high point of this liturgy, the consecration of the chrism. The prayer (GeV 385–88 = H 335), chanted, takes the form of a magnificent preface. It begins with the usual dialogue and consists of an anamnetic section and an epicletic section, the first laying the foundation for the petitions in the second. The anamnesis recalls how olives, creatures of God pressed into oil and used for anointing priests and kings of old, prophesied realities yet to come, especially the anointing of Jesus with the Spirit at his baptism, making him the Christ, the Anointed of the Lord. The epiclesis entreats the Father to sanctify the chrism by his blessing and "to mingle with it the virtue of the Holy Spirit, in cooperation with the power of Christ, thy Son, for whose name this chrism derives its name . . . that unto all who shall be reborn of water and the Holy Ghost it may be a chrism of salvation and give them participation in eternal life."

Having mixed the balsam with the consecrated oil, the bishop addresses a salutation to the sacred chrism, chanting, *Ave, sanctum chrisma*, or "Hail, holy chrism!" three times, each time on a higher note, then kisses the lip of the ampulla. The twelve priests do the same, genuflecting three times before the ampulla, each time chanting, *Ave, sanctum chrisma* on a higher note, then, like the bishop, kissing the lip of the ampulla. Such lavish outpourings of honor are more understandable when we recall the teaching of Cyril of Jerusalem, who maintains that by the invocation of the Holy Spirit the consecrated oil undergoes a transformation similar to that of the eucharistic bread. "Beware of supposing this to be plain ointment," he warns, "for as the bread of the Eucharist, after the invocation of the Holy Spirit, is mere

---

[47] "La Consécration des Saintes Huiles le Jeudi-Saint," *La vie et les arts liturgiques* 63 (1920) 224 (trans. mine).

bread no longer, but the body of Christ, so also this holy ointment is no more simple ointment."[48]

The exorcism and blessing of the oil of catechumens follow. The bishop and twelve priests breathe over the ampulla of this third oil as they did over the chrism. The prayer of exorcism, added to the Old Gelasian in Gaul (GeV 389) and absent from the *Hadrianum*, asks that every evil spirit depart from the oil so that the bodies anointed with it "may be sanctified into receiving spiritual grace." The prayer of blessing (GeV 384 = H 336) asks that should any taint of the enemy remain in those approaching "the laver of blessed regeneration, may it depart at the touch of this sanctified oil. Let there remain no home for spiritual wickedness, no opportunity for virtue to flee, no possibility for evil to lurk in ambush." On the contrary, the prayer asks, "May this prepared ointment help them forward to that salvation which they are to receive by the birth of heavenly regeneration in the sacrament of baptism."

Then the bishop and twelve priests salute the oil of catechumens in the same way as they did the chrism, this time chanting, *Ave, sanctum oleum*, "Hail, holy oil!" After this the ampullas of chrism and the oil of catechumens are carried in procession to the sacristy as the cantors and choir sing the remaining verses of *O Redemptor, sume carmen*. The bishop returns to the altar and finishes the Mass.

2. *The Reformed Rite of Blessing Oils*

After Vatican II reform of the blessing of oils and the consecration of chrism aimed mainly at pruning away the exorcisms and curbing the ceremonial displays that accumulated in medieval times north of the Alps in order to recover the strength of the original Roman tradition residing in the purity and eloquence of the prayers themselves.[49] The postconciliar rite was promulgated by the Sacred Congregation

---

[48] Cyril of Jerusalem, *Lecture XXI* (*Third Lecture on the Mysteries*) 3, trans. Edward Hamilton Gifford, in NPNF VII, 150. Interpretation of the rest of this sentence in Greek is controversial and is reflected in translations. Gifford's text declares that the consecrated oil "is Christ's gift of grace and, by the advent of the Holy Ghost, is made fit to impart his divine nature." McCauley and Stephenson's translation in FC 63, 170, states that it "becomes the gracious gift of Christ and the Holy Spirit, producing the advent [presence?] of his deity."

[49] For the steps leading up to the promulgation of the reformed rites, see Bugnini, *Reform*, 798–99.

for Divine Worship on December 3, 1970.[50] The introduction, no. 1, declares that "the chrism Mass is one of the principal expressions of the fullness of the bishop's priesthood and signifies the close unity of the priests with him." Later no. 14 calls the priests who concelebrate with the bishop "his witnesses and the co-workers in the ministry of the holy chrism"—phrases lifted from the Roman Pontifical of 1595–96.

After recalling that the Christian liturgy has assimilated the "Old Testament usage of anointing kings, priests, and prophets with consecratory oil because the name of Christ, whom they prefigured, means 'the anointed of the Lord,'" no. 2 of the introduction teaches that "chrism is a sign: by baptism Christians are plunged into the paschal mystery of Christ; they die with him, are buried with him, and rise with him; they are sharers in his royal and prophetic priesthood. By confirmation Christians receive the spiritual anointing of the Spirit who is given to them." No. 2 adds that "by the oil of catechumens the effect of the baptismal exorcisms is extended. Before they go to the font of life to be reborn the candidates for baptism are strengthened to renounce sin and the devil."

The new rite no longer insists on balsam but permits any "perfumes or other sweet smelling matter" to be mixed with the oil (no. 4). The mixing may take place either "privately before the rite of consecration or may be done by the bishop during the liturgical service" (no. 5). The second option is much better. Since the perfume is what makes chrism different from the other oils, it is highly desirable that the entire assembly see, hear, and smell it when it is poured into the oil—especially so if the second consecratory prayer is chosen because it refers to "this mixture of oil and perfume" (no. 25).

The oil of the sick may still be blessed, as in the past, before the end of the eucharistic prayer—any one of them—and other oils after Communion (no. 11), specifically "after the prayer after communion" (no. 21). The introduction adds, "For pastoral reasons, however, the entire rite of blessing may be celebrated after the liturgy of the word" (no. 12). Paul Turner notes that "the traditional arrangement seems almost illogical to those familiar with the post–Vatican II rites of baptism, confirmation, ordination, marriage, and anointing of the sick. In every case, the featured ritual takes place after the Liturgy of the Word. That is why the rubrics now permit the prayers over the oils to follow

[50] Texts are in *Rites* I, 704–13.

that model."[51] This is the one chosen by the Holy Father every year at Saint John Lateran. Otherwise the oil of the sick, though less important, would be blessed at a more important place in the Mass than the chrism. Besides, blessings performed after the prayer after Communion for all practical purposes are blessings performed after *Mass*. The bishop blesses the oils at a table in the center of the sanctuary with concelebrants standing in a semicircle around him (no. 21), the bishop facing the people (no. 22), not the altar as was the case previously.

There are still two grand processions. In the first, described in detail in nos. 16–18, the balsam and oils are brought up with the bread and wine during the preparation of the gifts, identified in a loud voice, and handed to the bishop. In the second, set forth in no. 27, the oils are carried behind the censer and cross to the sacristy after the final blessing. The hymn of choice in both processions is the traditional *O Redemptor, sume carmen*. In many places the oils are carried by the deans or lay representatives, ideally candidates for baptism and confirmation, who deliver them to the parishes or at least take them to some convenient place where pastors or their delegates can pick them up.

As for the prayers, all the exorcisms of the former rite have been eliminated. The core of the blessing of the oil of the sick (no. 20) remains, as before, the epiclesis of GeV 382 and H 334, *Emitte Spiritum tuum Sanctum Paraclitum*, except that *Paraclitum* is now frivolously rendered "man's Helper and Friend." Previously, the prayer began with this petition. The 1970 version prefaces it with "Lord God, loving Father, / you bring healing to the sick / through your Son Jesus Christ." The Latin behind "Lord God, loving Father" is *Deus, totius consolationis Pater*, "God, Father of all consolation," an obvious reference to 2 Corinthians 1:3, eminently fitting in such a prayer but passed over in the English translation. The prayer still looks to the recovery of health on the part of those anointed with this oil, asking that "they may be freed from pain and illness / and made well again in body, mind, and soul."

In the reformed rite the oils are blessed in the order of their ascending importance. Thus, the oil of catechumens, which used to be blessed last, is now blessed after the oil of the sick (no. 21). The introduction, no. 2, teaches that this oil strengthens the candidates with the power to renounce sin and the devil before going to the font of life for rebirth. This idea, prominent in the Latin text of the first half

---

[51] Turner, *Glory*, 33.

of the prayer (no. 22), a new one, is softened in English, which fails to include that God made oil a *signum roboris*, or "sign of strength," and omits the petition *concede fortitudinem*, "grant fortitude." The second half is well phrased:

> Bring them to a deeper understanding of the gospel,
> help them to accept the challenge of Christian living,
> and lead them to the joy of new birth
> in the family of your Church.

The blessing of oils culminates in the consecration of chrism. After pouring the balsam or other perfumed substance into the oil (no. 23), the bishop then enjoins all to pray that God

> will bless this oil
> so that all who are anointed with it
> may be inwardly transformed
> and come to share in eternal salvation. (no. 24)

This solemn invitation, a new element, engages the entire congregation in the liturgical action to follow. The bishop may then "breathe over the opening of the vessel of the chrism" (no. 25), but no longer three times in the form of a cross, as was the previous practice. And now that exorcisms have been removed, the exsufflation is no longer exorcistic but epicletic in significance, recalling the action of the risen Lord in John 20:22: "He breathed on them and said, 'Receive the Holy Spirit.'"

The 1970 ritual offers a choice between two consecratory prayers (no. 25).[52] The first is practically the same as the one in the 1596 Pontifical, taken from GeV 385–88 and H 335. The main difference is that it no longer takes the form of a preface and consequently has a new opening sentence and no introductory dialogue. The second formula is a new composition.[53] Both prayers have an anamnetic section followed by an epicletic section that begins, "And so . . ." At this point in both prayers, "all the celebrants extend their right hands toward the chrism, without saying anything, until the end of the prayer" (no. 25).

---

[52] For their sources, see Anthony Ward, SM, "Sources of the Postconciliar Blessings of the Holy Oils and the Chrism," EL 125 (2011) 190–233.

[53] For theological comments on it, see Giuseppe Ferraro, SJ, "La seconda formula della Consacrazione del Crisma," EL 125 (2011) 129–41.

Whereas the anamnetic section of the first prayer includes several Old Testament figures, its counterpart in the new prayer dwells almost entirely on the saving work of Christ. Both prayers mention that through the anointing with chrism the newly baptized are granted a share in Christ's royal, priestly, and prophetic mission. This, of course, reflects the meaning of the first postbaptismal anointing before which the bishop or priest prays,

> The God of power and Father of our Lord Jesus Christ
> has freed you from sin
> and brought you to new life
> through water and the Holy Spirit.
>
> He now anoints you with the chrism of salvation,
> so that, united with his people,
> you may remain for ever a member of Christ
> who is Priest, Prophet, and King.[54]

The newer prayer, besides mentioning the mixture of perfume with the oil, gives clearer expression to the postconciliar theology of confirmation as imparting the gift of the Holy Spirit. It asks the Father to

> make this mixture of oil and perfume
> a sign and source ✛ of your blessing.
> Pour out the gifts of your Holy Spirit
> on our brothers and sisters who will be anointed with it.

The first prayer, composed centuries before the current formula of confirmation was adopted, does not state that the anointing with chrism by the bishop confers the Holy Spirit. It simply asks, "Let this be indeed the chrism of salvation / for those who will be born again of water and the Holy Spirit." The prayer ends, "May they come to share eternal life." The second prayer finishes with a much more elaborate eschatological vision:

> Above all, Father, we pray
> that through this sign of your anointing
> you will grant increase to your Church
> until it reaches the eternal glory

[54] RCIA no. 228, in *Rites* I, 160.

where you, Father, will be the all in all,
together with Christ your Son,
in the unity of the Holy Spirit,
for ever and ever.

Though both prayers are outstanding, the second might be better
suited for use in today's church.

3. *The 1956 Chrism Mass*

Until the restoration of Holy Week by Pius XII, announced on November 16, 1955, and implemented in 1956, the oil of the sick and the
oil of catechumens were blessed and chrism confected at the cathedral
by the bishop during the Mass *in Cena Domini*, or Mass of the Lord's
Supper, celebrated everywhere on Holy Thursday morning. Pius XII
decreed that henceforth the Mass of the Lord's Supper be celebrated
in the evening but that oils still be blessed in the morning, no longer
at the Mass of the Lord's Supper but at one specially composed for
this purpose—the chrism Mass.[55] The collect, secret, and preface were
taken from the long-defunct *Missa chrismalis* of the Old Gelasian (GeV
375, 377, 378). The collect, which derives from the original Gelasian
core prior to the addition of prayers for consecrating chrism, focuses
on the role priests play in the sacrament of baptism and calls the faithful a consecrated people, perhaps alluding to Exodus 19:6 and 1 Peter
2:9. It prays, "Lord God, who dost use the ministry of priests in re-
generating thy people, grant us persevering subjection to thy will, so
that thy people who have been consecrated to thee may by thy grace
increase in our day in merits and in number."

The preface, inserted into the Gelasian formulary in Gaul with the
prayer for confecting chrism, extols the spiritual power of this mixture
of olive oil and balsam. By way of contrast, the secret contains nothing
pertinent to any of the oils or any of the sacraments. Since the Gelasian
Mass lacks a post-Communion, one from the *Veronensis* (V 245) was
selected to fill the void in the OHS. Two readings were added to the
prayers. The epistle was James 5:13-16. It recommends that the elders
of the church pray over the sick, "anointing them with oil," adding
that "the prayer of faith will save the sick and the Lord will raise them
up." The gospel, Mark 6:7-13, reports that the Twelve "cast out many
devils and anointed with oil many that were sick and healed them."

---

[55] Texts of the Mass are in OHS, pp. 61–66.

The communion antiphon is two verses from the same pericope, Mark 6:12-13.

Those responsible for reforming the Roman Missal after the Second Vatican Council judged Pius XII's chrism Mass to be incoherent. The collect recalls the role priests have in consecrating people to God through baptism; both readings are about anointing the sick; the preface extols the efficacy of chrism in perfecting the spiritual rebirth that takes place in the font; the communion antiphon, taken from the gospel, is about anointing the sick. The secret and post-Communion say nothing about either the oils or the sacraments of initiation.

The task of the reformers, then, was to find a unifying theme or image to govern the choice and arrangement of the chants, readings, and prayers of the postconciliar chrism Mass. According to Annibale Bugnini,[56] it was Paul VI himself who recommended that the Mass be a "feast of the priesthood." Since this is the Mass at which the oil of catechumens is blessed and sacred chrism consecrated, oils used in baptism and confirmation, and since the Second Vatican Council's Dogmatic Constitution on the Church, *Lumen Gentium*, no. 10, grounds the universal priesthood in these two sacraments,[57] one immediately thinks that this "feast of the priesthood" will be a Mass celebrating the royal priesthood of all the baptized. And indeed it is.

4. The Postconciliar Chrism Mass

Prayers and spoken formulas remain unchanged in all three editions of the Missal of Paul VI. Rubrics, however, have augmented. Rubric 4 in the 2002 Missal was the only one in the 1970 and 1975 editions. We will return to it shortly. Rubrics 1, 2, 3, and 5 are additions to the third typical edition. Except for the first, they all pertain to the time of blessing oils and derive from the Rite of the Blessing of Oils, nos. 9–12 in the Roman Pontifical.[58] As translated in the 2011 Roman Missal, rubric 5,

---

[56] Bugnini, *Reform*, 117.

[57] *Lumen Gentium*, no. 10, teaches that "the baptized, by regeneration and the anointing of the Holy Spirit, are consecrated to be a spiritual house and a holy priesthood." We recall, too, that no. 2 of the introduction to the Rite of the Blessing of Oils declares that "chrism is a sign: by baptism Christians are plunged into the paschal mystery of Christ; they die with him, are buried with him, and rise with him; they are sharers in his royal and prophetic priesthood." *Rites* I, 704.

[58] Texts in *Rites* I, 705–6.

corresponding to nos. 11–12 in the Rite of the Blessing of Oils, states: "In accord with traditional practice, the blessing of the Oil of the Sick takes place before the end of the Eucharistic Prayer, but the blessing of the Oil of Catechumens and the consecration of the Chrism take place after Communion." It adds, "Nevertheless, for pastoral reasons it is permitted for the entire rite of blessing to take place after the Liturgy of the Word." For reasons already given, this is certainly the option to be preferred.

The entrance antiphon, taken from the second reading, is a stirring acclamation on the part of all the baptized: "Jesus Christ has made us into a kingdom, priests for his God and Father" (Rev 1:6). The splendid new collect expands upon the entrance antiphon, affirming that God has made this gathering of the faithful—laity and clergy—share the same consecration by which he consecrated his Son when, anointing him with his Spirit, he raised him from the dead and "made him Christ and Lord."[59] The trinitarian dimension of the paschal mystery is here brilliantly set forth.[60]

The postconciliar Lectionary replaces Pius XII's epistle and gospel with three readings very closely connected to each other and most appropriate for the changed theme of the Mass. The first is Isaiah 61:1-3a, 6a, 8b-9. It begins, "The spirit of the Lord God is upon me, because the LORD has anointed me." The strength of this spirit impels the prophet to embark on a mission of liberation leading to the restoration of mourning Zion, the future inhabitants of which "shall be called priests of the LORD, ministers of our God."

The second reading is Revelation 1:5-8. In the center is the full doxology from which the entrance antiphon is taken: "To him who loves us and freed us from our sins by his blood, and made us to be a kingdom, priests serving his God and Father, to him be glory and dominion forever and ever." In the greeting before the doxology Jesus Christ is called "the faithful witness, the firstborn of the dead, and the ruler of the kings of the earth," three titles that "evoke the passion, the resurrection and the exaltation of Christ"[61]—in other words, the paschal mystery in its fullness.

---

[59] For the sources of the prayers of the chrism Mass, see Cuthbert Johnson, OSB, and Anthony Ward, SM, "Sources of the Orations for Holy Week in the 2000 'Missale Romanum,'" EL 123 (2009) 347–53.

[60] See CCC no. 648 under the title "The Resurrection—A Work of the Holy Trinity."

[61] Jean-Louis D'Aragon, SJ, "The Apocalypse," in JBC 64:19.

The gospel, Luke 4:16-21, is the perfect counterpart of the first reading. Jesus, at the very beginning of his public ministry, enters the synagogue in Nazareth, reads Isaiah 61:1-2, and declares, "Today this scripture has been fulfilled in your hearing." Jesus, then, is the Anointed of the Lord—Messiah in Hebrew, Christ in Greek. The Father, in raising him from the dead, pours out upon all believers the same Spirit with which he anointed Jesus, thereby making them, in the words of the collect, "sharers in his consecration."

The entrance antiphon, collect, and all three readings of this eucharistic celebration are extraordinarily well coordinated and, after the homily, could culminate in the blessing of oils. But they do not. They lead instead to the renewal of priestly promises, the second of three instances of what might be called presbyteral intrusion into the chrism Mass.

5. The Presbyteral Intrusion

The first instance of this intrusion is concelebration. In a 1961 article in *La Maison-Dieu* Pierre Jounel registered disappointment with the chrism Mass produced by Pius XII and stated that it "will become the most solemn and expressive manifestation of the diocesan church only on condition that," among other things, "concelebration be restored."[62] Putting this statement in historical context, he and others were voicing the desire that at the chrism Mass priests concelebrate not only the consecration of the chrism with the bishop but the Eucharist as well. Their wish was fulfilled when the Constitution on the Sacred Liturgy, promulgated on December 4, 1963, declared that "concelebration whereby the unity of the priesthood is appropriately manifested" be permitted on certain occasions, the first of which is "on the Thursday of the Lord's Supper, not only at the Mass of the Chrism, but also at the evening Mass" (no. 57, 1). Only in 1965, two years later, remarks Bugnini, "after lengthy preparation and ten months of experimentation," did eucharistic concelebration make "its radiant entrance into the liturgical practice of the Church on the very anniversary of the institution of the Eucharist and the priesthood."[63]

Here we find early formulations of ideas that subsequently will be repeated many times: that Thursday of the Lord's Supper is the

---

[62] Pierre Jounel, "Le jeudi saint, II: La tradition de l'Eglise," *La Maison-Dieu* 68 (1961) 25 (trans. mine).

[63] Bugnini, *Reform*, 117.

anniversary of the institution of the ministerial priesthood as well as of the Eucharist and that it is eminently fitting for the bishop and presbyters to concelebrate on that day, whether at the chrism Mass or at the evening Mass, as an expression of the oneness of the priesthood. With this, the chrism Mass, until then entirely bound up with baptism and confirmation, acquires links with holy orders, and Paul VI's feast of the priesthood, besides celebrating the priesthood of all the baptized, becomes an occasion for extolling the uniqueness and essential difference of the priesthood of the ordained.

A second instance of presbyteral intrusion into the chrism Mass is renewal of priestly promises after the homily. The desire for some such renewal was first voiced by Paul VI in his encyclical on priestly celibacy, *Sacerdotalis Caelibatus*, published on June 25, 1967. In no. 82 of that document he suggests that "each priest on the anniversary of his ordination or all together on the Thursday of the Lord's Supper, that sacred day on which the priesthood was instituted, renew the full and faithful dedication they once made to Christ the Lord."[64] This is fairly general. On November 4, 1969, the Sacred Congregation for the Clergy added much more precision to this suggestion in a circular letter addressed to the presidents of conferences of bishops on continuing education and formation of the clergy, especially the younger clergy. No. 9 reads, "To strengthen his spiritual life and sense of the priesthood it is strongly recommended that on the morning of Holy Thursday every priest, whether present at the chrism Mass or not, renew the act by which he dedicated himself to Christ and promised to carry out his priestly obligations, especially to observe celibacy and to render obedience to his bishop (or religious superior)."[65] The emphasis here has shifted to celibacy and obedience.

A decisive development came only four months later when on March 6, 1970, the Sacred Congregation for Divine Worship published texts for the renewal of priestly commitment called for by the Congregation for the Clergy. It also included a new preface, not called for by the Congregation for the Clergy. The preface is the third instance of presbyteral intrusion into the chrism Mass. The document from

[64] Translation mine from *Acta Apostolicae Sedis* 59 (1967) 689. The full text of the encyclical is on pp. 657–97.

[65] Translation in DOL doc. 333, no. 2763. Paul Turner reminds us in *Glory*, p. 36, that Cardinal John Wright, an American, was prefect of the congregation at that time.

the Congregation for Divine Worship summarizes the content of the promises of commitment and of the preface and announces that they are included in the reformed Missal of Paul VI that will be used for the first time on Holy Thursday of that year, March 26, 1970. It sums up the promises of commitment as follows: "Just as religious annually renew the vows of their profession, so also it is proper that priests renew the promises made to the bishop at their ordination. The bishop entreats the congregation to pray for his priests and for himself." Then comes a summary of the preface. "The preface," it says, " recalls the institution of the ministerial priesthood, over and above the royal priesthood of believers, and lists its duties: to offer sacrifice; to bear the message of salvation; to make people holy through the sacraments; to be an example by their virtue."

After the summaries the document presents the full texts of two rubrics, the promises and the preface. The first rubric states, "The bishop concelebrates this Mass with his presbyterate and during it blesses the oils. It serves as an expression of the communion between the priests and their bishop. It is therefore of great advantage that, if at all possible, all the priests take part in the Mass and receive communion, even under both kinds. As a sign of the unity of the diocese's presbyterate, the priests who concelebrate with the bishop are to be from different sectors of the diocese." The second rubric is about the homily. It states, "In the homily the bishop is to urge his priests to be loyal to the fulfillment of their office and to invite them to make a public renewal of their commitment to priestly service."[66] In the 1970 and 1975 editions of the *Missale Romanum* of Paul VI these two rubrics are printed together at the beginning of the chrism Mass, above the entrance antiphon. In the 2002 edition what was the first rubric has become rubric 4. It appears above the entrance antiphon with four other rubrics lifted, as we saw, from the Rite of the Blessing of Oils. In the 2002 Missal the rubric about the homily is rubric 8. It is no longer at the beginning of the Mass but, with some expansion, placed above the renewal of priestly promises. Having set forth these three instances of presbyteral intrusion into the chrism Mass—concelebration, renewal of priestly promises, and the preface—some critical comments are now in order.

[66] English translation of the document from the Congregation of Divine Worship can be found in DOL doc. 315, nos. 2556–58. The Latin text is in *Notitiae* 6 (1970) 86–87.

6. Critical Remarks

A. MANIFESTATION OF COMMUNION BETWEEN PRIESTS AND BISHOP

The first rubric in the document issued by the Congregation for Divine Worship on March 6, 1970, now rubric 4 in the chrism Mass of the 2002 Missal, as translated in 2011, states, "This Mass, which the bishop concelebrates with *his* presbyterate, should be, as it were, a manifestation of the Priests' communion with *their* Bishop" (emphasis mine). The rubric about the homily in the document of the Congregation for Divine Worship instructs the bishop "to urge *his* priests to be loyal to the fulfillment of their office" (emphasis mine). Modified and become rubric 8 in the 2002 Missal, it asserts that the bishop "speaks to the people and to *his* Priests about priestly anointing, urging the Priests to be faithful in their office" (emphasis mine).[67] Noteworthy are the possessive pronouns "his" and "their" used with priests and bishop. The priests are "his priests." The bishop is "their bishop." This is not said of the baptized. Rubric 8 in the 2002 Missal refers to the faithful gathered around the bishop as "the people," not *his* people. The danger of emphasizing the bond between bishop and priests at the chrism Mass is that, in the words of rubric 4, the "manifestation of the Priests' communion with their Bishop" may overshadow the primary purpose of this liturgical event, which is to bless oils for use especially in the sacraments of initiation at the Paschal Vigil.

This is most likely to occur when the number of concelebrants and the space allotted them is out of proportion to the rest of the congregation. Although rubric 4 of the chrism Mass in the 2002 Missal recognizes concelebration as a manifestation of communion between priests and bishop, it does not foresee every priest in attendance concelebrating. Rather, it distinguishes between priests who participate and priests who concelebrate. All participate; some concelebrate. It declares that "it is desirable that all Priests participate in it [the chrism Mass], insofar as is possible, and during it receive Communion even under both kinds. To signify the unity of the presbyterate of the diocese, the Priests who concelebrate with the Bishop should be from different regions of the diocese."

---

[67] This is the rubric as found in the 2011 translation of the Missal, not that of the document from the Congregation for Divine Worship printed in DOL doc. 315, no. 2558. Italics in these rubrics are mine.

This part of what is now rubric 4 is a reformulation of what was said in the document from the Congregation for Divine Worship. Foreseeing the possibility of the number of concelebrants being disproportionately large, the document declares, "If the number of priests is not too great, all may concelebrate with the bishop; otherwise the concelebrants are to be selected either from different parts of the diocese or from among the different heads of diocesan programs." Like rubric 4, it adds, "It is well for those who do not concelebrate to receive communion and under both kinds, even if they have already celebrated Mass for the benefit of the faithful or will do so later."[68] The document, of course, gives no criteria for determining when the number of concelebrants is too great.

B. HOMILY

The rubric about the homily in the March 6, 1970, document from the Congregation for Divine Worship declares, "In the homily the bishop is to urge his priests to be loyal to the fulfillment of their office and to invite them to make a public renewal of their commitment to priestly service."[69] The homily, then, is intended for the priests, and its purpose is to encourage fidelity. It is not for the entire body of faithful but something between the bishop and his priests—another expression of the bond between them. The rubric is printed without change in the 1970 and 1975 missals.

While retaining the exhortation to loyalty in the original version, rubric 8 in the 2002 Missal considerably enlarges the first part of the text. It reads, "After the reading of the Gospel, the Bishop preaches the Homily in which, taking his starting point from the text of the readings proclaimed in the Liturgy of the Word, he speaks to the people and to his Priests about priestly anointing, urging the Priests to be faithful in their office and inviting them to renew publicly their priestly promises." The homily is now addressed not only to the priests but to the people as well. This is admirable. But there are other difficulties. The "priestly anointing" about which the bishop is to speak is ambiguous. It could refer to the common priesthood, the hierarchical priesthood, or both.[70] It may mean that the bishop should

[68] Ibid., no. 2556, last two paragraphs.

[69] Ibid., no. 2558.

[70] In footnote 57 we already cited the Second Vatican Council's Dogmatic Constitution on the Church, *Lumen Gentium*, no. 10, as teaching that "the baptized, by regeneration and the anointing of the Holy Spirit, are consecrated to be a spiritual house and a holy priesthood." Without mentioning baptism and

begin his homily with the priestly anointing of all the baptized, then move to the responsibilities proper to the ordained, and conclude by inviting the priests to renew their "priestly promises."

Rubric 8 expects the bishop to take as the starting point of his homily "the text of the readings proclaimed in the Liturgy of the Word." While praiseworthy in principle, in the present case this is quite a challenge because, as we saw, the three readings at the chrism Mass give wonderful expression to the priestly character of all the faithful in virtue of their baptism but contain not a hint about the special office, the sacred duties, or the commitment to which the bishop is to urge "his priests" to renew, and, in fact, the Lectionary does not list any of these readings for use at ordination Masses. Furthermore, none of the christological images in the renewal of priestly promises—Christ the Head and Shepherd, Christ the High Priest, Christ the Master and Servant of all—are found in the readings, and none of the images in the second reading—Christ the faithful witness, the firstborn of the dead, the ruler of kings of the earth, the pierced one, the Alpha and Omega—occur in the renewal. One can only conclude that the 1970 formula of renewal was composed independently of the readings. So for a bishop in his homily to arrive at the obligations of presbyteral ministry, "taking his starting point from the text of the readings," as rubric 8 expects, requires a great deal of ingenuity.

C. THE DAY CHRIST SHARED HIS PRIESTHOOD

After the homily, says rubric 9, the bishop invites the priests to renew their priestly promises

> on the anniversary of that day
> when Christ our Lord conferred his priesthood
> on his Apostles and on us.

---

confirmation, the council's Decree on the Ministry and Life of Priests, no. 2, likewise states that the Lord Jesus "has made his whole Mystical Body share in the anointing by the Spirit by which he himself has been anointed. For in him all the faithful are made a holy and royal priesthood." A few paragraphs later, however, the same document applies the image of anointing to the ministerial priesthood, saying that "the sacerdotal office of priests is conferred by that special sacrament through which priests, by the anointing of the Holy Spirit, are marked with a special character and are so configured to Christ the Priest that they can act in the person of Christ the Head."

This is the translation that went into effect on the first Sunday of Advent in 2011. The previous translation was bolder. It had the bishop declare that

> today we celebrate the memory of the first eucharist,
> at which our Lord Jesus Christ
> shared his priesthood with his apostles and with us.

The glaring incongruity in this declaration is that the Mass at which priests renew their commitment is not the one commemorating the Last Supper at which the Eucharist and ministerial priesthood were instituted, that is, the Mass *in Cena Domini*.[71] Nor is the day yet *Feria V in Cena Domini*, Thursday of the Lord's Supper, as it used to be before the calendrical changes of 1969. It becomes that only at the start of the evening Mass. When the oils are blessed it is *Feria V Hebdomadae Sanctae*, Thursday of Holy Week, or some day close to it, and the Mass is the *Missa chrismatis*, which has nothing to do with the Last Supper or with the institution of the Eucharist and ministerial priesthood, but everything to do with oils used in the sacraments of initiation.

D. PRIESTLY PROMISES

The name of the act of renewal that priests make at the chrism Mass is the "Renewal of Priestly Promises." The expression "priestly promises" also occurs in rubric 8 of this Mass. It declares that the bishop in his homily should invite priests "to renew publicly their priestly promises." The word "promises" returns in the first two questions that the bishop directs to the priests. The second specifies that the promises in question were made at their ordination. From the context we can presume that the first does likewise. It asks,

> [A]re you resolved to renew,
> in the presence of your Bishop and God's holy people,
> the promises you once made?

---

[71] Rubric 9 in RM 2011 about the homily at the evening Mass states clearly that "the institution of the Holy Eucharist and of the priestly Order" are among "the principal mysteries that are commemorated in this Mass"—not, we may add, in the chrism Mass. Referring to the evening Mass, the 1988 circular letter *Paschalis Sollemnitatis*, no. 45, likewise declares that "careful attention should be given to the mysteries that are commemorated in this Mass: the institution of the eucharist, the institution of the priesthood and Christ's command of brotherly love. The homily should explain these points."

The second question is

> Are you resolved to be more united with the Lord Jesus
> and more closely conformed to him,
> denying yourselves and confirming those promises
> about sacred duties toward Christ's Church
> which, prompted by love of him,
> you willingly and joyfully pledged
> on the day of your priestly ordination?

The March 6, 1970, document from the Congregation for Divine Worship, in its summary of the "Promises of Commitment," is even more explicit, declaring that "it is proper that priests renew the promises made to the bishop at their ordination." We note that in all these instances the word "promises" is always in the plural. At ordination, however, a priest makes only one promise: to respect and obey his bishop. He is asked other questions. But their purpose is to ascertain his willingness to undertake the office. They are not promises.

Aspirants to the priesthood, of course, promise to remain celibate—not, however, at their priestly ordination but before being ordained to the diaconate. As we saw, celibacy and obedience were in the foreground of the November 4, 1969, letter of the Congregation for the Clergy, which, echoing the suggestion made by Paul VI in his encyclical on priestly celibacy, "strongly recommended that on the morning of Holy Thursday every priest, whether present at the chrism Mass or not, renew the act by which he dedicated himself to Christ and promised to carry out his priestly obligations, especially to observe celibacy and to render obedience to his bishop."[72]

This is the letter that prompted the Congregation for Divine Worship on March 6, 1970, to issue texts to be used for such a renewal during the chrism Mass. Yet the formula for the renewal, despite its length and verbosity, mentions neither celibacy nor obedience. If during the turbulent years following Vatican II the real motive for introducing this renewal was to elicit from priests an annual recommitment to celibacy and obedience, would it not have been preferable to have but one question focused squarely on that? Based on the letter of the Congregation for the Clergy, the question could be: "Are you resolved to renew the act by which you dedicated yourselves to Christ and

[72] DOL doc. 333, no. 2763.

promised to carry out your priestly obligations, especially to observe celibacy and to render obedience to your bishop?"

Finally, the document from the Congregation for Divine Worship compares the renewal of priestly promises at the chrism Mass to the annual renewal of vows by religious. "Just as religious annually renew the vows of their profession," it says, "it is proper that priests renew the promises made to the bishop at their ordination."[73] The basis for this comparison is hard to fathom. The pronunciation of vows is the essential act of religious profession. The promise of obedience is only a preliminary to ordination, the essential act of which is the imposition of hands and the prayer of the bishop. And in any case, as was just pointed out, it is not the promise of obedience made to the bishop at their presbyteral ordination that priests renew at the chrism Mass, nor their promise to remain celibate—at least not in any explicit way. The January 16, 1988, circular letter of the Congregation for Divine Worship, *Paschalis Sollemnitatis*, by the way, in its treatment of the chrism Mass says nothing about the renewal of priestly promises. Yet it was this very congregation that issued the texts for the renewal on March 6, 1970.

E. PREFACE

The preface of Pius XII's chrism Mass, taken from the Old Gelasian Sacramentary (GeV 378), centers entirely on the efficacy of the ointment, entreating God to "make this chrism, thy creature, an effective sign of life and salvation for those who are to become new creatures in the sacred bath of baptism." Alluding to the perfume mixed with the oil, it asks that "each of them, sanctified by this anointing, may give forth as a sacred temple the pure odor of a life pleasing to thee." It concludes with a reference to the royal priesthood conferred at baptism as well as to the white garment: "Invested with the dignity of king, priest and prophet by the sacred rite which thou hast instituted, may they be, by thy gift, clothed with the garment of immortality."[74]

The preface issued by the Congregation for Divine Worship together with texts to be used for the renewal of priestly promises is quite different. In the 2011 translation of the Missal it opens by emphasizing that there is but one priesthood in the church and that it is synonymous with the person of Christ:

[73] DOL doc 315, no. 2557.
[74] Translation from *Saint Andrew Daily Missal* (Bruges: Abbey of St. André, 1956) 462.

For by the anointing of the Holy Spirit
you made your Only Begotten Son
High Priest of the new and eternal covenant,
and by your wondrous design were pleased to decree
that his one Priesthood should continue in the Church.

With only passing mention of the royal priesthood of all the redeemed, the second part of the preface quickly turns to the ordained,
saying that

Christ not only adorns with a royal priesthood
the people he has made his own [1 Pet 2:9],
but with a brother's kindness he also chooses men
to become sharers in his sacred ministry
through the laying on of hands.

The prayer correctly points out that the essential gesture in the conferral of holy orders is the imposition of hands. Anointing of the
hands of a presbyter or the head of a bishop with chrism are explanatory rites.[75] In confirmation, on the other hand, chrism applied to the
forehead is the sacramental matter itself. Sacred chrism and hence
the chrism Mass are primarily about initiation, not ordination. The
reason the chrism is consecrated on this Thursday or earlier in the
week is not because of anything Jesus said or did at the Last Supper
but because the paschal Triduum will culminate in the sacraments of
initiation at the great vigil during which the bishop in the cathedral
or priests in parishes will sign the foreheads of the newly baptized
with this fragrant ointment, saying, "Be sealed with the gift of the
Holy Spirit."

The third part of the preface sums up the principal duties of the ordained: to sustain their brothers and sisters by the eucharistic sacrifice

---

[75] The Rite of Christian Initiation of Adults also classifies the postbaptismal
anointing of the crown of the head with chrism as an explanatory rite and allows it only in cases when confirmation is separated from baptism. See no. 228
in *Rites* I, 160. Many are puzzled by this restriction because the prayer before
the anointing asks that the newly baptized "may remain forever a member of
Christ / who is Priest, Prophet, and King." Since this anointing signifies something altogether different from the signing of the forehead with chrism by the
bishop to impart the Holy Spirit, why should those confirmed immediately
after baptism be deprived of it?

and other sacraments, by teaching, and by the witness of exemplary lives. As might be expected, these broadly parallel the duties set forth in the third question of the renewal of priestly promises. The subtitle of the preface is accurate: "The Priesthood of Christ and the Ministry of Priests," meaning *ordained* priests. The summary of the preface in the document of the Congregation for Divine Worship is quite pointed, saying that "the preface recalls the institution of the ministerial priesthood, *over and above* the royal priesthood of believers, and lists its duties" (emphasis mine). This preface is ideal for the ordination of bishops and priests but totally incongruent with the other prayers and the readings of the chrism Mass, all of which are about the priesthood of the faithful.

Short of retrieving the preface of Pius XII's chrism Mass, a far better choice for this occasion would be Preface I of the Sundays in Ordinary Time. After recalling that "through his Paschal Mystery" Christ "accomplished the marvelous deed, / by which he has freed us from the yoke of sin and death," the preface goes on to assert that he summoned us "to the glory of being now called a chosen race, a royal priesthood, / a holy nation, a people for your own possession, / to proclaim everywhere your mighty works." This portrayal of the Christian vocation, taken directly from 1 Peter 2:9, quoting Exodus 19:5-6, is an eloquent echo of the entrance antiphon, the collect, the second reading, and both prayers for consecrating chrism.[76] Hearing these phrases again in the preface would create an extraordinary bond between the Liturgy of the Word, the blessing of oils, and the eucharistic liturgy at this "feast of the priesthood."

We close with some suggestions for the next revision of the Roman Missal.

7. Suggestions

A. THE MASS

Have ministers wear purple vestments, and eliminate the Gloria. This will emphasize that the chrism Mass takes place on the last day of

---

[76] The first prayer asks that "[t]hrough this sign of chrism" God would grant "royal, priestly, and prophetic honor" to those anointed with it. The second prayer recalls that through the anointing with holy chrism God transforms those reborn in baptism "into the likeness of Christ" and gives them "a share in his royal, priestly, and prophetic work." Rite of the Blessing of Oils, no. 25, in *Rites* I, 712–13.

Lent, or close to it, not on Thursday of the Lord's Supper. White vestments and the Gloria are probably leftovers from the time when oils were blessed at the Mass *in Cena Domini* and the whole of Thursday was *Feria V in Cena Domini*.

By all means sing the entrance antiphon printed in the Missal,[77] not another hymn or song, and find a melody as powerful as the text. It sets the tone for all that follows.

For the penitential act, draft christological acclamations incorporating images from the second reading.[78] This will unify the introductory rites, connecting the entrance procession to the collect and pointing the way to the readings. Avoid the *Confiteor*.

Acknowledge the presence of candidates for confirmation and accord them places of honor. This Mass is mainly about them. Consider including them, or some of them, in the entrance procession.

Give careful thought to what the documents say about concelebrants. If it is not possible to limit their number, arrange them so as not to overwhelm the rest of the assembly.

B. RENEWAL OF PRIESTLY PROMISES

Make the formula more succinct, one question, and clarify its purpose. If it is a renewal of dedication to priestly ministry, use question 3. If it is a renewal of obedience and celibacy, use a question based on the 1970 letter of the Congregation for the Clergy. Rubric 9 states that "after the Homily, the Bishop speaks with the Priests in these *or similar words*" (emphasis mine). Therefore, he is not bound to use the texts printed in the Missal.

Ideally, take it out of the chrism Mass and do it at the end of the annual retreat or at some other significant gathering of clergy. Or else put it after Communion—assuming that all three oils are blessed after the homily.

Change "Renewal of Priestly Promises" to "Renewal of Priestly Commitment."

[77] Or at least the first half of it, "Jesus Christ has made us into a kingdom, priests for his God and Father." To this could be added, "To him be glory forever."

[78] For example, "You are the faithful witness, firstborn of the dead, and ruler of the kings of the earth: Lord, have mercy. You made us to be a kingdom, priests to serve your God and Father: Christ, have mercy. You are coming on the clouds and every eye will see you, even those who pierced you: Lord, have mercy."

Eliminate prayers for priests and bishop from the act of renewal and include them in the prayer of the faithful.

C. PREFACE

Restore the preface of Pius XII's chrism Mass, or else use Preface I of the Sundays in Ordinary Time.

Chapter 5

The Paschal Triduum

A. HOLY WEEK AND TRIDUUM

The 1947 encyclical of Pius XII on the sacred liturgy, *Mediator Dei*, provides a very vivid picture of how Holy Week was understood at that time. "In Holy Week," states no. 158, "when the most bitter sufferings of Jesus Christ are put before us by the liturgy, the Church invites us to come to Calvary and follow the blood-stained footsteps of the divine Redeemer, to carry the cross willingly with Him, to reproduce in our own hearts His spirit of expiation and atonement, and to die together with him."[1] The week, with no mention of a Triduum, focuses entirely on the expiatory character of the physical sufferings of Christ, said to be "most bitter." Remarks on the resurrection are reserved for the next paragraph on the paschal season.

Maxima Redemptionis Nostrae Mysteria, The Greatest Mysteries of our Redemption, the November 16, 1955, decree and instruction announcing the restoration of the Holy Week liturgies, makes passing reference to the origin of this week. It explains that once the Sunday before Easter became the day for celebrating the entrance of Jesus into Jerusalem, "a special liturgical week took its rise which, because of the excellence of the mysteries celebrated, was called 'Holy' and was enriched by very splendid and sacred rites."[2] Here, as in *Mediator Dei*, the fundamental unit is the week. Holy Week is the sixth and final week of Lent and extends from "the Second Passion Sunday, or Palm Sunday," states the instruction, "to the Mass of the Easter Vigil, inclusive" (II, 6).

Unlike the encyclical, however, the originality of the 1955 document is to make reference to the Triduum. Always designated "Sacred Triduum," it is the last three days of Holy Week and, hence, the last three days of Lent. The general decree calls them "Thursday of the Lord's Supper, Friday of the Passion and Death of the Lord, and Holy

---

[1] In Jackson, *Abundance*, 161.
[2] First paragraph, unnumbered.

Saturday" (II, 5). The general rubrics of the Roman Missal of 1962, no. 75, say much the same: "The week from the Second Passion or Palm Sunday until Holy Saturday inclusive is called *Holy Week*; the last three days of the same week are designated by the name *Sacred Triduum*" (emphasis in original). Easter Sunday is not part of the Triduum. It begins with the Mass of the Easter Vigil, the same moment at which Lent, Holy Week, and the Sacred Triduum come to an end. Since at least the ninth century, the Triduum was understood as the three days Jesus spent in the tomb, was characterized by sadness, mourning, and grief,[3] and represented the nadir of "the most bitter sufferings of Jesus Christ" set forth throughout the week, all of which were reversed on Easter Sunday by unbounded joy over the resurrection.

The 1969 Universal Norms on the Liturgical Year and the Calendar introduces momentous changes into the calculation and content of the Triduum, making it an autonomous entity independent of both Lent and Holy Week and according it the distinction of being the apex of the liturgical year. It does this by placing the death and resurrection of Christ within the larger category of the paschal mystery, thereby giving expression to a renewed understanding of their relationship in the economy of salvation. No. 18 lays down the theological principle that "since Christ accomplished his work of human redemption and of the perfect glorification of God principally through his Paschal Mystery, in which by dying he has destroyed our death, and by rising restored our life, the sacred Paschal Triduum of the Passion and Resurrection of the Lord shines forth as the high point of the entire liturgical year." No. 19 discloses the new way of reckoning the Triduum. "The Paschal Triduum of the Passion and Resurrection of the Lord begins with the evening Mass of the Lord's Supper, has its center in the Easter Vigil, and closes with Vespers (Evening Prayer) of the Sunday of the Resurrection."

We see, then, that the Triduum is now called the *paschal* Triduum or, more frequently, the *sacred paschal* Triduum,[4] that it celebrates the paschal mystery, understood to be the life-giving death of the Lord as well as his resurrection, that it extends through Easter Sunday, but

[3] See my "Holy Thursday Reservation: From Confusion to Clarity," *Worship* 81 (2007) 98–120, here 104–5.

[4] In the phrase "sacred paschal Triduum" the word "sacred," left over from the nomenclature of Pius XII's epoch, adds nothing to the content of the three days. I prefer "paschal Triduum," as in the Universal Norms, no. 19.

that it begins only on Thursday evening with the Mass of the Lord's Supper. Consequently, the day hours of Holy Thursday are still Lent and are not yet the Triduum. The Triduum, for its part, is no longer the last three days of Lent. Lent and Triduum are two distinct periods. This has a major impact on Holy Week, for now the week is split into two parts, the first five days belonging to Lent and the last two to the Triduum. And given the exalted status that no. 18 of the Universal Norms confers upon the Triduum as "the high point of the liturgical year," the last two days of the week are far more important than the first five. As a result, the week as such has less status as a liturgical unit in the Missal of Paul VI than it had in Pius XII's restored *Ordo* and is now somewhat overshadowed by the two much more pivotal periods of Lent and Triduum.

Nos. 18 and 19 of the Universal Norms just cited both contain the expression "Paschal Triduum of the Passion and Resurrection of the Lord." Great care must be taken not to think that the Triduum celebrates the passion and resurrection of the Lord successively—that is, one after the other, beginning with the passion on Good Friday and ending with the resurrection on Easter Sunday, the vigil being the transition from one to the other. Rather, both are aspects of the one paschal mystery included in the liturgies of all three days. This is a dramatically different vision of the relationship between the death and resurrection of Christ than that contained in Pius XII's *Mediator Dei* and even *Maxima Redemptionis Nostrae Mysteria*.

Some clarification may be in order here. Like Passover, the English words "Pasch" and "paschal" ultimately derive from the Aramaic form of the Hebrew term *pesach*, rendered in Greek and Latin as *pascha*. Christine Mohrmann has shown that Christians in the early centuries used the word *pascha* in two senses: *passio* and *transitus*, or "passion" and "passage."[5]

The biblical foundation for *pascha* as *passio* is the slaughter of the Passover lamb, described in Exodus 12 but interpreted christologically by Saint Paul, who tells the Corinthians, *Pascha nostrum immolatus est Christus*, "Our paschal lamb, Christ, has been sacrificed" (1 Cor 5:7). *Pascha* as *transitus*, on the other hand, derives from Israel's passage

[5] "Pascha, Passio, Transitus," *Etudes sur le latin des chrétiens* I (Roma: Edizioni di storia e letteratura, 1961) 205–22. See also Raniero Cantalamessa, *Easter in the Early Church* (Collegeville, MN: Liturgical Press, 1993) 1–23, and my "Paschal Vigil: Passage and Passage," *Worship* 79 (2005) 98–130, here 101–9.

through the Red Sea, recounted in Exodus 14:15-31. Saint Augustine synthesizes these two meanings by invoking John 13:1 to affirm that the very passion of Christ is his passage from this world to the Father and that through faith and sacraments Christians join him in both.

Qualifying the Triduum as paschal emphasizes that it celebrates simultaneously both aspects of the mystery of redemption: the Lord's passion, including his entire kenotic descent from the bosom of the Father to the depths of hell, and his glorious passage from below the earth to above the heavens, culminating in the outpouring of the Holy Spirit to make the rest of humanity partakers of his new existence beyond death. This means that the Pasch of Christ is fully completed only by being realized in the church, by being realized in his brothers and sisters with whom he, in virtue of the incarnation, is one in substance. Furthermore, it is in view of this that God created the universe. At the most profound and least-known level, then, this is what the Triduum celebrates: the Pasch of Christ ecclesially actualized as the perfection of salvation and goal of creation. The following pages aim to show how in the liturgies of each of the three days Christ renders himself present symbolically or sacramentally in order to make the assembled faithful participants in his passion as well as in his passage, in his death as well as in his resurrection, and so bring his own Pasch to full realization.

B. EVENING MASS OF THE LORD'S SUPPER

1. The Restored Order of Pius XII

Preliminaries. Until 1956, Mass on Holy Thursday was celebrated in parishes at the usual hour of weekday Mass: around seven or seven thirty in the morning. Few of the faithful were present at this commemoration of the Last Supper and the institution of the Eucharist, but many, individually or in groups, came throughout the day and especially in the early evening to adore the Blessed Sacrament reserved in the ornately decorated repository until the Good Friday service the next morning.

The general decree of November 16, 1955, announced that henceforth this Mass would be celebrated in the evening. "On Holy Thursday, the Mass of the Chrism is celebrated after Terce, but the Mass of the Lord's Supper must be celebrated in the evening, at the most suitable hour; not, however, before 5 nor after 8 p.m." (II, 7). Besides being the hour when the Last Supper actually took place, it was hoped that transferring the Mass to the evening—after work and after school—would enable people to attend in greater numbers and, of course, receive Holy Communion. The response of the faithful exceeded by far all expectations.[6]

But changing the hour of the Mass also drastically reduced the amount of time remaining after it for adoration. In effect Pius XII had shifted Holy Thursday's center from personal devotion to sacramental celebration, from Eucharist as object adored to Eucharist as supper shared. This was consonant with a principle articulated in the seventh paragraph of the general decree: "The liturgical rites of the Sacred Week possess not only a singular dignity but also a particular sacramental power and efficacy for nourishing the Christian life; nor can these rites be sufficiently compensated for by those exercises of devotion which are usually called extraliturgical and which are performed during the sacred triduum in the hours after noon."

Another innovation was permission to perform the washing of feet during the evening Mass. The instruction of November 16, 1955, explained that this was intended "to manifest the Lord's commandment of brotherly love" and to encourage the faithful "to be generous in the works of Christian charity on this day" (I, 2, b). In a word, the footwashing ceremony on this night was to remind the faithful of the social dimensions of the eucharistic celebration and of the Lord's presence not only in the consecrated bread but also in the neighbor, especially the needy.

Prayers. The orations, readings, and chants in the evening Mass of the restored *Ordo* of Pius XII, repeated in the 1962 Missal, are the same as those in the Tridentine Missal of 1570. The three presidential prayers are first found in the Sacramentary of Pope Hadrian (H 328, 329, and 337). Of these only the secret mentions the Eucharist. Recalling the command of Christ heard in the epistle, it asks that he "render our sacrifice acceptable to thee, who on this day taught his disciples

---

[6] Bishop Edwin V. O'Hara of Kansas City, MO, reported to an international congress on pastoral liturgy held on September 18–22, 1956, at Assisi that the restored Order was "by far the greatest Holy Week in memory, both as to the numbers who attended and especially as to the number who received holy Communion." A frequent complaint, he admitted, was overcrowding and disappointment at not being able to get into church for Mass and Communion on Holy Thursday and Good Friday. See his "The Assisi Report on Holy Week in the United States in 1956," *Worship* 30 (1956) 548–55, here 550.

to do this in remembrance of him." The post-Communion makes the general request that "the rite we perform in this mortal life may win us life immortal with thee." The collect, borrowed from after the first reading on Good Friday, contrasts the fates of Judas and the good thief. Both men did wrong. The good thief repented and "received the reward of his confession." Judas did not and "received the punishment of his guilt." The prayer asks that "even as in his passion our Lord Jesus Christ gave to each retribution according to his merits, so having cleared away our former guilt, he may bestow on us the grace of his resurrection."

Readings. Mention of Judas in the collect leads directly to the way Paul in the epistle, 1 Corinthians 11:20-32, begins his account of the institution of the Eucharist: "The Lord Jesus, on the night he was betrayed [*in qua nocte tradebatur*] . . ." The apostle, of course, does not disclose what night that was. We learn of it from the Synoptic Gospels, which make institution of the Eucharist part of their passion narratives, thereby paschalizing it. A very literal translation of the Latin text of this section of the epistle would be, "I received from the Lord what I handed over [*tradidi*] to you, that the Lord Jesus on the night he was handed over [*tradebatur*] took bread and, giving thanks, broke it and said, 'Take and eat. This is my body, which will be handed over [*tradetur*] for you.'" We notice that the same Latin word, *tradere*, which in general means "to hand over" or "to deliver," is here used three times, each time in a different sense. It is used first in the sense of "to transmit" or "to bequeath," then in the sense of "to betray," and finally in the sense of "to give oneself up" or "to surrender."

Although in the Latin version of 1 Corinthians 11:23 Jesus identifies the bread with his body "which will be handed over for you," *quod pro vobis tradetur*, the Greek has no verb. It reads, "which is for you." This is what is found in postconciliar lectionaries, which contain translations of the Greek New Testament, not the Latin one. By way of contrast, in both Mark 14:22 and Matthew 26:26 Jesus says of the bread, "This is my body," with no mention of its being given. The same is found in the preconciliar text of the Roman Canon, in which Jesus declares, *Hoc est enim corpus meum*. The statement "which will be given up for you," from the Latin version of 1 Corinthians 11:23, is, however, added to Jesus' words over the bread in the supper narratives of all postconciliar eucharistic prayers, including the Roman Canon, now Eucharistic Prayer I. So there are now two versions of the supper narrative in the Roman Canon: one in the ordinary form, the other in the extraordinary form. The one in the ordinary form contains the addition that the body "will be given up for you," thereby emphasizing the sacrificial character of Jesus' death and hence also of the Eucharist. The one in the extraordinary form does not.

Eucharistic Prayer III introduces its account of the institution of the Eucharist with the Pauline formula "on the night he was betrayed," thereby bringing out the contrast between Judas's handing over of Jesus and Jesus' handing over of himself expressed in his words over the bread. The Roman Canon has a proper *communicantes* and a proper *Hanc igitur* for use at the evening Mass on Holy Thursday. In the 2011 translation of the Missal the *communicantes* identifies it as "the most sacred day / on which our Lord Jesus Christ / was handed over for our sake [*pro nobis est traditus*]," whereas the *Hanc igitur* presents it as the day on which "our Lord Jesus Christ / handed on [*tradidit*] the mysteries of his Body and Blood / for his disciples to celebrate."

All three meanings of *tradere* weave in and out of the Holy Thursday liturgy to affirm that on the same night in which Jesus is handed over by Judas, he hands himself over in oblation to the Father and hands over to the apostles the sacramental form in which that oblation is made forever present in the church. At the root of these different connotations of *tradere* is a deeper theological current—the portrait of Jesus as a passive victim, betrayed and executed by malicious evildoers, and the portrait of him as priest and king freely surrendering himself to the one from whom he eternally comes forth as Son and to whom he returns in the death that is his glorification and triumph over the prince of this world.

The gospel is John 13:1-15, the opening scene in John's Last Supper narrative, the longest such narrative of the four gospels. It begins with the footwashing, continues with the farewell discourse, and culminates in the High Priestly Prayer. But, unlike the Synoptic Gospels, in this one Jesus does nothing with bread and wine and says nothing about his body and blood. Nor is this supper a Passover meal as in the Synoptics, for John aligns Passover with the death of Jesus on Friday afternoon. The other gospels align it with the supper on Thursday evening—each for his own theological motives: John to invest the death of Jesus with paschal value; the Synoptics to invest the Eucharist with paschal value.

Though mutually contradictory from a historical point of view, they are identical from a theological one inasmuch as the eucharistic meal is the sacramental form in which Christ's life-giving death subsists. For this reason Paul writes in 1 Corinthians 11:26, "As often as you eat this bread and drink the cup, you proclaim the Lord's death until he comes." The Eucharist and the cross are two forms of one and the same paschal event. Pope John Paul II even states that the Eucharist "is in an outstanding way the sacrament of the paschal mystery,"[7] and Pope Benedict XVI writes that even if the Last Supper, historically speaking, was not the Jewish Passover meal, during it Jesus gave the disciples "something new: he gave them himself as the true Lamb and thereby instituted *his* Passover" (emphasis in original).[8]

The opening lines in the gospel of Holy Thursday night are: "Now before the festival of the Passover, Jesus knew that his hour had come to depart from this world and go to the Father. Having loved his own who were in the world, he loved them to the end" (John 13:1). This statement, the foundational text of Augustine's interpretation of *Pascha*, applies not only to the footwashing but to all that comes after it. The entire passion, in other words, is the hour of Jesus, the time ordained in the divinely established plan of salvation when the weak, perishable, mortal humanity that he assumed in becoming flesh is totally transformed and made radiant by his return to the Father. This hour is eternally enduring and followed by no other. Henceforth Jesus exists forever in the death that is his life, in the oblation that is his glorification, in the self-abasement that is his exaltation.[9]

As an act of humility that cleanses and grants communion, the footwashing gesture, coupled with the discourse and prayer following it, anticipates and explains in advance all that the passion means and accomplishes. Judas is mentioned several times. The betrayal is imminent and Jesus knows it. But by taking the initiative to disrobe, stoop

---

[7] Encyclical letter *Ecclesia de Eucharistia* (Città del Vaticano: Libreria Editrice Vaticana, 2003) no. 3.

[8] Pope Benedict XVI, *Jesus of Nazareth*, part 2, *Holy Week: From the Entrance into Jerusalem to the Resurrection* (San Francisco: Ignatius Press, 2011) 113. Benedict continues on p. 115 by recognizing that for both Paul and John "the death and resurrection of Christ have become the Passover that endures. On this basis one can understand how it was that very early on, Jesus' Last Supper—which includes not only a prophecy but a real anticipation of the Cross and resurrection in the eucharistic gifts—was regarded as a Passover: as *his* Passover. And so it was" (emphasis in original).

[9] See CCC, nos. 730 and 1085 especially, as well as nos. 2746–49.

down, and perform the servile act of washing the feet of disciples and servants, the Lord and Master reveals the paradox of the Cross—that the ensuing passion, far from being the tragic consequence of Judas's treachery, is freely embraced as the Father's plan for bringing the world back to himself, that his life is being not taken but given, and that in reality his going away is a return to one whom he has never left. It is, in other words, the full human actualization of an uninterrupted bond of communion, the goal of which is to prepare a place for us, that where he has gone we may follow (John 14:2-3).

The rite of footwashing. The gospel episode ends with Jesus returning to the table and telling his disciples, "If I, your Lord and Teacher, have washed your feet, you also ought to wash one another's feet. For I have set you an example, that you should do as I have done to you" (John 13:14-15). Probably for this reason a ceremonial washing of feet on this day, begun in Spain in the seventh century, becomes a custom adopted more or less everywhere.[10] Until the reform of Pius XII, however, it was limited to bishops and prelates who performed it not during the morning Mass but later in the afternoon or evening, usually at the cathedral or, in the case of religious men, at the collegiate church. The first antiphon sung during the ceremony, taken from John 13:34, begins, "I give you a new commandment [*Mandatum novum do vobis*], that you love one another / as I have loved you." From the first word of the Latin text of this antiphon, the footwashing rite is commonly known as the *mandatum*, and the day in some places is called Maundy Thursday.

The originality of Pius XII's initiative is to permit the *mandatum* for pastoral reasons to be done during the evening Mass and by the priest who celebrates that Mass. Although the Tridentine Missal, which contains texts for the ceremony after those of the Mass, does not indicate the number of those whose feet are washed, rubrics 16, 17, and 20 in the 1956 *Ordo* four times specifies that they are twelve men, *duodecim viri*. This makes the ceremony much more explicitly imitative—a ritual mimesis of the gospel narrative. Like the palm procession, then, it is best understood as a performed anamnesis—the chanted antiphons

---

[10] On the liturgical history of footwashing, its meaning, and current discussion about washing the feet of women, see Peter Jeffery, "Mandatum Novum Do Vobis: Toward a Renewal of the Holy Thursday Footwashing Rite," *Worship* 64 (1990) 107–41.

retelling the biblical event while it is being liturgically enacted. With this in mind it would have been better if the *mandatum* followed immediately upon the gospel rather than being separated from it by the homily.

No. I, 2, b of the instruction of November 16, 1955, and the recommended content of the homily in rubric 13 of the OHS present the meaning of the *mandatum* as being mainly moral—a reminder of the obligation of charity toward each other implied in the eucharistic celebration. This is reinforced by the chant *Ubi caritas* near the end of the footwashing, as well as by the communion antiphon from John 13:12-13, 15 that ends, "I have given you an example that you also may do likewise." This obligation of loving one another, especially the poor, is vastly important and must never be downplayed. But in addition to that, the liturgical footwashing, like the original one in the Upper Room, has christological meaning insofar as it expresses in gesture the truth of Jesus' person and mission. It also has sacramental meaning, not in the sense that it points to specific sacraments—though as a washing with water it has unmistakable baptismal connotations—but that it is a symbolic acting out of the paradox of Christian life and indeed the whole of human existence: that through self-forgetful love of neighbor and generous service of others, we, like Christ in whom our life is hidden, plunge ever more deeply into the mystery of trinitarian communion. Or rather in the self-sacrificing love of one another the eternal and infinite love of Father, Son, and Spirit expresses itself in the time and space of this world, thereby filling creation with divine sanctity.

But if such love opens onto the eternity and infinity of God, then the limits of time and space, including the ultimate limit, death, have been overcome, and those who so love have already entered upon life eternal. In sum, through the footwashing on Holy Thursday night we act out our conviction that by imitating the example of our Lord and Master and fulfilling his command to wash each other's feet—that is, to serve those most in need—we participate in his hour and with him pass from this world to the Father.

The *mandatum* in Pius XII's *Ordo* ends with the priest reciting the Lord's Prayer, some versicles and responses, and a concluding oration. These go back to the time when the ceremony took place outside of Mass. The Missal of Paul VI eliminated them.

Reservation of the sacrament. Besides the washing of feet on Holy Thursday, another innovation in 1956 of even greater magnitude was permission for the faithful to receive Holy Communion at the Good Friday liturgy. As will be explained in the next section, since the early thirteenth century only the priest received. To this end he consecrated two large hosts at the Mass on Thursday morning, one of which he consumed. After Mass he carried the other in an elaborate procession to the repository where, as was mentioned earlier, it was adored for the rest of the day. From the viewpoint of the faithful this was the worst of all possibilities—praying in adoration to a host that they would never receive. In some places the repository was thought to represent the sepulcher in which Jesus was buried, the locking of its door recalling the sealing of the tomb, and prayer before it imitating the women keeping watch. The procession to the repository expanded into a dramatization of the funeral of the lifeless Lord. The circular letter *Paschalis Sollemnitatis*, no. 55, is firm in declaring that "the place where the tabernacle or pyx is situated must not be made to resemble a tomb, and the expression *tomb* is to be avoided for the chapel of repose is not prepared so as to represent the 'Lord's burial' but for the custody of the eucharistic bread that will be distributed in communion on Good Friday."

Permission for the faithful to receive Holy Communion on Good Friday profoundly impacted the character of Holy Thursday reservation. It became immediately evident that what is borne in procession and stored in the repository is no longer a solitary wafer eventually to be consumed by the priest but a quantity of consecrated bread sufficient to be shared by the whole congregation on Good Friday. In other words, the repository—purged of funereal symbolism—is seen to contain the community's Communion.[11]

The uniqueness of Holy Thursday reservation is its inseparable link with the eucharistic banquet. What is reserved derives from the community's Communion on Thursday evening and will be the community's Communion on Friday afternoon. At the moment of being reserved it is briefly adored by the entire congregation and later for longer periods by individuals and groups. The purpose for which the Body of the Lord is reserved, however, is not to be adored but to be received. Holy Thursday reservation and Good Friday Communion contain annual reminders of truths forgotten for centuries and always in

[11] For a fuller treatment of this topic, see my "Holy Thursday Reservation" in note 3.

danger of receding from consciousness. The last rubric for Holy Thursday evening in the third typical edition of the Missal of Paul VI is a short but theologically significant statement: "If the celebration of the Passion of the Lord on the following Friday does not take place in the same church, the Mass is concluded in the usual way and the Blessed Sacrament is placed in the tabernacle." No procession. This shows yet again that the purpose of transferring the sacrament in procession on Thursday is for the sake of Communion on Friday.

The procession to the repository after the Mass of the Lord's Supper is quite different from other processions with the Blessed Sacrament. On Holy Thursday what is carried is a vessel full of Communion bread that remains part of the larger eucharistic action, not a single, unbroken host made the center of attention in what is sometimes referred to as "cult of the Eucharist outside of Mass." Furthermore, what is carried in procession, reserved, and adored on Holy Thursday remains veiled and concealed until brought forth to be received. On other occasions the host is displayed in a monstrance, adored, and put back in the tabernacle without being received. When exposed perpetually, its origin and destiny hold no interest for those praying to it.

If exposition of an unbroken host in a monstrance indefinitely prolongs the elevation of the Mass, introduced at Paris in 1210, Holy Thursday reservation antedates that practice by at least five centuries and derives not from the elevation but from Communion. In effect the Evening Mass of the Lord's Supper is a Mass with two Communions—one that evening, the other the next afternoon. Thus Holy Thursday and Good Friday go together in the same way that the Cenacle and the cross go together. The self-surrender of Jesus in the Cenacle anticipates the cross and makes it redemptive. The cross corporeally actualizes and makes eternally enduring the self-surrender expressed in the Cenacle and there given ritual shape.

The Order of 1956 concludes by stating that after silent adoration of the sacrament, the celebrant, still vested, returns to the sanctuary and begins performing the final action of the evening, the *altarium denudatio*, or stripping of the altars. During it Psalm 21 is recited with verse 19 as the antiphon, "They divided my garments among them and cast lots for my robe." The ceremony, then, symbolized Jesus being stripped of his garments. In the postconciliar Missal removal of altar cloths is no longer part of the service. Rubric 41 in the 2011 translation, repeating rubric 19 in RM 1970, simply says, "At an appropriate time, the altar is stripped."

2. *The Missal of Paul VI*

Entrance rite. In the Missal of Paul VI the evening Mass on Holy Thursday inaugurates the paschal Triduum, the high point of the liturgical year. The entrance procession on this night should receive special emphasis and be led by incense, cross, and candles—perhaps six candles. Bells should be rung longer than usual and the organ prelude should be grander, for on this night the entrance rite is a rite of passage bringing Lent to a close and opening onto the three days for which Lent prepares. At this moment too the name of the day changes from Thursday of Holy Week to Thursday of the Lord's Supper.

The entrance antiphon, *Nos autem*, retained from MR 1962, is inspired by Galatians 6:14 and is a splendid overture to what is celebrated not only at this Mass but throughout the Triduum. "We should glory in the Cross of our Lord Jesus," it sings in the 2011 translation, "in whom is our salvation, life and resurrection." With these words of Saint Paul in mind, Cyril of Jerusalem exclaims that "the Catholic Church glories in every action of Christ, but her glory of glories is the cross."[12] In the Tridentine Missal the same entrance antiphon, *Nos autem*, appears also on Tuesday of Holy Week. The *Ordo* of Pius XII retains it, and hence the 1962 Missal does so as well. But the Missal of Paul VI provides another text on Tuesday, thereby making the Mass on Thursday evening the only one at which *Nos autem* is sung besides the feast of the Exaltation of the Holy Cross.

Readings. Paul's recollection of the institution of the Eucharist in 1 Corinthians 11:23-26 and John's account of the footwashing are still read at the postconciliar Mass *in Cena Domini*. Perhaps the most noticeable change is the addition of Exodus 12:1-8, 11-14, the foundational text for *pascha* as *passio*, as the first reading. In the 1570 Missal and in the OHS this passage is the second reading on Good Friday. The Lectionary transfers it to Holy Thursday evening—and with good reason. It recounts the origin of Passover and, hence, the origin of the meal at which Jesus, according to the Synoptic Gospels, instituted the Eucharist. In changing the day, however, the Lectionary also changes the length of the reading and its focal point. When it was on Good Friday,

---

[12] Cyril of Jerusalem, *Catechesis* XIII, 1, trans. Leo P. McCauley, SJ, and Anthony A. Stephenson, in FC 64, 4.

it ended at Exodus 12:11 and the focal point was the parallel between the slaughter of the lambs and the death of Jesus, which John makes to coincide with the slaying of the lambs in the temple precincts, thereby portraying him as the fulfillment of Israel's Passover.

When moved to Holy Thursday, the passage was extended to Exodus 12:14, which reads, "This day shall be a day of remembrance for you." Now the focal point is the parallel between the anamnetic aspect of Passover and the command of Jesus to be heard twice in the second reading, "Do this in remembrance of me" (1 Cor 11:24-25). The meal, which until then was a remembrance of the Passover sacrifice (Exod 12:26-27), is made into a remembrance of Jesus and his sacrifice. Pope Benedict XVI writes, "In instituting the sacrament of the Eucharist, Jesus anticipates and makes present the sacrifice of the Cross and the victory of the resurrection. At the same time, he reveals that he himself is the *true* sacrificial lamb, destined in the Father's plan from the foundation of the world."[13]

Prayers. The Missal of Paul VI replaces the three presidential prayers and the preface of the 1956 OHS.[14] Recalling that the name of this Mass is Mass of the Lord's Supper and the name of the day is Thursday of the Lord's Supper, it is significant to note that the word "supper," *cena* in Latin, appears in both the collect and the prayer after Communion. Obviously, these prayers are meant for this Mass. Drawing a parallel between the Lord's Supper celebrated now on earth and the eschatological banquet that awaits us in heaven, the prayer after Communion, based on one in the *Missale Gothicum* (Go 214), asks that "just as we are renewed / by the Supper of your Son / in this present age, so we may enjoy his banquet for all eternity."

The collect, a new composition, likewise uses the word "supper." It prays,

> O God, who have called us to participate
> in this most sacred Supper,
> in which your Only Begotten Son,

[13] Pope Benedict XVI, *Sacramentum Caritatis* (Città del Vaticano: Libreria Editrice Vaticana, 2007) no. 10 (emphasis in original).

[14] For their sources, see Anthony Ward, SM, "Euchology for the Mass 'In Cena Domini' of the 2002 *Missale Romanum*," *Notitiae* 45 (2008) 611–32, and "Sources of the Orations for the Mass 'In Cena Domini' of the 2002 'Missale Romanum,'" EL 123 (2009) 105–28.

when about to hand himself over to death,
entrusted to the Church a sacrifice new for all eternity,
the banquet of his love,
grant, we pray,
that we may draw from so great a mystery,
the fullness of charity and of life.

Perhaps inspired by the Constitution on the Sacred Liturgy, 47, it voices an amazingly dense doctrinal synthesis, declaring that the Eucharist is "the most sacred Supper," entrusted to the church by Christ, inseparable from his handing himself over to death; that it is sacrifice and banquet; and that participation in it imparts love and life—life, we might say, that consists in love. The collect is an amazing example of theology prayed. Much of its content is developed at greater length in Pope Benedict XVI's apostolic exhortation *Sacramentum Caritatis*, following the synod of bishops on the Eucharist in October of 2005.

The prayer over the offerings is taken from the Ninth Sunday after Pentecost in the Tridentine Missal and is very ancient, going back to the Verona collection of papal Masses (V 93) and to the Old Gelasian (GeV 170 and 1186). It too articulates a crucial point of doctrine, that "whenever the memorial of this sacrifice is celebrated, / the work of our redemption is accomplished." The Eucharist, then, does not merely apply the effects of Christ's redemptive work but makes present the work itself—or rather, makes present Christ in his redemptive act. Thus the church's liturgical act and Christ's redemptive act are one. The word "memorial" in the prayer is highly significant, for it recalls the statement in the first reading about Passover being a "day of remembrance" (Exod 12:14) and the two commands of Jesus in the second reading, "Do this in remembrance of me" (1 Cor 11:24-25). Unfortunately, this prayer is not unique to the Holy Thursday evening Mass but is used also on the Second Sunday of Ordinary Time and in the votive Mass of Christ the High Priest. This being the case, one can wonder why the secret of Pius XII's Mass *in Cena Domini*, from H 329, was not kept. Its mention of Christ teaching his disciples on this day "to do this in remembrance of him" could not be more appropriate.

The command of Jesus to "do this" is incorporated into the institution narratives of all postconciliar eucharistic prayers, including the Roman Canon, and reads, "Do this in memory of me." The General Instruction of the Roman Missal, 72, invokes it to justify its explanation of the structure of the eucharistic meal. The received text of the Roman

Canon, however, has a different formulation. It is not a command but a declaration. In the 1962 Missal it is: "As often as you do these things, you shall do them in remembrance of me." The expression "as often as," *quotiescumque*, here is similar to "whenever," *quoties*, in the prayer over the offerings just discussed. What is far more important to notice is that just as the words Jesus speaks over the bread in the Roman Canon are different in the ordinary form and the extraordinary form, so are the words that follow what he says about the wine. A final difference is that in the ordinary form after the institution narrative, Eucharistic Prayer I, the Roman Canon, has a memorial acclamation introduced by "The mystery of faith." There is no such acclamation in the extraordinary form, and the phrase *mysterium fidei*, though not found in any of the biblical accounts, is included in what Jesus says over the chalice.

The *Ordo* of Pius XII, like the 1570 Roman Missal, directs that the preface of the Holy Cross be used on Holy Thursday, as it is at all Masses during the last two weeks of Lent. The Missal of Paul VI replaces it with Preface I of the Most Holy Eucharist, a 1964 revision by Dom Anselmo Lentini of the preface for Holy Thursday in the Paris Missal of 1738, itself based on earlier sources.[15] It is very similar in content and phraseology to the prayer over the offerings, declaring that Christ "is the true and eternal priest, who instituted the pattern of an everlasting sacrifice and was the first to offer himself as the saving victim, commanding us to make this offering as his memorial."

Chants. We already noted that the entrance antiphon of the Thursday evening celebration is the same in the restored Order of Pius XII and the Missal of Paul VI. But other chants have changed and we must take note of them.

In the 1956 *Ordo* the first antiphon sung during the footwashing ceremony is *Mandatum novum do vobis*, "I give you a new commandment," taken from John 13:34. Since 1970 the Lectionary uses this same text as a gospel acclamation—an excellent choice, even though these words of Jesus are not heard in the passage about to be read, which ends at 13:15. The Missal of Paul VI alters the order of the antiphons sung during the footwashing. In the new sequence *Mandatum novum do vobis* is no longer first. In the first two editions it was fifth. In the third edition it is sixth. If the footwashing rite, like the palm

---

[15] See Ward, "Euchology for the Mass 'In Cena Domini,'" 621–30.

procession, is interpreted as an anamnetic enactment of the gospel just proclaimed, it would be preferable if the words used before the reading were also used at the start of the enactment, and it would also be preferable if the enactment followed the gospel, not the homily. The reformed Missal no longer specifies the number of those to have their feet washed, thereby returning to the situation prior to 1956. The mimetic aspect of the rite is clearest, of course, when those whose feet are washed are twelve.

The postconciliar Missal changes the place at which the hymn *Ubi caritas* is sung. It is no longer chanted near the end of the footwashing but during the procession with the gifts—which, of course, did not exist at the time of Pius XII. The 2002 edition of the Missal contains a revised version of the antiphon. Instead of *Ubi caritas et amor, Deus ibi est*, the text reads, *Ubi caritas est vera, Deus ibi est*, translated in the 2011 Missal as "Where true charity is dwelling, God is present there."

In the *Ordo* of Pius XII, as in the Tridentine Missal, the gradual, chanted after the epistle, is the sublime *Christus factus est* from Philippians 2:8-9, "Christ became obedient for us unto death, for which cause God also hath exalted him." The Lectionary moves this chant to Palm Sunday and Good Friday, making it the prelude to the passion on each of those days. In its place on Thursday evening is a responsorial psalm consisting of verses from Psalm 115 and words from 1 Corinthians 10:16 as the refrain: "The cup of blessings that we bless is a communion with the blood of Christ," texts that are obviously eucharistic.

The communion antiphon in Pius XII's *Ordo*, likewise taken from the Tridentine Missal, is John 13:12-13, 15. It repeats what Jesus told his disciples after washing their feet: "I have given you an example, that you also may do likewise." The first two editions of the Missal of Paul VI abandon it altogether. The third edition retrieves it, making it the second antiphon chanted during the washing of feet. This is why there are seven antiphons in the 2011 Missal and why "I give you a new commandment," *Mandatum novum do vobis*, is the sixth one, whereas in the two previous editions there were only six antiphons and "I give you a new commandment" was the fifth. The new communion antiphon in the Missal of Paul VI, not from the gospel, summarizes the Pauline institution narrative heard in the second reading, thereby sharpening the eucharistic focus of the Mass. In the antiphon the word *tradere* returns, for in it Jesus declares that his body "will be given up for you," *quod pro vobis tradetur*. After declaring the chalice to be the new covenant in his blood, he issues the command from 1 Corinthians 11:25, "Do this, whenever you receive it, in memory of me."

3. Conclusion

The thematic content of this Mass in the reformed Order of 1956 is multifaceted and diffused. Three texts mention the cross. The introit exhorts us to glory "in the cross of our Lord Jesus Christ," the gradual recalls that Christ became obedient unto death, "death on a cross," and the preface of the Holy Cross gives thanks to God, who determined that the human race be saved "through the wood of the cross." The collect calls to mind how Christ in his passion gave Judas "the punishment of his guilt" and the good thief "the reward of his confession." The gospel recounts the footwashing episode, the closing words of which are repeated in the communion antiphon, "I have given you an example, that you also may do likewise." Besides the insertions in the Roman Canon proper to the occasion, only two texts refer to the Eucharist: the epistle and the secret. The preconciliar Mass *in Cena Domini*, then, in large measure stands in continuity with the rest of Holy Week. Indeed, some of its texts are borrowed from other days of this week. The introit, for example, is from Wednesday, and the collect is from Good Friday. The institution of the Eucharist is only one of several thematic threads and, considering the formulary as a whole, occupies a fairly modest place within the much broader context of the mystery of the cross. Doctrinal content is confined to the hymn *Pange lingua*, chanted during the procession to the repository. The same hymn accompanies the Corpus Christi procession, but, except for it and part of the epistle, the Holy Thursday Mass has nothing in common with that of Corpus Christi, which is filled with eucharistic doctrine, especially the sequence, *Lauda, Sion*.

By way of contrast, the postconciliar formulary is squarely focused on the Eucharist—almost exclusively so. Only the entrance antiphon, gospel, and footwashing chants, which are all that remain of the previous formulary, are without explicit eucharistic content. The three new presidential prayers are strongly doctrinal in content, presenting the Eucharist as Christ's gift to the church, memorial of his sacrifice, banquet of his love, actualization of the work of our redemption, source of charity and life, and foretaste in this present age of eternal bliss. The preface, for its part, portrays Christ as both priest and victim and the Eucharist as the pattern of an everlasting sacrifice, the memorial of which he commanded us to offer, adding that the eating of his flesh strengthens us and the drinking of his blood washes us clean. Both the responsorial psalm and its refrain and the changed communion antiphon are explicitly eucharistic. The gradual and *communio* that they replaced were not. The addition of Exodus 12:1-8, 11-14 as an Old Testament reading is most appropriate, for it connects recollection of the Last Supper on this night with institution of the Jewish Passover and so brings out the paschal dimension of the Eucharist, lacking in the 1956 OHS but prominent in magisterial documents of the past four decades. Furthermore, since the Triduum is now characterized as paschal, which was not the case before the 1969 Universal Norms, inclusion of this passage results in the Liturgy of the Word of this Mass having readings that express both meanings of *Pascha*: Pasch as passion in the reading from Exodus about the slaughter of the lamb and the smearing of its blood; Pasch as passage in the opening lines of the gospel about Jesus declaring that the hour had come for him to pass from this world to the Father.

C. FRIDAY OF THE PASSION OF THE LORD

1. Name, Time, and Color

The Missal of 1570 assigns Good Friday the name *Feria VI in Parasceve*. This unusual term *Parasceve* comes from the Greek word for "to put in order" or "to prepare" and means "day of preparation."[16] The Synoptics use it to refer to the day on which Jesus dies, a Friday, and explain it as the day of preparation for the Sabbath, the day on which no work was permitted (Mark 15:42; Matt 27:62; Luke 23: 54). For them Passover begins on Thursday evening, the evening of the Last Supper. John uses the word three times, all three in his passion narrative (19:14, 31, 42). For him too it designates the Friday on which Jesus dies. But for him, unlike the other gospels, that Friday evening marks the onset of Passover. Consequently, he explains the meaning of the word to be "the day of preparation for the Passover" (19:14). This may be a touch of Johannine irony in which the author reduces the entire significance of the Jewish Passover to being preparation for the one inaugurated by the death of Christ.

In MR 1570 priest and ministers wear black vestments, also worn at requiem Masses and for burying the dead, thus reinforcing a funereal aspect of the liturgy. Since the early ninth century, the Triduum,

---

[16] Arndt-Gingrich, *"paraskeué,"* p. 627.

consisting of Holy Thursday, Good Friday, and Holy Saturday, was taken as a commemoration of the Lord's three days in the grave and, as was already pointed out, the procession with the reserved sacrament on Holy Thursday as a funeral cortege and the repository as the tomb in which Jesus is buried.[17]

The general decree and instruction of November 16, 1955, and the *Ordo Hebdomadae Sanctae* of 1956 change the name of the day to "Friday of the Passion and Death of the Lord." The general decree also announced a change in time of the service from the early morning to the afternoon "and indeed about 3 p.m." (II, 8). Both changes are reflected in a new title of the day's liturgy: "Solemn Afternoon Liturgical Action of the Passion and Death of the Lord."

Pius XII's *Ordo* for the first time divides the liturgy into four parts, each numbered: I. Readings; II. Solemn Orations; III. Adoration of the Cross; and IV. Communion. Priest and deacon wear black stoles for the first part (no. 3). For the second part the priest puts on a black cope, the deacon a black dalmatic, and the subdeacon a black tunic (no. 12). They all take off their outer garments for the third part (no. 14). For the fourth part the priest and deacon take off their black stoles and put on purple vestments—the priest stole and chasuble, the deacon stole and dalmatic. The subdeacon puts on a purple tunic (no. 22). The wearing of black vestments gives a somber tone to the first three parts and emphasizes the second half of the title, the Lord's death. Only in the Communion service with the change from black to purple vestments does the weight of grief and mourning lift a bit. Yet this overwhelmingly sorrowful view of Good Friday finds little basis in the liturgical texts.

The 1969 Universal Norms, no. 20, drops mention of death from the name of the day, replacing it with "Friday of the Passion of the Lord." The Missal of Paul VI does the same for the title of the liturgy, calling it "The Celebration of the Passion of the Lord," a phrase repeated in rubrics 2 and 4. Grounded in the Gospel of John, the liturgy now centers on the passion, a single whole beginning in the Cenacle and culminating on the cross. It is the hour of Jesus. His death of course is included, but it is understood to be his exaltation, the culminating moment of his victorious passage from this world to the Father. "The passion in John," writes Bruce Vawter, CM, "is part of a drama of triumph, in which can already be discerned the fruits of victory made secure

---

[17] See my "Holy Thursday Reservation: From Confusion to Clarity," *Worship* 81 (2007) 104–9.

forever through Jesus' resurrection and glorification."[18] This vision of Good Friday is reflected in the directive that priest and ministers wear no longer black but red vestments, the color of martyrdom, and wear the same ones throughout the service.

2. Entrance

In the 1570 Missal the service begins with the priest and ministers going to the altar and prostrating before it in prayer. Meanwhile, acolytes spread a single cloth on the altar. Then the priest and ministers go up to the altar, usually on three steps, and kiss it, after which the priest goes to the epistle side of the altar where he stands and reads to himself in a low voice the biblical passages that other ministers are reading aloud to the congregation.

The 1956 *Ordo* is quite different. It specifies that the altar is completely bare—without cross, candles, or cloth (no. 1). The celebrant, deacon, and subdeacon approach the altar in a procession through the church. After the prostration the priest stands before the steps of the altar and recites an oration, then goes to a stool (*sedilia*). No longer required to read the lessons to himself, he and the rest of the congregation sit and listen to the Word of God as it is proclaimed from a lectern (nos. 7 and 9). The bare altar, an entrance procession, the priest sitting down after an opening prayer, and the Scriptures being read at a lectern anticipate details of the postconciliar Order of Mass.

One of the rare changes in the texts of the liturgy made by Pius XII is the addition of an opening prayer. The oration is taken from Good Friday in the Old Gelasian (GeV 398), where it was recited after the first reading. Recalling that Christ by his passion loosened the bonds of death, the heritage of the first sin, it asks that as we have necessarily "borne the likeness of earthly nature, so we may by sanctification bear the likeness of heavenly grace."

The Missal of Paul VI makes a slight modification in how the service begins. According to rubric 6, after the prostration the priest goes to the chair, not to the foot of the altar, and there, facing the people, recites the opening prayer. The Missal offers a choice between two orations. The second is the one introduced in the reformed Order of Pius XII. The first, far superior to it, was the third of three prayers to be said after Communion in the OHS. Taken from Monday of the sixth week of Lent in the Old Gelasian (GeV 334), it declares that Christ "by the

[18] Bruce Vawter, CM, "The Gospel According to John," JBC 63:136.

shedding of his blood established the paschal mystery." To those accustomed to identify *Pascha* with the resurrection of Christ and hence with Easter, this may sound surprising. But it serves as a reminder that for both John and Paul the Jewish Passover is fulfilled in the death of Christ. This is what the Fourth Gospel intends to show by making the death of Jesus coincide with the sacrifice of the Passover lambs. It is what Paul means when he tells the Corinthians that "our paschal lamb, Christ, has been sacrificed" (1 Cor 5:7).

Because of the link between the crucifixion and Passover, Jewish Christians understood *Pascha* to mean the passion of Jesus and in the second and third centuries celebrated it on the same day as the Jewish Passover, not on the following Sunday as other Christians did and as eventually became standard. Since Passover is the fourteenth night of the lunar month of Nisan, the night of the full moon, Christians who celebrated *Pascha* on this night, regardless of the day of the week on which it fell, are called Quartodecimans, from *quartodecima*, the Latin word for "fourteenth."[19] The reference in the first of the two opening prayers to Christ, establishing the paschal mystery "by the shedding of his blood" is, therefore, a precious expression of a fundamental Quartodeciman conviction and is particularly striking as the first words spoken at this liturgy because they bring out the unmistakable paschal character of this Friday of the Passion, the first full day of the paschal Triduum. Before the calendrical changes of 1969, *Pascha* was limited to Easter Sunday and referred to the resurrection. The Triduum, not being paschal, was called sacred.

Unlike the 1956 *Ordo*, the Missal of Paul VI groups the solemn prayers with the readings under the heading of "Liturgy of the Word." Consequently its celebration of the passion consists of three parts instead of four: Liturgy of the Word, adoration of the cross, and Holy Communion.

3. Liturgy of the Word

Readings in the reformed Order of 1956 are the same as those in the 1570 Missal. The first is Hosea 6:1-6, in which an unfaithful people exhort each other to repentance, confident of being healed, restored, and forgiven by a loving God. "After two days he will revive us," they tell each other; "on the third day he will raise us up." Though nowhere

[19] For more on this, see Bradshaw-Johnson, "The Quartodeciman Celebration," *Origins of Feasts*, 39–47, and the following chapter, "The Date of the Festival," 48–59.

cited in the New Testament, in liturgical context these words would be taken as prophetic of Christ's resurrection on the third day (1 Cor 15:4; Luke 24:7, 45). At the time this passage was selected, Easter Sunday may have still been the third day of a Triduum that consisted of Friday, Saturday, and Sunday, not Thursday, Friday, and Saturday.

The reading from Hosea leads to a chant from the book of Habakkuk (Hab 3), called a tract in the 1570 Missal. The Order of Pius XII changes its name to a responsory, a step in the direction of the postconciliar term "responsorial psalm." The chant is followed by the prayer about Judas being punished for his guilt and the good thief being rewarded for his confession—the prayer also used as the collect of the Mass of the Lord's Supper.

The second reading is likewise from the Old Testament: the instructions in Exodus 12:1-11 about the origins of Passover, the slaughtering of the lamb, the smearing of its blood, and the eating of its roasted flesh, now read at the evening Mass on Holy Thursday. Its use on Good Friday in ancient lectionaries may be another indication that the three-day celebration of Passover fulfilled in Christ began on that day. After it comes a chant from Psalm 139:2-10, 14, the name of which Pius XII's reform changes from tract to responsory. The 1956 OHS, no. 9, states that these two Old Testament passages are read from a lectern in the sanctuary and that everyone, priest included, sits and listens to them—signs of what will become the Liturgy of the Word after the Second Vatican Council.

The Lectionary of Paul VI replaces both of these readings from the Old Testament. Having assigned the first three Servant Songs from Isaiah to Monday, Tuesday, and Wednesday of Holy Week, respectively, it substitutes for the reading from Hosea the fourth Servant Song, Isaiah 52:13–53:12. The Tridentine Missal used a slightly shorter form of this passage as a second Old Testament reading on Wednesday of Holy Week. Good Friday is a far more appropriate day for it because it recounts how, in the inscrutability of the divine plan, the suffering of one innocent person, willingly borne, brings healing, prosperity, and long life not only to him but to everyone else, including his persecutors. Carroll Stuhlmueller, CP, writes that "the doctrine of expiatory suffering finds supreme expression in these lines."[20]

The text consists of four parts. In the first, 52:13-15, God announces the exaltation of his Servant: "See, my servant shall prosper. He shall be exalted and lifted up and shall be very high." In the second part,

[20] Carroll Stuhlmueller, CP, "Deutero-Isaiah," JBC 22:43.

53:1-6, those who tormented him express astonishment at this un-expected turn of events, for they realize that he whom they afflicted had done no wrong, that *they* were the guilty ones, deserving the very punishment they had meted out to him, and that, paradoxically, his wounds had brought them healing. The prophet adds in the third part, 53:7-10, that all this unfolded in accord with the will of the Lord, who considered the death of the Servant as an offering for sin to be rewarded with length of days. Finally, in the fourth part, 53:11-12, God speaks again: "The righteous one, my servant, shall make many righteous. . . . He poured out himself to death, and was numbered with the transgressors; yet he bore the sins of many, and made intercession for the transgressors." The key word here is "many." This last part of the passage is affirming that the Servant's suffering is universally ef-ficacious, taking away the guilt not only of one people, his own, but of the many others as well—that is, all people. Stuhlmueller asserts that "a strong case can be advanced that converted Gentiles proclaim this most sublime revelation of the Old Testament from 53:1 onward."[21]

Using the word "many," Jesus twice identifies himself as the Suffer-ing Servant. In Matthew 20:28 he asserts that "the Son of Man came not to be served but to serve, and to give his life as a ransom for many." Still more specific is the declaration he makes in Matthew 26:28 when giving the cup to his disciples at the Last Supper: "This is my blood of the covenant which is poured out for many for the forgiveness of sins." Here, Jesus interprets his impending death as a sacrifice that will, like the suffering of the Servant, obtain forgiveness of sins for all.[22]

Saint Paul uses the term "many" in Romans 5:18-19 when contrast-ing Christ with Adam and the effects of their actions on the rest of humanity. "Just as one man's trespass led to condemnation for all, so one man's act of righteousness leads to justification and life for all. For just as by the one man's disobedience the many were made sinners, so by the one man's obedience the many will be made righteous." In writing that by one man's disobedience the many were made sinners,

---

[21] Ibid., 22:43. In this same section the author presents passages in the New Testament identifying Jesus as the Suffering Servant.

[22] This declaration, with slight modification, is what Jesus says of the cup in the institution narratives of Roman eucharistic prayers. In 2006 Pope Benedict XVI determined that *multis* in the Latin text be translated as "many," thereby assuring that the same word is used in the Isaian Servant Song, in Matt 20:28, in the Matthean account of the Last Supper, and in the eucharistic prayers.

the apostle is not implying that some were not made sinners. And in writing that by one man's obedience the many will be made righteous, he is not implying that some will not be made righteous. Here, as elsewhere, "many" means "all." As a responsorial psalm after the first reading are verses from Psalm 30 with the refrain "Father, into your hands I commend my spirit," words of the dying Jesus in Luke 23:46.

Having transferred the Passover instructions of Exodus 12:1-11 to the Thursday Mass *in Cena Domini*, the Lectionary of Paul VI appoints as a second reading on Good Friday a teaching on the priesthood of Christ from Hebrews 4:14-16; 5:7-9. The preface on Thursday evening acclaimed Christ as "the true and eternal Priest." This reading expands that theme.

Just as the fourth Servant Song begins by announcing the exaltation of one struck down, so this passage opens by proclaiming the present status of Jesus as one who, after the abasement of his passion, is now raised on high to the very dwelling place of God. "We have a great high priest," it declares, "who has passed through the heavens." The author repeats this twice, saying in 8:1 that we have a high priest who, in the words of Psalm 109:1, "is seated at the right hand of the throne of the Majesty in the heavens," and in 9:24 that "he entered into heaven itself, now to appear in the presence of God on our behalf." The same theme is sounded in the first paragraph of the letter, again referring to Psalm 109:1: "When he had made purification for sins, he sat down at the right hand of the Majesty on high."

The fact that Jesus, having poured out his blood, now sits enthroned in heaven is central to the whole argument of the letter, for it proves that his one sacrifice, unlike all others, is uniquely efficacious—that it really does cleanse from sin, that it really does make holy, that it really does lead to union with God. Not only is Jesus one with God, he is also one with us. The Good Friday reading declares that "we do not have a high priest who is unable to sympathize with our weaknesses, but we have one who in every respect has been tested as we are, yet without sin (4:15). He, therefore, is the perfect mediator (8:6; 9:15), a *pontifex* uniquely capable of bridging the chasm between God and humans, heaven and earth. And enduring forever, like Melchizedek, his priesthood and his sacrifice render all others obsolete.

As a chant before the gospel, OLM prescribes the magnificent *Christus factus est*, formerly the gradual on Thursday evening sung after the institution narrative of Saint Paul. The text is Philippians 2:8-9, the central portion of an ancient christological hymn: "Christ for our sake became obedient unto death, death on a cross, because of which God highly exalted him." In its new location it distills into a single sentence what the liturgy of this day celebrates: the passion of the Lord as both humiliation and exaltation.

The climax of the Liturgy of the Word on Good Friday both before and after Vatican II is the reading of the passion according to John. It is of paramount importance to understand how this passion differs from that of the Synoptics and to avoid running them together.[23] Here, we call attention to some of the episodes proper to this gospel. After the supper Jesus and his disciples go to a garden (18:1), but there is no agony: no prayer for the cup to pass, no sweat turned to blood, no sleeping disciples. Resolute, Jesus tells Peter, "Am I not to drink the cup that the Father has given me?" (18:11). In a similar vein, shortly after entering Jerusalem he had told Andrew and Philip, "Now my soul is troubled. And what should I say—'Father, save me from this hour?' No, it is for this reason that I have come to this hour. Father, glorify your name" (12:27). He adds, "Now the ruler of this world will be driven out. And I, when I am lifted up from the earth, will draw all people to myself" (12:31-32). The evangelist remarks that "he said this to indicate the kind of death he was to die" (12:33), disclosing for the first time that the crucifixion would be an exaltation, indeed an ascension, a passage from this world to the Father (13:1), and that, once united to the Father in his death, he would draw all things back to himself, even as in the beginning all things came to be through him (1:3).

When Judas, the soldiers, and the police arrive at the garden seeking Jesus of Nazareth, Jesus replies, "I am he" (18:6), at which "they stepped back and fell to the ground" (18:6). We must point out that here both the Greek and the Latin texts have not "I am he" but "I am." To comprehend the reaction of those who hear these words, we must recall that "I am" is the personal name of God revealed to Moses in the burning bush (Exod 3:14). On the lips of Jesus, they disclose him to be the bearer and revealer of the divine name.[24] In an earlier discussion about his identity Jesus had declared, "When you have lifted up the Son of Man, then you will realize that I am he" (8:28). Here too the Greek and Latin texts have not "I am he" but "I am." As the

[23] Unsurpassed in this regard is still Raymond Brown, SS, "The Passion According to John," *Worship* 49 (1975) 126–34, reprinted in his *A Crucified Christ in Holy Week* (Collegeville, MN: Liturgical Press) 57–71.

[24] This theme had been developing throughout the gospel in the series of "I am" sayings. See Vawter, JBC 63:94 and 63:158.

culmination of the self-revelation of God begun at the burning bush, the exaltation of Jesus on the cross is nothing less than a theophany. Although the scene in the garden ends with the arrest of Jesus (18:12), in reality he surrenders himself, offers himself, hands himself over—as was noted in our discussion of *tradere*. "No one takes [my life] from me," he says, "but I lay it down of my own accord" (10:18).

In the trial before Pilate there is a great difference between the Gospel of John and the Synoptics. In the latter, Pilate asks Jesus, "Are you the King of the Jews?" Jesus answers, "You say so" (Mark 15:2; Matt 27:11; Luke 23:3), after which he remains silent. This calls to mind what is said of the Suffering Servant: "He was oppressed and he was afflicted, yet he did not open his mouth; like a lamb that is led to the slaughter, and like a sheep that before its shearers is silent, so he did not open his mouth" (Isa 53:7). In the Fourth Gospel, however, Jesus, the Word made flesh (1:14), engages in a lengthy dialogue with Pilate.

Sidestepping Pilate's question about whether he was a king, Jesus declares, "For this was I born and for this I came into the world, to testify to the truth." At this Pilate scoffs, "What is truth?" (18:37-38). Despite this open contempt for the truth, Pilate professes the truth of Jesus' universal kingship. When the chief priests object to the phrase "King of the Jews" in the inscription attached to the cross and demand that it be changed to "This man said, I am King of the Jews," Pilate is unyielding: "What I have written I have written" (19:19-22). The inscription, in Hebrew, Latin, and Greek (19:20), suggests that Jesus is the universal king. As the Suffering Servant would make many righteous and bear the sins of many (Isa 53:11-12), so Christ by his blood ransoms "saints from every tribe and language and people and nation" (Rev 5:9) and receives their homage.

In the Gospel of John, Jesus, at the moment of his death, does not say, "My God, my God, why have you forsaken me?" from Psalm 21:1, as in Mark 15:34 and Matthew 27:46, nor "Father, into your hands I commend my spirit," from Psalm 30:5, as in Luke 23:46, but rather, "It is finished" (John 19:30). These words recall those of the High Priestly Prayer in 17:4-5: "I have glorified you on earth by finishing the work you gave me to do. So now, Father, glorify me in your presence with the glory that I had in your presence before the world existed." Lifted up from the earth (12:32), sanctified (17:19), and empowered to confer eternal life (17:2), Jesus at last says, "It is finished."

At this point the Synoptics declare that Jesus "breathed his last" (Mark 15:37; Matt 27:50; Luke 27:46). John, however, writes in 19:30 that he "gave up his spirit." This evangelist "intends the reader to think of the Spirit that is given as a result of Jesus' glorification (7:39; 20:23)."[25] For John, then, the crucifixion is not only the ascension of Jesus. It is also the outpouring of the Holy Spirit. Proof of this follows immediately. "One of the soldiers pierced his side with a spear and at once blood and water came out" (19:34). But blood and water are both symbols of life. Raymond Brown explains that

> the other Gospels mark Jesus' death with miraculous signs in the ambience: the Temple curtain is torn; tombs open and bodies of the saints come forth; and an expression of faith is evoked from a Roman centurion. But the Fourth Gospel localizes the sign in the body of Jesus itself: when the side of Jesus is pierced, there comes forth blood and water (19:34). In 7:38-39 we heard: "From within him shall flow rivers of living water," with the explanation that the water symbolized the Spirit which would be given when Jesus had been glorified. That is now fulfilled, for the admixture of blood to the water is the sign that Jesus has passed from this world to the Father and been glorified (12:23; 13:1).[26]

Briefly put, the Gospel of John distinguishes itself from the other three in affirming that Jesus in his death is living and life-giving.

Since the reading of the passion has been lengthy and the congregation has been standing throughout, a choral interlude might provide a moment of relief before the homily. It would be difficult to find a more fitting text than the following verses from a hymn of Prudentius:

> For a while salvation's Leader gave Himself
>   to realms of Death,
> That He might the dead, long buried, guide
>   in their return to light,
> When the chains that had been welded by that
>   primal sin were loosed. . . .
>
> Then when death He had destroyed and
>   mankind restored to life,
> That great Victor mounts triumphant to the
>   Father's throne above,
> And the glory of His Passion bears with
>   Him to Heaven's height.

---

[25] Ibid., 63:171.
[26] Brown, *Crucified Christ*, 66–67.

Hail! Thou King of all the living; hail! Thou
   Judge of all the dead;
At the right hand of Thy Father, Thou art
   throned in highest power,
And from thence, just Judge of sinners,
   Thou shalt one day come again.[27]

So as not to further extend this section, we treat the intercessory prayers under a new heading, aware that the Missal of Paul VI considers them part of the Liturgy of the Word.

4. Intercessory Prayers

The fundamental unit of these intercessions is an invitatory stating the intention, a brief pause for silent prayer, and the oration. The Tridentine Missal of 1570 contains a series of nine intercessions. They have no heading, are not numbered, and have no subtitles. The priest, at the epistle side of the altar, recites both the invitatory and the oration. The texts are from the Sacramentary of Pope Hadrian, H 338–55. The Old Gelasian has the same series (GeV 400–417) with slightly different wording. An introductory rubric (GeV 399) refers to what follows as "solemn orations." The same Sacramentary indicates that after the invitatory the deacon announces, *Flectamus genua*, "Let us kneel," then, *Levate*, "Rise," indicating that between the invitatory and the oration everyone prayed silently on bended knee. The basic structure of the intercessions remains unchanged to the present day. Details, however, vary in the 1956 *Ordo* and in each of the three editions of the Missal of Paul VI.

In the 1956 reformed Order of Holy Week the intercessions are the second part of the liturgical action of Good Friday and bear the general heading of "Solemn Orations," taken from GeV 399, to which is added "Also Called Prayers of the Faithful." The priest still recites both the invitatory and the oration, but he does so at the center of the altar. Each intercession is numbered and given a subtitle. There are nine intercessions, and the texts are exactly the same as those in MR 1570, except for the fourth, which prays for all who hold public office instead of for the emperor. The title of the seventh, "For the Unity of the Church," may be a bit misleading. Unchanged from MR 1570 and

[27] "A Hymn for Every Hour," trans M. Clement Eagan, CCVI, in FC 43, 67–68.

H 350 and 351, it is a prayer for "heretics and schismatics." The invitatory asks that "our Lord God would rescue them from all their errors." The oration entreats God to turn his gaze on "souls deceived and led astray by the devil. May they cast off the evil of their heresy and in true repentance of their errors return to the unity of thy truth."

The Missal of Paul VI changes the name of the intercessions to *Oratio universalis*—translated "General Intercessions" in 1974 but "Solemn Intercessions" in 2011—and considers them to be no longer an independent part of the service but the conclusion to the Liturgy of the Word. Though the faithful may still kneel for prayer after the traditional invitation, then rise for the oration, they may "remain either kneeling or standing throughout the entire period of the prayers." Unlike the litanic form of the usual prayer of the faithful, participation of the congregation in the Good Friday intercessions is more physical than verbal. Without a change of posture to mark the difference between the invitation and the prayer, the intercessions can quickly become a long and boring string of words. The 1975 typical edition permits a deacon to read the invitatories at the ambo but reserves recitation of the orations to the priest either at the chair or at the altar. The third typical edition in rubric 12 authorizes conferences of bishops to "provide other invitations to introduce the prayer of the Priest." It is silent about acclamations of the people before the prayer and whether the priest may choose from the list of intercessions those most appropriate for local circumstances. Both were permitted in the 1970 and 1975 typical editions. Turner says that "this acclamation has been suppressed."[28] In the absence of a deacon, the latest edition permits a lay minister to read the invitations. This is crucial from a pastoral viewpoint, for the change in voices, like a change in posture, is a great help in distinguishing between the invitation and the prayer.

The postconciliar Missal continues to number the intercessions and provide subtitles. It retains seven of the nine intercessions of Pius XII's *Ordo* but after the first three changes their order. It provides a new subtitle, invitatory, and oration for the Jewish people, recognizing that they are the ones to whom God first spoke and asking that they attain fullness of redemption. It abandons the formulas for heretics and schismatics as well as those for the conversion of infidels and replaces them with three new categories: the unity of Christians, based on one

---

[28] Turner, *Glory*, 87.

baptism; those who do not believe in Christ; and those who do not believe in God, thus producing a series of ten intercessions.

If the intercessions bequeathed to the Tridentine Missal from the *Hadrianum* reflect the situation of sixth- or seventh-century Christendom in which the world was ruled by a Christian emperor and in which the subjugation of barbarians, conversion of Jews and pagans, renunciation of idols, and return of heretics and schismatics were major concerns—religious as well as political—those in the Missal of Paul VI stem from a post-Christian world in which a more modest church values freedom of conscience, religious liberty, ecumenism, and interreligious dialogue.

The intercessions in the 1962 Roman Missal, of course, are the same as those in the 1956 *Ordo*, including those for the conversion of heretics and schismatics, Jews and pagans, except that Jews are no longer called "perfidious." When in 2007 Pope Benedict XVI gave permission for it to be used as an extraordinary form of the Roman Rite, he insisted that the invitatory and oration for the Jews be replaced. And they were, starting in 2008—not, however, with those in the current Missal of Paul VI but with other compositions.[29] These have met with a good deal of criticism, because, for example, the invitatory entreats God to illuminate the hearts of the Jewish people, "that they may acknowledge Jesus Christ, the savior of all mankind."[30]

5. Adoration of the Cross

Exposition and adoration of the cross on Good Friday, like the palm procession on the previous Sunday, originated in Jerusalem and from there spread to other churches.[31] The object of adoration is the true cross discovered by the empress Helena, mother of Constantine, in the early fourth century. Egeria recounts that about eight o'clock Friday morning the wood of the cross is taken out of its gold and silver box and placed before the bishop on a table on Golgotha. "All the people,

[29] For the sources, see Anthony Ward, SM, "Sources of the New Good Friday Intercession for the Jews in the 1962 'Missale Romanum,'" EL 122 (2008) 250–55.

[30] For a recent critique, see Rita Ferrone, "Anti-Jewish Elements in the Extraordinary Form," *Worship* 84 (2010) 498–513. More recent still is Benjamin Leven, "The Good Friday Prayer for Jews: A 'Borderline Case' of Christian Prayer," *Studia Liturgica* 41 (2011) 78–91.

[31] See my "Veneration of the Cross," *Worship* 52 (1978) 2–13, reprinted in Maxwell E. Johnson, ed., *Between Memory and Hope*, 143–53.

catechumens as well as faithful," she reports, "come up one by one to the table. They stoop down over it, kiss the wood, and move on."[32]

In the papal liturgy of late seventh- or early eighth-century Rome there was a procession from the Lateran to the nearby Basilica of the Holy Cross starting at 2:00 p.m. In it a deacon bears the precious wood in a gold reliquary. In front of it walks the pope carrying a thurifer with incense. All the ministers are barefoot. During the procession Psalm 118 is chanted. Upon arrival at the basilica around three o'clock, the deacon places the cross on the altar, the pope prostrates before it in prayer, then all kiss it. The readings and intercessory prayers follow.[33] In Roman churches served by presbyters there is no procession. Instead, at three o'clock the cross is placed on the altar. After the readings, intercessions, and Lord's Prayer, "all adore the holy cross," says the Old Gelasian, "and communicate" (GeV 418). Here we recognize the sequence of parts as they still are today: biblical readings, intercessory prayers, adoration of the cross, and Communion.

Starting in the late eighth century north of the Alps, the rather spare Roman approach to adoring the cross is progressively embellished with chants and gestures expressive of homage. One of the oldest chants is the antiphon *Ecce lignum crucis*, "Behold the wood of the cross on which hung the salvation of the world. Come, let us adore." At first it is sung during adoration, later as the cross is being exposed. The text is composed of phrases strongly reminiscent of various accounts of the finding of the true cross. Saint Paulinus, for example, states that "once you think that you *behold the wood on which* our *salvation*, the Lord of Majesty, *was hanged* with nails whilst the world trembled, you, too, must tremble, but you must also rejoice."[34] Another pertinent text is furnished by Rufinus, who reports that as Helena searched for the cross she prayed that God would reveal to her "the blessed *wood on which hung* our *salvation*."[35] The chant *Ecce lignum crucis* and others similar to it suppose that a relic of the true cross, or at least a cross, is being shown and reverenced.

---

[32] Egeria, *Itinerarium* 37, 2, in Wilkinson, *Egeria's Travels*, 137.

[33] *Ordo* XXIII, 9–21, in Andrieu, OR III, 270–72.

[34] Paulinus of Nola, *Letter* 31, 1, trans. P. G. Walsh, ACW 36, 126 (emphasis mine).

[35] Rufinus, *Historia ecclesiastica* I, 7, in PL 21, 476C (trans. and emphasis mine).

Ordo XXXI, stemming from the second half of the ninth century, is of particular interest, for it shows that exposition of the sacred wood has been made into a theophany—which, of course, is fully consistent with Saint John's view of the crucifixion as the revelation of divine glory. The cross, covered with a veil, is carried to the front of the altar by two acolytes. They stop three times along the way. Each time they do so, chanters bow and sing in Greek, "Holy God, holy Mighty One, holy Immortal One, have mercy on us." The choir answers with the same words in Latin. After the third time the bishop unveils the cross all at once and acclaims in a loud voice, "Behold the wood of the cross."[36]

The cross is here regarded as the revelation of God himself, as the manifestation of his presence and saving power. Hence, its appearance calls forth the awesome *Trisagion*. The custom mentioned in the Romano-Germanic Pontifical[37] of genuflecting or even prostrating before the sacred wood is likewise consistent with this understanding. Pseudo-Alcuin comments: "When we adore this cross, our whole body clings to the earth; and him whom we adore, we mentally discern as if hanging upon it."[38] This passage may be dependent on Jerome's description of Paula's pilgrimage to Jerusalem: "Prostrate before the cross, she adored him whom she discerned as if hanging upon it."[39] These texts show that the figure of the Crucified is not affixed to the cross but discerned only mentally.

The *Trisagion* is usually sung not during exposition of the cross, as in *Ordo* XXXI, but with the first part of the *Improperia*, or Reproaches, the opening stanza of which is from Micah 6:3-4 and the third from Isaiah 5:1-4. The genre of reproach, therefore, is rooted in Israel's prophets. Hansjörg Auf der Maur points out that the Good Friday Reproaches should not be understood as lamentations spoken by the Man of Sorrows but by the *Kyrios* lifted up on the cross. They are, he continues, reminders of how throughout human history the gracious initiatives of a loving God have met with rejection by his ungrateful people, both Jewish and Christian.[40]

---

[36] *Ordo* XXXI, 46–47, in Andrieu, OR III, 498.

[37] RGP XCIX, 331–33, in Vogel-Elze II, 91–92.

[38] Pseudo-Alcuin, *De divinis officiis liber* XVIII, in PL 101, 1210C (trans. mine).

[39] Jerome, *Epistola* 108, 9, in PL 22, 883 (trans. mine).

[40] Auf der Maur, *Le celebrazioni nel ritmo del tempo* I, 173–74. In these pages the author displays awareness that some regard the *Improperia* as anti-Semitic and that they should be removed from the liturgy. He maintains that their

The theophanic aspect of the unveiling of the cross leads to the idea of its being a royal throne from which the divine presence rules. In the desert the Lord directed Moses to construct a wooden ark surmounted by a covering, called the propitiatory, or throne of mercy, at each side of which were winged figures, or cherubim. "There I shall come to meet you," he promises, "there, from above the throne of mercy" (Exod 25:22). Each year on the Day of Atonement the high priest was required to sprinkle the blood of sacrificed animals on the propitiatory and to burn incense before it (Lev 16:11-16) with a view to obtaining forgiveness. This is the background for the teaching in the second reading on Good Friday from the Letter to the Hebrews that Christ, by the sprinkling of his blood, once for all accomplished what all previous sacrifices failed to do, that he is the "source of eternal salvation" (Heb 5:9), and that the wood of his cross supplants the former throne of mercy as the meeting place between the Lord of hosts and mortals. Catching sight of it, the people of the new covenant remove their shoes as did Moses (Exod 3:5) and Joshua (Josh 5:15) in the presence of the Holy One and in the *Trisagion* cry for mercy. The bearing of incense by the pontiff before the relic of the cross in the ancient papal rite may be an evocation of the action of the high priest on the Day of Atonement.

Medieval rituals also prescribe that the hymn *Pange lingua* with its recurring refrain *Crux fidelis* should be sung during either adoration or Communion.[41] This splendid composition was written by Venantius Fortunatus in 569 for the reception of a relic of the true cross sent to Queen Radegunde at Poitiers by the Byzantine emperor Julian II. As the wood of the cross appears, it prompts the narration of how Christ in the fullness of time assumed our flesh and redeemed the human race by his death on a tree, thereby restoring creation by means of the very material that caused its fall. The precious wood, then, is a sign of victory—a trophy. This hymn, like the *Vexilla regis*, composed by Fortunatus for the same occasion, is an outstanding example of how the cross was understood in the West and what kind of response it stirred.

Old Testament roots and the close reciprocal connection between the Jewish and Christian tradition of reproach should caution us against drawing that conclusion.

[41] See *Ordo* XXXI, 50, in Andrieu, OR III, 498, and RGP XCIX, 334, in Vogel-Elze II, 92.

It is an excellent commentary not only on adoration of the cross but on the entire Good Friday liturgy.

During the eleventh and twelfth centuries Frankish and Germanic practices were brought down to Rome and given fresh expression in the Roman Pontifical of the Twelfth Century. According to this document, the pope removes his shoes and prostrates three times before the cross, which is covered with a veil. Then he intones *Ecce lignum crucis* three times, each time unveiling a portion of the cross. The Reproaches with the *Trisagion, Pange lingua,* and other anthems are sung during adoration.[42] This in essence is the rite transmitted to later centuries through the Tridentine Missal, except that the priest exposes the cross first and only then removes his shoes, prostrates, and kisses it.

While preserving the fundamental configuration, texts, and gestures of MR 1570, the reformed *Ordo* of Pius XII introduces a few details never seen in any previous service book. It says that on the cross should be the Crucified (no. 14), that the priest, after unveiling the cross, kisses the feet of the Crucified (no. 17), and that the faithful do likewise—men first, then women (no. 18). Fortunately, all these statements are eliminated from the first edition of the postconciliar Missal in 1970 and have not returned. They are, however, still in the 1962 *Missale Romanum,* the extraordinary expression of the Roman Rite.

An original element in the Missal of Paul VI is two forms for exposing the cross. Both involve processions—possibly inspired by the seventh- or eighth-century papal practice. In the first form a veiled cross is carried from the sacristy through the church to the center of the sanctuary, where, as in the past, it is unveiled in three stages. At each stage "Behold the wood of the cross" is sung, to which all respond, "Come let us adore," then kneel for a moment of silent adoration. The second form is new. An unveiled cross is carried from the door of the church to the sanctuary. Along the way it is raised three times, acclaimed, and adored as in the first form. As is the case for the eucharistic species, rubric 18 declares that the preferred gesture for adoring the cross is now a simple genuflection, though it still permits a kiss or other sign appropriate to the region. The same rubric says that the priest is the first to approach the cross "with the chasuble and his shoes removed, if appropriate." Turner remarks that "the rubrics have never suggested that the faithful remove their shoes at

---

[42] XXXI, 7–9, in Andrieu, PRMA I, 236.

this time, but there is nothing to forbid them if they would find this appropriate."[43]

Rubric 19 rightly insists that "[o]nly one Cross should be offered for adoration" and that if the size of the congregation makes individual adoration by everyone impossible, "the Priest, after some of the clergy and faithful have adored," stands before the altar, "invites the people in a few words to adore the Holy Cross," then holds it up for a short time for the faithful "to adore it in silence." Though the intent of this directive is fundamentally sound, objection could be made to three details. First, if all cannot adore individually, it would be better if none were allowed to do so and everyone made a corporate act of adoration. Second, the assembly has already been invited to adoration three times during the showing of the cross. The recommendation that the priest invite "the people in a few words to adore the Holy Cross" after some have already done so is superfluous, interrupts the flow of the action, and risks becoming an unfocused ramble. Third, adoration in silence is always praiseworthy. But in the present case the chanting of the *Trisagion* and a few verses of the hymn *Pange lingua* after silent adoration would be desirable. The cross could also be incensed.

The singing of the *Stabat mater* "or another suitable chant in memory of the compassion of the Blessed Virgin Mary," permitted at the end of no. 20 in the third edition of the Missal of Paul VI but not in the first two, runs counter to what is laid down in the circular letter *Paschalis Sollemnitatis*, no. 72, that "commemorations of the sorrows of the Blessed Virgin Mary" and other such devotions "should be assigned to a time of day that makes it quite clear that the liturgical celebration by its very nature far surpasses them in importance."

6. Holy Communion

The description of the late seventh- or early eighth-century papal liturgy at the Basilica of the Holy Cross on Good Friday relates that the pontiff and deacons do not receive Holy Communion but that after their departure anyone wishing to do so receives from what was set aside from the sacrifice on Thursday or else receives at one of the titular churches.[44] The Old Gelasian Sacramentary, used in the latter, states that after the solemn orations "all adore the holy cross and communicate" (GeV 418). Communion on Good Friday, then, is not due to the

---

[43] Turner, *Glory*, 99.
[44] *Ordo* XXIII, 22, in Andrieu, OR III, 272.

pope but is an initiative of the faithful themselves and attests a deeply rooted desire on their part for sacramental union with the living Lord on the day that recalls his death.

Since it is the presbyteral format of the Good Friday liturgy that is disseminated north of the Alps and not the papal one, rubrics in Frankish sacramentaries and *ordines* are unanimous in stating that after adoration of the cross everyone receives Communion. What is copied in liturgical books, however, does not always correspond to actual practice. It is widely known that in the Middle Ages the majority of the baptized rarely received Holy Communion.[45] The Pontifical of the Roman Curia, compiled during the papacy of Innocent III (1198–1216), declares that on Good Friday only the pontiff communicates.[46] This declaration, however, was thought to be a prohibition, and consequently, with few exceptions, in subsequent centuries the priest alone received Communion, and the faithful were excluded.

The instruction of November 16, 1955, grants permission for the faithful once again to receive Holy Communion on Good Friday (I, 2, c). But it does so in conjunction with remarks about the meaning of the rest of the liturgy, especially adoration of the cross. It first asserts that after the readings and intercessory prayers "the holy cross, trophy of our redemption, is most devoutly adored by the family of Christ, clergy and people" (I, 2, c). Mention of the cross being adored by both clergy and people prepares for the next statement on reception of Communion by the entire congregation. "As was the custom for many centuries," continues the instruction, "all who desire and who are properly prepared, may also come to Holy Communion, with this intention above all: that, by devoutly receiving the body of the Lord, delivered up for all on this day, they may obtain more abundantly the fruits of redemption" (I, 2, c).

Henceforth, on the day that recalls Christ's redemptive death on behalf of all, all—not just the priest—have access to his sacramental Body, even as everyone, clergy and people, adore his holy cross. Besides grounding general Communion in the universality of redemption, the instruction restores its close connection with adoration of the cross. The latter is homage paid to the trophy of redemption; the former is sacramental union with the person of the Redeemer. Thus the

---

[45] See Joseph A. Jungmann, SJ, *The Mass of the Roman Rite*, 2 vols. (New York: Benziger Brothers, Inc., 1955) II, 359–67.

[46] XLIII, 15 left column, 18 right column, in Andrieu, PRMA II, 469.

intimate bond between these two parts of the Good Friday service, so obvious in the Old Gelasian and other early sources, once again shines forth. In this connection, too, we must recall that the first reading in Pius XII's service is Exodus 12:1-11, which enjoins the Israelites to eat the flesh of the roasted lamb with unleavened bread and bitter herbs. Restoration of general Communion, then, enables the faithful once again to eat the flesh of him whose passion brings to fulfillment all that was prefigured in Israel's Passover.

The OHS makes a number of ceremonial modifications worthy of note. First of all, it eliminates all the accretions surrounding the priest's Communion that gave it the appearance of a Mass without a eucharistic prayer and returns it to its original integrity as a Communion rite, prepared for by recitation of the Lord's Prayer and its embolism. An important detail, however, is that the *Pater Noster* is to be prayed aloud no longer by the priest alone but by the priest *et omnes praesentes*, "and all present," specifies no. 26. We saw earlier that in the first part of the service rubrics 7 and 9 stipulate that all sit and listen to the readings and that the priest no longer stands at the altar reading to himself the same texts being proclaimed aloud to the faithful. All these changes are aimed at communion: communion in the Word, communion in prayer, and finally communion in the Body of Christ.

Another change is in the procession after adoration of the cross in which hosts to be consumed in Communion are brought from the repository to the altar. Pius XII's *Ordo* replaces the hymn of MR 1570, *Vexilla regis*, with three short antiphons. The first and third, like the *Agnus Dei* at Mass, are addressed to Christ and are affirmations of his Real Presence in the consecrated bread: "We adore thee, O Christ, and we bless thee," and "Savior of the world, save us." In addition, all three include reference to his redemptive work, suggesting that Christ is present not statically but dynamically, in the very act of redeeming the world. Finally, all three mention the cross, thereby binding together the last two parts of the liturgy, adoration of the cross and Communion. The Missal of Paul VI, on the other hand, wants the hosts to be brought from the repository to the altar in as short and direct a way as possible, in effect eliminating the procession. This has the happy result of enabling Communion to follow immediately upon adoration of the cross and hence strengthening the connection between them. But unfortunately it entails omitting the three antiphons introduced by Pius XII.

In the 1570 Missal after the priest receives Holy Communion, he and other ministers go directly to the sacristy in silence. The reformed Order of 1956 adds three prayers from the Old Gelasian to be recited after all have communicated: *Super populum tuum* (GeV 219), *Omnipotens et misericors Deus* (GeV 344), and *Reminiscere miserationum tuarum* (GeV 334). The text of the third is exactly as found in the Old Gelasian. But the first two are given insertions to make them more suitable for their use on Good Friday. The first begins by asking God to bless his people, after which is inserted the relative clause "who with devout hearts have recalled the passion and death of thy Son." The second prayer opens with the invocation "Almighty and merciful God," to which is appended the relative clause "who has restored us by the passion and death of thy Christ." Here we must recall the title of the service in Pius XII's *Ordo*: "Solemn Afternoon Liturgical Action of the Passion and Death of the Lord." We notice that inclusion of the words "passion and death" in the relative clauses inserted into the first two prayers is consistent with understanding the service to be a commemoration of the passion and death of the Lord, as expressed in the title.

The Missal of Paul VI changes the placement and function of these three prayers. It makes the third, *Reminiscere*, the first of two possible opening prayers—the preferred one because it declares that Christ, "by the shedding of his Blood, / established the Paschal Mystery." It uses the second prayer as the prayer after Communion, changing the invocation from *Omnipotens et misericors Deus*, "Almighty and merciful God," to *Omnipotens sempiterne Deus*, "Almighty ever-living God," which is what it is in GeV 344. Finally, it makes Pius XII's first prayer after Communion to be a prayer over the people, recited with hands extended over them.

More important, however, it changes the wording of the two relative clauses inserted into the prayers in 1956 in ways congruent with the new name of the day, "Friday of the Passion of the Lord," and the new title of the service, "The Celebration of the Passion of the Lord"—not passion and *death*. Pius XII's second prayer, now the prayer after Communion, no longer addresses God "who hast restored us by the passion and death of thy Christ," but God "who have restored us to life / by the blessed Death and *Resurrection* of your Christ" (emphasis mine). Similarly, the new prayer over the people, formerly the first prayer after Communion, invokes divine blessing no longer upon a people "who with devout hearts have recalled the passion and death of thy Son," but upon those "who have honored the Death of your Son / *in the hope of their resurrection*" (emphasis mine), omitting "with devout hearts."

These alterations in the final two prayers of the service—so easy to pass over unnoticed—are consistent with the interpretation of the entire Good Friday liturgy in the Missal and Lectionary of Paul VI and indicate, in short, that Friday of the Passion of the Lord commemorates no longer an ignominious passion ending in death but a glorious passion crowned with resurrection.

7. Conclusion

The afternoon hour, the passion of John, the solemn intercessions, adoration of the cross, and Holy Communion are common to the Good Friday liturgy in the restored Order of 1956 and in the Missal of Paul VI. In 1956, however, the day belonged to Lent. Despite the first reading from Exodus 12 about the origins of Passover and despite the passion according to John, which makes the death of Jesus coincide with the onset of Passover, it was not considered paschal. More than anything else, the wearing of black vestments and the inclusion of the Lord's death in the name of the day and in the title of the service make the liturgy overwhelmingly sorrowful, lugubrious, and funereal—blinding participants to the triumphal and life-giving character of the passion of Christ expressed in the gospel, in the chants during the exposition and adoration of the cross, and in the prayers, especially the three after Communion.

The Universal Norms of 1969 set a new direction by changing the name of the day to "Friday of the Passion of the Lord" and investing it with paschal character by recalculating the Triduum and declaring it to be a three-day celebration of the paschal mystery, understood as both the passion and the resurrection of the Lord. The Missal of Paul VI advances what the norms began by calling the service "The Celebration of the Passion of the Lord," by changing the color of vestments from black to red, and by introducing the opening prayer about Christ establishing the paschal mystery "by the shedding of his blood." The Lectionary replaces the first reading of 1956 with the fourth Servant Song, an obvious prefiguration of the passion, and the second one with the passage from the Letter to the Hebrews about the suffering of Christ, freely accepted, being the act of "a great high priest who has passed through the heavens" (Heb 4:14). It also adds as a gospel acclamation *Christus factus est*, ending with the soaring *propter quod et Deus exaltavit illum*, "because of which God highly exalted him." Consequently, all three readings, each in its own way, portray the passion of Jesus as a glorification, an exaltation, an ascension, and prepare the way for the wood of the cross to be lifted up and acclaimed by cantors,

Noblest tree of all created,
Richly jeweled and embossed:
Post by Lamb's blood consecrated;
Spar that saves the tempest-tossed;
Scaffold-beam which, elevated,
Carries what the world has cost![47]

to which all add,

Faithful Cross the Saints rely on,
Noble tree beyond compare!
Never was there such a scion,
Never leaf or flower so rare.

The consecrated bread shared on the afternoon of Friday of the Passion derives from the Mass *in Cena Domini* on the previous evening and brings out the inseparable link between these two liturgies. Without Communion on Friday reservation of the sacrament on Thursday would lose its purpose. The reason for reserving the sacrament on Thursday is not adoration later that night but Communion the next day. This practice represents the stubborn perdurance and official recognition on this Friday of a stream of primitive tradition focused more on what Paul Bradshaw calls "feeding on the life-giving Jesus" than on celebrating the holy sacrifice. "This dominant emphasis," he continues, "explains why the reception of communion in separation from the eucharistic action proper . . . emerged so soon in the life of the church and became so widely established: they [the faithful] needed, not to celebrate the Eucharist often, but to feed on Christ all the time."[48]

In Communion on Good Friday Christ is received not as he once was in past historical time but as he lives forever in eschatological plenitude—the victim who is victor, whose immolation is his glorification, whose passion is passage from this world to the Father. Put more simply, in Communion the risen Christ is received, the anticipation and assurance of our own resurrection, for he promised, "Those who eat my flesh and drink my blood have eternal life and I will raise them up on the last day" (John 6:54). Hence the prayer after Communion on

[47] This is the 2011 translation of the ninth stanza of the hymn *Pange lingua*, sung during adoration of the cross.
[48] Paul Bradshaw, "The Eucharistic Sayings of Jesus," *Studia Liturgica* 35 (2005) 11.

Good Friday includes mention of both the death and the resurrection of Christ, saying,

> Almighty ever-living God,
> who have restored us to life
> by the blessed Death and Resurrection of your Christ,
> preserve in us the work of your mercy.

Communion, then, perhaps more explicitly than other parts of the Good Friday liturgy, emphasizes the role of the resurrection in the economy of salvation and assures that on that afternoon as well as at the Paschal Vigil both aspects of *Pascha*—the passion of Christ as well as his passage—are celebrated.

D. EASTER SUNDAY OF THE RESURRECTION OF THE LORD: VIGIL IN THE NIGHT

1. Overview

The most significant differences between the Paschal Vigil restored by Pius XII, reproduced in the 1962 Missal, and that of the Missal of Paul VI are found not in the readings, prayers, and rubrics—though these do contain some differences—but in the day, time, and structure of the celebration.

Day. When restoration of the vigil was first announced on February 9, 1951, changes in the service as it had hitherto existed in the *Missale Romanum* were published in *Acta Apostolicae Sedis* under the title of *Rubricae Sabbato Sancto Servandae si Vigilia Paschalis Instaurata Peragitur* (Rubrics to be observed on Holy Saturday when the restored Paschal Vigil takes place).[49] The essential message here is that the vigil represents a change of rubrics on Holy Saturday. The title of the service book issued by the Vatican for use at the 1951 vigil is practically the same: *Ordo Sabbati Sancti Quando Vigilia Paschalis Instaurata Peragitur* (Order of Holy Saturday when the restored Paschal Vigil takes place).

---

[49] Sacra Congregatio Rituum, "Decretum de solemni vigilia paschali instauranda," AAS 42 (January 10, 1951) 130–37 (trans. mine). Paragraphs are not numbered. For an account of the formation of this document, see Giampietro, *Development of the Liturgical Reform*, 35–56, and, more recently, his "Ricordando il nuovo *Ordo Instauratus* della Veglia Pasquale: Febbraio 1951," *Notitiae* 48 (2011) 33–63.

Five years later in the *Ordo Hebdomadae Sanctae Instauratus* of 1956, texts for the vigil are still given under the heading of *Sabbato Sancto*, "Holy Saturday." We see, then, that although Pius XII moved the service from Saturday morning to Saturday night and restored its ancient name, Paschal Vigil, abandoned in sacramentaries and missals since the eighth century,[50] he did not change the day. It was still celebrated on Holy Saturday. The Roman Missal of 1962 keeps it there.

The first edition of the Missal of Paul VI, however, changes the day. It places the vigil after *Sabbato Sancto* under a new heading, *Dominica Paschae in Resurrectione Domini*. The second and third typical editions maintain this heading and placement. Since 1970, then, the vigil has been celebrated on "Easter Sunday of the Resurrection of the Lord," as the heading is now translated. To distinguish it from what in MR 1570 is the one Mass of Easter Sunday, the Missal calls the vigil "The Easter Vigil in the Holy Night" and the other one "The Mass during the Day." So there are now two Easter Sunday Masses. As nos. 4 and 5 of the instruction on the vigil designate them, the first is the "Mass of the Vigil," or "Mass of the Night." The other is the "Mass during the Day."

Time. The decree of February 9, 1951, announcing the restoration of the vigil begins by recalling that in ancient times this vigil took place during the hours of the night *quae Domini praecedunt Resurrectionem*, "which precede the resurrection of the Lord." It then points out that at present, as a result of historical investigations, there has arisen a strong desire to restore the vigil to its original time during the night hours *quae dominicam Resurrectionis antecedunt*, "which precede the Sunday of the Resurrection." It adds that many bishops and religious superiors have requested permission to hold the vigil during the night *inter sabbatum sanctum et dominicam Resurrectionis*, "between Holy Saturday and Sunday of the Resurrection." Here we see that the Lord's resurrection is identified with Easter Sunday. The vigil on Saturday night is not yet Easter but precedes it and leads up to it.

The first rubric of the vigil in both the 1951 *Acta Apostolicae Sedis* article and the *Ordo Sabbati Sancti* service book of the same year specifies that the vigil should start at an hour "that enables the solemn Mass of the Paschal Vigil to begin around midnight," *quae permittat incipere missam solemnem vigiliae paschalis circa mediam noctem*.[51] Four years later no.

---

[50] See Bruylants I, no. 89.

[51] In the AAS article this is titulus II, caput I, 1 on p. 131.

9 of the general decree of November 16, 1955, announcing the reform of Holy Week repeats this requirement: "The solemn Easter Vigil is to be celebrated at the proper hour, namely, a time which will permit that the solemn Mass of the Vigil begin at about midnight which falls between Holy Saturday and Easter Sunday." The instruction accompanying the decree states that "the sacred Vigil is concluded with the solemn Mass of the Resurrection" (I, 2 d). In these texts three points stand out: (1) the vigil and the Mass are two distinct entities; (2) the vigil takes place on Holy Saturday, the Mass on Easter Sunday; (3) midnight is the turning point from one to the other. It is also, we should add, the moment of transition from Lent to Easter, from the forty days of obligatory fasting to the season of rejoicing. In fact, it was precisely restoration of the vigil for the church universal that led Pius XII in the decree of November 16, 1955, to extend the Lenten fast to midnight on Holy Saturday.[52]

By way of contrast the Missal of Paul VI so broadens the time frame of the vigil that midnight no longer has any significance. No. 3 of the instruction under the title of "The Easter Vigil in the Holy Night" states in the 2011 translation that "the entire celebration of the Easter Vigil must take place during the night, so that it begins after nightfall and ends before daybreak on the Sunday."[53] No. 4 continues: "The Mass of the Vigil, even if it is celebrated before midnight, is a paschal Mass [*Missa paschalis*] of the Sunday of the Resurrection."[54] What is significant now is not the moment midway through the night, but simply the *night*. Liturgically speaking, Easter Sunday no longer begins at midnight but at whatever hour the vigil begins. And since Easter is synonymous with the Lord's resurrection, at least in English transla-

---

[52] The general decree states that "the abstinence and fast prescribed for Lent, which hitherto has ceased on Holy Saturday after noon, according to canon 1252, par. 4, will cease in the future at midnight of the same Holy Saturday" (III, 10).

[53] The general decree of February 11, 1955, allowed, for pastoral reasons and with approval of the local ordinary, the starting time of the vigil to be anticipated but not "before twilight, or certainly not before sunset" (II, 9).

[54] The phrase *Missa pachalis* might have been better rendered as "Easter Mass." The rubric is saying that even though the Mass of the vigil may begin before midnight, it is considered to be an Easter Mass, that is, a Mass of Easter Sunday. This point also eluded the previous translation, which read, "Even if the vigil Mass takes place before midnight, the Easter Mass of the resurrection is celebrated."

tions of the documents we are considering, celebration of the resurrection begins no longer only with the Mass of the vigil but with the vigil itself. The vigil, then, is no longer spent in expectation of the resurrection, the celebration of which commences with the Mass. Rather, the resurrection is celebrated in the whole of the vigil. This is why ministers wear white vestments from the outset and why everyone stands during the Litany of the Saints. The period of expectation no longer takes place during the vigil that precedes the Mass but during all the hours of Holy Saturday that precede the vigil. The first paragraph of the instruction about Holy Saturday on the page before Easter Sunday in the current Missal states, "On Holy Saturday the Church waits at the Lord's tomb in prayer and fasting, meditating on his Passion and Death and on his Descent into Hell, and awaiting his Resurrection."[55]

Another indication of change in the time when Easter Sunday and, consequently, celebration of the resurrection begin is seen in a tiny alteration in the wording of no. 2 in the initial instruction about the vigil in the third typical edition of the Missal of Paul VI. The first two editions state that in the second part of the vigil new members of the church are born *appropinquante die resurrectionis*, "as the day of resurrection approaches" (RM 1985), meaning that "the day of resurrection," or Easter Sunday, comes at some time after the baptismal service. In the third edition this text is modified. It now states that new members are born *appropinquante die*, "as day approaches" (RM 2011). By eliminating the word *resurrectionis*, the revisers acknowledge that the day of resurrection does not begin at some unspecified time after the baptismal service but begins with the vigil itself.

In light of this we must return to the brief instruction about Holy Saturday on the page before the vigil in the current Missal. What is now no. 2 in the 2011 translation says that the solemn vigil is "the anticipation by night of the Resurrection, when the time comes for paschal joys." The previous translation was worse. It reads, "Only after the solemn vigil during the night, held in anticipation of the resurrection, does the Easter celebration begin, with a spirit of joy." This statement, already present in the first typical edition of 1970, is lifted from the instruction of February 16, 1955, which declares that on Holy Saturday "after the solemn Vigil or nocturnal expectation of the

---

[55] This text is a modification of what is said in the instruction of November 16, 1955, that Holy Saturday "is a day of the greatest sorrow when the Church lingers at the Lord's tomb, meditating upon his passion and death" (I, 2, d).

resurrection," the church "gives way to paschal joys" (I, 2, d). When first written, this was true—and still is true in the extraordinary form. But it is superseded by what is said elsewhere in the Missal of Paul VI. Retention of such an outdated text in the third typical edition is puzzling.

Structure. Besides changing the day and broadening the time frame of the vigil, the Missal of Paul VI also alters its structure. We saw that the *Ordo Sabbati Sancti* of 1951 and the *Ordo Hebdomadae Sanctae Instauratus* of 1956 made a sharp distinction between the vigil and the Mass of the vigil, and that midnight was the turning point from one to the other. We shall now show that the Gloria of the Mass was meant to coincide with midnight.

The vigil of Pius XII consists of the opening ceremonies surrounding the paschal candle, four Old Testament readings with their canticles and prayers, and the blessing of baptismal water, followed by renewal of baptismal promises and sprinkling of the congregation. Throughout the vigil it is still Lent. Ministers wear purple vestments, except for the deacon who wears white to chant the *Exsultet* and the priest who puts on a white stole and cope before the renewal of baptismal promises.

During the second part of the Litany of the Saints near the end of the vigil, ministers go to the sacristy and change to white vestments. Meanwhile, the altar is prepared, the candles are lit, and flowers are set in place. With the return of the ministers, Mass begins with the chanting of the *Kyrie* and incensing of the altar—prayers at the foot of the altar being omitted. When the priest solemnly intones *Gloria in excelsis Deo*, bells are rung[56] and statues and crucifixes—veiled in purple throughout Passiontide—are uncovered. It is midnight. Easter Sunday has arrived. The sorrow of mourning the Lord's death gives way to the joy of celebrating his resurrection. The collect, going back to GeV 454 and H 377, the epoch when catechumens were still baptized at the vigil, prays, "O God, who dost illuminate this most holy night by the glory of the Lord's resurrection, preserve in the new children of thy family the Spirit of adoption." The other parts of the Mass follow as usual—epistle and gospel, offertory, preface, Canon, and Communion.

---

[56] The instruction of November 16, 1955, urges that "in places where there are several churches, whether the sacred ceremonies are celebrated in all of them at the same time or at different times, the bells of all the churches are to be rung together with the bells of the cathedral church" (25, b).

If in the service of Pius XII midnight is the temporal moment marking the transition from the vigil to the Mass, from Saturday to Sunday, from Lent to Easter, from fast to feast, the Gloria is the liturgical moment. The postconciliar vigil, however, dissolves this moment. The structure of the vigil in the Missal of Paul VI consists of four parts, each named and numbered: (1) "The Solemn Beginning of the Vigil or Lucernarium," (2) "The Liturgy of the Word," (3) "Baptismal Liturgy," and finally (4) "The Liturgy of the Eucharist."[57] In this arrangement there is no longer any distinction between the vigil and the Mass of the vigil. Once again we see how outdated is no. 2 of the instruction about Holy Saturday, originally written in 1955: "The Church abstains from the Sacrifice of the Mass, with the sacred table left bare, until after the solemn Vigil." This was true for the *Ordo* of Pius XII and still holds for the extraordinary form, but in the postconciliar Missal the Eucharist does not follow the vigil but is its final and climactic part. The priest does not wear a cope for the vigil and change to a chasuble for the Mass. Rather, priest and deacon from the beginning of the vigil wear white vestments "as at Mass," states no. 6. Hence, it is untenable and anachronistic to consider the Gloria to be a turning point from the vigil to the Mass, from awaiting the resurrection to celebrating it.

Nor does the Gloria mark the end of Lent or the end of the Triduum. In the 1969 calendar Lent ends at the evening Mass on Holy Thursday, and the Triduum continues through Vespers of Easter Sunday. Finally, the vigil no longer brings forty days of obligatory fasting to a close. Since the apostolic constitution *Paenitemini* of February 11, 1966, there are only two obligatory fast days, Ash Wednesday and Good Friday, and, in any case, the 1969 Universal Norms on the Liturgical Year and the Calendar, no. 27, presents Lent not as a period of fasting but as "ordered to preparing for the celebration of Easter." As we saw earlier, the vigil does not necessarily even mark the passage from Saturday to Sunday. All these considerations prompt us to propose a reinterpretation of what is celebrated at the vigil. But first we must compare each section of the vigil in the current Missal with their counterparts in the restored Order of Pius XII. This amounts to comparing the ordinary form of the vigil with the extraordinary form.

---

[57] No. 2 of the instruction on the vigil explains the progression from one part to the other, as does no. 81 of the circular letter *Paschalis Sollemnitatis*.

2. Individual Parts

A. FIRST PART: THE SOLEMN BEGINNING OR LUCERNARIUM

The Missal of Paul VI, unlike the OHS of Pius XII, provides a short introduction to the vigil emphasizing its eschatological character. "By most ancient tradition," no. 1 points out, "this is the night of keeping vigil for the Lord (Exod 12:42), in which, following the Gospel admonition (Luke 12:35-37), the faithful, carrying lighted lamps [*lucernas ardentes*] in their hands, should be like those looking for the Lord when he returns, so that at his coming he may find them awake and have them sit at his table." This paragraph alludes to the earliest stage of the celebration of *Pascha* by Christians who observed the feast not on the same day as the Jewish Passover, as did the Quartodecimans, but on the Sunday following it. The Friday and Saturday before this Sunday had no liturgies but were days of strict fast commemorating the absence of the bridegroom (Mark 2:19-20) and expressing hope for his imminent return (John 16:16). It is called the paschal fast and is distinct from the Lenten fast.[58] The Eucharist at the end of the vigil "very early on the first day of the week" (Mark 16:2) was the sacramental fulfillment of this hope, an anticipated Parousia.[59]

The title of the first part of the vigil is *Sollemne Initium Vigiliae seu Lucernarium*, "The Solemn Beginning of the Vigil or Lucernarium." The Latin word *lucernarium*, formerly translated "service of light," comes from *lucerna*, meaning "lamp," and refers to the ancient practice of lighting oil lamps in homes and churches at the onset of evening. We have seen that the introduction to the vigil describes the assembled faithful as "carrying lighted lamps, *lucernas ardentes*, in their hands." The word *lucernarium* occurs not only in the title but also in no. 2 of the instruction, which says that the first part of the vigil includes "the Lucernarium and Easter Proclamation."

---

[58] No. 1 of the instruction on the Triduum preceding Thursday of the Lord's Supper in the 2011 Missal declares, "The Paschal Fast should also be kept sacred. It is to be celebrated everywhere on the Friday of the Lord's Passion and, where appropriate, prolonged also through Holy Saturday." This repeats the Constitution on the Sacred Liturgy, no. 110, and the 1969 Universal Norms, no. 20. Because this fast was originally ordered to Communion at the Paschal Vigil, to restore its integrity some want to eliminate Communion on Good Friday. See my "The Good Friday Communion Debate," *Worship* 81 (2007) 2-23.

[59] See my "The Three Days and the Forty Days," 3-4.

Texts and rubrics of the lucernarium are shown under three subtitles: "The Blessing of the Fire and Preparation of the Candle," "Procession," and "The Easter Proclamation (Exsultet)." The corresponding headings in the 1956 *Ordo* are "Blessing of the New Fire," "Blessing the Paschal Candle," and "Procession and Easter Proclamation." The main difference between the two is that the OHS combines the procession with the *Exsultet* in the third heading, whereas the Missal of Paul VI allows it to stand alone as the second heading, thereby indicating that the procession connects preparation of the candle outside the church with the paschal proclamation inside. This manner of grouping and identifying the material more accurately reflects the tripartite structure of the paschal lucernarium in mid-fifth-century Jerusalem where this part of the vigil originated. There, the faithful first gathered in the rotunda over the tomb of Jesus where light was kindled and distributed. Then, carrying lighted candles, they walked in procession across a courtyard to the basilica. After reconvening in the basilica, they entered upon the twelve readings of the vigil, each followed by prayer on bended knee.[60]

The third typical edition of the Missal of Paul VI makes a few additions to the start of the vigil. It requires that the service begin, as does every Eucharist, with the sign of the cross and the priest greeting the assembly. Then comes the short admonition (no. 9) dating from 1970. In it the priest tells the faithful that the gathering on this most sacred night is dedicated to keeping "the memorial / of the Lord's paschal solemnity" by "listening to his word and celebrating his mysteries," in "the sure hope / of sharing his triumph over death / and living with him in God."

The word "mysteries" here refers to baptism and Eucharist. The admonition articulates the important truth that the vigil is not primarily about commemorating the Lord's victory over death in the past but about sacramentally sharing it in the present. The memorial of the Lord's *Pascha* consists in its being actualized in the church and so made complete.

The postconciliar Missal no longer requires, as does OHS, that the new fire be struck from flint and that from it coals be kindled. Instead, rubric 8 declares that "a blazing fire is prepared." Consequently, the words "new fire struck from flint" are excised from the prayer for blessing the fire. The circular letter *Paschalis Sollemnitatis*, no. 82, says of the fire that its "flames should be such that they genuinely dispel

---

[60] For further details, see my "Paschal *Lucernarium*: Structure and Symbolism," *Worship* 82 (2008) 98–118, especially 101–7.

the darkness and light up the night." Other changes in the lucernarium are that the processional cross is omitted, the new fire is not sprinkled or incensed after being blessed, insertion of five grains of incense into the paschal candle is optional, and the prayer for blessing the candle, *Veniat*, used in the 1570 Missal to bless the five grains of incense, is eliminated. For this reason the heading "Blessing of the Paschal Candle" is replaced by "Preparation of the Candle." During the procession into church there is no longer a genuflection when responding to the threefold acclamation of the candle as "Light of Christ." Finally, a lay cantor may sing the *Exsultet* when necessary.

We see, then, that the Missal of Paul VI continues the simplification of these opening ceremonies begun by Pius XII and accords even greater prominence to the paschal candle—the preparing of it by the inscription and ornamentation, the lighting of it from the new fire, the carrying of it from outside to inside, the acclaiming of it as "Light of Christ," the sharing of its flame with all present, and finally its being honored with incense after being raised aloft and set in the holder from which it will shed its joyful light upon the world for the next fifty days. The paschal proclamation recounts all the saving events God wrought by night. Preferably sung by candlelight, it brings the lucernarium to a close.

B. SECOND PART: THE LITURGY OF THE WORD

The number of readings at the vigil and the way they are counted vary considerably in liturgical books. The Old Gelasian lists ten Old Testament readings, each followed by an oration (GeV 431–41). When the epistle and gospel of the Mass are added, the total number of readings is twelve. The Sacramentary of Pope Hadrian, on the other hand, has only four readings from the Old Testament during the vigil (H 362, 364, 366, 368), followed by the two New Testament readings of the Mass for a total of six. But since each was read in both Latin and Greek, the total number of readings is again twelve. The Tridentine Missal of 1570 reflects a further development. Although the readings of the Mass remain fixed at two, the epistle and the gospel, the number of Old Testament readings preceding them at the vigil is increased to twelve.[61] In all the sources an oration accompanies each reading from the Old Testament, applying its content to baptism or to the

---

[61] For details about the number of readings, see Chavasse, *Gélasien*, 107–26.

redemptive work of Christ. Perhaps this is why the readings of the vigil are called "Prophecies" in the Tridentine Missal.

The 1951 reform of Pius XII, no doubt imitating the *Hadrianum*, reduces the number of Old Testament readings and their corresponding orations to four. They are the first, fourth, eighth, and eleventh of MR 1570. Each of the last three of these issues upon a canticle. The first reading is the Priestly author's story of creation in Genesis 1:1–2:2. The second is the crossing of the sea in Exodus 14:24–15:1, leading into the canticle of the sea. The third is the Lord's promise in Isaiah 4:2-6 to wash away the filth of a remnant in Jerusalem and to establish his presence there. It leads to the canticle of the vineyard. The fourth is the final instruction of Moses in Deuteronomy 31:22-30, leading to the canticle he entrusted to all Israel.

The OHS of Pius XII enjoins, as does the Tridentine Missal, that after each reading and, where applicable, the canticle following it, all rise when the priest says *Oremus*, kneel in silent prayer when the deacon says *Flectamus genua*, and rise again when he says *Levate*. The priest then recites the oration. This is the same routine observed during the intercessory prayers on Good Friday. This is because Pius XII's vigil takes place while it is still Lent. Hence prayer in the penitential posture of kneeling is prescribed. We must recall that the Old Testament readings of the preconciliar vigil were followed not by the New Testament ones but by the blessing of baptismal water. The epistle and gospel belonged not to the vigil but to the Mass, which began only after the congregation had renewed its baptismal promises and had been sprinkled with holy water.

As was already noted, the Missal of Paul VI significantly alters the structure of the vigil by combining the two New Testament readings with those of the Old Testament to form the second part of the vigil, the Liturgy of the Word, and by making the baptismal section a third part after the homily. Just as it provided a short statement for the priest to use when introducing the vigil as a whole, so does it provide one for introducing the readings and prayers. "Let us meditate on how God in times past saved his people," the priest urges, "and in these, the last days, has sent his Son as our Redeemer. / Let us pray that our God may complete this paschal work of salvation / by the fullness of redemption." The priest is saying in effect that all the wonders about to be recounted in both testaments are but the beginning of marvelous realities that reach completion only in the sacraments soon to be celebrated. This is to say that in the sacramental deeds of the church

God brings to perfection the redemptive deeds proclaimed in the Scriptures.

The postconciliar Lectionary provides nine readings for the vigil—seven from the Old Testament, two from the New—each followed by a responsorial psalm or canticle and an oration.[62] The third edition of the Missal in no. 20 recommends that all "should be read whenever this can be done, so that the character of the Vigil, which demands an extended period of time, may be preserved."[63] Nevertheless, the number of Old Testament readings may be reduced when pastoral circumstances necessitate it. No. 21 of the third edition insists, however, that "[a]t least three readings should be read from the Old Testament, both from the Law and from the Prophets, and their respective Responsorial Psalms should be sung." This is a change and is based on the 1988 circular letter, *Paschalis Sollemnitatis*, no. 85. The first two editions of the Missal as well as a rubric at the beginning of the vigil in the Lectionary allowed as few as two Old Testament readings in urgent cases and did not require that they be from the Law and Prophets. The reading about the crossing of the sea in Exodus 14 and its canticle must never be omitted.

At the end of each reading and responsorial psalm, states no. 23, "all rise, the Priest says 'Let us pray' and, after all have prayed for a while in silence, he says the prayer corresponding to the reading." Unlike the practice enjoined by MR 1570 and OHS, the faithful no longer kneel for prayer after the readings, and hence the deacon no longer says *Flectamus genua* and *Levate*. The reason is because the postconciliar vigil is celebrated during the Easter season, not Lent, and during this season kneeling, like fasting, is forbidden in order to show that we "have been raised with Christ" (Col 3:1). This should apply also to the eucharistic prayer.

Comparing the readings in the Lectionary with those in earlier sources, the first reading is still the same as it was in MR 1570 and the *Ordo* of Pius XII: the creation account in Genesis 1:1–2:2. A shorter form of this reading is available in the Lectionary. It is Genesis 1:1, 26-31a, limited to the creation of human beings. The full form is recommended because of extensive parallels between it and the third

---

[62] For the choice and sources of these prayers, see Anthony Ward, SM, "The Orations after the Readings at the Easter Vigil in the 2002 'Missale Romanum,'" EL 123 (2009) 460–507.

[63] The 1988 circular letter *Paschalis Sollemnitatis*, no. 85, says the same.

reading, the passage through the sea.[64] The oration corresponding to the first reading, from GeV 433, asks that

> those you have redeemed understand
> that there exists nothing more marvelous
> than the world's creation in the beginning
> except that, at the end of the ages,
> Christ our Passover has been sacrificed.

The prayer contrasts the end of time with its beginning, redemption with creation, to affirm that God's creative work concludes in an even more wonderful way than it began. The alternate oration, from H 363 and used after the first reading in MR 1570 and the OHS, is better recited when the short form of the reading is chosen, because it mentions not the creation of the world but only the creation of the human race.

The second reading, Genesis 22:1-18, recounts Abraham's sacrifice of his only son, Isaac. This one too has an abbreviated form. The corresponding prayer declares that by "pouring out the grace of adoption / throughout the whole world" God actually does make Abraham to be "father of nations," as was promised. The third reading is Israel's passage through the sea—the second reading in Pius XII's vigil and the fourth in MR 1570. The text is about twice as long as it used to be because it now begins at Exodus 14:15 instead of Exodus 14:21, and it still issues upon the canticle of the sea, which likewise includes more verses than before. The first of the two prayers corresponding to this reading is the same in all three sources under consideration and is found in both the Old Gelasian (GeV 435) and the *Hadrianum* (H 365). It acknowledges that what God "once bestowed on a single people, / freeing them from Pharaoh's persecution," he now brings about "for the salvation of the nations / through the waters of rebirth." The alternate prayer, from GeV 620, affirms that "the Red Sea prefigures the sacred font / and the nation delivered from slavery / foreshadows the Christian people." This concludes readings from the Law. The next four are from the prophetic books.

The fourth reading is Isaiah 54:5-14, not in MR 1570 or OHS. In it the Holy One of Israel affirms that his love is everlasting and irrevocable. The corresponding prayer, from GeV 436, entreats him to surpass what he "pledged to the Patriarchs by reason of their faith, / and through

---

[64] See below, p. 223.

sacred adoption increase the children of your promise." The fifth reading is Isaiah 55:1-11, also the fifth reading in MR 1570, but the latter begins with Isaiah 54:17 instead of 55:1. Besides inviting all who thirst to "come to the waters" and be renewed as a free gift of divine love, it relates how the Word of the Lord efficaciously accomplishes what it is sent to do. The corresponding prayer, from GeV 441, sees "the mysteries of this present age"—namely, the sacraments of initiation—already disclosed in the preaching of the prophets. The sixth reading, from Baruch 3:9-15, 31–4:4, likewise the sixth reading in MR 1570 but consisting of 3:9-38, is a summons to hear the commandments of life and learn wisdom. The corresponding prayer, from H 369, entreats God to protect those he washes clean in the water of baptism.

In the seventh reading, Ezekiel 36:16-17a, 18-28, not in MR 1570 or OHS, the Lord God promises: "I will sprinkle clean water upon you. . . . A new heart I will give you. . . . I will put my spirit within you." The corresponding prayer is particularly profound because of its ecclesial emphasis, the universality of its breadth, and the role of Christ in both redemption and creation. Alluding to a theme recurring throughout the letter to the Ephesians but expressed succinctly in 1:10, it prays that all things be "restored to integrity through Christ, / just as by him they came into being." The alternate prayer, very appropriate after the last Old Testament reading, articulates the hermeneutical principal underlying all these orations, that "the pages of both Testaments / instruct and prepare us to celebrate the Paschal Mystery."

"After the last reading from the Old Testament with its Responsorial Psalm and its prayer," says rubric 31, "the altar candles are lit, and the Priest intones the hymn Gloria in excelsis Deo (Glory to God in the highest), which is taken up by all, while bells are rung." Lighting the altar candles at this point seems to be a relic of the preconciliar arrangement in which the Gloria marked the end of the vigil and the beginning of the Mass. After the Gloria the priest recites the collect, the same one as in OHS and extending back to GeV 454 and H 377. "Stir up in your Church," it asks, "a spirit of adoption, / so that, renewed in body and mind, / we may render you undivided service." The reading from the apostle follows, no longer Colossians 3:1-4 as in the past but Romans 6:3-11, a fitting prelude to the baptismal liturgy about to take place. "After the Epistle has been read," rubric 34 declares, "all rise, then the Priest solemnly intones the Alleluia three times, raising his voice by a step each time." Then the gospel is proclaimed: Matthew 28:1-10 in Year A, Mark 16:1-7 in Year B, and Luke 24:1-12 in Year

C. Prior to the 1970 Lectionary, Matthew 28:1-7 was read every year and still is in the 1962 Missal. The second part of the postconciliar vigil ends with the homily, which, says rubric 36, "even if brief, is not to be omitted."

C. THIRD PART: BAPTISMAL LITURGY

The writings of Tertullian from the early third century indicate that blessing of water was already an essential component of the baptismal liturgy together with renunciation of Satan, profession of faith, and immersion.[65] He is also among the first to state that "Passover provides the day of most solemnity for baptism."[66] Centuries before publication of the Roman Missal of 1570 baptism ceased to be conferred on Holy Saturday morning. Water, however, continued to be blessed during the service and used for baptisms throughout the year, thereby maintaining a connection between baptism and Easter. With the promulgation of the Rite of Christian Initiation of Adults, called for by the Second Vatican Council, baptism again became an integral part of the Paschal Vigil. A major step in this direction is the 1951 *Ordo Sabbati Sancti* of Pius XII, reproduced in his *Ordo Hebdomadae Sanctae Instauratus* of 1956, which introduced renewal of baptismal promises by all present. In the following paragraphs we will examine MR 1570, the books of Pius XII, and the postconciliar Missal to observe how baptism assumes a progressively more prominent place in the vigil as we move from one to the next. This is a complicated undertaking. To avoid getting lost in details and in the multiple options offered by the postconciliar rites, it is well to keep an eye on the two actions common to all these documents: the blessing of water and the sprinkling of the congregation.

MR 1570. In the Tridentine Missal the water is blessed at the font, wherever it is located. After the twelfth reading from the Old Testament the priest, vested in purple cope, and other ministers walk there in procession from the sanctuary. During the procession is sung Psalm 41:2-4, *Sicut cervus,* listed as the last of four Old Testament canticles

---

[65] Texts in E. C. Whitaker, *Documents of the Baptismal Liturgy,* 2nd ed. (London: SPCK, 1970), 7–10.

[66] *De baptismo* 20, in Whitaker, *Documents,* 9. On paschal baptism, see Paul F. Bradshaw, " 'Diem baptismo sollemniorem': Initiation and Easter in Christian Antiquity," in Maxwell E. Johnson, ed., *Living Water,* 137–47.

in one of the ancient antiphonals (AMS 79a–b). It begins, "As the hart panteth after the fountains of water, so my soul panteth after thee, O God." The word "fountains" translates *fontes* in Latin, which of course evokes the baptismal font. Upon arrival there the priest recites an oration based upon a baptismal interpretation of the psalm. It asks God to look upon "thy people about to be reborn, who like the hart pant after the fountain of thy waters: and mercifully grant that the thirst of their faith may, by the sacrament of baptism, hallow their souls and bodies."[67] The psalm is noted and text of the oration given in both the Old Gelasian (GeV 442) and the *Hadrianum* (H 370, 372).

The long prayer of blessing, likewise common to the Old Gelasian (GeV 445–48) and the *Hadrianum* (H 374a–c), begins with the preface dialogue and is chanted on the preface tone. It is interrupted several times by symbolic gestures and culminates with the priest inserting the paschal candle into the water three times while chanting each time on a higher pitch, "May the virtue of the Holy Spirit descend into all the water of this font." Then, breathing three times upon the water—in the form of the Greek letter psi, specifies a 1920 missal—he adds, "and make the whole substance of this water fruitful for regeneration." Immediately thereafter the priest sprinkles the people with the blessed water. Meanwhile, another minister withdraws some of the water from the font to be used for blessing homes and other places.

Having returned to the baptistery after the sprinkling, the priest first pours oil of catechumens, then sacred chrism, then both into the water while saying prescribed prayers. Then the congregation kneels, and the Litany of the Saints is sung. Meanwhile, candles around the altar are lit, and ministers go to the sacristy where they change from purple to white vestments. As the *Kyrie* is being chanted, they enter the sanctuary and begin the Mass. The possibility of conferring baptism at this service on Holy Saturday morning is recognized by MR 1570 but hardly expected.

Reform of Pius XII. The restored vigil of 1951 on Saturday night divides the Litany of the Saints into two parts. The first part, invoking the three Persons of the Trinity and the names of the Saints, begins after the last Old Testament reading with its canticle and

---

[67] Translations of the psalm and oration are from the Baronius translation of the 1962 Missal, though there they are found *after* the blessing of water, not before.

corresponding oration. The rest is chanted after the congregation is sprinkled with blessed water. More important, Pius XII requires that the water be blessed not at the font but in the sanctuary where the faithful can see it. The text, melody, and gestures of the blessing are the same as those in MR 1570, but now the blessing is recited facing the people. At its end some of the water is set aside for sprinkling the congregation. After the oils are added the rest is carried in procession to the baptistery. *Sicut cervus* is sung during the procession; its accompanying prayer is recited after the water is poured into the font.

The possibility of baptism being conferred at Pius XII's vigil is more likely than it was previously, but it is limited to places where the liturgical movement of the first half of the twentieth century was particularly fruitful and is by no means widespread. Realizing that in most places no one will be baptized, Pius XII does the next best thing. He enjoins that once ministers have returned to the sanctuary after pouring the water into the font, the entire assembly, holding candles lit from the paschal candle, renews its baptismal promises—and does so not in Latin but, in the words of OHS, no. 26, *in lingua vernacula*, "in the vernacular tongue." This permission, already included in the 1951 vigil, was a milestone in the introduction of modern languages into the Roman Rite.

Having put on a white stole and cope, and with midnight only moments away, the priest introduces this unprecedented action, saying, "The Lenten observance now completed, let us renew the promises of baptism by which formerly we renounced Satan and . . . promised to serve God faithfully in his holy Catholic Church." After the tripartite interrogative renunciation of Satan, the profession of faith, and the concluding prayer, the priest sprinkles everyone with water reserved for this purpose before the oils were added to it. The second half of the litany, beginning *Propitius esto*, is then sung. The faithful kneel, ministers go the sacristy, candles on the altar are lit, and flowers are set in place. During the *Kyrie* the ministers emerge in white vestments. It is midnight. Mass has begun. The austerities of Lent give way to the joys of Easter as the Gloria is intoned and bells rung.

Postconciliar developments. A momentous advance in the Missal of Paul VI, taken in conjunction with the Rite of Christian Initiation of Adults, is that baptism at the Paschal Vigil not only is a possibility, as it was previously, but is expected. Henceforth, a vigil without baptism is incomplete, the exception. This is obvious from the title of the third part of the service, "Baptismal Liturgy." It begins not after the Old Testament readings but after the gospel and homily, which conclude the second part of the vigil, the Liturgy of the Word, and takes place at the font if it can be seen by the faithful. If not, it takes place in the sanctuary where a vessel of water has been prepared. After the candidates are presented, the entire Litany of the Saints is chanted "with all standing," says rubric 41, "because it is Easter Time." The priest then blesses the water using a shorter prayer with extensive revisions.[68] The preface dialogue has been removed, as have all the symbolic gestures except insertion of the paschal candle into the water, which is optional. An innovation is an acclamation by the people after the blessing: "Springs of water, bless the Lord; / praise and exalt him above all forever," from the canticle of the three young men in the fiery furnace (Dan 3:77). Oils are no longer mixed with the water.

Using formulas in the Roman Ritual, the candidates then "make the required renunciation"[69] and profession of faith, are baptized,[70] receive the baptismal garment,[71] and are given a candle lighted from the paschal candle.[72] Finally, rubric 53 of the 2011 translation adds that "if adults have been baptized, the Bishop or, in his absence, the Priest who has conferred Baptism, should at once administer the Sacrament of Confirmation to them in the sanctuary." Paul Turner, an authority on confirmation, states that "this information is all new to the third edition of the Missal."[73] Rubric 44 in the 1985 translation said that

---

[68] On the differences between the postconciliar version of this blessing and that found in previous sources, see Dominic Serra, "The Blessing of Baptismal Water at the Paschal Vigil: Ancient Texts and Modern Revisions," *Worship* 64 (1990) 142–56.

[69] This is the expression in no. 48 of the 2011 translation. The 1985 translation, no. 44, said the candidates "renounce the devil." RCIA, no 224, calls the gesture "renunciation of sin."

[70] In RCIA, no. 226, immersion is option A, and the pouring of water is option B.

[71] This is the expression of RCIA, no. 229, which says that "the garment may be white or of a color that conforms to local custom." Rubric 51 of the 2011 translation declares that "a white garment is given to each."

[72] The third edition, nos. 48–51, explains all this in far greater detail than the one paragraph, no. 44, in the first two editions, showing how much more prominent the initiation rites have become at the vigil.

[73] Turner, *Glory*, 154. It would be wise to study carefully all that he says about the third part of the vigil on pp. 145–60.

"adults are confirmed immediately after baptism if a bishop or priest with the faculty to confirm is present." The Missal does not mention the possibility of deferring confirmation, as does the RCIA.[74]

After the rites of baptism and confirmation are completed, the faithful renew their baptismal promises—the practice introduced in 1956—and are sprinkled with blessed water.[75] An innovation in the Missal of Paul VI is that during the sprinkling the faithful sing *Vidi aquam*, translated in no. 56 as

> I saw water flowing from the Temple,
> from its right-hand side, alleluia;
> and all to whom this water came were saved
> and shall say: Alleluia, alleluia.

Or they may sing "another chant that is baptismal in character," says no. 56. When introducing the renewal of baptismal promises, the priest continues to say in no. 55 what he did in OHS, "[n]ow that our Lenten observance is concluded. . . ." This gives the impression that Lent has just ended, as was the case at the time of Pius XII. In fact, Lent now ends with the evening Mass on Holy Thursday. Since these words risk perpetuating the misconception that Lent ends at some point during the vigil, it would be better to rephrase or omit them, as is permitted by the last sentence of rubric 55.

The third part of the vigil concludes with the neophytes being led to their places among the faithful and the priest, at the chair, directing the universal prayer in which the newly baptized participate for the first time. "If the blessing of baptismal water has not taken place in the baptistery," rubric 57 directs that "the Deacon and the ministers reverently carry the vessel of water to the font." But the *Sicut cervus* is not chanted, nor is its accompanying oration said. Fortunately, this lovely text has not disappeared from the vigil. It is the responsorial psalm after the seventh reading, Ezekiel 36:16-17a, 18-28, in which the Lord promises to sprinkle clean water upon his people and give them a new heart. The refrain is Psalm 41:2, translated in *The Revised Grail Psalms* as:

---

[74] RCIA, nos. 14, 24, 228, 230.

[75] If there were no baptisms and the font was not blessed, the priest blesses water using the formula provided in no. 54, which is different from that used to bless baptismal water.

Like the deer that yearns
for running streams,
so my soul is yearning
for you, my God.[76]

D. FOURTH PART: THE LITURGY OF THE EUCHARIST

In the restored *Ordo* of Pius XII the sprinkling of the congregation
with blessed water after the renewal of baptismal promises concludes
the vigil and, as close as possible to midnight, opens onto the Mass,
which begins with the *Kyrie* and Gloria and continues as usual with
the epistle and gospel. After that comes the offertory, though on
this night the offertory chant is omitted, as is the *Agnus Dei* and kiss
of peace. A shortened form of Easter Sunday Lauds, now Morning
Prayer, is chanted after Communion, and two alleluias are added to
the usual dismissal, *Ite, missa est*, and its response, *Deo gratias*. The
Missal of Paul VI, be it said once again, combines the Gloria, epistle,
and gospel with the Old Testament readings in a single unit, the Liturgy of the Word. This is followed by the baptismal liturgy. The fourth
part of the vigil, then, the eucharistic liturgy, begins with the preparation of the gifts. It makes a few changes after the Our Father. It restores
the sign of peace and *Agnus Dei*; replaces Lauds with the communion
antiphon from the day Mass, "Christ our Passover has been sacrificed"
(1 Cor 5:7-8);[77] includes a solemn blessing, though the final blessing
from the baptismal liturgy may also be used; and provides a choice
between two dismissal formulas.

The secret and post-Communion as well as the preface, proper *communicantes*, and *Hanc igitur* of the 1956 OHS are the same as those
in the Tridentine Missal and come from the Sacramentary of Pope

---

[76] *The Revised Grail Psalms*, prepared by the monks of Conception Abbey in
Missouri (Chicago: GIA Publications, Inc., 2010). In the Lectionary a note after
the psalm says that when baptism is celebrated the responsorial psalm following the fifth reading is used, or else Ps 50.

[77] This is the communion antiphon printed in the first typical edition of the
postconciliar Missal in 1970. The 1988 circular letter, no. 91, suggests an alternative: "It is appropriate that at Communion there be sung Psalm 117 with the
antiphon '*Pascha nostrum*,' or Psalm 33 with the antiphon 'Alleluia, Alleluia,
Alleluia,' or some other song of Easter exultation." The triple alleluia was part
of Lauds, which the Missal eliminated. Singing it with Ps 33 has never been
incorporated into the Missal of Paul VI, but the third typical edition says that
with the antiphon from 1 Cor 5:7-8 "Psalm 117 may appropriately be sung."

Hadrian (H 378–82). Of these only the post-Communion is missing from the Mass in the Old Gelasian. The others are GeV 455, 458, 459, and 460. The Missal of Paul VI keeps all these prayers.[78] Taken together with the collect, then, the Mass formulary is extraordinarily stable. In the latest translation the prayer over the offerings asks that "what has begun in the paschal mysteries" may bring us to "the healing of eternity." Dom Bernard Botte interprets this as referring to the sacrifice of Christ made present in the eucharistic celebration.[79] The prayer after Communion also looks to the Eucharist, praying that "this paschal Sacrament" make those nourished by it "one in mind and heart." The proper *Hanc igitur* of the Roman Canon prays for those whom God willed "to give new birth by water and the Holy Spirit, / granting them forgiveness of all their sins."

Already in 1970 the first typical edition of the Missal of Paul VI declared in rubric 51 that at the preparation of the gifts "it is fitting that the bread and wine be brought forward by the newly baptized." To this the third typical edition adds in rubric 60 that "if they are children," the gifts are brought forward "by their parents or godparents." The latest edition of the Missal also adds three other rubrics that were not in the first two editions. None of these rubrics are new. They are lifted from the Rite of Christian Initiation of Adults, nos. 241–43. Including them in the fourth part of the Paschal Vigil, however, highlights the uniqueness of this Eucharist and its postbaptismal character. Rubric 63 specifies that "a commemoration is made of the baptized and their godparents" in all eucharistic prayers in a way proper to each prayer. Rubric 64 states that before the invitation to Communion "the Priest may briefly address the newly baptized about receiving their first Communion and about the excellence of this great mystery, which is the climax of Initiation and the center of the entire Christian life." Finally, rubric 65 encourages Communion under both kinds, going so far as to list all who should so receive: "It is desirable that the newly baptized receive Holy Communion under both kinds, together with their godfathers, godmothers, and Catholic parents and spouses, as well as their lay catechists. It is even appropriate that, with the

[78] For their sources, see Anthony Ward, SM, "The Easter Mass Formularies for the Vigil Mass and the Mass 'in die' in the 2002 'Missale Romanum,'" EL 124 (2010) 90–128.

[79] "Paschalibus initiata mysteriis," EL 61 (1947) 77–87.

consent of the Diocesan Bishop, where the occasion suggests this, all the faithful be admitted to Holy Communion under both kinds."

In many ways these directives are the climax of the restoration of the sacramental dimension of the vigil begun in 1951 when Pius XII inserted renewal of baptismal promises by the congregation after the blessing of water. Baptism became much more prominent in 1970 when the first edition of the Missal of Paul VI made it the third part of the vigil. At that time conferral of the sacrament was only a possibility. Significantly, the first rubric of this section, no. 37, declared, "If there are candidates to be baptized, they are called forward." There was still nothing in the Missal about the First Communion of the newly baptized. In the third typical edition of 2002 conferral of baptism is not a mere possibility. It is expected. Rubric 37 now declares, "After the Homily the Baptismal Liturgy begins."

These changes make clear that the vigil is not a mere commemoration of the resurrection of Jesus but the sacramental actualization of the entire paschal mystery, the Lord's passion as well as his passage, in the church. The vigil is primarily about Christian initiation. The addition of rubrics 63, 64, and 65 in the 2002 Missal, however, emphasizes that initiation does not culminate in baptism or even confirmation but in Holy Communion; that the Eucharist, too, is a sacrament of initiation; and that at the Paschal Vigil not only are the elect baptized and confirmed, but the newly baptized and newly confirmed also join the rest of the faithful at the Eucharist for the first time and with them commune in the Body and Blood of Christ. This, then, is one of the most amazing aspects of the third typical edition of the Missal of Paul VI, the ordinary form of the Roman Rite. The extraordinary form goes no further than the 1956 *Ordo* of Pius XII. Having reached the end of this lengthy comparison, we can at last offer a theological interpretation of the postconciliar vigil.

3. Theological Interpretation

Preliminaries. All three editions of the Missal of Paul VI place the nocturnal vigil under the general title of *Dominica Paschae in Resurrectione Domini,* "Easter Sunday of the Resurrection of the Lord." From the viewpoint of liturgical time, then, the vigil is no longer part of Holy Saturday as it was when Pope Pius XII restored it in 1951. It now belongs to Easter Sunday, the day that the Missal immediately qualifies as "The Resurrection of the Lord," thus making

Easter and the resurrection of the Lord synonymous. The vigil, of course, does celebrate the Lord's resurrection. But it celebrates vastly more than that. It also celebrates his passion and, most of all, our communion in both, beginning at baptism and continuing at every Eucharist.[80] Since its restoration in 1951, the vigil has commonly been called the Easter Vigil and is still called that in the 2011 translation of the third typical edition of the Roman Missal. But because of the identification of Easter with the Lord's resurrection, this expresses only half of what is celebrated on this night. The Latin name for the service is *Vigilia Paschalis*, "Paschal Vigil." This term is much more satisfactory for our purposes because it indicates that the vigil, like the other days of the Triduum, celebrates both aspects of *Pascha*, *passio* and *transitus*, the Lord's life-giving passion as well as his passage from humiliation to glory.[81] We now want to reflect on the four parts of the vigil to see how in the liturgical action of each of them Christ renders himself present in such a way as to make the assembled faithful participants in his passion as well as in his passage, thereby completing in them the plan of salvation, bringing history to eschatological plenitude, and accomplishing the purpose for which the world was created.

A. FIRST PART: THE SOLEMN BEGINNING OR LUCERNARIUM

The first part of the vigil consists of the preparation and lighting of the paschal candle from new fire outside the church, the procession into church, and, after all have reassembled, the chanting of the *Exsultet*. The vigil must begin after nightfall and end before daybreak (no. 6). It is a watch through the night—because, as the introduction to the service points out (no. 1), the first Passover occurred during the night (Exod 12:42) and also because the Lord instructed his followers to await his coming "with lamps burning" (Luke 12:35-37).

---

[80] See my "Paschal Vigil: Passion and Passage," *Worship* 79 (2005) 98–130.

[81] *Vigilia Paschalis* was translated "Paschal Vigil" in the texts submitted to the Vatican by English-speaking conferences of bishops. An official in the Congregation for Divine Worship, assisted by a small group of collaborators, changed it to "Easter Vigil" in both the Universal Norms and the Missal, together with hundreds of other alterations. One sentence in the Universal Norms, however, eluded them. It is no. 28, which states that "from the beginning of Lent until the Paschal Vigil, the *Alleluia* is not said." See also chap. 4, p. 114, n. 20 above.

The vigil, then, has an anamnetic and an epicletic dimension. While calling past events to mind, it prays that future ones come to pass. In it the dawn of creation and the dawn of creation's consummation meet. Genesis and Parousia intersect in the enduring Now of the paschal Christ.

The burning candle, as candle, already evokes sacrifice, for it gives light by consuming itself. The inscription and five wax nails, together with the *Exsultet*, historicize its meaning, transforming it into a *paschal* candle and enabling its light to become the light of *Christ*.

After the fire is blessed the priest, with a stylus, inscribes upon the candle a cross, the first and last letters of the Greek alphabet, and the current year, saying,

> Christ yesterday and today
> the Beginning and the End
> the Alpha
> and the Omega
> All time belongs to him
> and all the ages. (no. 11)

The inscription reflects *pascha* as *transitus*. In the book of Revelation, Alpha and Omega, the Beginning and the End, the First and the Last, are all titles of the one seated on the throne (Rev 1:4, 17; 21:6; 22:13), "the one who is and who was and who is to come (Rev 1:4, 8; 4:8; 11:17; 16:5). Amplifications of the divine name "I Am," revealed to Moses in the burning bush (Exod 3:4), these express the eternity, omnipotence, and uniqueness of "the Almighty" (Rev 1:8). Applied to Christ, they emphasize that he, having arrived at the goal of his passage, shares the universal dominion of the *Pantocrator*. The tracing of the current year upon the surface of the candle inserts our fleeting moment of history into the ever-enduring actuality of him who "is the same yesterday and today and forever" (Heb 13:8) and so consecrates it.

The priest then fixes to the candle five wax nails in the form of a cross, praying,

> By his holy
> and glorious wounds,
> may Christ the Lord
> guard us
> and protect us." (no. 12)

This recalls *pascha* as *passio*. With these ornaments the paschal candle is made an image of the Jesus who on the evening of the first day of the week and eight days later stood among his disciples and "showed them his hands and his side" (John 20:20). Even as the heavenly Lamb in his immolation *stands* (Rev 5:6), so the Living One (Luke 24:5; Rev 1:18) in his death *lives*. The pierced side never closes. The wounds never heal. They are the signs by which Christ, glorified on the cross, henceforth identifies himself—the proof that in his emptiness he is filled with all power in heaven and on earth (Matt 28:18), that in his self-abasement he is highly exalted (Phil 2:9), and that precisely through his passion he passes from this world to the Father (John 13:1).

The culminating point of these introductory rites is the lighting of the candle from the new fire. When doing so, the priest says, "May the light of Christ rising in glory / dispel the darkness of our hearts and minds" (no. 14). The lighting of the candle is, in fact, a symbolic enactment of this very rising. Yet the one "rising in glory" continues to display his wounds, also "glorious," *vulnera gloriosa*. The preparation and lighting of the candle is followed by the procession into church during which the candle is lifted up three times and acclaimed "The Light of Christ," to which all respond, "Thanks be to God." Meanwhile, all light their candles from the paschal candle and so commune in its light. It is important to note here the symbolic value not only of the candle as an object seen but of its *light*, and especially the sharing of its light.

Christ as light is a major theme in the Gospel of John. Having already been designated by the prologue as "the true light" (John 1:9), Jesus proclaims himself to be "the light of the world" in 8:12 and 9:5. As the Jewish Passover draws nigh (John 11:55), and with it the hour of his passion and passage, Jesus declares, "The light will be with you only a little longer now" (John 12:35; JB). At the Last Supper as soon as the betrayer had taken the morsel of bread, "Satan entered into him" (John 13:27), and he left the room. John adds, "And it was night" (John 13:30). Consequently, the newly kindled light symbolized by the paschal candle, the light of Christ "rising in glory," has eschatological significance. It is light dawning from beyond the world, from beyond death. It is uncreated light and hence unending. Most of all, it is light shining in darkness (John 1:5), darkness that cannot overcome it but that, as the mystics know well, the light does not eliminate.

Just as the resurrection of the Crucified does not close his open side or heal his hands and feet, neither does the light destroy the darkness in which it shines; rather, it allows itself to be seen precisely therein, thus making the darkness itself luminous even as the passage makes the passion glorious. This, then, is the light kindled, acclaimed, and shared at the vigil. In the procession this is the light we "follow" (John 8:12) and in which we "walk" (John 12:35). This is the light that will enlighten those to be baptized and make them "children of light" (John 12:36).

The procession from outside to inside, from natural to humanly constructed space, is an enacted anamnesis of the passage from chaos to cosmos "in the beginning" (Gen 1:1) and of Israel's historical passage out of Egypt through the sea—biblical episodes soon to be narrated. But it raises each one, creation and history, to a higher level, the level of their eschatological fulfillment, for the light leading this procession is neither that of sun or moon or stars nor that of a column of fire (Exod 13:21; 14:19, 24) but the light of one gloriously rising out of death and "coming into the world" (John 1:9) as the goal of creation and the destiny of history, even while being their source, as the inscription on the candle attests.

The lighting of the candle coupled with the ensuing procession and the lighting of the candles of the congregation are the Parousia in the church of the person of Christ in the act of his Pasch, enabling those who await him to commune in the death that is his life and there discover the ultimate meaning of their existence on earth and journey through time. By recalling past passages and giving expression to others currently in process—the initiatory passage of those about to be baptized, the penitential passage of sinners to pardon, and the continual passage of each believer out of self into deeper communion with others—the procession ecclesially actualizes the ever-actual passage of Christ. Once set upon the candlestick prepared for it at the ambo or in the middle of the sanctuary, the paschal candle stands as a radiant axis defining the center of the symbolic universe progressively taking shape during the vigil.

The deacon then chants the *Exsultet*, known as the *Praeconium paschale*, or Paschal proclamation (nos. 18–19). After calling upon the heavenly choirs, the earth, and Mother Church to join together in singing the praise of the candle, *cerei laudem*, the deacon embarks on a long anamnetic section recounting the marvelous deeds God accomplished at night, introducing each one with the expression *Haec nox est*, "This is the night." It begins with Passover and the exodus from Egypt—the two foundational events for the Christian understanding of *pascha*.

These, however, are but prefigurations of an even greater Pasch "in which is slain the Lamb, the one true Lamb, / whose Blood anoints the doorposts of believers." The Pasch accomplished by the triumphant passion and passage of Christ continues to be accomplished in the sacraments of the church. "This is the night," exclaims the deacon,

> when once you led our forebears, Israel's children,
> from slavery in Egypt
> and made them pass dry-shod through the Red Sea. . . .

> This is the night
> that even now, throughout the world,
> sets Christian believers apart from worldly vices
> and from the gloom of sin,
> leading them to grace
> and joining them to his holy ones.

> This is the night,
> when Christ broke the prison-bars of death
> and rose victorious from the underworld.

This, then, is a "truly blessed night," a *vere beata nox*.

The *Exsultet* concludes with a petition:

> Therefore, O Lord,
> we pray you that this candle,
> hallowed to the honor of your name,
> may persevere undimmed. . . .

> May this flame be found still burning
> by the Morning Star:
> the one Morning Star who never sets,
> Christ your Son,
> who, coming back from death's domain,
> has shed his peaceful light on humanity.

This majestic supplication—which functions as the epicletic counterpart to the foregoing anamnesis, but without mentioning the Holy Spirit—asks in effect that the marvelous reality coming into existence during this night endure and expand until the day dawns when he who now makes himself present in sign appears in person.

The body of faithful, now gathered together inside the church and communing in the light of Christ, is ready to listen to the Word of God, which will lift them to another level.

Introducing this part of the vigil, the priest first exhorts the faithful to "meditate on how God in times past saved his people / and in these, the last days, has sent his Son as our Redeemer." Then he urges them to pray "that our God may complete this paschal work of salvation / by the fullness of redemption" (no. 22). The Liturgy of the Word, then, has an anamnetic and epicletic structure. The readings recall the saving work of God. The prayers ask that it be brought to completion. As will soon become evident, this completing of the work of salvation occurs sacramentally in baptism and Eucharist.

The word "complete," which translates the Latin *perficiat*, is key. It means that the Redeemer's "paschal work of salvation" is not yet finished. This "paschal work," the priest says, belongs to "the last days" (Heb 1:2), to the eschatological era, and so is ever actual. What is prayed for is that this ever-actual paschal work of Christ be actualized in *us*, in the church, and thereby attain perfection, for it was unto this that the work was undertaken. The liturgical event does not merely apply the fruits of a saving event already completed in another time and place. Rather, the liturgical actualization is an essential dimension of the saving event itself and in fact is its perfection. In other words, in the liturgical act the Redeemer makes full his redemptive act.

Of the seven Old Testament readings provided in the Lectionary the first three are the richest: the creation of the world (Gen 1:1–2:2), the sacrifice of Isaac (Gen 22:1-18), and the passage through the sea (Exod 14:15–15:1)—the third having already been mentioned in the *Exsultet*. The sacrifice of Isaac prefigures that of Christ and reflects *pascha* as *passio*. Genesis 22:12 and 16 refer to Isaac as "your son, your only son," to which 22:2 adds "whom you love." Jesus is similarly designated by the Father at his baptism and transfiguration. Abraham and Isaac walk for three days, the amount of time that Jesus spends "in the heart of the earth" (Matt 12:40) before being raised "on the third day" (Luke 24:7, 46; Acts 10:10; 1 Cor 15:4) as he had prophesied three times (Matt 16:21; 17:23; 20:19; 27:64). On the way to Mount Moriah Isaac carries on his shoulders the wood to which he will be bound (Gen 22:6), as Jesus carries the wood of his cross to the hill of Calvary (John 19:17). In the end, though, Isaac, offered up in obedience to the divine will, is delivered from death by the same God who decreed it. In his oblation Isaac, like Jesus, *lives*. Being set free, he anticipates in the patriarchal period what will later transpire in Egypt when all the firstborn of Israel are spared by the slaughter of a lamb that "God himself will provide" (Gen 22:8). At the end of the reading God repeats his promise that the descendants of Abraham will be "as numerous as the stars of heaven and as the sand on the seashore (Gen 22:17). The prayer after the reading sees this fulfilled in the *paschale sacramentum*, meaning baptism, in which God multiplies the children of the promise "by pouring out the grace of adoption / throughout the whole world," thereby making Abraham to be the "father of nations."

The first and third readings—the creation account in Genesis 1:1–2:2 and the crossing of the sea in Exodus 14:15–15:1—despite obvious differences, have much in common. The author of Genesis 1 depicts God's creative activity as a series of divisions, separations, and passages—light from darkness (1:4), waters above from waters below (1:7), dry land from sea (1:10), day from night (1:14), birds from fish (1:21), and cattle from reptiles (1:24). Then he makes human beings in his own image (1:26), set above all other creatures. His work complete, he rests on the seventh day and hallows it as the day of rest set apart from the other six. And since to sanctify something means to set it apart, we see that God by the very way in which he creates the world likewise sanctifies it.

All these transitions from evening to morning, from one day to the next, from work to rest already anticipate the momentous divisions, separations, and passages to be recounted in the exodus from Egypt. The parting of the sea in Exodus 14:16, 22 is reminiscent of the dividing of the waters in Genesis 1:17. The emergence of dry land between the walls of water in Exodus 14:21-22, 29 recalls Genesis 1:10. The passage from night in Exodus 14:20 to day in Exodus 14:24 echoes the refrain "and there was evening and there was morning" in Genesis 1:5, 8, 13, 19, 23, 31. In the passage from night to morning in Exodus 14, Israel passes through the sea, those who put their faith in the Lord are set apart from the stubborn of heart who oppose him, and the living are separated from the dead (Exod 14:30).

Through these similarities between the work of creation and the work of salvation the sacred writers are telling us that creation is oriented toward salvation and that salvation is the crowning of creation. But there is something more. All the passages described in these stories are surpassed by the passage of Christ, not a passage from one thing to another or from one place on earth to another but an eschatological one—a passage from this world to the Father. This passage of Christ, therefore, is the definitive accomplishment of what all the others pointed to: rest in the presence of the Holy One who, though totally set apart from creation, totally gives himself to it throughout salvation history in order to separate it from sin, sanctify it, and unite it to himself. This is the ever-actual passion and passage that attain perfection in being sacramentally actualized in the church so that we, while still living in creation and history, might already commune with their origin and goal and so become perfect ourselves—or at least make progress toward it.

The prayer after Genesis 1 invites us to realize that redemption is an even more marvelous work of God than is creation, and it ends by citing 1 Corinthians 5:7, the earliest reference to our *Pascha* being the crucified Christ. It reads,

> Almighty ever-living God,
> who are wonderful in the ordering of all your works,
> may those you have redeemed understand
> that there exists nothing more marvelous
> than the world's creation in the beginning
> except that, at the end of the ages,
> Christ our Passover has been sacrificed.

Mention here of "beginning" and "end" recalls the inscription on the paschal candle. The alternate prayer following the reading from Exodus states that the Red Sea prefigures the sacred font and asks that all nations "may be reborn by partaking of your Spirit." The next four readings are from the Prophets, and practically all the orations following them make mention of baptism, though not necessarily using that term.

Before Vatican II the epistle was Colossians 3:1-4. It emphasized *pascha* as *transitus*: "If you have been raised with Christ, seek the things that are above." The postconciliar Lectionary changes it to Romans 6:3-11, which conveys quite a different message, one more in keeping with *pascha* as *passio*. "Do you not know," Paul asks, "that all of us who have been baptized into Christ Jesus were baptized into his death?" He continues, "If we have been united with him in a death like his, we will certainly be united with him in a resurrection like his" (Rom 6:5). But not yet. Here, the resurrection is still in the future. At present all we do is "walk in newness of life" (Rom 6:4). With the homily after the gospel the second part of the vigil comes to an end. It consists of anamnesis and epiclesis. Through carefully chosen readings from the Word of God it makes memory of the great events of salvation history, prefigured in creation and definitively realized in the passion and passage of Christ. After each one it asks God to bring his plan of salvation to perfection in the gathered assembly and particularly in those about to be baptized.

C. THIRD PART: BAPTISMAL LITURGY

All that the community has been praying for in the second part of the vigil begins to be realized in this part. Here, the rites of Christian initiation and those of the vigil intersect. The collect after the Gloria begged God to "stir up in your Church a spirit of adoption." Before blessing the font the priest makes much the same entreaty, "Send forth the spirit of adoption," *spiritum adoptionis emitte* (no. 43), but this time it is on behalf of those about to be baptized. The verb "to send forth" is probably from Psalm 103:30, which in *The Revised Grail Psalms* reads, "You send forth your spirit, and they are created, / and you renew the face of the earth." Here, however, God is being asked to send forth something more specific: "the spirit of adoption," a phrase lifted from Romans 8:15 where it is counterposed to "the spirit of slavery." Paul writes, "All who are led by the Spirit of God are children of God. For you did not receive a spirit of slavery to fall back into fear, but you received a spirit of adoption." Similar ideas are expressed in Galatians 4:4-7. Now for the apostle the Spirit is the generative principle of the Father by which he raised Jesus from the dead and revealed him as Son. This petition at the start of the baptismal liturgy is beseeching the Father to send the same life-giving Spirit upon the candidates for baptism in order to make them his adopted children in Christ. The history of salvation is about to be perfected in the sacramental actualization of the ever-actual Pasch of Christ.

The prayer for blessing the baptismal water (nos. 44 and 46) consists of an anamnetic section and an epicletic section. The anamnetic section is a lengthy invocation, repeating the word *Deus*, "God," five times, each followed by a relative clause describing how at creation and throughout history God uses water to bring about salvation. This leads to three petitions in the epicletic section entreating God by the power of the Holy Spirit to bring to completion in this sacramental moment the eschatological fulfillment of all his work in creation and history just recalled.

The prayer begins with the affirmation that through sacramental signs the invisible power of God accomplishes "a wondrous effect." This reflects the classic definition of a sacrament as an efficacious sign or sign of grace. As signs, sacraments make use of sensible elements—things that can be seen and touched—to express and establish spiritual realities beyond the realm of sense. In baptism the sensible element is water. The second line of the blessing makes an astounding declaration. It says that God in many ways prepared water, his creature, "to show forth the grace of Baptism."

The anamnetic section of the blessing recounts the ways in which God prepared water for this noble function. The first way is that, as was heard in the first reading, the Spirit of God hovered over the primeval waters *ut iam tunc virtutem sanctificandi aquarum natura conciperet*, "so that the very substance of water / would even then take to itself the power to sanctify." The prayer is telling us that in the major steps of salvation history God was not only preparing water to be the future sign of baptismal grace but had actually created it for this purpose, so that in bringing sinners to rebirth, water itself attains all that it was created to be. This is to say once again that creation is fulfilled in salvation and that salvation is perfected in the sacraments of the church. The prayer then relates how God made the flood a foreshadowing of regeneration and the passage through the sea a prefiguration of baptism; how Christ at his baptism in the waters of the Jordan was anointed with the Holy Spirit; how on the cross blood and water issued from his side; and how, once risen, he commanded his disciples to baptize all nations.

Having taken salvation history to its eschatological term in the passion and passage of Christ, anamnesis yields to the three petitions of the epicletic section. The first is short. It asks God to look upon the face of his church and "graciously unseal for her the fountain of Baptism." The second is longer. It asks that this water receive the grace of Christ from the Holy Spirit in order that human nature, created in the divine image (Gen 1:26-27), having been "washed clean through the Sacrament of Baptism / from all the squalor of the life of old," may "rise to the life of newborn children / through water and the Holy Spirit," an obvious reference to John 3:5. Through baptism, then, human beings become what they were created to be: images of God. The sacramental economy of the church brings to full realization what humans are destined to be in virtue of their creation.

At this point the paschal candle may be lowered into the font. Then comes the third petition, an explicit invocation of the Holy Spirit, made even more climactic by insertion of the word *quaesumus*, reminiscent of the "Therefore, O Lord, we pray" near the end of the *Exsultet*. The priest calls out, *Descendat, quaesumus, Domine, in hanc plenitudinem fontis per Filium tuum virtus Spiritus Sancti,* "May the power of the Holy Spirit, / O Lord, we pray, / come down through your Son / into the fullness of this font." The purpose of this entreaty, the prayer immediately adds, is that "all who have been buried with Christ / by Baptism into death [Rom 6:4] / may rise again to life with him." This is surprising because the anamnetic section made no reference to the Pauline theology of baptism in Romans 6:3-11, and, as we have seen, in that letter the resurrection of the baptized is a future hope, not a present reality.

Through the words of the blessing the water to be used for baptism, in addition to being a natural symbol, acquires historical significance through its use in the economy of salvation and eschatological significance by its connection with the Pasch of Christ, the event that completes salvation history and makes it eternally enduring. Most of all, through the *virtus Spiritus Sancti,* or "power of the Holy Spirit," invoked upon it, water becomes the divinely instituted instrument for the sacramental actualization in the church of the ever-actual Pasch of Christ. Through the *virtus Spiritus Sancti* invoked upon it, the water is made capable of doing what of itself it cannot do, contain and impart the Spirit, so that all who enter it are "born of water and spirit" (John 3:5) and so made adopted children of the Father. In sum, through the *virtus Spiritus Sancti* water becomes all that it was created to be but could never become of itself, those reborn in it are restored to the divine image in which they were created, the economy of creation reaches completion in salvation, and salvation is perfected in the sacramental act of the church.

After the elect have been baptized and confirmed, the rest of the assembly renews its baptismal faith and is sprinkled with the blessed water while singing *Vidi aquam* or another chant baptismal in character. The universal prayer brings the third part of the vigil to a close.

D. FOURTH PART: THE LITURGY OF THE EUCHARIST

Celebration of the Eucharist is the culmination of the vigil, of the Triduum, and of the long journey of Christian initiation. This one is very different in character from the Mass *in Cena Domini* not only because of the presence and Communion for the first time of the newly baptized but because it is preceded on Friday and ideally also on Saturday by the paschal fast recalling the departure of the bridegroom (Mark 2:19-20).[82] This makes the Eucharist toward which the fast is

---

[82] On the paschal fast, see above, p. 202, n. 58.

directed to be like a nuptial banquet served by the bridegroom himself to those awaiting his return[83] or like the postresurrection meals described in the New Testament (Luke 24:28-32; John 21:9-13; Acts 10:41)—in other words, a Parousia in sacramental form.[84]

The preface declares that the principal motive for giving thanks on this night is that *Pascha nostrum immolatus est Christus*, "Christ our Passover has been sacrificed"—words that return in the communion antiphon. This direct quote from 1 Corinthians 5:7, the New Testament foundation for *pascha* as *passio*, leaves no doubt that the Paschal Vigil celebrates not only the Lord's resurrection but also his passion. The preface continues by declaring that Christ "is the true Lamb / who has taken away the sins of the world." At the beginning of Jesus' ministry John the Baptist twice acclaims him as "the Lamb of God," the first time adding, "who takes away the sin of the world" (John 1:29, 35), thereby linking him not only with the Passover victim but also with the mysterious Suffering Servant whom Isaiah 53:7 depicts as "a lamb that is led to the slaughter. The image of the sacrificed lamb recurs in the First Letter of Peter but with the further specification of the expiatory value of its blood. "You were ransomed from the futile ways inherited from your ancestors not with perishable things like silver and gold, but with the precious blood of Christ, like that of a lamb without defect or blemish" (1 Pet 1:18-19).

The *Exsultet* likewise sings of Christ "the one true Lamb, / whose Blood anoints the doorposts of believers." This takes us back to the very origins of Passover. For countless generations before the time of Moses nomadic herdsmen on the night of the full moon following the spring equinox, before moving their flocks to new pastures, would sacrifice a year-old lamb or goat, then smear its blood on their tent posts to keep "the destroyer" (Exod 12:23) at bay and to reclaim their world from surrounding chaos. At the same time of year, agricultural

[83] After referring to "the gospel admonition" (Luke 12:35-37), no. 1 of the introduction to the vigil in the Missal portrays the faithful as "looking for the Lord when he returns, so that at his coming he may find them awake and have them sit at his table."

[84] On the relationship between postresurrection meals and the Last Supper in the development of the theology of the Eucharist, see Oscar Cullmann, "The Meaning of the Lord's Supper in Primitive Christianity," in Oscar Cullmann and F. J. Leenhardt, *Essays on the Lord's Supper*, Ecumenical Studies in Worship 1 (Richmond: John Knox Press, 1963, 4th printing) 5–23.

peoples would eat bread baked without yeast to protect their crops against corruption by noxious organisms. These rites were bound up with the reproductive cycle of animals and the growth cycle of plants. Their performance year after year was dictated by nature and required no positive command.

In Exodus 12:1-28 the diverse elements of these hitherto separate festivals are found fused into what is intended to be a single whole, though the two names, Passover and Unleavened Bread, reflect its composite character.[85] Details of the narrative need not be repeated here. Suffice it to note that now all the ritual prescriptions are attributed to the God who revealed his name to Moses (Exod 3:14) and together constitute a remembrance of how he chose Israel to be his own and to this end delivered her from the bondage of Egypt. From the raw materials of earlier nature feasts has emerged a historical one, the yearly repetition of which is meant to move the people ever closer to full attainment of the goal for which they were chosen and redeemed: covenant union with the Lord. Once made historical, however, the significance and purpose of the ritual enactment are no longer apparent from the actions themselves. They must be narrated, verbally transmitted from generation to generation. Hence Exodus 12:14 stipulates, "This day shall be a day of remembrance for you." Exodus 12:25-27 adds, "And when your children ask you, 'What do you mean by this observance?' You shall say, 'It is the passover sacrifice to the LORD, for he passed over the houses of the Israelites in Egypt, when he struck down the Egyptians but spared our houses.'"

Unlike John, who aligns Passover with the death of Jesus in order to portray him as the true paschal lamb, the Synoptics, especially Luke (Luke 22:14-15), align it with the Last Supper, thereby making it a Passover meal, the annual anamnesis of Israel's redemption in view of covenant union. Pope Benedict XVI writes that this meal "was a remembrance of the past, but at the same time a prophetic remembrance, the proclamation of a deliverance yet to come. . . . This is the context in which Jesus introduces the newness of his gift. In the prayer of praise, the *Berakah*, he does not simply thank the Father for the great events of past history, but also for his own 'exaltation.'" The pontiff continues, "In

---

[85] A lucid and fairly recent exposition of the origin and development of these two feasts is that of Baruch M. Bokser, "Unleavened Bread and Passover, Feasts of," in *Anchor Bible Dictionary*, ed. David Noel Freedman, 6 vols. (Doubleday: New York, 1992) 6, 755–65.

instituting the sacrament of the Eucharist, Jesus anticipates and makes present the sacrifice of the Cross and the victory of the resurrection. At the same time, he reveals that he himself is the *true* sacrificial lamb, destined in the Father's plan from the foundation of the world. . . . By placing his gift in this context, Jesus shows the salvific meaning of his death and resurrection, a mystery which renews history and the whole cosmos."[86] By identifying the broken bread and shared cup with himself in the act of handing himself over in sacrifice to inaugurate the new covenant, Jesus transforms the annual anamnesis of Israel's redemption into his own anamnesis—the eschatological fulfillment and ever-present actuality of what all past history and nature itself are destined for.

In the Eucharist of the Paschal Vigil, then, the baptized of every time and place "do" (1 Cor 11:24-25; Luke 22:19) the anamnesis of the Lord. In the power of the Holy Spirit—earlier called down upon the water of the font but now invoked upon the eucharistic elements and themselves—they commune in the Lord's Pasch at the always new and never-ending hour of its accomplishment. This is to say once again that salvation, ever actual in Christ, is perfected in its sacramental actualization in the church.

4. Conclusions

1. All four parts of the vigil celebrate one and the same reality, the Lord's Pasch understood as both his passion and his passage. But they do so through different signs and images, words and gestures. The mystery celebrated remains constant throughout the service. Only the manner of its symbolic expression changes.

2. The vigil does not develop in linear fashion, beginning at one point and ending at another. Rather, it consists of recurring cycles that keep turning on themselves. But the theme does not advance from one to the other. Only the forms of expression change, not the thematic content. In saying that the vigil celebrates the death and resurrection of Christ, then, care must be taken not to think that it begins with the death and ends with the resurrection and that at some point there is a transition from one to the other—like the Gloria in Pius XII's vigil.

3. Although there is no thematic development at the vigil, there is development of another kind. The images and symbols through which the one mystery is made present become more divine, dense, and

---

[86] Pope Benedict XVI, *Sacramentum Caritatis*, no. 10.

enduring as the service progresses. The lucernarium is entirely ecclesiastical, that is, human in origin. The biblical readings, on the other hand, are the Word of God. But as spoken words they are immaterial and pass away as soon as they are uttered. Baptism is a sacrament, divinely instituted, and the use of water makes it concrete and tangible. The Eucharist too is a sacrament. Unlike the water of baptism, however, which confers grace without being changed into Christ, the bread and wine become the Lord's Body and Blood and remain so even after the celebration has ended. Hence the Eucharist is the most substantial and enduring form of Christ's presence in the church. The other sacraments are ordered toward it, as is the entire Paschal Vigil.

4. In each part of the vigil there is also an upward progression in the levels of symbolism from natural to historical to eschatological. The words of orations and blessings accompanying the ritual actions disclose how elements of creation (light, water, oil, bread, and wine), already having symbolic value in the natural order, acquire new significance from how they are used in salvation history and finally attain the eschatological plenitude toward which they are destined by becoming signs or sacraments of the Lord's ever-actual Pasch actualized in the church. As the vigil moves forward, therefore, the Spirit is invoked with increased frequency and intensity to effect this transformation of nature and history into what they are meant to be—manifestations of divine glory humanly shared.

5. Each part of the vigil, then, is directed toward ecclesial participation in the Lord's Pasch. The paschal candle is lit so that from it the faithful may light their own candles and so share in the light of Christ gloriously rising. The Word of God is proclaimed, that its creative power may bind the listeners together in him who is its fulfillment. Water is blessed, that from it sinners may be born anew in the life-giving Spirit of the crucified Christ. Bread and wine are consecrated, that by them all present, while still in the world and still in time, may already commune in the wedding supper of the Lamb. In each part of the vigil, and becoming more profound and lasting as each part leads to the next, salvation is perfected and creation reaches its goal.

E. EASTER SUNDAY: MASS DURING THE DAY

1. The Roman Missal of 1962

Preliminaries. The 1956 reform of Pius XII was a reform of Holy Week. It did not include Easter Sunday. The Mass for this day in the

1962 Missal is exactly as it was in the Tridentine Missal of 1570. The orations, preface, *communicantes*, and *Hanc igitur* are from the *Hadrianum* (H 383–88). The two readings are from the oldest lectionaries. The chants are found in the six earliest manuscripts of the Roman Antiphonal, though the introit and communion are missing from one (AMS 80). The sequence, *Victimae paschali laudes*, is the work of Wipo of Burgundy, who died after 1046.[87]

In the ancient sacramentaries, lectionaries, and antiphonals the Mass of Easter Sunday follows immediately upon that of Holy Saturday. Not so in the preconciliar Roman Missal. In the 1570 *editio typica* and continuing through the 1962 edition, the Ordinary of the Mass, prefaces, and *Canon Missae* are inserted between the Mass of Holy Saturday and that of Easter Sunday, thereby producing a disjunction between Holy Week and Easter, the passion and the resurrection. Since before 1956 the service on Holy Saturday took place early that morning when only a handful of the faithful was present, the Mass on Sunday morning, attended by a multitude, was perceived to be and indeed *was* the Easter Mass.

Pasch as passage. The phrase *Dominica Resurrectionis*, "Sunday of the Resurrection," in the title above the Mass in the missals of both 1570 and 1962 suggests that recollection of the Lord's passion and death during the past week has given way to a triumphant celebration of his resurrection. Several texts in the formulary support this view. Chief among them is the gospel, Mark 16:1-7, in which a young man clothed in white announces to the women as they enter the sepulcher, "He is risen. He is not here." The proper *communicantes* of the Roman Canon declares that we are "keeping the most holy day of the resurrection of our Lord Jesus Christ."

The introit places phrases adapted from Psalm 138:18, 5-6 on the lips of Jesus: *Resurrexi et adhuc tecum sum*, "I arose and am still with thee." The offertory is probably thinking of the earthquake in Matthew's account of the resurrection (Matt 28:2) when it sings in the words of Psalm 75:9-10: "The earth trembled and was still when God arose in judgment." In the second half of the sequence Mary Magdalene declares that she beheld "the tomb of Christ who now liveth and likewise the glory of the Risen," adding, "Yea, Christ my hope is arisen," to which is heard the reply, "we know that Christ is risen, henceforth

---

[87] M. I. J. Rousseau, "Victimae Paschali Laudes," NCE 14, 645.

ever living." The collect is less direct. It asserts that God, through his Son, "conquered death and threw open to us the gate of everlasting life." But it does not disclose how or when and, unlike the collect of the vigil, makes no mention of the resurrection.

Pasch as passion. By way of contrast, the epistle, 1 Corinthians 5:7-8, is not at all about the resurrection of Christ but about his death, specifically its paschal value—"Christ our Pasch has been immolated"— bringing to perfection the redemption begun by the slaughter of the Passover lambs in Egypt. We recall that this text of Paul, together with the passion according to John, is the New Testament foundation for the Christian interpretation of *pascha* as *passio*. The declaration *Pascha nostrum immolatus est Christus* returns in the Alleluia verse, the preface, and the communion antiphon. The image of the Passover lamb fulfilled in the death of Christ also lies behind the first part of the *Victimae paschali laudes*: "Christians! To the paschal victim offer your thankful praises. The lamb the sheep redeemeth: Christ, who only is sinless, reconcileth sinners to the Father." All these passages link the Mass of Easter Sunday with the service on Good Friday. Despite its separation from the Holy Week liturgies in the liturgical books and the impression given by its title, this Mass is as much about the Lord's passion as it is about his resurrection.

It was already pointed out that the collect makes no mention of the resurrection. Nor do the other two sacerdotal orations. The secret declares that "our eternal healing," reserved for the eschatological future, derives from "what has been begun by the paschal mysteries," which Dom Botte interprets as being the sacrifice of Christ, the true paschal lamb.[88] The post-Communion affirms that God satisfies the hunger of his people "with the sacraments of Easter."[89]

The texts for the Mass of Easter Sunday in MR 1962, then, display a remarkable balance between the two meanings of *pascha*—*transitus* and *passio*—a balance that is unexpected in light of the title *Dominica Resurrectionis*. This title, however, is not ancient. Headings for Masses on this day in the earliest sacramentaries are not narrowly focused on

---

[88] "Paschalibus initiata mysteriis," EL 61 (1947) 87.

[89] In this prayer the phrase *paschalibus sacramentis* is translated "sacraments of Easter" in the Baronius translation of RM 1962 but "paschal mysteries" in the 2011 translation of the same prayer at the vigil.

the resurrection. The Old Gelasian has *Dominicum paschae*; the *Hadrianum, Dominica sancta.*[90]

2. *The Roman Missal of Paul VI*

The 1969 Universal Norms on the Liturgical Year and the Calendar, no. 19, makes Sunday of the Resurrection the third day of the paschal Triduum, thereby connecting it to the two previous days to form a three-day unit celebrating the Lord's Pasch in the double sense of his blessed passion as well as his glorious passage from death to life. In 1970 the first typical edition of the Missal of Paul VI placed the vigil during the night and the Mass during the day under a common title, the first half of which is from the Old Gelasian, *Dominica paschae in resurrectione Domini*, "Easter Sunday of the Resurrection of the Lord." Since then, the Paschal Vigil has been considered as taking place no longer on Holy Saturday but on Easter Sunday. Consequently, the Mass that was formerly called the Mass of Easter Sunday is now the second of two Easter Masses, the first celebrated as part of the vigil, or *in vigilia*, and the second later in the day, or *in die.*

Prayers. The postconciliar Missal replaces the collect of its predecessor with that of the Easter Sunday Mass in the Old Gelasian (GeV 463).[91] In Latin the first part of the prayer is the same as the one in MR 1962 taken from H 383. In the 2011 translation it prays,

> O God, who on this day,
> through your Only Begotten Son,
> have conquered death
> and unlocked for us the path to eternity. . .

The second half, however, is different. Instead of asking God to "give effect to our desires," it prays that

> we who keep
> the solemnity of the Lord's Resurrection
> may, through the renewal brought by your Spirit,
> rise up in the light of life.

---

[90] See Bruylants I, no. 90.

[91] For the sources of the prayers of this Mass, see Anthony Ward, SM, "The Easter Mass Formularies for the Vigil Mass and the Mass 'in die' in the 2000 'Missale Romanum,'" EL 124 (2010) 90–128.

Explicit mention of the action of the Spirit on what is said to be "the solemnity of the Lord's Resurrection" is welcome.

Since the secret and post-Communion of the Easter Sunday Mass in RM 1962 are the same as those of the Paschal Vigil, the Missal of Paul VI replaces them with other prayers. As a new prayer over the gifts the reformers chose the secret of Easter Wednesday in the 1962 Missal, which comes from H 409. Anticipating the doctrine of *Ecclesia de Eucharistia* by many centuries, it affirms that by offering the eucharistic sacrifice the church "is wondrously reborn and nourished."[92] The new prayer after Communion, from the Sacramentary of Bergamo, no. 564, also makes explicit mention of the church. "Look upon your Church, O God," it asks, "with unfailing love and favor, / so that, renewed by the paschal mysteries, / she may come to the glory of the resurrection." Here, the resurrection is presented as the eschatological destiny of the church. The sacraments—here called "paschal mysteries"—are the means that enable the pilgrim church to reach its heavenly goal and indeed to commune in it already on earth.

Readings. The Lectionary assigns Acts 10:34a, 37-43 as the first reading, a most appropriate selection for the third day of the Triduum because in it Peter explains that Christ was put to death by being hung on a tree but that "God raised him on the third day." This primitive discourse is of capital importance because it affirms that Jesus did not bring himself back to life but was raised from the dead by God, that is, the Father. Here we are at the heart of the trinitarian dimension of the resurrection. Under the heading of "The Resurrection—A Work of the Holy Trinity," the *Catechism of the Catholic Church*, no. 648, explains: "The Father's power 'raised up' Christ his Son and by doing so perfectly introduced his Son's humanity, including his body, into the Trinity. Jesus is conclusively revealed as 'Son of God in power according to the Spirit of holiness by his resurrection from the dead.' St. Paul insists on the manifestation of God's power through the working of the Spirit who gave life to Jesus' dead humanity and called it to the glorious state of Lordship." The reading from Acts also declares that the way in which the disciples came to know the reality of Christ's resurrection

---

[92] The Latin has *renascitur et nutritur*. This is how the prayer reads in GeV 470. The text in H 409, however, is *nascitur et nutritur*, "born and nourished," not "reborn and nourished." In MR 1962 it is *pascitur et nutritur*, "fed and nourished."

is that they "ate and drank with him after he rose from the dead." The eucharistic implications of this statement are enormous.[93]

The second reading for the Mass of Easter Day is Colossians 3:1-4, formerly used at the vigil but replaced by Romans 6:3-11. Unlike the passage from Romans, this one makes no mention of baptism or of Christ's death and burial. The focus is on Christ "seated at the right hand of God" and on the Christian as having been "raised with Christ," seeking "the things that are above" and destined "to be revealed with him in glory." The epistle from the Easter Sunday Mass in RM 1962, 1 Corinthians 5:7-8, is retained as an optional second reading.

Having shifted Mark 16:1-7, formerly read on Easter Sunday, to the Paschal Vigil in Year B, the postconciliar Lectionary has to find another gospel for the Mass *in die Paschae*.

It chooses John 20:1-9, the report of Mary Magdalene about the Lord's body being missing from the place where it had been buried, followed by the race of Simon Peter and the Beloved Disciple to the tomb.[94] It is important to notice that in this passage, unlike the gospels at the vigil, there is no celestial figure in the sepulcher announcing, "He is risen." After the homily, renewal of baptismal promises may take place, as at the vigil. In this case the Creed is omitted.

Chants. The Missal of Paul VI keeps *Resurrexi et adhuc tecum sum*, "I have risen and I am with you still," from Psalm 138:18, 5-6 as the entrance antiphon but adds an alternative consisting of the declaration in Luke 24:34, "The Lord has truly risen," with a doxology from Revelation 1:6, "To him be glory and power for all the ages of eternity." The gospel acclamation and communion antiphon remain *Pascha nostrum immolatus est Christus* from 1 Corinthians 5:7-8. The sequence, *Victimae paschali laudes*, is sung after the second reading.

Without 1 Corinthians 5:7-8 as a second reading, references to *pascha* as *passio* are limited to the Alleluia verse, communion antiphon, the first part of the sequence, and, of course, the preface. The traditional

---

[93] See Oscar Cullmann, "The Meaning of the Lord's Supper in Primitive Christianity," in Cullmann-Leenhardt, *Essays on the Lord's Supper*, 5–23, especially 5–16.

[94] The Lectionary permits the gospel of the vigil to be read at this Mass as well. At an evening Mass it permits Luke 24:13-35, the Emmaus story, meant for Wednesday of Easter week, to be read because of its mention of being nearly evening and the day being almost over.

entrance antiphon and all three readings are about the resurrection. The petition of the collect identifies the day as "the solemnity of the Lord's Resurrection," and the prayer after Communion asks that the church "may come to the glory of the resurrection." The day Mass of Easter in RM 2011, then, is very coherent and each of its components of high quality. But despite its being the third day of the paschal Triduum and despite the new heading, *Dominica Paschae*, the two meanings of *pascha* are not as well balanced in this formulary as they are in the Easter Sunday Mass of the 1962 Missal. *Pascha* as *transitus* predominates.

The third petition in the solemn blessing for the vigil and Mass of Easter day in the latest edition of the Missal of Paul VI, not in the first two editions, is the clearest expression of *Pascha* as resurrection to the exclusion of the passion and in opposition to it. The priest prays,

> Now that the days of the Lord's Passion have drawn to a close,
> may you who celebrate the gladness of the Paschal Feast
> come with Christ's help, and exulting in spirit,
> to those feasts that are celebrated in eternal joy.

The solemn blessing is not obligatory, and at the two Masses on the Sunday of the Resurrection it would be better either to omit it or, at the vigil, to use the one from the rite of baptism of adults. On the other hand, the solemn blessing for optional use during Easter Time, no. 6 in the collection of solemn blessings following the Order of Mass, is splendid. The first invocation recalls that God, "by the Resurrection of his Only Begotten Son" conferred "the gift of redemption and of adoption." The third prays that all

> who have already risen with Christ
> in Baptism through faith,
> by living in a right manner on this earth,
> be united with him in the homeland of heaven.

Chapter 6

Easter Time

A. CALCULATION

In the early third and fourth centuries the Easter season is fifty consecutive days devoted to celebrating the resurrection of Christ and the bestowal of the Holy Spirit as two aspects of a single act by which the Father regenerates fallen humanity.[1] The entire period is called Pentecost and is characterized by unbounded joy, the chanting of "alleluia," standing for prayer, and exclusion of fasting. Only after the First Council of Constantinople in 381 determines that the Spirit of God is a Divine Person equal to the Father and the Son does the fiftieth day become an independent feast commemorating the great event described in Acts 2:1-13 and, of course, having the same name. At roughly the same time and inspired by Acts 1:1-11, the fortieth day emerges as an independent feast commemorating the ascension of Jesus. In this way the chronology of Acts reshapes the older fifty-day unit.

Toward the mid-seventh century, Pentecost acquires an octave in imitation of the one appended to what had by then become the feast of the Resurrection.[2] Thus does the Easter season obtain the three subdivisions set forth in no. 76 of the general rubrics of the Roman Missal of 1962. "The Easter season [*tempus paschale*]," the rubric says, "runs from the beginning of the Mass of the Paschal Vigil until None inclusive of the Saturday within the octave of Pentecost." It includes three parts: (a) the season of Easter, *tempus Paschatis*, running from the beginning of the Mass of the Paschal Vigil until None inclusive of the Vigil of the Ascension; (b) the season of the Ascension, *tempus Ascensionis*, running from First Vespers of the Ascension until None inclusive of the Vigil of Pentecost; and (c) the octave of Pentecost, running from

---

[1] See my "The Fifty Days and the Fiftieth Day," *Worship* 55 (1981) 194–218, reprinted in Maxwell E. Johnson, ed., *Between Memory and Hope*, 223–46; see also the more recent Bradshaw-Johnson, *Origins of Feasts*, 69–74.

[2] Chavasse, *Gélasien*, 250.

the Mass of the Vigil of Pentecost until None inclusive of the following Saturday.

We see, then, how indefinite the length of the season has become—and remains in the extraordinary form. Sometimes it extends through the octave of Pentecost, a week longer than the original fifty days. Sometimes it is limited to the forty days between the resurrection and Ascension, ten days shorter than the original fifty. Sometimes it is restricted to the octave of Easter, not mentioned in the 1962 general rubrics but seen already in the Old Gelasian Sacramentary of the seventh century, which marks Masses after the octave as *post clausum Paschae*, "after the close of Easter."[3] The 1570 Missal of Pius V restricts Easter to one day, Easter Sunday, identifying the other days of the week as days *post Pascha*, or "after Easter." To some extent variation in the length of the season is due to the splitting up of the paschal mystery into three separate parts—the resurrection, the ascension, and the conferral of the Spirit—and the tendency to associate Easter, or *Pascha*, only with the resurrection.

The 1969 Universal Norms on the Liturgical Year and the Calendar decisively clarifies the length and character of *tempus paschale*. Immediately after the section on the paschal Triduum, no. 22 declares that "the fifty days from the Sunday of the Resurrection to Pentecost Sunday are celebrated in joy and exultation as one feast day, indeed as one 'great Sunday.'" Easter, then, is no longer one day or even eight. It is fifty days beginning with the Sunday of the Resurrection, *Dominica Resurrectionis*, and ending with Pentecost Sunday, *Dominica Pentecostes*. "This sacred period of fifty days concludes with Pentecost Sunday," says the Universal Norms, no. 23. Since Pentecost is conclusive in character, its octave is eliminated. All fifty of these days are Easter, and all the Sundays are Easter Sundays. In designating not only the first day but the entire period as *Pascha*, Easter, the Universal Norms is obviously using the word "Easter" in the same way as third- and fourth-century writers use the word "Pentecost": a fifty-day unit celebrated with rejoicing and exultation as a single whole, a "symbol of the world to come," a "great Sunday," a "first installment" of eternal life, as Saint Athanasius wrote in 329.[4]

---

[3] See the six Masses *post clausum Paschae* in GeV 541–71. They are discussed in Chavasse, *Gélasien*, 238–44.

[4] Athanasius, *Festal Letter* 1, 10, in Cantalamessa, text 58, p. 70. The phrase "great Sunday" in the Universal Norms, no. 22, comes from this passage of Athanasius.

The numerical value of Easter Time in the Missal of Paul VI is expressed in the collect of the vigil Mass of Pentecost, taken from GeV 637, which states that God "willed the Paschal Mystery / to be encompassed as a sign in fifty days." The length of the season is also specified in no. 2 of the instruction on Holy Saturday. The 2011 translation declares that on Easter night "the time comes for paschal joys, the abundance of which overflows to occupy fifty days." We already noted that these paragraphs of the Missal are taken from the November 16, 1955, document of the Sacred Congregation of Rites. The instruction in that document states that at the end of the vigil, sorrow "gives way to paschal joys whose abundance flows over into the *following* days" (emphasis mine). Here, the number of days is not indicated because, as we just saw, before the 1969 Universal Norms the length of the Easter season was quite fluid.

Having pointed out differences in how the season as a whole is calculated, we now compare and contrast the first week, then the octave day, and finally the Sunday Masses in our two missals.

B. THE FIRST WEEK

1. Nomenclature

The 1962 Missal identifies Monday through Friday, but not Saturday, of the week beginning with Easter Sunday as days *infra octavam Paschae*, or days "within the octave of Easter." All three editions of the Missal of Paul VI and the two editions of the Lectionary do the same but include Saturday as well. The general rubrics of RM 1962, no. 63, define an octave as the celebration of a feast for eight consecutive days. The octaves of Easter and Pentecost, adds no. 66, are octaves of the first class, and days within them have the rank of first class. The 1969 Universal Norms has the same understanding of an octave. No. 24 declares that "the first eight days of Easter Time constitute the Octave of Easter and are celebrated as Solemnities of the Lord."

This understanding of the word "octave" and its application to Easter is no older than the first quarter of the twentieth century, being found for the first time in a Roman Missal printed in 1921 but not in one printed in 1920. Prior to that, at least in Roman books, the octave referred to only one day, the eighth, in this case the Sunday after Easter Sunday. The Roman Missal of 1570, for example, provides no other identification of Monday through Friday of Easter week than days *post Pascha*. Saturday is *Sabbato in albis*. The next day is the *octava Paschae*, or the octave of Easter, implying, as was pointed out above, that the previous Sunday alone is *Pascha*, or Easter.

The importance of this first week is shown by the fact that both the Old Gelasian and the Sacramentary of Pope Hadrian have proper Masses for each day, continuing the practice begun on Wednesday of Quinquagesima week, our Ash Wednesday, and not found at any other time of the year. Although the week eventually absorbed some of the resurrection thematic, its original character was and still is strongly baptismal. Throughout the week those initiated at the Paschal Vigil wore their baptismal garments to the eucharistic celebration as well as to Vespers, which at the Lateran ended each day with a procession to the font and the chapel of the cross where, during the Paschal Vigil, confirmation was administered.[5] Early Roman liturgical books designate these days not as the octave but as *ebdomada alba*, or "white week," referring to the color of the baptismal robes. The heading above the first of the Masses for these days in the Old Gelasian (GeV 468) is "Orations and Prayers of the Whole White (Week)." In the *Hadrianum* the day after Easter Sunday is Monday *in albas* (title 89), and the next Sunday is Sunday *post albas* (title 95). Two of the ancient antiphonals designate all the Sundays after Easter as *post albas* (AMS 87–91).

This is the week during which Saint Ambrose preached his sermons on the mysteries or sacraments of initiation to the newly baptized in Milan. Saint Cyril did the same in Jerusalem. At Hippo Saint Augustine preached twice a day to both neophytes and the other faithful. Egeria provides a graphic description of hagiopolite mystagogy in action. "During the eight days from Easter Day to the eighth day . . . the bishop stands leaning against the inner screen in the cave of the Anastasis," the rotunda built by Constantine over the tomb of Jesus. "The newly baptized come into the Anastasis," she continues, "and any of the faithful who wish to hear the Mysteries," that is, the meaning of the initiation rites at the Paschal Vigil. "The bishop relates what has been done, and interprets it, and, as he does so, the applause is so loud that it can be heard outside the church. Indeed the way he expounds the mysteries and interprets them cannot fail to move his hearers."[6]

Jounel observes that, "unfortunately, there is no trace of Roman baptismal catechesis. The homilies of Gregory the Great for the Easter

---

[5] See Pierre Jounel, "Les vêpres de Pâques," *La Maison-Dieu* 49 (1957) 96–111.

[6] Egeria, *Itinerarium* 47, 1–2, in Wilkinson, *Egeria's Travels*, 145–46. "Anastasis" in Greek means "resurrection."

octave make no reference to the newly baptized. In the homily he delivered on the Gospel of John in the Lateran on the octave Sunday he addresses his recommendations to the people alone: 'We are ending the Easter festival but we must live in such a way as to reach the eternal festival.' " Jounel remarks that "by calling the octave Sunday *die dominico post albas* [the Sunday after the white garments]," the *Hadrianum* "stresses the fact that the newly baptized had put off their white garments on Saturday."[7] We will return to this matter shortly.

2. *Masses in the 1962 Missal*

A. MONDAY THROUGH FRIDAY

Prayers for the Masses of Easter week in the 1962 Missal come from the Sacramentary of Pope Hadrian (H 392–434), which also provides orations to be recited at Vespers, at the baptismal font, and at other chapels each evening. A special feature of these Masses is that the sequence *Victimae paschali laudes*, preface, *communicantes, Hanc igitur*, and dismissal of Easter Sunday are repeated every day. Throughout the week the gradual is *Haec dies*, "This is the day which the Lord hath made: let us rejoice and be glad in it," from Psalm 117:24, followed each day, except Tuesday, by a different verse of the same psalm. These repetitions give unity and direction to the week.

Like the Masses of Lent, in ancient times these too were celebrated by the pope and Roman faithful in a different church each day. "The stational arrangement of Easter Week is worthy of comment," remarks John Baldovin. "Each major basilica is visited in order of the patron's importance for the city." After listing the basilicas and the days they were visited, he observes that "this scheme constitutes a grand, well-conceived tour of the Christian city, calling to mind octaves at Jerusalem. It is as if the neophytes and the rest of the faithful were being introduced to the saints important for the life of the city as they commemorated the Risen Savior."[8] The place of celebration to a large extent determines the choice and arrangement of readings.

---

[7] Jounel, *Church* IV, 59. The homily of Gregory the Great that he quotes is *Homilia* 26, *In octava paschae* 10 (PL 76, 1202 D–1203 A).

[8] Baldovin, *Urban Character* 156. Egeria lists the churches in Jerusalem where the Easter week liturgies were celebrated in *Itinerarium* 39, 2, in Wilkinson, *Egeria's Travels*, 135.

Prayers and readings on Monday, Tuesday, and Wednesday deal not so much with baptism as with the resurrection. The stational church on Monday is Saint Peter's, and the liturgy centers on the chief of the apostles. The epistle is Peter's proclamation of the resurrection to Cornelius and his household in Acts 10:34-43. His remarking that the risen Christ showed himself not to all but only to those whom God chose and "who ate and drank with him after he rose from the dead" is the prelude to what the gospel, Luke 24:13-35, relates about the Lord's self-revelation to the disciples on the road to Emmaus in the breaking of the bread, concluding with their going back to Jerusalem and being told by the Eleven, "The Lord has risen indeed, and he has appeared to Simon!"—words used as the communion antiphon. The secret and post-Communion on Easter Monday are the same as those of the Paschal Vigil and Easter Sunday. Our discussion of the octave day will explain why.

The stational church on Tuesday is the Basilica of Saint Paul-Outside-the-Walls. The epistle is Acts 13:26-33. In it the Apostle to the Gentiles announces to the children of Abraham and "others who fear God" that in raising Jesus from the dead God makes forgiveness of sins possible for all. Consistent with this universal outlook, the second verse of the gradual is taken not from Psalm 117, as it is on other days of the week, but from Psalm 106:2-3, which summons the redeemed to praise the Lord, the redeemed whom he "gathered from far-off lands, / from east and west, north and south," as *The Revised Grail Psalms* translates the Hebrew. The gospel, Luke 24:36-47, is the continuation of Monday's pericope. After eating a piece of broiled fish, Christ declares that "repentance and forgiveness of sins is to be preached *to all nations*" (emphasis mine). Saint Paul returns in the communion antiphon to say, "If you be risen with Christ, seek the things that are above" (Col 3:1-2).

The collect on Wednesday makes explicit mention of the resurrection of Christ: "O God, who dost fill us with joy when year by year we solemnize the resurrection of the Lord, grant that keeping these feasts now will make us worthy of the happiness of heaven." Since Wednesday's gospel is the third weekday narration of a postresurrection appearance, the choice is John 21:1-17, the episode at the Sea of Tiberias, which, the evangelist notes, "was the third time that Jesus appeared to the disciples after he was raised from the dead." The stational church is Saint Lawrence. Mention of the charcoal fire in verse 9 may be an allusion to this saint's being burned alive on a gridiron.[9] In the epistle, Acts 3:13-15, 17-19, Peter tells the Israelites in Solomon's Portico, "You killed the Author of life, whom God raised from the dead. To this we are witnesses." The Greek word here translated "witnesses" also means "martyrs" and certainly evokes the heroic Roman deacon in whose basilica the liturgy is being celebrated. A portion of the offertory chant from Psalm 77:23-25, "He gave them the bread of heaven," may allude to an action near the end of the gospel: "Jesus came and took the bread and gave it to them."

On Thursday the theme of the readings and prayers shifts to baptism. The collect is extraordinary—an ideal prayer in today's multicultural, ecumenical context: "O God, who hast united divers nations in the confession of thy name, grant that all who have been born again in the font of baptism, may be one in mind by faith and one in love by deed." The secret prays that the Christian people "be renewed by the confession of thy name and by baptism." Mass on Thursday is celebrated at the Basilica of the Holy Apostles, dedicated to Philip and James. The epistle, Acts 8:26-40, tells how a deacon named Philip baptizes an Ethiopian eunuch. The gospel narrates the encounter of Jesus with Mary Magdalene in John 20:11-18. Although she is the first to see the Lord in the Fourth Gospel, the liturgy withholds the episode until the appearances to Peter and other apostles have been recounted.

The Mass on Friday is celebrated at the Pantheon, known as Santa Maria ad Martyres. The epistle, 1 Peter 3:18-22, declares that at the time of Noah "eight persons were saved through water" and that "baptism, which this prefigured, now saves you." The gospel, Matthew 28:16-20, reports the risen Lord revealing himself to the Eleven on a mountain in Galilee and commanding them to baptize "in the name of the Father, and of the Son and of the Holy Spirit." The core of the gospel is repeated in the communion antiphon. The secret discloses that the eucharistic sacrifice is being offered "in atonement for the sins of those who are born anew and to hasten the coming of heavenly help."

---

[9] This is the suggestion of Antoine Chavasse in *L' Eglise en Prière* (Tournai: Desclée & Cie., 1961) 715, to whom I am indebted for the some of the material in this section.

As was pointed out earlier, MR 1962 identifies Monday through Friday of Easter week as being *infra octavam Paschae*. Saturday is not so designated. It has a different identification: Saturday *in albis*. The full Latin phrase is *in albis depositis* or *in albis deponendis* and means the day on which the neophytes, probably after Vespers, lay aside the white baptismal garments they have been wearing at liturgical services all week. This action brings the rites of initiation to an end. From now on those baptized at the Paschal Vigil will no longer be distinguishable from the other faithful by their white robes. Given the importance of this moment, it is surprising to discover that the title *Sabbato in albis* is found only in the early ninth-century Lectionary of Alcuin (A XCVIIII).

The other two ancient lectionaries, the gospel books, the sacramentaries, and the antiphonals simply identify the day as *Feria septima*, "the seventh day," or *Sabbato*, "Saturday." Except for the Lectionary of Alcuin, then, *Sabbato in albis* is of recent coinage. The fourteenth-century Sacramentary of the Curia still has only *Sabbato* as its heading. The phrase *in albis* is added to it in the first printed edition of the Roman Missal in 1474 and retained in the various editions of the Tridentine Missal, including that of 1962.[10] It was already pointed out that the title of the next day, Sunday, in the *Hadrianum* is *Die dominica post albas*, enabling Jounel to assert that "the newly baptized had put off their white garments on Saturday."[11] This is borne out by the content of the Mass formulary.

The stational church on this Saturday is the Lateran Basilica, scene of the sacramental climax of the initiation process on the previous Saturday when the newly baptized were given the white garments they are about to take off. The communion antiphon reminds them and the other faithful, "All ye who have been baptized in Christ, have put on Christ" (Gal 3:27). The NRSV reads, "As many of you as were baptized into Christ have *clothed* yourselves with Christ" (emphasis mine). The opening word of the epistle, 1 Peter 2:1-10 is *Deponentes*, which means "putting aside." Of course it evokes the putting aside of the white garments. In the biblical text, however, it has a moral meaning. "Putting

---

[10] For a list of the titles, see Bruylants I, no. 97.

[11] Jounel, *Church* IV, 59. Two of the six ancient antiphonals also designate this Sunday as *post alba*. See AMS 87.

aside all malice and all guile, as newborn babes desire the rational milk without guile" (trans. mine).

The gospel, John 20:1-19, also emphasizes cloth—not baptismal robes, but the burial garments of Jesus. When Peter and the Beloved Disciple arrive at the tomb, they discover it to be open but not empty. The Beloved Disciple sees "the linen wrappings lying there." Simon Peter sees them and something else: "the cloth that had been on Jesus' head, not lying with the linen wrappings but rolled up in a place by itself." All week long the *Victimae paschali laudes* has been relating that Mary Magdalene, who reported the open tomb to Peter, also saw "the shroud and napkin resting."[12] Mention of "the cloth that had been on Jesus' head" reminds us that besides white robes neophytes were also given, at least in some places, cloth bands with which to cover the place where their heads had been anointed with sacred chrism.[13]

This Saturday brings to a close more than just the wearing of the white robes. Liturgically, it also brings a close to the weeklong paschal celebration begun at the vigil on the previous Saturday. On this day the characteristic features of the Masses of Easter week are heard for the last time: the gradual *Haec dies* and the sequence *Victimae paschali laudes*; the proper *communicantes* and *Hanc igitur*; and the *Ite, missa est* with double alleluia. Moreover, the collect, from H 429, prays that "we who have reverently celebrated the paschal festival, may through it deserve to possess eternal joys." Use of the past tense here suggests that the paschal festival of which it speaks is now over. Expressions such as "paschal festival," "paschal solemnity," "paschal mysteries," "paschal sacraments," and "paschal joys"—so frequent in the prayers of this week—are never heard during the next seven weeks, not even on the feasts of Ascension and Pentecost or during the octave of Pentecost.

Judging from the prayers, then, not only does Easter *week* end on this day. The Easter season ends too. This is confirmed by the designation of subsequent Sundays in RM 1962 as Sundays *after* Easter. The Old Gelasian designates them as Sundays *post clausum Paschae*, "after the close of Easter." Although no. 76 of the general rubrics of RM 1962 declares that the Easter season extends through the octave of Pentecost, for the prayers and titles in this Missal it ends on Saturday *in*

---

[12] From the English translation of the 1962 Missal published by Baronius Press.

[13] Righetti, *Manuale* II, 290.

albis. On the other hand, as is explained after the epistle, this day also inaugurates a practice that will continue until the Vigil of Pentecost: replacement of the gradual by four Alleluias and two verses. The order is a first Alleluia, repeated with a verse, followed by a second Alleluia and verse, then repetition of the second Alleluia.

C. OCTAVE DAY

In the 1962 Missal the name of the Sunday after Easter Sunday is composed of two parts: *Dominica in albis* and *in octava Paschae.* The words *in albis* were added only in the 1604 Roman Missal,[14] thus producing two days *in albis,* Saturday and Sunday. As we just saw, in ancient times the newly baptized laid aside their white garments on Saturday, not Sunday. Of the two parts of this Sunday's title, then, the second part, *octava Paschae,* "octave of Easter," is the older. Significantly, here the word "octave" has its primitive meaning of "eighth day," not "eight days." The Old Gelasian, followed by the Sacramentary of Gellone, are the first to designate the day as *octava Paschae.*[15] Other Frankish Gelasians follow the *Hadrianum* and call it *Dominica post albas.* Starting in the eleventh century, missals revert to *octava,* which remains unchanged through the Tridentine Missal, including that of 1962.[16]

Chavasse argues that the Old Gelasian's designation of the Sunday in question as *octava Paschae,* though found in the present state of the text, is not primitive. At an earlier stage the eighth day was Saturday, not Sunday, and marked the octave of baptism administered at the vigil on the previous Saturday. This is obvious from the collect of the Gelasian Mass on the Saturday of Easter week, which prays for those "the octave of whose sacred regeneration we celebrate" (GeV 499; trans. mine). With the decline of adult initiation the octave day shifted from Saturday to Sunday, probably under Pope Honorius (625–30), ceasing to be the octave of paschal baptism and becoming instead the *octava Paschae,* "octave of Easter." Easter is here understood as an eight-day celebration of the resurrection of Christ beginning on what the Old Gelasian calls *Dominicum Paschae,* "Easter Sunday." In its final state, then, Easter in the Gelasian begins on *Dominicum Paschae* and ends on *octava Paschae.*

[14] Bruylants I, no. 98.
[15] Except for the Epistolary of Würzburg, the early lectionaries and four of the ancient antiphonals do the same.
[16] Again, see the titles in Bruylants I, no. 98.

Attachment of the Sunday after Easter to Easter week, Chavasse continues, required adjustments in lectionaries and sacramentaries. In the Old Gelasian the words *die dominico* had to be added to *octava Paschae* in Sunday's title because previously the eighth day was Saturday. In the *Hadrianum*, the six Masses from Monday through Saturday of the original Easter week were moved forward one day, becoming in that document, as well as in RM 1962, Masses from Tuesday through Sunday. This explains why the collect on Sunday is a recasting of Saturday's collect, asking that "we who have celebrated the paschal feast, may retain its fruits." The introit may also have been taken from Saturday, because the text is from Saturday's epistle, *Quasi modo geniti infantes*, "As newborn babes, desire the rational milk without guile" (1 Pet 2:2). The offertory, about the angel of the Lord descending from heaven (Matt 2:2, 5-6), is borrowed from Monday of Easter week and is out of place here. Finally, when the block of six Masses in the *Hadrianum* was moved forward one day, the Sunday after Easter Sunday acquired texts, but Easter Monday was left empty. To fill the void a new collect was found, but the secret and post-Communion repeat those of Holy Saturday and Easter Sunday.[17]

The obvious gospel choice on the octave day is John 20:19-31—the appearance of Jesus to the disciples on the first day of the week when Thomas was absent, and his appearance "eight days later" when Thomas was present. The two Alleluia verses are a wonderful prelude to this episode. "On the day of my resurrection," the Lord promises in the first, "I will go before you into Galilee." The second continues, "After eight days, the doors being shut, Jesus stood in the midst of his disciples and said, 'Peace be with you.'" The communion antiphon repeats the Lord's command to Thomas, "Put in thy hand and know the place of the nails, alleluia; and be not faithless but believing, alleluia, alleluia."

---

[17] Chavasse explains this in detail in *Gélasien*, 235–41, and provides a very brief summary in *Eglise*, 714–15.

Other authors have different opinions on these matters. Adolf Adam, for example, referring to Easter week, writes, "Originally it ended on Sunday, which was therefore called 'Sunday in white garments' (*dominica in albis*). From the seventh century on the neophytes set aside their white garments on Saturday; this was due to the fact that the Vigil Mass had by now been moved back to Holy Saturday." *Liturgical Year*, 86. This is an English translation of a German original dating from 1979.

The epistle, 1 John 5:4-18, declares that Christians are "born of God" through faith in "the one who came by water and blood, Jesus Christ, not with the water only but with the water and the blood." These words, together with John 19:34, must lie behind the image of Jesus, Divine Mercy, whose hands are pierced and from whose chest emanates two rays, one white and the other red, representing the water and blood issuing from the heart of Christ on the cross. The epistle in RM 1962 is read every year on the Sunday after Easter, but paradoxically the day is not called Divine Mercy Sunday.

When we recall Chavasse's explanation of how the Mass formulary of the present octave day was put together and that all the characteristic liturgical features of the days *infra octavam* have ceased—the gradual and sequence, the proper *communicantes* and *Hanc igitur*, the *Ite, missa est, alleluia, alleluia*—it can be maintained that this Sunday is the *octava Paschae* in name only and that the real climax of Easter week, or white week, the real eighth day, remains Saturday. It is worth noting here that the Missal of Paul VI removes *in albis* from the titles of both Saturday and Sunday. Like the other days of the week, Saturday is now "within the Octave of Easter."

3. Masses in the Missal of Paul VI

a. Preliminaries

As we saw, formularies for the Masses of this week in the Tridentine Missal were extremely local in origin. Texts were selected and arranged in function of the specific sites within the city of Rome where these Masses were celebrated. Even though it has been centuries since the Holy Father presided at Eucharist in any of these churches on these days, the 1962 Missal continues to print their names. By way of contrast the Missal of Paul VI eliminates the names of Roman churches during Easter week, Lent, and all other days. Its Masses are meant for use anywhere in the world. They are not local compositions that were eventually adopted elsewhere. From the outset they are destined for the universal church.

Texts are the same in all three typical editions of the Missal and have much in common with their predecessors in previous Mass books. Introit antiphons are the same, though starting in 1970 an alternate is provided on Monday. Three of the six communion antiphons are the same: the three taken from gospels still read during this week. The three from gospels that are no longer read had to be replaced. The Gloria is chanted every day. The gradual *Haec dies* may replace the responsorial psalm, according to the General Instruction of the Roman Missal, no. 61. The sequence *Victimae paschali laudes* may still be sung, but it is optional. Paschal Preface I is required throughout the week with the words "on this day above all," as in the past. The proper *communicantes* and *Hanc igitur* are used with Eucharistic Prayer I. Two alleluias are added to whatever dismissal formula is chosen. Finally, in both missals the days of the Easter octave are markedly baptismal in character and enjoy the highest possible rank: first-class feasts in RM 1962, solemnities in the new Missal. So during this week there is much continuity in the texts of our two missals. This will not be so in later weeks or on Sundays.

b. Readings

As the introduction to the Lectionary, no. 101, states, "The Gospel readings during the Easter Octave are accounts of the Lord's appearances." This is also the case in RM 1962. But the Lectionary has two selections not found in the old Missal: Matthew 28:8-15 on Monday and Mark 16:9-15 on Saturday. This is because it transferred two pericopes of Easter week in RM 1962 to other days: Matthew 16:16-20 from Friday to the solemnity of the Ascension and John 20:1-9 from Saturday to the day Mass of Easter Sunday. Moreover, the sequence of the passages is different. In RM 1962 the day on which a particular passage is read depends mainly on the church where the liturgy is taking place. The Lectionary arranges the appearances in chronological order, in so far as it can be determined.

Monday's gospel, Matthew 28:8-15, one of the two not in RM 1962, begins with Jesus encountering the women departing from the tomb on the first day of the week to announce to the disciples what the angel had said to them. It continues with the chief priests and elders giving a bribe to the guards and enjoining them to tell people that the disciples of Jesus stole his body while they were asleep. Still on the first day of the week and at the tomb, Tuesday's gospel relates how Mary Magdalene "stood weeping outside the tomb," then saw Jesus but did not recognize him until he spoke her name.

The event in Wednesday's gospel, Luke 24:13-35, takes place on the first day of the week—not, however, at the tomb but on the road to Emmaus where Jesus, after interpreting the Scriptures, makes himself known "in the breaking of the bread." A new communion antiphon is the last sentence of the gospel, "The disciples recognized the Lord

Jesus in the breaking of the bread." Thursday's gospel, Luke 24:35-48, continues that of Wednesday. As the two disciples after returning to Jerusalem were recounting to the Eleven what had happened to them on the road, Jesus stood among them, showed them his hands and feet, opened their minds to understand the Scriptures, and declared that "repentance and forgiveness of sins should be preached in his name to all nations."

The time of Friday's gospel, John 21:1-14, is no longer the first day of the week, and the setting is no longer in or near Jerusalem but at the Sea of Tiberias in Galilee, where the disciples, having caught nothing all night, at the command of Jesus haul in 153 fish, large ones. Bruce Vawter contends that "there can hardly be any doubt that ch. 21 is an appendix added to the Gospel that had already been concluded with ch. 21."[18] As on Wednesday the communion antiphon is from the gospel: "Jesus said to his disciples: Come and eat. / And he took the bread and gave it to them, alleluia" (John 21:12-13). Saturday's gospel, Mark 16:9-15, may also be regarded as an appendix, for it is one of three conclusions attached to a gospel that seems to have ended at 16:8.[19] It is the so-called longer or canonical ending, synthesizing the appearance stories heard individually throughout the week. It ends with the command to "go into all the world and proclaim the good news to the whole creation." Inexplicably, the Lectionary omits the next verse with its reference to baptism: "The one who believes and is baptized will be saved" (Mark 16:16).

The introduction to the Lectionary, no. 101, explains that on Sundays as well as on weekdays throughout the Easter season "the first reading is a semicontinuous reading from the Acts of the Apostles." This book, a sequel to the Gospel of Luke, narrates how Christ, though ascended into heaven and physically absent, continues to act in the church, making it grow numerically and expand geographically under the impetus of the Spirit imparted at Pentecost. While the Easter octave mainly dwells on the resurrection, Ascension and Pentecost are already joined to it through the readings from Acts.

On Monday is read Peter's discourse on the day of Pentecost from Acts 2:14, 22-33, leading on Tuesday to Acts 2:36-41, the baptism of some three thousand souls. This is the only mention of baptism in the

---

[18] Vawter, JBC 63:180.
[19] See Edward J. Mally, SJ, "The Gospel According to Mark," JBC 42:96–100.

readings of the Easter octave. On Wednesday through Saturday Acts recounts the healing of a man lame from birth by Peter and John on their way to the temple in 3:1-10, the discourse of Peter that follows it in 3:11-26, and the consequent imprisonment of Peter and James in 4:1-12. Obviously, these incidents have no direct connection with the appearance stories of the gospels. During this week and throughout the rest of the season the two weekday readings are on independent tracks. But the liturgy's juxtaposing of events from the end of the gospels and the beginning of Acts enables the faithful to ponder day after day the paschal mystery as a whole: the resurrection of Jesus, his enthronement in heaven, and his continued activity in the church by the power of the Spirit.

c. Prayers

The collects of Wednesday, Thursday, and Friday of Easter week are the same as they were in RM 1962. That of Monday in the old Missal is now on Saturday of the fourth week of Easter, with some changes in light of GeV 474. In its place is the collect of Tuesday in RM 1962, which brings the church and baptism to the fore at the beginning of this week. It prays,

> O God, who give constant increase
> to your Church by new offspring,
> grant that your servants may hold fast in their lives
> to the Sacrament they have received in faith.

The collect on Saturday, which replaces the one in RM 1962, is from GeV 500, but the petition that the elect be clothed with blessed immortality is from GeV 516. It too speaks of the faithful increasing in number by the addition of those reborn in baptism:

> O God, who by the abundance of your grace
> give increase to the peoples who believe in you, . . .
> clothe with blessed immortality
> those reborn through the Sacrament of Baptism.

As for the other prayers, it was pointed out that the secret and post-Communion of Easter Monday in RM 1962 are the same as those of the Paschal Vigil and Easter Sunday and that they simply fill the void created by the shifting of the six Masses from Monday through Saturday in the *Hadrianum* to Tuesday through Sunday. The Missal of Paul

VI retains these prayers at the Paschal Vigil but provides other ones for the day Mass of Easter Sunday. It does the same on Easter Monday, transferring the secret of Thursday in RM 1962 to Monday and securing a new prayer after Communion from GeV 498 but adding to it "those you have set on the way of eternal salvation" from GeV 503.

Easter Friday's prayer after Communion, taken from the Sacramentary of Bergamo 573, asks God to watch over those he has saved "that, redeemed by the Passion of your Son, / they may rejoice in his Resurrection." Mention of the passion on this day of the week is appropriate. Interestingly, the version of this prayer in GeV 532, addressed to Jesus, refers not to those whom he has saved, *salvasti*, but to those whom he has washed, *lavasti*.

In sum, the prayers for this week in the 1962 Missal are all of good quality. Besides eliminating the doublets on Easter Monday, the substitutions and transfer of days in the postconciliar reform seem aimed at increasing references to baptism and paschal sacraments, integrating them with references to the resurrection and distributing them more evenly throughout the week.[20] Having completed our investigation of the first week, we now turn to the Sunday Masses of Easter Time.

C. SUNDAY MASSES

1. Sundays in the 1962 Missal

a. Nomenclature

The 1962 Missal contains four Masses for what it calls the Second, Third, Fourth, and Fifth Sundays *post Pascha*, "after Easter," and a fifth for the Sunday *post Ascensionem*, "after the Ascension." The designation *post Pascha* is relatively recent, dating only from the first printed edition of the Roman Missal in 1474. Before that these Sundays were counted not from Easter Sunday but from the *octava Paschae* and hence were known as "Sundays after the Octave of Easter." Two of the ancient antiphonals call them Sundays *post albas*, "after white week." The Old Gelasian is unique in using the expression *post clausum Paschae*, "after the close of Easter."

The Old Gelasian is also unique in designating the Sunday before Pentecost as *Quinta dominica post clausum Paschae*, "Fifth Sunday after the Close of Easter." The other early sources—sacramentaries,

---

[20] For the sources of these prayers, see Anthony Ward, SM, "The Missal Orations of the Easter Octave from Monday to Sunday," EL 125 (2011) 63–111.

lectionaries, antiphonals—call it "Sunday after the Ascension of the Lord." The first printed edition of the Roman Missal in 1474, followed by the Tridentine Missal of 1570, calls it the Sunday *infra octavam Ascensionis*, "within the octave of the Ascension." Since RM 1962 abolished all octaves except those of Christmas, Easter, and Pentecost, it dropped this title and reverted to "Sunday after the Ascension."[21] What should be noted here is that in all these sources Easter is either one day, Easter Sunday, or eight days, the octave, but never the whole period from Easter to Pentecost, as it will become in the postconciliar calendar of 1969.

b. Chants

Jounel remarks that "it is the antiphonal that best expresses on each Sunday the joy of the community sharing the victory of its Lord over sin and death."[22] Many of these chants are outbursts of sheer joy. *Jubilate Deo* (Ps 65:1) is heard three times[23] and *Cantate Domino* (Pss 97:1; 95:2) twice. *Lauda, anima mea* (Ps 145:2) occurs only once but is particularly intense: "Praise the Lord, O my soul: in my life I will praise the Lord. I will sing to my God as long as I shall be. Alleluia" (Ps 145:2).

Other chants, especially Alleluia verses, recount details of the resurrection story. The first Alleluia on the second Sunday, for example, is Luke 24:35: "The disciples knew the Lord Jesus in the breaking of the bread." The second Alleluia of the following Sunday is from the same episode: "It behooved Christ to suffer and to rise again, and so to enter into his glory" (Luke 24:46). The second Alleluia on the fourth Sunday is Romans 6:9: "Christ, rising from the dead, dieth now no more. Death shall no more have dominion over him." The first Alleluia on the fifth Sunday is a free composition: "Christ is risen and hath shown upon us whom he redeemed with his blood."

c. Readings

The gospel passages for these five Sundays are already found in the oldest type of Roman evangelary, dating from 650. All are drawn from John but are not continuous, and the reason they are arranged as they

---

[21] For the titles of these Sundays, see Bruylants I, nos. 100–103.

[22] Jounel, "Le dimanche e le temps de Pâques, II: La tradition de l'église," *La Maison-Dieu* 67 (1961) 180.

[23] Introit antiphon of the third Sunday, offertory of the fourth, introit psalm of the fifth.

are is not clear.[24] When they were put together, Ascension and Pentecost were already independent feasts, and they reflect a linear progression from the resurrection of Christ to his ascension into heaven and the coming of the Paraclete. The second Sunday is popularly known as Good Shepherd Sunday because in the gospel, John 10:11-16, Jesus declares, "I am the good shepherd. I lay down my life for the sheep." The second Alleluia, John 10:14, is from this passage: "I know my sheep and mine know me."

On the third Sunday in John 16:16-22 Jesus announces his departure from the disciples and his return "after a little while." The communion antiphon repeats the first verse: "A little while and you shall not see me, alleluia; and again a little while and you shall see me because I go to the Father, alleluia, alleluia." Though Ascension has not yet been celebrated, the selection on the fourth Sunday looks to Pentecost. Jesus discloses in John 16:5-14 that his going to the Father is the condition for his sending the Paraclete. Once again the communion antiphon is from the gospel: "When the Paraclete, the Spirit of truth, is come, he will convince the world of sin and of justice and of judgment, alleluia" (John 16:8).

On the fifth Sunday, when the feast of the Ascension is imminent, the gospel is John 16:23-30, in which Jesus announces, "I came from the Father and have come into the world. Again I am leaving the world and am going to the Father." On the Sunday after Ascension Jesus again takes up the theme of the Paraclete, also called Advocate and Consoler. In John 15:26–16:4 Jesus declares that "when the Advocate comes, whom I will send you from the Father, the Spirit of truth who comes from the Father, he will testify on my behalf." The lengthy communion antiphon is not from this passage but from the farewell discourse: "Father, while I was with them, I kept them whom thou gavest me, alleluia. But now I come to thee. I pray not that thou shouldst take them out of the world but that thou shouldst keep them from evil, alleluia, alleluia" (John 17:12-13, 15).

The five epistles are already found in the late sixth-century Epistolary of Würzburg. The one on the second Sunday, 1 Peter 2:21-25, is an ideal complement to the gospel about the Good Shepherd. It begins with a reference to Christ's expiatory suffering: "He himself bore our sins in his body on the cross." It then cites Isaiah 53:5, a well-known line from the fourth Servant Song: "By his wounds you have been

[24] Auf der Maur, *Le celebrazioni nel ritmo del tempo* I, 186.

healed." The last sentence leads directly to the gospel: "You were going away like sheep, but now you have returned to the shepherd and guardian of your souls." As appropriate as this epistle is, the four others—1 Peter 2:11-20 on the third Sunday, James 1:17-21 on the fourth Sunday, James 1:22-27 on the fifth Sunday, and 1 Peter 4:7-11 on the Sunday after Ascension—have no connection with either the season or the gospels that follow them.

d. Prayers

Unlike all the other prayers in the 1962 Missal that we have considered, none of the prayers of the Sundays after the octave day come from the *Hadrianum*. This sacramentary contains Masses for Easter week, Ascension, and Pentecost and its octave but none for the Sundays between the Sunday *post albas* and Pentecost. The absence of formularies for this period means that in the ancient papal liturgy, to which the *Hadrianum* witnesses, Easter ends on the Sunday *post albas*. It is followed by Ascension and Pentecost, celebrated as independent feasts forty and fifty days, respectively, after Easter. But an Easter season as such is nonexistent.

This is a major deficiency. But it is not the only one. The *Hadrianum* also lacks Masses for the Sundays after Epiphany and the Sundays after Pentecost.

For this venerable sacramentary, thought to derive from Pope Gregory the Great, to be usable throughout the year, the missing Masses had to added in the form of a supplement. Though for a long time thought to be the work of Alcuin of York, "it is now apparent that the Supplement was assembled in Septimania ca. 810–15, during the reign of King Louis the Pious, by Saint Benedict of Aniane (+821), the monastic founder and reformer par excellence of the Carolingian period."[25]

Masses for the second, third, fourth, and fifth Sundays after Easter and the Sunday after Ascension in RM 1962, then, are not from the Sacramentary of Pope Hadrian. They are the first five of six formularies in the Old Gelasian (GeV 541–71) meant for the six Sundays between Easter and Pentecost.[26] They probably reached the Roman

---

[25] Vogel, *Medieval Liturgy*, 86.

[26] This may be confusing. Because the Mass of the octave of Easter in RM 1962 is the *Hadrianum*'s Mass of the Sunday *post albas*, "after white week" (H 435–39), the Mass that the Old Gelasian intends for the First Sunday after

Missal not directly but through the Carolingian supplement (Sup 1114–31). The heading above the first of these six formularies is "Orations and Prayers for the Sunday after the Octave of Easter." Here the word "octave" can only mean Easter Saturday or Saturday *in albis*. Otherwise there would be seven Sundays between Easter and Pentecost: the octave and these six—one too many. The prayers under this title, then, are intended for the Sunday after Easter Saturday and stem from the time before that Sunday became the *octava Paschae*. In its original place, the collect that is on the second Sunday in RM 1962, Good Shepherd Sunday, would have recalled the redemptive event celebrated during Easter week: "O God, who, by the humility of thy Son, didst lift up a fallen world, grant . . . that those whom thou hast snatched from the perils of endless death, thou mayest cause to rejoice in everlasting joys."

The other five formularies are meant for Sundays that the Old Gelasian identifies as *post clausum Paschae*, "after the close of Easter," and numbers two to six. This means that the first of the six formularies, the one to be used on the Sunday after Easter Saturday, is the first Sunday *post clausum Paschae*. This shows yet again that for the Old Gelasian, the close of Easter is Easter Saturday, the eighth day after the great vigil and baptisms on Holy Saturday. Deriving from a time when the Sunday after Easter was not yet *octava Paschae* and the sixth Sunday was not yet called the Sunday after Ascension, these six Mass sets are very old, have affinities with the Verona collection of papal Masses, and were probably incorporated into the Old Gelasian as an already-existing group.[27]

As was already pointed out, none of the prayers of these formularies in RM 1962 use the word "paschal" or refer to any aspect of the paschal mystery. Nor should we expect them to do so. They derive from Masses meant for *post clausum Paschae*, after Easter has ended, and could just as well be used in Ordinary Time. In fact, the sixth Mass of the Gelasian block (GeV 566–71) is found in RM 1962 on the First Sunday after Pentecost. No doubt this is the weakest part of the Tridentine Missal. We now investigate how postconciliar reformers reconstructed it.

Easter (GeV 541–45) appears in RM 1962 on the second Sunday, and the Mass that the Old Gelasian intends for the Sixth Sunday after Easter (GeV 566–71) appears in RM 1962 on the First Sunday after Pentecost.

[27] Chavasse, *Gélasien*, 241–44.

2. Sundays in the Missal of Paul VI

a. Nomenclature

A major change in the Missal of Paul VI and other postconciliar liturgical books is that the Sundays of this season are called no longer Sundays *after* Easter but Sundays *of* Easter. The 1969 Universal Norms on the Liturgical Year and the Calendar, no. 23, states, "The Sundays of this time of year are considered to be Sundays of Easter and are called, after Easter Sunday itself, the Second, Third, Fourth, Fifth, Sixth, and Seventh Sundays of Easter." Just as Easter is no longer one day but fifty days, so is Easter Sunday no longer one day. Rather, all seven Sundays of Easter are Easter Sundays, *dominicae Paschae*, the first being distinguished from the others by being called Sunday of the Resurrection, *dominica Resurrectionis*. The others are identified numerically from two to seven, the eighth being Pentecost.

Consistent with this understanding, all three editions of the Missal of Paul VI as well as both editions of the Lectionary eliminate *in albis* and *octava Paschae* from the title of the second Sunday. They also replace "Sunday after the Ascension" in RM 1962 with "Seventh Sunday of Easter," thereby giving all the Sundays between the Resurrection and Pentecost the same status and character. All are Sundays of Easter. In this context the insertion of *seu de divina Misericordia* beneath the title of the second Sunday in the third typical edition of the *Missale Romanum* in 2002 is disconcerting.[28] What officially is a subtitle printed in small, lowercase letters has for a large segment of the Catholic populace become the name of the day, Divine Mercy Sunday, supplanting the Second Sunday of Easter.

Be that as it may, the designation of Monday through Saturday of the first week as days *infra octavam Paschae*, "within the octave of Easter," coupled with elimination of *octava* from the title of the second Sunday paradoxically results in an octave that consists of only seven days, issuing upon an eighth day that is no longer called the octave. A further paradox is that although in the Tridentine Missal the characteristic features of the octave days cease on Sunday—*Haec dies, Victimae paschali laudes*, the proper *communicantes* and *Hanc igitur*, the two

---

[28] For background, see Antonella Meneghetti, "Tempo di Quaresima e di Pasqua," *Rivista liturgica* 90 (2003) 595–600, here 595, and Maurizio Barba, *Il Messale Romano:Tradizione e progresso nella terza edizione tipica*, Monumenta Studia Instrumenta Liturgica 34 (Città de Vaticano: Libreria Editrice Vaticana) 68.

alleluias after *Ite, missa est*—in the Missal of Paul VI they do not, or at least not necessarily. This suggests that the second Sunday may still be the octave day, though no longer so called. Let us look further into this possibility.

In the first two editions of the postconciliar Missal a rubric following the prayer after Communion on Easter Day prescribes that the dismissal with double alleluia be used *per totam octavam*, "throughout the whole octave," but without specifying when the octave ends. The third edition of 2002 omits this rubric but following the prayer after Communion on the second Sunday declares that for the dismissal of the people there is sung or said, "Go forth, the Mass is ended, alleluia, alleluia," thus implying that this Sunday is still part of the octave. Another rubric just above this one allows the solemn blessing of Easter Sunday to be used on this day too. On subsequent Sundays the solemn blessing of Easter Time must be used. The second Sunday is thereby connected to the Sunday of the Resurrection and distinguished from the other Sundays.

Furthermore, a rubric under the prayer over the offerings on the second Sunday requires that Preface I of Easter be used with the insertion "on this day above all." The option of using a different preface of Easter or Preface I with the insertion "in this time above all" begins only on Monday of the second week. The second Sunday, then, seems to be within the octave. In all three editions of the Missal of Paul VI a rubric above Preface I of Easter, no. 45 in the third edition, states that "on Easter Sunday and throughout the Octave of Easter, is said 'on this day'; on the other days of Easter Time, is said 'in this time.'" Use of the word "octave" here is decisive. Since the Missal calls for the same insertion on the second Sunday as it does during the octave, it must regard that Sunday as being the octave. From all this we may conclude that, if in the 1962 Missal the Sunday after Easter is an octave in name only but not in fact, in the postconciliar Missal the Second Sunday of Easter is an octave in fact but not in name.

b. Gospels

All the Sunday gospels of Easter Time are from John, except on the third Sunday in Years A and B when they are from Luke 24:13-35 and 35-48, respectively, the episode on the road to Emmaus and its sequel. The introduction to the Lectionary, no. 100, states, "The Gospel readings for the first three Sundays recount the appearances of the risen Christ." This is not altogether accurate. On the first Sunday, the Sunday of the Resurrection, at the Paschal Vigil in all three years is read the accounts in the Synoptic Gospels of the women visiting the tomb of Jesus early on the first day of the week and being told, "He is not here." Only in Year A, however, at the end of Matthew 28:1-10, does Jesus appear. He greets the women, and they take hold of his feet and worship him. At the Mass during the day on Easter Sunday John 20:1-9 is read on all three years. It tells of Mary Magdalene discovering the tomb open and reporting it to Peter and the Beloved Disciple, who then run toward the tomb. But Jesus does not appear. Only one of the four gospel selections on the first Sunday, therefore, narrates an appearance.

The appearance stories, properly speaking, begin only on the second Sunday when John 20:19-31 is read in all three years. The same passage is read on the Sunday after Easter, the octave day, in RM 1962. The text is in two parts. In the first part Jesus shows his hands and side to the disciples on the evening of the first day of the week, breathes on them, and imparts the Holy Spirit. This part will return on Pentecost Sunday. The second section is the reason this incident is read on the second Sunday, for it recounts the interaction between Jesus and Thomas "eight days later."

Appearances continue on the third Sunday with the two pericopes not from John: Luke 24:13-35, the two disciples on the road to Emmaus in Year A, and its continuation, Luke 24:35-48, in Year B. In Year C is the appearance by the Sea of Tiberias in John 21:1-19. It consists of the catch of 153 large fish in 21:1-14 and the questioning of Simon Peter in 21:15-19. The long form of the reading includes both of these; the short form only the second. All three of these gospels have something important in common. They describe postresurrection meals. In Year A the two disciples urge Jesus to stay with them. At table "he took bread, blessed and broke it, and gave it to them" (Luke 24:30). Later they tell the Eleven "how he had been made known to them in the breaking of the bread" (Luke 24:35). In Year B, after assuring his disciples that a ghost does not have flesh and bones as he does, he asks whether they have anything to eat. "They gave him a piece of broiled fish, and he took it and ate it in their presence" (Luke 24:43). In Year C, as the disciples come ashore, they see a charcoal fire with fish and bread on it. After inviting them to have breakfast, Jesus "came and took the bread and gave it to them, and he did the same with the fish" (John 21:13). All these incidents have obvious eucharistic overtones that could well be elaborated in postbaptismal catechesis or mystagogy prescribed in the Rite of Christian Initiation of Adults, nos. 244–48.

Surprisingly, the appearance to the women and the bribing of the guards in Matthew 28:8-15, read on Easter Monday, the appearance to Mary Magdalene in John 20:11-19, read on Easter Tuesday, and the summary of the appearances in the longer ending of Mark (16:9-15), read on Easter Saturday, are not read on any Sunday. This is unfortunate. The first two could have alternated with John 20:1-9 at the day Mass of Easter Sunday. The third could have been placed before Mark 16:15-20 on Ascension and would have made the point that the account of Jesus being taken up to heaven and seated at the right hand of God took place on the same day as all the appearances summarized in Mark 16:9-15 and not forty days "after his suffering" as in Acts 1:3.

"The readings about the Good Shepherd are assigned to the Fourth Sunday," states the introduction to the Lectionary, no. 100, again somewhat inaccurately because the expression "Good Shepherd" is heard on the lips of Jesus only in Year B, not the other years. In the old Missal the Good Shepherd gospel is on the previous Sunday, its second Sunday after Easter. The Lectionary moves it back one week so as not to interrupt the series of appearance stories on the first three Sundays.

In all three years, gospels of the fourth Sunday are from the same chapter of John, chapter 10. Like the meal narratives on the third Sunday, these passages have much in common while at the same time remaining distinct. In John 10:1-10, read in Year A, Jesus contrasts the shepherd of a flock with a stranger. Because sheep recognize the voice of their shepherd, he says, they follow him but run away from strangers. A comment of Bruce Vawter, CM, is enlightening. He writes that in Palestine "the sheep of a village were kept in a common fold, where each shepherd would call out his own sheep and lead them away to pasturage."[29] In other words, there is mutual recognition, a bond of communion between the shepherd and the sheep that the stranger lacks, and it is essential for the survival and growth of the flock. This leads Jesus to twice affirm, "I am the gate," meaning that he provides access to nourishment, protection, and rest and that only through him is life attained.

This theme is further developed in John 10:11-18, read in Year B. Here Jesus twice declares, "I am the good shepherd," proclaiming himself as the one who will bring about the restoration, healing, and prosperity that the Lord God promised in Ezekiel 34:11-16. After saying several times that he lays down his life for his sheep, near the end

---

[29] Vawter, "The Gospel According to John," JBC 63:117.

of the pericope he adds that he has "power to take it up again." Vawter explains that "in his exaltation Christ takes up life not only for himself but also for all who live through his work of salvation."[30] In John 10:27-30, read in Year C, Jesus sums up what his work of salvation brings to those who hear his voice and follow: "I give them eternal life and they will never perish." Throughout the fifty days of Easter the faithful recall their insertion into the work of salvation through faith and baptism, and in the Eucharist they deepen their imperishable communion with Christ in the act of taking up his life again.

"On the Fifth, Sixth, and Seventh Sundays," remarks the introduction to the Lectionary, no. 100, "there are excerpts from the Lord's discourse and prayer at the end of the Last Supper." The fourth Sunday, then, is the turning point for the gospels of Easter. The first three Sundays feature appearance stories; the last three contain selections from the farewell discourse and the High Priestly Prayer. Because Jesus in these latter selections speaks of his departure from this world and the sending of the Paraclete, there is a tendency to interpret them in light of the solemnities of Ascension and Pentecost, which they lead up to. We must remember, however, that the account of Jesus being taken up to heaven forty days after the passion and the account of the coming of the Holy Spirit on the Jewish feast of Pentecost are found in the first two chapters of Acts but are not in John, from which the gospels on these Sundays are taken. The introduction to the Lectionary, no 100, reminds us of the original setting of the farewell discourse and the High Priestly Prayer: the Last Supper. Efforts must be made, therefore, to understand these passages first of all in their Johannine context without resorting to the Lukan chronology.

Excerpts from the farewell discourse are spread over two Sundays, the fifth and the sixth, and so, like other Sundays, have common themes. Moreover, in Years A and B the gospel of the sixth Sunday begins where the gospel of the fifth Sunday left off. They are like a single long pericope spread over two successive Sundays. On the fifth Sunday in Year A Jesus tells his disciples in John 14:1-12 that he is going to the Father. On the next Sunday in 14:15-21 he adds that this will not result in their being left orphans, because the Father will send them the Paraclete, the Spirit of truth, who will enable them, while still in the world, to dwell with him in the Father's house. In Year B on the fifth Sunday Jesus declares himself to be the true vine in John 15:1-8

[30] Ibid., 63:118.

and that to remain alive the disciples must abide in him even as he abides in the Father. On the next Sunday, in John 15:9-17, he explains that this abiding consists in self-sacrificing love. He makes such love a commandment for his followers. "This is my commandment," he says, "that you love one another as I have loved you. No one has greater love than this, to lay down one's life for one's friends." Mention of laying down one's life recalls what the Good Shepherd said on the fourth Sunday. In Year B there is no mention of the Holy Spirit on either the fifth or the sixth Sunday.

In Year C the gospel of the sixth Sunday does not continue that of the fifth Sunday, but the two are closely connected by the theme of mutual love. On the fifth Sunday is the beginning of the farewell discourse. In John 13:31-33a, 34-35, immediately after Judas takes the morsel of bread and exits the supper room, Jesus announces that now he is glorified, that God will be glorified in him, and that the disciples are to love one another as he loved them. The gospel on the sixth Sunday skips to the end of the following chapter. In John 14:23-29 Jesus promises that the Father will love those who love him and that "we will come to them and make our home with them." Like the gospel in Year A, this one too includes words about the Holy Spirit whom the Father will send: "He will teach you everything and remind you of all that I have said to you."

On the seventh Sunday the entire prayer of Jesus is read from year to year, beginning in Year A with John 17:1-11a. The evangelist opened the supper narrative in 13:1 by stating that "before the festival of the Passover, Jesus knew that his hour had come to depart from this world and go to the Father." Now, at the end of the supper, the word "hour" returns, this time on the lips of Jesus. "Father, the hour has come," he prays, "glorify your Son so that the Son may glorify you." The Lectionary ends the pericope in the middle of verse 11.

The text in Year B, John 17:11b-19, continues with the rest of verse 11: "Holy Father, protect them in your name." Qualifying the Father by the adjective "holy" in the opening words of this invocation is of the utmost importance because the pericope ends with Jesus declaring, "For their sakes I sanctify myself, so that they also may be sanctified in truth." Because the Father is holy, going to him makes Jesus holy. His passage from this world to the Father in the hour of his passion, then, is not only a glorification bringing the identity of each person to blinding clarity but also a sanctification, a total transformation of his humanity by the utterly transcendent holiness of the one to whom he goes. And because of the abiding union of the exalted Jesus with his own in the world, the passage that sanctifies him at the same time sanctifies them. Further, their sanctification is the goal of his passage, and love of them is the motive for his undertaking it. "For their sakes I sanctify myself," he says, "so that they also may be sanctified."

The prayer concludes in Year C with Jesus in John 17:20-26 requesting for all future believers "that they may all be one. As you, Father, are in me and I am in you, may they also be in us." He continues, "I made your name known to them, and I will make it known, so that the love with which you have loved me may be in them, and I in them." Touching on various aspects of the inexhaustible mystery of divine love revealed in Christ and communicated to the church, the gospels of the fifth, sixth, and seventh Sundays in Year C may be the most coherent of all.

c. Second Reading, Year A

The second reading during the Easter season is taken from three different books of the New Testament read on alternating years. None are letters of Saint Paul. The introduction to the Lectionary, no. 100, explains, "For the reading from the Apostles, the First Letter of Peter is in Year A, the First Letter of John in Year B, the Book of Revelation in Year C. These are the texts that seem to fit in especially well with the spirit of joyous faith and sure hope proper to this season." Rarely does the second reading have any direct connection with the other two. This is not so during the Easter season. On each Sunday of this season in all three years the second reading contains anticipated resonances of the gospel to follow. In Year A is read the First Letter of Peter. This work has attracted much scholarly attention because of its baptismal content. "The allusions to baptism in the first part (1:3–4:11) are so numerous," writes Joseph Fitzmyer, "that this section should be regarded as a baptismal exhortation incorporated into the letter."[31] Readings from the second through the sixth Sunday come from this section. On the seventh Sunday is read 4:13-16, verses that "recapitulate the baptismal exhortation and apply it to the present reality."[32] This is why the RCIA, no. 247, declares that the readings in Year A are "particularly suitable" for postbaptismal mystagogy.

---

[31] Joseph Fitzmyer, "The First Epistle of Peter," JBC 58:4.
[32] Ibid., 58:24.

On the second Sunday, when Jesus in the gospel (John 20:19-31) tells Thomas, "Blessed are those who have not seen and yet have come to believe" (John 20:29), Peter declares in the second reading (1 Pet 1:3-9), "Though you do not see him now, you believe in him." In the gospel of the third Sunday (Luke 24:13-35) Jesus asks the two disciples on the road to Emmaus, "Was it not necessary that the Messiah should suffer these things and then enter into his glory?" The second reading (1 Pet 1:17-21) says that God "raised him from the dead and gave him glory."

In the gospel of the fourth Sunday, John 10:1-10, Jesus says that a shepherd "calls his own sheep by name and leads them out" and that "the sheep follow him because they know his voice." Not this passage but the second reading, 1 Peter 2:20b-25, identifies the shepherd as Christ. In suffering patiently, it says, Christ left an example "that you should follow in his steps." It concludes, "You were going astray like sheep, but now you have returned to the shepherd and guardian of your souls."

In the gospel of the fifth Sunday, John 14:1-12, taken from the farewell discourse, the departing Jesus assures his troubled disciples, "I will come again and will take you to myself, so that where I am, there you may be also."[33] The second reading, 1 Peter 2:4-9, calls those whom Christ takes to himself "a chosen race, a royal priesthood, a holy nation, God's own people." He also calls them "a spiritual house," which may be what Jesus means when he says in the gospel that there are many dwelling places in his Father's house and that "I go to prepare a place for you." Vawter explains that "the Father's 'house' is wherever God is, and whoever is with God is his 'house'; one of Paul's favorite metaphors for the Church is this house of God (1 Cor 3:10-17). In the present context, therefore, the 'many dwelling places' of the Father's house may also refer to the many members of the Church on earth, where Christ will also be."[34]

The common element on the sixth Sunday is the Spirit. The second reading, 1 Peter 3:15-18, declares that Christ was "put to death in the flesh, but made alive in the Spirit."[35] "At the resurrection," comments Fitzmyer, "Christ became *pneuma*. Raised by the Father's glory (*doxa*,

---

[33] Vawter remarks that although "these words can refer naturally enough to the Parousia," they refer "also to Christ's invisible return through the Spirit." JBC 63:143.

[34] Ibid., 63:143.

[35] In the NRSV "spirit" is not capitalized in this passage.

Rom 6:4), Christ was endowed with a power (*dynamis*, Phil 3:10) making him a 'vivifying Spirit' (1 Cor 15:45)."[36] In the gospel, again from the farewell discourse, Jesus in John 14:15-21 says that at his request the Father will give "the Spirit of truth" and that "he abides with you, and he will be in you." The Spirit enables all who believe in Christ to share the new life of his resurrection. Paul tells the Romans in 8:11: "If the Spirit of him who raised Jesus from the dead dwells in you, he who raised Christ from the dead will give life to your mortal bodies also through his Spirit that dwells in you."

In the gospel on the seventh Sunday, John 17:1-11a, the beginning of the High Priestly Prayer, Jesus addresses the Father, "Father, glorify your Son so that the Son may glorify you. I glorified you on earth by finishing the work that you gave me to do. So now, Father, glorify me in your own presence with the glory that I had in your presence before the world existed." The second reading, 1 Peter 4:13-16, is not from the baptismal exhortation as on previous Sundays but from the final recapitulation in which the author sums up his message for persecuted Christians. "Because the Spirit of glory, which is the Spirit of God, is resting on you," he tells them, "if any of you suffers as a Christian, do not consider it a disgrace, but glorify God because you bear this name."[37] In other words, just as Christ in his passion glorified the Father and in turn was glorified by him, suffering Christians should do likewise, confident of shouting for joy "when his glory is revealed."

d. Second Reading, Year B

In Year B readings from the First Letter of John also evoke the gospel. On the second Sunday, insistence that Jesus came "not with the water only but with the water and the blood" in 1 John 5:1-6 calls to mind the water and blood issuing from the pierced side of Jesus that in the gospel, John 20:19-31, Thomas is commanded to touch. In the gospel of the third Sunday, Luke 24:35-48, Jesus says of the Messiah that "repentance and forgiveness of sins is to be proclaimed in his name to all nations." The second reading, 1 John 2:1-5a, states that Christ "is the atoning sacrifice for our sins, and not for ours only but for the sins of the whole world." On the fourth Sunday the Good Shepherd declares in John 10:11-18, "I know my own and my own know me." Not so the world. According to the second reading, 1 John 3:1-2, "it did not

---

[36] Fitzmyer, JBC 58:20.
[37] In the NRSV "spirit of glory" is not capitalized in this passage.

know him." The world here may be the "other sheep" of John 10:16 whom the shepherd must also bring into his fold.

The unifying theme of the fifth Sunday is mutual abiding. The gospel about the vine and the branches, John 15:1-8, uses the word "abide" eight times. The second reading, 1 John 3:18-24, declares, "All who obey his commandments abide in him, and he abides in them." It concludes, "And by this we know that he abides in us, by the Spirit he has given us." On the sixth Sunday the unifying theme shifts to love. In the gospel, John 15:9-17, Jesus declares, "As the Father has loved me, so I have loved you; abide in my love," then, "This is my commandment, that you love one another." Identical expressions occur throughout the second reading, 1 John 4:7-10, which begins, "Beloved, let us love one another, for love is of God."

The second reading on the seventh Sunday, 1 John 4:11-16, takes up where it left off the previous week but, as on the fifth Sunday, mentions the gift of the Spirit, eminently appropriate at the approach of Pentecost: "By this we know that we abide in him and he in us, because he has given us of his Spirit." In the gospel of the seventh Sunday, John 17:11b-19, in the middle section of the High Priestly Prayer, Jesus calls his Father "holy" and characterizes his own passion as an act that sanctifies or consecrates him and those who are one with him. Vawter asserts that "Christ certainly means that this work of consecration will be done by the Spirit of Truth (cf. 16:13)."[38] If so, the link between the two readings on this Sunday is that the Spirit mentioned in the second reading is the one who brings about the sanctification of Christ and us spoken of in the gospel.

e. Second Reading, Year C

In Year C the second reading is from the book of Revelation. It too connects with the gospels. On the second Sunday in Revelation 1:9-11a, 12-13, 17-19, one like the Son of Man announces, "I am the first and the last, and the living one." Yet, as the gospel describes in John 20:19-31, he continues to bear and display his wounds. Because his passion is a going to the Father, in his death he lives. As "the living one" he makes others live by breathing on them and imparting the Spirit by which he himself lives, thereby enabling them to live in death with him.

On the third Sunday Jesus reveals himself at the Sea of Tiberias in John 21:1-19. Recognizing him, Peter jumps into the sea, then, at the

---

[38] Vawter, JBC 63:155.

Lord's command, hauls ashore the net "full of large fish, a hundred fifty-three of them." Jesus then says, "Come and have breakfast." In the second reading, Revelation 5:11-14, the visionary of Patmos hears "every creature in heaven and on earth and under the earth and *in the sea* and *all that is in them*" (emphasis mine) singing praise "to the one seated on the throne and to the Lamb." Jean-Louis D'Aragon, SJ, observes that "the whole created universe, including 'the sea,' has the mission to glorify God and the Lamb."[39] The second reading on this Sunday in Year A, 1 Peter 1:17-21, also mentions the Lamb, saying, "You were ransomed . . . with the precious blood of Christ, like that of a lamb without defect or blemish." The second reading in Year B, 1 John 2:1-5, does not mention the Lamb but states that Christ "is the atoning sacrifice for our sins." Perhaps these references to the sacrificed Lamb in the second reading on this Sunday in all three years are meant to set forth the content of the Eucharist alluded to in the meals recounted in the gospels on these same Sundays.

On the fourth Sunday, when the Good Shepherd in John 10:27-30 declares that "my sheep hear my voice" and that "I give them eternal life and they will never perish," Revelation 7:9, 14b-17 discloses the heavenly bliss of Christians who on earth shed their blood in union with him: "The Lamb at the center of the throne will be their shepherd, and he will guide them to springs of the water of life." The second reading on the next two Sundays is drawn from the same chapter of the book of Revelation, chapter 21. On the fifth Sunday the "new Jerusalem, coming down out of heaven from God, prepared as a bride adorned for her husband," in Revelation 21:1-5a is the climactic realization of the glorification of which Jesus speaks in John 13:31-33a, 34-35. On the sixth Sunday the Spirit is the connecting link. In John 14:23-29 Jesus says that "the Holy Spirit, whom the Father will send in my name, will teach you everything, and remind you of all that I have said to you." In the opening words of the second reading, Revelation 21:10-14, 22-23, John confesses that it is "in the spirit" that an angel shows him "the holy city Jerusalem coming down out of heaven from God." On the seventh Sunday in Year C, both the second reading and the gospel are endings. The second reading is the end of the book of Revelation (22:12-14, 16-17, 20). The gospel, John 17:20-26, is the end of the High Priestly Prayer.

[39] "The Apocalypse," JBC 64:36.

f. First Reading

There are no readings from the Old Testament during Easter Time. "The first reading is from the Acts of the Apostles," says the introduction to the Lectionary, no. 100, "in a three-year cycle of parallel and progressive selections; material is presented on the life of the early Church, its witness, and its growth." By "progressive" the introduction means that in any given year the narrative moves forward from Sunday to Sunday. By "parallel" it means that on any given Sunday there is a common theme in all three years. In this season the first reading is independent of the other two.

The second Sunday has the three familiar and perhaps idealized summaries of the activities of the primitive Christian community in Jerusalem: Acts 2:42-47 in Year A, Acts 4:32-35 in Year B, and Acts 5:12-16 in Year C. Their content is similar, though they differ in detail. Each year the third Sunday features one of the five discourses of Peter, delivered at various places in Jerusalem: Acts 2:14a, 22-28 in Year A, preached on the day of Pentecost; Acts 3:13-15, 17-19 in Year B, in the Portico of Solomon after healing a cripple; Acts 5:27b-32, 40b-41 in Year C, before the Sanhedrin after being delivered from prison by an angel. In Acts these are the first, second, and fourth sermons of the apostle. All are formulations of the apostolic kerygma that Jesus was handed over to death but that God raised him to life. They are the core of what will later become the written gospels.

Selections on the next three Sundays deal with the numerical growth of the Christian community, its spread beyond Jerusalem, its leadership structures, and the continued activity of the Holy Spirit. The fourth Sunday records the beginnings of expansion. In Year A the passage from Acts 2:14a, 36-41 continues the one from the previous Sunday. It repeats "on the day of Pentecost" and reports the first conversions and baptisms resulting from Peter's inaugural discourse. Year B contains Peter's third discourse, Acts 4:8-12, delivered before the Sanhedrin after being arrested and interrogated. Hostility, opposition, and persecution on the part of religious authorities in Jerusalem cause Christians to flee the city and seek refuge in Judea and Samaria, where, of course, they continue to proclaim the Good News. In Year C Paul and Barnabas, on their first missionary journey, preach in the synagogue of Antioch in Pisidia (Acts 13:14, 43-52), are rejected, and turn to the Gentiles.

The fifth Sunday describes the emergence of service personnel or ministries within the expanding church: seven assistants in Year A; an apostolic college into which Paul is incorporated in Year B; and a body of elders in Year C. In Year A the Christian community is still confined to Jerusalem but is increasing. The tension between Hebrews and Hellenists set forth on this Sunday in Acts 6:1-7 is resolved by the selection of seven assistants who in fact are deacons, though not so called. They are presented to the apostles, who pray and impose hands on them. All are Hellenists. As Greek speakers they initiate the mission to the Gentiles. In Year B Acts 9:26-31 tells how the recently converted Saul comes to Jerusalem and is introduced to the college of apostles by Barnabas. He argues with the Hellenists mentioned in Year A. In Year C Paul and Barnabas, already preaching to the Gentiles, encourage the faithful in Acts 14:21b-27 to persevere in the faith and install elders or presbyters in every church. Unlike the seven assistants in Year A, the elders are not elected but appointed.

The Spirit was mentioned on the fourth and fifth Sundays in Years A and B but only in passing. On the sixth Sunday he is in the foreground. Years A and B recount two major outpourings of the Spirit, and Year C acknowledges his role in the momentous decision that determined the future course of Christian history. In Year A the church is beginning to spread beyond Jerusalem. Philip, one of the seven assistants named on the previous Sunday and a Hellenist, is preaching Christ in Samaria on his own. Multitudes are accepting his message. When the apostles at Jerusalem heard this, Peter and John came down and, as told in Acts 8:5-8, 14-17, "prayed for them that they might receive the Holy Spirit (for as yet the Spirit had not come upon any of them; they had only been baptized in the name of the Lord Jesus). Then Peter and John laid their hands on them, and they received the Holy Spirit." In this event, called "the Samaritan Pentecost," Luke is emphasizing that "the gift of the Spirit comes through the Church, represented by the Twelve in Jerusalem."[40]

In Year B on the sixth Sunday Acts 10:25-26, 34-35, 44-48 recounts the fifth great discourse of Peter, then "the Gentile Pentecost,"[41] leading to the baptism of Cornelius and his entire household. "While Peter was still speaking," Luke says, "the Holy Spirit fell upon all who

[40] Richard J. Dillon and Joseph A. Fitzmyer, SJ, "Acts of the Apostles," JBC 45:47.

[41] The expressions "Samaritan Pentecost" and "Gentile Pentecost" are from Dillon-Fitzmyer, JBC 45:47.

heard the word," and they spoke in tongues. Peter asks, "Can anyone withhold the water for baptizing these people who have received the Holy Spirit just as we have?" The reading from Acts 15:1-2, 22-29 on the sixth Sunday in Year C is the letter that Paul and Barnabas together with Judas and Silas take from Jerusalem to Antioch, saying, "It has seemed good to the Holy Spirit and to us" that Gentile converts not be obliged to observe the Mosaic law. This "is the turning point in Luke's story, when the apostolic and presbyteral college of Jerusalem officially recognizes the evangelization of the Gentiles," and "the Christian Church officially breaks out of its Jewish matrix."[42]

On the seventh Sunday, between Ascension and Pentecost, Years A and B relate two episodes that Acts says followed the Lord's being taken up to heaven: in Year A the Eleven, Mary, other women, and the brothers remaining in continuous prayer in Jerusalem (Acts 1:12-14), and in Year B the choice of Matthias (Acts 1:15-17, 20a, 20c-26). Year C recalls the stoning of Stephen, the first martyr, in Acts 7:55-60. It begins with his vision. "Filled with the Holy Spirit, he gazed into heaven and saw the glory of God and Jesus standing at the right hand of God."

g. Prayers

Prayers in the 1962 Missal for the second through the fifth Sundays after Easter as well as for that of the Sunday after Ascension have no paschal content because, as we saw, in the present state of the source from which they ultimately derive, the Old Gelasian, celebration of the resurrection ceases on the Sunday it calls the octave of Easter, and the Masses in question are understood as being celebrated "after the close of Easter." With rare exceptions the Missal of Paul VI shifts these prayers to Ordinary Time or other occasions and replaces them with others that are replete with references to the various facets of the paschal mystery and hence are eminently appropriate for what are now Sundays of Easter. These Sundays in the postconciliar Missal, then, are quite different than their predecessors.

The collect and prayer over the offerings on the second Sunday continue the theme of baptism from the Paschal Vigil and days within the octave. The collect, from the *Missale Gothicum* (Go 309),[43] is particularly

---

[42] Ibid., 45:72.

[43] For the sources of the orations of the Second Sunday of Easter, see Anthony Ward, SM, "The Missal Orations of the Easter Octave from Monday to Sunday," EL 125 (2011) 112–19, 122. The third typical edition of the Missal of

striking. Invoking the "God of everlasting mercy," it asks that all the faithful

> may grasp and rightly understand
> in what font they have been washed,
> by whose Spirit they have been reborn,
> by whose Blood they have been redeemed.

The petition is no doubt inspired by 1 John 5:6, read on this Sunday in Year B. This passage speaks of Jesus Christ as "the one who came by water and blood, . . . not with water only, but with the water and the blood. And the Spirit is the one that testifies, for the Spirit is the truth." The prayer over the offerings was the secret of Easter Thursday in RM 1962. It asks God to accept the oblations of those "brought to new birth," that, "renewed by confession of your name and by Baptism, / they may attain unending happiness."

Two orations on the third Sunday are filled with expressions of joy, characteristic of the fifty days of Easter since earliest times. In the collect, composed of GeV 515 and V 1148, the faithful exult at being adopted as children of God in the present and at having the hope of resurrection in the future. It prays:

> May your people exult for ever, O God,
> in renewed youthfulness of spirit,
> so that, rejoicing now in the restored glory of our adoption,
> we may look forward in confident hope
> to the rejoicing of the day of resurrection.

The prayer after Communion, used also on Saturday within the octave of Easter, makes a similar request, asking that the faithful "may attain in their flesh / the incorruptible glory of the resurrection"—words inspired by a sermon of Pope Leo the Great preached at the Paschal Vigil in 443.[44] The prayer over the offerings, used on the octave of Easter in

---

Paul VI contains a votive Mass of the Mercy of God, the collect of which is the same as that of the Second Sunday of Easter. A rubric above the entrance antiphon says, "This Mass may not be said on the Second Sunday of Easter." Obviously, there is a connection between the collect of the second Sunday and devotion to Divine Mercy.

[44] Leo declares that "always rising from relapses to wholeness, we might deserve to arrive at that incorruptible resurrection of glorified flesh." *Sermon*

RM 1962, characterizes the church as "exultant" at having been given "cause for such great gladness."

The theme of joy returns on the next three Sundays as well. The prayer over the offerings on the fourth Sunday, from H 430, also used on Saturday within the octave of Easter in both missals, requests that "the renewal constantly at work within us / may be the cause of our unending joy." In the collect of the fifth Sunday the faithful ask to "come to the joys of life eternal." That of the sixth Sunday characterizes the entire season as "days of joy." This calls to mind the statement in the Universal Norms, no. 22, that "the fifty days from the Sunday of the Resurrection to Pentecost Sunday are celebrated in joy and exultation as one feast day." Lastly, the third section of all five Easter prefaces declares that we are "overcome with paschal joy."

On the fourth Sunday, when the gospel in all three years is from John 10 in which Jesus likens himself to a shepherd, the collect, from GeV 524, asks that "the humble flock may reach / where the brave Shepherd has gone before." Inexplicably, the Missal omits the petition that God would grant those reborn of the Holy Spirit to enter his kingdom. The prayer after Communion on the fourth Sunday, from GeV 272, invokes the Father as "kind Shepherd," praying,

> Look upon your flock, kind Shepherd,
> and be pleased to settle in eternal pastures
> the sheep you have redeemed
> by the Precious Blood of your Son.

Two of the prayers on the fifth Sunday center on renewal. The collect, pieced together from two prayers in the Sacramentary of Bergamo (B 577 and 571), prays that those whom God was "pleased to make new in Holy Baptism" may "come to the joys of life eternal." In the first two editions of the Missal of Paul VI this oration was on Saturday of the fourth week of Easter. Perhaps it was moved from there to the fifth Sunday because its reference to being made new in holy baptism complements the request in the prayer after Communion that the Eucharist enable the faithful "to pass from former ways to newness of

---

71, 6, trans. Freeland and Conway, in FC 93, 315. Latin text in PL 54, 389 D or in the edition of Antoine Chavasse in CCL 138 A, 440. The prayer is found with a different ending on Friday of Easter week in H 426 and RM 1962. See also GeV 533.

life."[45] This petition is from V 1297, but the rest of the prayer is the same as the post-Communion of Monday within the octave of Pentecost in RM 1962, which is from H 534. There, the petition asks God to defend the communicants from the fury of their foes.

We saw that the collect of the third Sunday portrays the baptized as looking forward with hope to "the day of resurrection." The prayer after Communion asks that they "attain in their flesh / the incorruptible glory of the resurrection." In both cases the resurrection in question is that of the faithful, expected on the last day. Only on the sixth Sunday do prayers speak of Christ's resurrection. The collect of that Sunday speaks of Easter Time as "days of joy" kept "in honor of the risen Lord," phrases lifted from a preface in V 229. In a sentence from GeV 467, the prayer after Communion recalls how God restored the faithful to eternal life "in the Resurrection of Christ."

The ascension is in the foreground of prayers on the seventh Sunday. The collect alludes to Matthew 28:20, read on the solemnity of the Ascension in Year B. While believing that Christ is now with the Father in glory, it prays that we "may experience, as he promised, / until the end of the world, / his abiding presence among us." The prayer after Communion, from V 174, is more ecclesial. It asks that "there will be accomplished in the body of the whole Church / what has already come to pass in Christ her Head."

h. Prefaces

The 1962 Missal has only one preface for the entire period from the Paschal Vigil to the Vigil of the Ascension. It comes from the Sacramentary of Pope Hadrian, where it is used at the Mass on Holy Saturday night (H 379) and the Mass of Easter Sunday (H 385) and is listed on Monday and Thursday of Easter week (H 394 and 417), though it was probably used on other days as well, since it is the only preface of the Easter season, which, we recall, ended on the Sunday after Easter, called "Sunday after White Week" in title 95. In the Missal of Paul VI it is the first of five prefaces for Easter Time. In all five the first and third sections do not change. The first section always ends by declaring that

---

[45] On weekdays the third typical edition of the Missal of Paul VI replaces some nine collects in the first two editions with other ones in order to eliminate doublets. The new prayers are taken from either the Old Gelasian or the *Hadrianum* and are markedly paschal in content. They are listed with their sources in Maurizio Barba, "Il Temporale, l' 'Ordo Missae' e il Santorale del nuovo 'Missale Romanum,'" EL 116 (2002) 320–66, here 336–38.

the principal reason for giving thanks is because, as Paul wrote in 1 Corinthians 5:7, "Christ our Passover has been sacrificed." In similar fashion the third section always begins by confessing that we are "overcome with paschal joy." The second section, different in each of the five prefaces, relates the reasons why "it is truly right and just" to acclaim the Lord "at all times." Biblical quotations or allusions in these sections are extensive. We can point out but a few.

Preface I affirms that Christ "is the true Lamb / who has taken away the sins of the world," the exclamation of John the Baptist in John 1:29, the first time he saw Jesus coming toward him. Preface II, extracted from GeV 466, states that through Christ "the children of light rise to eternal life." The New Testament several times calls believers "children of light." Jesus urges the crowds in John 12:36 to "believe in the light, so that you may become children of light."[46] Earlier in John 8:12 he reveals himself as "the light of the world," promising that whoever follows him "will have the light of life," thus linking light and life as does the preface. The next line in Preface II states that Christ's death "is our ransom from death, / and in his rising the life of all has risen." The same idea is in Preface I: "By dying he has destroyed our death, / and by rising, restored our life."

The third preface is from the *Missale Gothicum* (Go 296). Its statement that Christ "defends us and ever pleads our cause" recalls the consoling words of John 2:1: "If anyone does sin, we have an advocate with the Father, Jesus Christ the righteous." The preface continues, "[H]e is the sacrificial Victim who dies no more." The Latin is *immolatus iam non moritur*. The words *iam non moritur* are from Romans 6:9, "Christ, being raised from the dead [*iam non moritur*] will never die again." In the preface, however, the reason Christ "will never die again" is not because he is "raised from the dead" but because he is *immolatus*, offered in sacrifice. This word *immolatus*, translated as "the sacrificial Victim," comes from 1 Corinthians 5:7, *Pascha nostrum immolatus est Christus*, "Christ our Passover has been sacrificed." To this the preface adds the marvelous Latin phrase *semper vivit occisus*, "he lives forever, slain," a reference to Revelation 5:6, the vision of "a Lamb standing as if it had been slaughtered." To grasp the full import of this statement, we must recall the obvious: if a victim destined for sacrifice is still standing, it has not yet been slaughtered, and once slaughtered, it can

---

[46] See also Luke 16:8; 1 Thess 5:5; Eph 5:8-9.

no longer stand. In saying that the celestial Lamb "stands as slain," the book of Revelation is emphasizing the simultaneous coexistence of death and life in the Lamb, that in its death, it lives. The idea of the preface, then, is that, though offered in sacrifice, Christ is not now dead but rather, precisely in his immolation, lives forever.

In declaring "the old order destroyed" and "integrity of life restored to us in Christ," the fourth preface, from GeV 487, may be alluding to what Paul wrote in 2 Corinthians 5:17, that "if anyone is in Christ, there is a new creation; everything old has passed away; see, everything has become new." This rejuvenation affects not only human beings but also the entire creation. In Christ, the preface says, "a universe cast down is renewed." Having been granted a vision of the final transformation of the world, the author of the book of Revelation testifies in 21:1, "I saw a new heaven and a new earth; for the first heaven and the first earth had passed away, and the sea was no more," adding in 21:5 that "the one who was seated on the throne said, 'See, I am making all things new.'" This preface is very similar in content to the first oration after the seventh reading of the Paschal Vigil, which prays,

[M]ay the whole world know and see
that what was cast down is raised up,
what had become old is made new,
and all things are restored to integrity through Christ,
just as by him they came into being.

The opening lines of Preface V, from GeV 476, summarize the teaching of the Letter to the Hebrews, chapters 7–10. "By the oblation of his Body," it says, Christ "brought the sacrifices of old to fulfillment / in the reality of the Cross." Mention of "the oblation of his Body" recalls in particular the statement in Hebrews 10:5 that "when Christ came into the world, he said [quoting Psalm 40:7], 'Sacrifices and offerings you have not desired, but a body you have prepared for me.'" Hebrews 10:10 concludes that "we have been sanctified by the offering of the body of Jesus Christ once for all." The second half of the preface states that "by commending himself to you for our salvation," Christ "showed himself the Priest, the Altar, and the Lamb of sacrifice." That Christ is priest is the central message of Hebrews 7–10. That he is Lamb is stated in two other prefaces. Preface I calls him "the true Lamb / who has taken away the sins of the world" (John 1:29, 39), and

Preface III extols him as "the sacrificial Victim who dies no more, / the Lamb, once slain, who lives for ever" (Rev 5:6, 12).[47] Taken together, Preface V is articulating the traditional doctrine that on the cross Christ is simultaneously priest and victim, the one who offers and the one who is offered.

The third image in the preface, Christ as altar, appears with the other two in the 1977 document of the Congregation for the Sacraments and Divine Worship, *Dedication of a Church and an Altar*, which states that "the ancient Fathers of the Church did not hesitate to assert that Christ was the victim, priest, and altar of his own sacrifice. For in the Letter to the Hebrews Christ is presented as the High Priest who is also the living altar of the heavenly temple" (IV, 1).[48] The concluding words of the prayer of dedication, no. 48, likewise identify Christ as "high priest and living altar." Finally, the proper preface for the rite of dedication, no. 60, calls him the "true priest and true victim" who offered himself to the Father "on the altar of the cross."

i. Mystagogy

Masses of the Sundays of Easter are also the privileged occasions for what nos. 244–51 of the Rite of Christian Initiation of Adults calls the period of postbaptismal catechesis or mystagogy. "This is a time," says no. 244, "for the community and the neophytes together to grow in deepening their grasp of the paschal mystery and in making it part of their lives through meditation on the Gospel, sharing in the eucharist, and doing the works of charity."

No. 245 explains more precisely the content and goal of catechesis during the weeks immediately following the sacraments of initiation at the vigil: "The neophytes are, as the term 'mystagogy' suggests, introduced into a fuller and more effective understanding of mysteries through the Gospel message they have learned and above all through their experience of the sacraments." The main setting for this postbaptismal catechesis on the sacraments or mysteries experienced at the vigil, says no. 247, "is the so-called Masses for neophytes, that is, the Sunday Masses of the Easter season. Besides being occasions for

[47] The word "lamb" is not in the Latin text of Preface III, which reads, *immolatus iam non moritur, sed semper vivit occisus*. A literal translation would be "offered in sacrifice, he is dead no longer but forever lives as slain." In Preface V the Latin says only that Christ is *agnus*, "Lamb," not "Lamb of sacrifice."

[48] The reference is to Heb 13:10, "We have an altar from which those who officiate in the tent have no right to eat."

the newly baptized to gather with the community and share in the mysteries, these celebrations include particularly suitable readings from the Lectionary, especially the readings for Year A." Finally, "to close the period of postbaptismal catechesis," no. 249 recommends that "some sort of celebration should be held at the end of the Easter season near Pentecost Sunday."

Speaking of Easter Time, the 1988 circular letter *Paschalis Sollemnitatis*, no. 102, declares that "for adults who have received Christian initiation during the Easter Vigil, the whole of this period is given over to mystagogical catechesis." No. 103 continues, "Throughout the Easter season, the neophytes should be assigned their own special place among the faithful. All neophytes should endeavor to participate at Mass along with their godparents. In the homily and, according to local circumstances, in the general intercessions, mention should be made of them. Some celebration should be held to conclude the period of mystagogical catechesis on or about Pentecost Sunday."

The changes in nomenclature, readings, and prayers as well as the attention given to the newly baptized make Easter Time in the Missal of Paul VI a vast improvement over its counterpart in the preconciliar Missal, now permitted as an extraordinary form of the Roman Rite.

Chapter 7

The Ascension of the Lord

Preliminaries. According to the general rubrics of the Roman Missal of 1962, no. 76b, this feast is the start of the second subdivision of the Easter season, *tempus Ascensionis*, or "Time of Ascension," which begins with First Vespers of the Ascension and runs through None of the Vigil of Pentecost when the third subdivision, "The Octave of Pentecost," begins. The 1969 Roman Calendar abolished these subdivisions in order to make the Easter season a single unit. Concerning Ascension, the Universal Norms on the Liturgical Year and the Calendar, no. 25, states: "On the fortieth day after Easter the Ascension of the Lord is celebrated, except where, not being observed as a Holyday of Obligation, it has been assigned to the Seventh Sunday of Easter." The possibility of transferring the solemnity reflects no. 7 of the Universal Norms: "Where the solemnities of the Epiphany, the Ascension and the Most Holy Body and Blood of Christ are not observed as Holydays of Obligation, they should be assigned to a Sunday"—"the Ascension," no. 7b adds, "to the Seventh Sunday of Easter."

The 1962 Missal has a Mass for the Vigil of the Ascension meant for the morning of Wednesday of the fifth week after Easter, the morning before Ascension Thursday. Except for the readings, the formulary is the same as that of the Fifth Sunday after Easter. It makes its appearance as a vigil only in 1474, the date of the first printed edition of the Roman Missal, and is reproduced in the Tridentine Missal of 1570.[1] In MR 1570 and 1962 the day before Ascension is also the third of the three Rogation Days or Lesser Litanies. When the procession takes place on these days, the Mass of Rogation is said, not that of the Vigil of the Ascension. When the Mass of the vigil *is* said, it does not yet belong to *tempus Ascensionis* but is the last Mass of *tempus Paschatis*, which, as stated in the general rubrics, no. 76a, runs until None on Wednesday.

---

[1] See Bruylants I, no. 105.

The Roman Calendar of 1969 abolishes vigils of this type: Masses on the mornings before feasts meant to prepare for the feasts but not part of the feasts for which they prepare.

For five solemnities, however, the Roman Missals of 1970 and 1975 provide vigil Masses of a new type: Masses celebrated on the evenings before solemnities that belong to the solemnities themselves. The solemnities with vigil Masses are the Nativity of the Lord, Pentecost, the Nativity of Saint John the Baptist, the solemnity of Saints Peter and Paul, and the Assumption.[2] To these the third typical edition of the Missal of Paul VI adds Epiphany and Ascension. The current Missal, then, has two Ascension Masses—one *in vigilia*, the other *in die*. The second is the immediate successor of the Ascension Mass in RM 1962. The other is new. We shall treat these Masses one after the other, showing the theological enrichment as we move from the Mass in the 1962 Missal to its successor in the 1970 Missal of Paul VI to the vigil Mass inserted in the 2002 *Missale Romanum* and repeated in the 2008 edition.

A. THE ROMAN MISSAL OF 1962

Prayers. The orations, proper preface, and *communicantes* in RM 1962 all come from the Sacramentary of Pope Hadrian (H 497–501) under the title of *Ascensa Domini*. The collect (H 497) asks that we who believe our Redeemer "to have ascended on this day into heaven, may also ourselves dwell in mind amid heavenly things." This recalls the rousing exhortation of Pope Leo the Great in his second sermon on the ascension: "Let us freely raise the eyes of our hearts to that height where Christ is. Let not earthly desires hold down the souls called upwards. Let perishable things not hold those ordained for eternity."[3] Although the secret (H 498) mentions "the glorious ascension" of Christ, its request is unrelated to it: "Grant that we may be freed from present perils and attain to everlasting life." The petition of the post-Communion (H 501) is well phrased but without connection to the feast. It asks that "we may obtain the invisible effects of what we have received under visible signs." The preface, on the other hand, taken from H 499, recounts that Christ, after his ascension, appeared openly to his disciples and in their sight was taken up to heaven. To this it appends the astounding theological

---

[2] The first two are called *Ad Missam Vigiliae*, whereas the last three are *Ad Missam in Vigilia*.

[3] Leo the Great, *Sermon* 74, 5, trans. Freeland and Conway, in FC 93, 328.

assertion "that he might make us sharers in his divinity." It thus makes our divinization the goal of his ascension. The proper *communicantes* (H 500) is equally profound. It states that we are celebrating the day when Christ "established at the right hand of thy glory the substance of our frail human nature, which he had taken to himself."

Readings. The epistle is Acts 1:1-11, the description of Jesus being taken out of sight by a cloud after appearing to his apostles during forty days. The gospel is Mark 16:14-20, the conclusion of the longer ending of this gospel. Besides telling that Jesus, on the same day as his resurrection, was taken up to heaven, it adds that he was seated at the right hand of God and that the Eleven went forth to preach everywhere. Mention of Jesus sitting at the right hand of God is, of course, a reference to Psalm 109:1, which, in *The Revised Grail Psalms*, reads,

> The LORD's revelation to my lord:
> "Sit at my right hand,
> until I make your foes your footstool."

Chants. The introit antiphon, *Viri Galilaei*, is a slight modification of Acts 1:11, the last two lines of the epistle. In the biblical text the two men in white robes ask the men of Galilee, "Why do you stand looking up toward heaven?" In the antiphon they ask, "Why wonder you, looking up to heaven?" Further, the antiphon replaces "this Jesus" with the pronoun "he" and reads, "He shall so come as you have seen him going up to heaven." In the Missal the opening line of Psalm 46, "Clap your hands, all ye nations," follows the antiphon. Verse 6 of the same psalm is chanted with the first Alleluia and at the offertory: "God is ascended with jubilee, and the Lord with the sound of a trumpet." Parts of the other ascension psalm, Psalm 67, are used elsewhere. Verse 19, "Ascending on high he hath led captivity captive," is sung with the second Alleluia. Verses 33 and 34 are the communion antiphon, "Sing ye to the Lord, who mounteth above the heaven of heavens to the East." Though not theologically noteworthy except for the preface and *communicantes*, the formulary is exceptionally unified and coherent because of the description of the ascension in each of the two readings, the introit being taken from the epistle, the chanting of the same psalm verses at different parts of the Mass (for example, Ps 46:6 at both the first Alleluia and the offertory), or the chanting of different verses of the same psalm (for example, Ps 67:18-19 at the second Alleluia and Ps 67:33-34 at Communion).

Prayers. This Mass goes back to the first typical edition of the Missal of Paul VI. It replaces the three prayers of RM 1962 with others rich in doctrinal content and directly linked to the event celebrated. Discussing the sources of this material, Anthony Ward writes that, besides the early sacramentaries, "on occasions the revisers, aware of the relation between the ancient Roman liturgy and the preaching of the Fathers, broadened their searches to draw on patristic writings for the composition of new prayers."[4] Such is the case with the collect introduced in 1970. It converts a statement of Pope Leo in his first sermon on the ascension into a prayer. Leo declares that "since the Ascension of Christ is our elevation, and since, where the glory of the Head has preceded us, there hope for the body is also invited, let us exult, dearly beloved, with worthy joy and be glad with a holy thanksgiving."[5] The collect prays, "Gladden us with holy joys, almighty God, and make us rejoice with devout thanksgiving, for the Ascension of Christ your Son is our exaltation, and where the Head has gone before in glory the Body is called to follow in hope." RM 1970 and 1975 omitted the collect of the 1962 Missal. The third typical edition of 2002 brought it back as an alternate.

The prayer over the offerings in the postconciliar Missal is that of the Mass *in Ascensa Domini* in the Old Gelasian (GeV 574). It asks that as we honor the ascension of Christ, "through this most holy exchange we too may rise to the heavenly realms." The new prayer after Communion is a combination of parts of two ancient orations in the Verona collection of papal Masses. The invocation, "Almighty ever-living God, / who allow those on earth to celebrate divine mysteries," is from V 689, whereas the petition that "Christian hope may draw us onward / to where our nature is united with you" is from V 185.

The union of human nature with God, found in the *communicantes* and in several other ancient orations,[6] is a frequent theme in the sermons of Pope Leo, including the two on the ascension. In the first he declares that "truly it was a great and indescribable source of rejoicing when, in the sight of the heavenly multitudes, the nature of our

---

[4] Anthony Ward, SM, "The Orations for the Solemnities of Ascension and Pentecost in the 2000 *Missale Romanum*," EL 124 (2010) 219.

[5] Leo the Great, *Sermon* 73, 4, in FC 93, 324.

[6] See Ward, "Ascension and Pentecost," 231–33.

human race ascended over the dignity of all heavenly creatures, to pass the angelic orders and to be raised beyond the heights of archangels. In its ascension it did not stop at any other height until this same nature was received at the seat of the eternal Father, to be associated on the throne of the glory of that One to whose nature it was joined in the Son."[7] In his second ascension sermon Leo likewise states that on this feast "we recall and rightly venerate that day when our lowly nature was carried in Christ above all the hosts of heaven, over all the angelic orders and beyond the height of all powers, to the seat of God the Father."[8]

The Missal of Paul VI retains the preface of the 1962 Missal as Preface II. Preface I is a new composition of comparable doctrinal density, but it is more expansive. The christological titles are particularly numerous and filled with biblical evocations: King of glory, conqueror of sin and death, mediator between God and man, judge of the world, Lord of hosts, our head and founder. Like the preface in RM 1962, this one ends with a statement of purpose: "He ascended, not to distance himself from our lowly state, / but that we, his members, might be confident of following / where he, our Head and Founder, has gone before"—an idea very similar to the second half of the collect formed from *Sermon* 73 of Saint Leo: "[T]he Ascension of Christ your Son / is our exaltation, / and where the Head has gone before in glory, / the Body is called to follow in hope."

Many of the expressions in this preface, moreover, are lifted from two prefaces and an oration in the Verona collection. "Mediator between God and humanity" is from V 176, "King of glory" and "Lord of hosts" are from V 177—both prefaces—and the request that his members "might be confidant of following / where he, our Head and Founder, has gone before" is from V 183, an oration. The phrase *judex mundi*, "judge of the world," in the new preface is found nowhere in the *Veronensis*, but the Last Judgment is closely associated with the ascension and even with the resurrection in the thought of Pope Leo, who declares in his second sermon on the ascension that Christ would remain at the right hand of the Father until "he would return to judge the living and the dead in the same flesh with which he ascended" and that "as the first witness of the heavenly messengers told that he had risen from the dead (Matt 28:1-7), so the service of the angels was

---

[7] Leo the Great, *Sermon* 73, 2, in FC 93, 324.
[8] Leo the Great, *Sermon* 74, 2, in FC 93, 325.

to announce that he would come to judge the world" (Matt 24:31).[9] Reflecting on the new prayers for the day Mass of the Ascension, Anthony Ward writes that "the reform of the Second Vatican Council brought to light many treasures from the ancient books, both whole orations and rich individual phrases, which the 1970 and subsequent revisers put to good use in compiling the new formularies."[10]

Readings. On the solemnity of the Ascension the Lectionary features the concluding paragraphs of all three Synoptic Gospels on alternate years. The gospel of the 1962 Missal, Mark 16:14-20, is assigned to Year B. But the reproach in verse 14 is omitted, and the pericope begins with verse 15, the Lord's command to proclaim the Good News to the whole creation. Year A has the conclusion of Matthew's gospel, Matthew 28:16-20, in which Jesus, after commissioning the Eleven to make disciples, to baptize, and to teach, assures them, "I am with you always, to the end of the age." Year C has the conclusion of Luke's gospel, Luke 24:46-53. This is another short account of the ascension that, as in Mark 16:19-20, takes place on the same day as the resurrection but contains the detail that Jesus lifted up his hands and blessed the disciples as he was being carried up to heaven.

The postconciliar Lectionary keeps Acts 1:1-11 as the first reading in all three years but adds a second reading from the New Testament "from the Apostles on Christ in exaltation at the right hand of the Father," says the general introduction, no. 102. The first choice is Ephesians 1:17-23. Like the ending of Mark's gospel, it too alludes to Psalm 109:1 when it declares that God seated Christ "at his right hand in the heavenly places," adding, in the words of Psalm 8:7, that God "put all things under his feet." The Lectionary offers two other New Testament readings for optional use. The first is Ephesians 4:1-13 for Year B. In it the text of Psalm 67:19 is altered to read, "When he ascended on high . . . he gave gifts to his people." Joseph A. Grassi, MM, explains that "the general sense is this: Christ ascended in victory into the heavens in order to give men on earth the gift of the Spirit to be exercised in the various ministries of the Church."[11] A shorter version of this passage is provided, but its use is not recommended because it omits verses 8-9, the citation of Psalm 67:19 and its application to the ascension, thereby

[9] Leo the Great, *Sermon* 74, 2 and 4, in FC 93, 326, and 328.
[10] Ward, "Ascension and Pentecost," 242.
[11] "The Letter to the Ephesians," JBC 56:30.

excluding the very portion of the passage that makes it suitable for this solemnity.

The other optional New Testament reading is Hebrews 9:24-28; 10:19-23, proposed for Year C. This one is reminiscent of the Good Friday liturgy. In contrast to the futility of the Jewish high priest entering the holy place year after year with the blood of sacrificed animals and failing to secure remission of sins, the author affirms that Christ, by shedding his blood once for all, "entered heaven itself, now to appear in the presence of God on our behalf." For the Letter to the Hebrews, then, the ascension is not what is described at the beginning of Acts but what took place on the cross.

Chants. The Missal of Paul VI keeps the introit of RM 1962, *Viri Galilaei*, but replaces its communion antiphon with the words of Jesus in Matthew 28:20, "Behold, I am with you always, / even to the end of the age," heard in the gospel reading in Year A and included in the gospel acclamation of all three years. Singing these words during Communion may suggest that this promise of Jesus is fulfilled in the Eucharist, especially the consecrated species. This would be narrower than Matthew intended. Pope Leo understood the Lord's abiding presence to be a broadly sacramental one. Jesus "made an end to his bodily presence in the sight of his disciples on the fortieth day after the resurrection," teaches the pontiff. "What was to be seen of our Redeemer has passed over into the Sacraments."[12] According to Leo, this sacramental presence known by faith is more real and more profound than physical presence known by sense perception. He has Jesus telling Mary Magdalene, who wanted to cling to him, "I do not want you to come to me bodily, nor to acknowledge me with the perception of your flesh. I am taking you to higher things. I am preparing greater things for you. When I have ascended to my Father, then you will feel me more perfectly and more truly."[13]

Readings in the 1962 Missal were both narratives—accounts of Jesus being taken up to heaven. The introit antiphon, prayers, and preface for the most part summarize the story or repeat details. The

---

[12] Leo the Great, *Sermon* 74, 2, in FC 93, 326. At the time of Leo the term "sacrament" did not yet have the technical meaning given it by the twelfth-century scholastics but, as Augustine taught, was the sign of any sacred or divine reality.

[13] Leo the Great, *Sermon* 74, 4, in FC 93, 327.

petition of the collect is moral—that our minds may dwell in heaven where Christ is. Only the preface makes the theological point that the purpose of Christ's ascension is to make us partake of his divinity—a point reinforced in the *communicantes*, which says that the substance of frail human nature is glorified with Christ's enthronement at the right hand of the Father. The addition of readings from Ephesians, Hebrews, and the end of Matthew's gospel in the postconciliar Lectionary interjects strong doctrinal components into the formulary, doctrinal components reflected in the new prayers and preface of the Missal of Paul VI. This progression from narrative to doctrine culminates in the three presidential prayers of the vigil Mass added in the 2002 *Missale Romanum* and conserved in the 2008 one.

C. THE VIGIL MASS OF THE 2008 MISSAL

The collect of the vigil Mass is based on that of the Mass *in Ascensa Domini* in the Old Gelasian (GeV 572). The Gelasian prayer, however, is addressed to Christ, whereas the one in MR 2002 and MR 2008 is addressed to the Father. This required changing "your promise" to "his promise." Like the collect in RM 1962, now an alternate at the day Mass, this one begins by recalling the narrative in Acts 1:9 that Christ "ascended to the heavens / as the Apostles looked on." It then asks that "in accordance with his promise, / we may be worthy for him to live with us always on earth, / and we with him in heaven." This is not the moral or psychological request of that other collect, now translated "that we . . . may in spirit dwell already in heavenly realms," but an ontological and ecclesial one based on the Lord's promise in Matthew 28:20 to remain with us always, on his declaration in John 14:2 of having prepared a place for us that "where I am, there you may be also," and on his desire expressed in John 17:24 that those given him by the Father "may be with me where I am."

The prayer over the offerings is an adaptation of the secret of the Sunday within the octave of the Ascension in the 1739 Paris Missal (MP 1493). It is inspired mainly by the Letter to the Hebrews, as the title "High Priest" applied to Christ would lead us to expect. It declares that the "Only Begotten Son, our High Priest, / is seated everliving at your right hand to intercede for us." Being seated at the right hand of God, of course, comes from Psalm 109:1. The rest is a citation of Hebrews 7:25. The plea "[g]rant that we may approach with confidence the throne of grace / and there obtain your mercy" is likewise from Hebrews, this time Hebrews 4:16, words also heard in the second reading of Good Friday in the postconciliar Lectionary. In accord with Hebrews 8:1 and 12:2, the prayer pictures Jesus "seated at the right hand of God" to be seated on one throne with God the Father. This is also the understanding of Leo the Great. In his first ascension sermon he says that Jesus "preserved the wounds of the nails and the lance" to show that the human nature "which had lain in the tomb was to take its place on the throne of God the Father."[14] He continues by emphasizing that the exaltation of Jesus did not stop "until this same nature was received at the seat of the eternal Father, to be associated on the throne of the glory of that one to whose nature it was joined in the Son."[15]

The prayer after Communion is also from the Sunday within the octave of the Ascension in the 1738 Paris Missal (MP 1495). It consists of two petitions, each drawn from the Letter to the Hebrews.[16] The first asks that the gifts received in Communion "kindle in our hearts a longing for the heavenly homeland." This is drawn from Hebrews 11:14-16, in which the author, after recalling the faith of Abel, Enoch, Noah, and Abraham, states that they were "seeking a homeland" (11:14), "a heavenly one" (11:16). The second petition is that the gifts "cause us to press forward, following in the Savior's footsteps, / to the place where for our sake he entered before us." In Latin the words "where for our sake he entered" are *quo praecursor pro nobis introivit*. Unfortunately, the word *praecursor*, meaning "precursor" or "forerunner," is untranslated. If it were, the prayer would ask that the gifts make us press forward to where the Savior "has entered on our behalf *as forerunner*." The word "forerunner" here refers to Hebrews 6:20, which states that we hope to enter the inner shrine "where Jesus, a forerunner on our behalf, has entered" as High Priest—*ubi praecursor pro nobis introivit Iesus*. Although the original prayer in the Paris Missal cited Hebrews 6:20 exactly, *qui praecursor pro nobis introivit Iesus*, compilers of the formulary in RM 2002 changed *Iesus* to *Salvator*, Savior.

The entrance antiphon of the vigil Mass is also taken from the Paris Missal (MP 1473), this time from the Mass of the Ascension. It is Psalm 67:33, 35:

> You kingdoms of the earth, sing to God;

---

[14] Leo the Great, *Sermon* 74, 3, in FC 93, 324.

[15] Leo the Great, *Sermon* 74, 4, in FC 93, 324.

[16] Surprisingly, Anthony Ward gives no biblical sources for this prayer in "Ascension and Pentecost," 224–25.

praise the Lord, who ascends above the highest heavens;
his majesty and might are in the clouds.

This is almost the same text as the communion antiphon in RM 1962, except that the latter lacks verse 35, "his majesty and might are in the clouds," and declares that the Lord ascends above the heaven of heavens *ad Orientem*, "to the East," a phrase in both the Vulgate and the *Nova Vulgata* but omitted from the entrance antiphon in both the Paris Missal and MR 2002. That Christ ascended to the East was important because it enabled Christians to maintain that he would also return from there and to pray facing East in expectation of that event. The communion antiphon is Hebrews 10:12, "Christ, offering a single sacrifice for sins, is seated forever at God's right hand." This text fits perfectly with the prayer over the offerings and the prayer after Communion, both of which are derived from the Letter to the Hebrews.

Except for the opening words of the collect, which refer to the ascension story in Acts, the three presidential prayers and the communion antiphon of the vigil Mass are drawn either from the promise at the end of Matthew's gospel or from a variety of passages from the Letter to the Hebrews. The themes of Christ's sacrifice, enthronement at the right hand of God, intercession on our behalf, and abiding presence on earth are more frequent than his being taken up to heaven. In the texts of the vigil Mass, then, doctrinal aspects of the feast have largely supplanted narratives of the event.

The solemn blessing for the Ascension of the Lord synthesizes the key images and themes of the two Masses of the solemnity: that Christ's piercing of the heavens unlocks the way for us "to ascend to where he is," that he will be seen again "when he comes as Judge," and that though "he is seated / with the Father in his majesty," he fulfills his promise to stay with us "until the end of time."

Chapter 8

Pentecost Sunday

A. VIGIL OF PENTECOST IN THE 1962 MISSAL

According to the general rubrics of the 1962 Roman Missal, no. 76c, the Mass of this vigil inaugurates the third subdivision of the Easter season, the octave of Pentecost, which runs until None inclusive of the following Saturday. The orations, preface, proper *communicantes*, and *Hanc igitur* of this Mass all come from a formulary in the Sacramentary of Pope Hadrian (H 520–25) preceded by the phrase *post ascensum fontis*, "after coming up from the font," and hence they were originally meant for a eucharistic celebration following the conferral of baptism at a nocturnal vigil modeled on that of Holy Saturday.

In the Tridentine Missal of 1570 the vigil has six Old Testament readings, called prophecies, all taken from Holy Saturday. Three are followed by tracts, also taken from Holy Saturday. After the readings is a procession to the font where baptismal water is blessed using formulas from Holy Saturday. Ministers wear purple vestments for the vigil, as on Holy Saturday, then change to red for the Mass. During the Gloria bells are rung, as on Holy Saturday. In sum, the Pentecost Vigil duplicates that of Holy Saturday but without the light service. Texts for the vigil together with those of the Mass continue to appear in subsequent editions of the Missal, though the service took place early Saturday morning and no one was baptized at it. No. 16 of the instruction on the reform of Holy Week, issued on November 16, 1955, ordered the vigil to be omitted and the Mass to begin with an introit taken from Wednesday of the fourth week of Lent, *Cum sanctificatus fuero in vobis*. Consequently, the 1962 Roman Missal no longer prints texts for the vigil, only those for the Mass.

Every prayer, reading, and chant of the Mass, except the Alleluia, mentions the Holy Spirit, frequently in connection with baptism or an aspect of it, such as cleansing or illumination. The introit antiphon, from Ezekiel 36:23-26, though recent, is a splendid overture to the entire Mass. In it the Lord declares, "I will pour upon you clean water and you shall be cleansed from all your filthiness: and I will give you a new spirit." The collect calls upon God by the illumination of the Holy Spirit to "confirm the hearts of those who have been born again by thy grace." The secret and post-Communion both ask God to "cleanse our hearts" by either the light or the infusion of the Holy Spirit. The *Hanc igitur*, taken from Easter, intercedes for those brought "to a new birth by water and the Holy Ghost."

The epistle, Acts 19:1-8, recounts how twelve men "were baptized in the name of the Lord Jesus." Then, "when Paul had laid hands on them, the Holy Spirit came upon them." This reading would be a splendid follow-up to the vigil when it still included baptism and confirmation. Though the gospel is John 14:15-21, the promise of another Paraclete, the communion antiphon, *Ultimo festivitatis die*, is not from it but from another important Johannine episode, John 7:37-39, in which Jesus, "on the last day of the festivity," said of the believer that "out of his belly shall flow rivers of living water," with the comment of the evangelist, "Now this he said of the Spirit which they should receive who believed in him."

As a postbaptismal eucharistic celebration, all the texts of this formulary are magnificent. Only two of them, however, say anything about the Pentecost event. The preface—not proper but that of the Holy Spirit—recalls that Christ, "ascending above all the heavens and sitting at thy right hand, this day poured out the promised Holy Spirit upon the children of adoption." The proper *communicantes* of the Roman Canon makes memory of "the most holy day of Pentecost, wherein the Holy Ghost appeared to the Apostles in countless tongues." The preface alone connects the outpouring of the Spirit with the ascension of Jesus. Neither of them mentions the resurrection.

B. MASS OF PENTECOST SUNDAY IN THE 1962 MISSAL

The centerpiece of this day's Eucharist is the epistle, Acts 2:1-11, recounting the spectacular eruption of the Holy Spirit upon the disciples gathered together in Jerusalem for the Jewish feast of Pentecost, fifty days after Passover: "Suddenly from heaven there came a sound like the rush of a violent wind, and it filled the entire house where they were sitting. Divided tongues, as of fire, appeared among them, and a tongue rested on each of them. All of them were filled with the Holy Spirit and began to speak in other languages, as the Spirit gave them ability."

The communion antiphon, *Factus est repente*, synthesizes the epistle. "Its quick syllabic texture and its abruptly rebounding leap of a fifth unmistakably suggest the sudden rush of wind that signifies the Holy Spirit," remarks James McKinnon.[1] "Suddenly there came a sound from heaven, as of a mighty wind," it sings, "and they were all filled with the Holy Ghost, speaking of the wonderful works of God." The opening words of the introit, *Spiritus Domini*, "The Spirit of the Lord hath filled the whole world," are applicable to the universal spread of the Gospel through the apostolic preaching, but they come from Wisdom 1:7, not from Acts. The preface and *communicantes* are the same as those of the vigil and relate, respectively, that Christ poured out the Spirit after ascending to heaven and being seated at the right hand of the Father, and that the Spirit appeared to the apostles in countless tongues.

Despite the dramatic character of the Pentecost story, the three sacerdotal orations, all from the *Hadrianum*, pass over it in silence. Nor do any of them link the outpouring of the Spirit to the resurrection and ascension of Christ or to the foundation of the church and the inauguration of its mission. They focus rather on the interior action of the Spirit within the individual, purifying and enlightening the heart. The collect (H 526), for example, recalls that on this day God "taught the hearts of the faithful by the light of the Holy Spirit." The secret (H 527) and post-Communion (H 531)—which are the same as those of the vigil—ask God to "cleanse our hearts by the light of the Holy Spirit" and to "render them fruitful by the inward sprinkling of his dew."

Although the verse from Psalm 103:30 sung with the Alleluia is cosmic in scope, asking the Spirit to "renew the face of the earth," the invocation that follows it looks inward: "Come, O Holy Spirit, fill the hearts of thy faithful and kindle in them the fire of thy love." The sequence, *Veni, Sancte Spiritus*, dating from the late twelfth century,[2] continues along similar lines, calling the Spirit "the soul's delightful guest" and entreating him, "O most blessed light divine, shine within these hearts of thine and our inmost being fill." This view, though legitimate, is at odds with the epistle's portrayal of the Spirit of God as an overwhelming public and ecclesial power, impelling recipients to set forth to the ends of the earth, fearlessly preaching and bearing witness. In the gospel, John 14:23-31, Jesus assures his disciples at the Last Supper that the Paraclete, to be sent by the Father, would call to their minds all that he said to them.

---

[1] McKinnon, *Advent Project*, 7.
[2] A. J. Kinnirney, "*Veni, Sancte Spiritus*," NCE 14 (1967) 600.

C. VIGIL MASS IN THE MISSAL OF PAUL VI

Already in 1970 the first typical edition of the Missal of Paul VI abolished the Vigil of Pentecost as it existed in the previous Missal, a Mass on Saturday morning, and replaced it with a Mass meant for Saturday evening, a vigil Mass in the postconciliar sense, containing different orations and readings, a proper preface, and some new chants. No longer a Eucharist following baptism and confirmation, there are fewer references to these sacraments, to cleansing, and to illumination. The collect of the 1962 Missal, asking God to confirm the hearts of those born again, is kept as an alternate that could be used if there are candidates for initiation on this day. But the introit from Ezekiel 36:22-26, promising clean water and a new spirit, is gone, as is the epistle from Acts 19:1-8, describing the twelve men being baptized and subsequently receiving the Holy Spirit through the imposition of hands. The *Hanc igitur* of Easter, interceding for those reborn of water and the Holy Spirit, is also gone. The obvious logic here is that, unless preceded by baptism, a Mass formulary cannot be postbaptismal. And in any case, baptism is administered no longer before Mass but *during* it.

Another noticeable difference between the two vigils is the reduction of references to the internal action of the Holy Spirit within the hearts of individuals. This is accomplished by providing three presidential orations and a preface that better reflect the Pentecost event described in Acts 2:1-11.[3] The new collect is the first in the Gelasian Mass for Pentecost Sunday (GeV 637). Alluding to the dispersal of peoples and confusion of languages at Babel, it asks that

> from out of the scattered nations
> the confusion of many tongues
> may be gathered by heavenly grace
> into one great confession of your name.[4]

---

[3] As was just noted, the collect of the 1962 Missal is kept as an alternate at the vigil Mass in the Missal of Paul VI. The other two prayers in the 1962 vigil, which are the same as those of Pentecost Sunday, together with the 1962 collect of Pentecost Sunday, appear in the first votive Mass of the Holy Spirit in the Missal of Paul VI. Since none of them refer to the Pentecost event, they function well in their new context.

[4] Since the prayer does not ask that the scattered nations be gathered into one *church*, Dom Philippe Rouillard considers it "particularly ecumenical." See his " 'Le vent souffle où il veut': Les messes de la Pentecôte dans le Missel romain," *Liturgie* 149 (2010) 129.

The prayer over the offerings opens with a grand epiclesis taken largely from the Sacramentary of Gellone (G 1772): "Pour out upon these gifts the blessing of your Spirit, we pray, O Lord." Then in words from V 1262 it prays that the message of salvation "may shine forth for the whole world," a possible allusion to the universality of the apostolic preaching. The new preface, which combines parts of two Pentecost prefaces in the Old Gelasian (GeV 634 and 641), also tells how the Holy Spirit,

> as the Church came to birth,
> opened to all peoples the knowledge of God
> and brought together the many languages of the earth
> in profession of the one faith.

The prayer after Communion, "economical in expression and stylishly crafted,"[5] is from the Sacramentary of Bergamo (B 775). It desires "that we may always be aflame with the same Spirit / whom you wondrously poured out on your Apostles." The new entrance antiphon, on the other hand, draws attention to the very element these prayers are intended to displace: "The love of God has been poured into our hearts / through the Spirit of God dwelling within us, alleluia" (Rom 5:5; 8:8).

As a gospel reading for the vigil Mass, John 7:37-39 replaces John 14:15-21. It begins with the words "On the last day of the festival, the great day . . ." In the context of John's gospel this refers to the feast of Booths or Tabernacles mentioned at the beginning of chapter 7. But the Lectionary wants us to understand it as Pentecost, the last of the fifty days of Easter, the period that the new collect presents as a divinely willed symbolic number, declaring that God "willed the Paschal Mystery / to be encompassed as a sign in fifty days."

On this "last day of the festival," the biblical text continues, Jesus invites anyone thirsty to come to him and drink, promising that rivers of living water will flow "out of his heart." The problem is to know whose heart Jesus is referring to, his own or that of the believer. Jesus' remark to the Samaritan woman in John 4:14 is invoked in support of the latter, but opinion is divided and different Bibles translate accordingly.[6] We saw that the communion antiphon in RM

---

[5] Ward, "Ascension and Pentecost," 238.
[6] See Vawter in JBC 63:105 with bibliography.

1962, *Ultimo festivitatis die*, consists of these verses. It reflects the view that the waters flow from the heart—or belly—of the believer: "He that believeth in me, out of his belly shall flow rivers of living water." Though the communion antiphon in the Missal of Paul VI begins in the same way as its counterpart in RM 1962, it limits itself to saying that "On the last day of the festival, Jesus stood and cried out: / If anyone thirsts, let him come to me and drink." By omitting the reference to rivers of living water, it avoids having to take sides about the one from whom they flow.

The final sentence of the gospel text is probably the reason why the passage was selected for this occasion. The evangelist comments that Jesus "said this about the Spirit, which believers in him were to receive; for as yet there was no Spirit because Jesus was not yet glorified." The words are of great importance theologically because they show that the bestowal of the Spirit is the consequence of Christ's glorification, whether understood as his death, his resurrection, or his enthronement at the Father's right hand. They are important liturgically because they link the solemnity of Pentecost with the paschal Triduum and the rest of Easter Time, especially Ascension. In applying "the last day of the festival, the great day," to Pentecost, the Lectionary rightly makes the outpouring of the Spirit and ecclesial communion in his life to be the goal toward which the whole paschal event is directed and in which it is perfected. The new preface, in giving thanks to the Father, declares that

> *bringing your Paschal Mystery to completion,*
> you bestowed the Holy Spirit today
> on those you made your adopted children
> by uniting them to your Only Begotten Son." (emphasis mine)

It then calls the Spirit the *principio nascentis Ecclesiae*, "the principle of the church coming to birth" (trans. mine). Once again the trinitarian and ecclesial dimensions of the paschal mystery shine forth.

For the New Testament reading the Lectionary passes over the one in RM 1962, the baptism of the twelve men in Acts 19:1-8, and chooses instead Romans 8:22-27, which states that "we have the first fruits of the Spirit," who "helps us in our weakness" and "intercedes with sighs too deep for words." This reading, says the general introduction to the Lectionary, no. 102, "shows the actual working of the Holy Spirit in the Church."

The Lectionary offers a choice between four possible readings from the Old Testament. The introduction to the Lectionary, no. 103, states that "any one of them may be used, in order to bring out the many aspects of Pentecost." The first is Genesis 11:1-9, the scattering of the peoples and the confusion of their language at Babel. The second is Exodus 19:3-8a, 16-20b, the covenant at Sinai, followed by the Lord's descent in thunder and lightning, fire and smoke to dictate the law. The third is Ezekiel 37:1-14, the prophet's invocation of the breath of God to make dry bones live. The fourth is Joel 2:28-32, the Lord's promise to pour out his spirit on all flesh and provoke visions and dreams in young and old. These readings go extremely well with each other[7] but evoke nothing of note in the New Testament reading or the gospel of the vigil Mass. Imagery and themes in all of them are readily connected to the outpouring of the Spirit at Pentecost and its impact on the apostolic community. Surprisingly, however, the story of Pentecost is not read at the vigil Mass. This is as puzzling as would be an Epiphany Mass without the story of the magi. The vast majority of Catholics who participate in the vigil Mass on Saturday evening will not go back on Sunday for the Mass during the day when Acts 2:1-11 is read and so will not hear about the startling episode that gives its name to this solemnity.

The third typical edition of the Missal of Paul VI permits all four of the above-mentioned Old Testament passages to be read at what it calls an extended form of the vigil Mass, which may also be combined with Vespers. As at the Paschal Vigil, each reading is followed by a responsorial psalm, a silent prayer, and a concluding oration.[8] The 1988 circular letter *Paschalis Sollemnitatis*, no. 107, encourages the extended form but remarks that it "is not baptismal as at the Easter Vigil, but is one of urgent prayer, after the example of the apostles and disciples, who persevered together in prayer with Mary, the mother of Jesus, as they awaited the Holy Spirit."

D. MASS DURING THE DAY IN THE MISSAL OF PAUL VI

As is the case in RM 1962, "For the Mass of Pentecost itself," says the introduction to the Lectionary, no. 102, "the account in the Acts of

---

[7] As the comments of Geoffrey F. Wood in JBC 25:17 illustrate.

[8] For the sources of these prayers, see Anthony Ward, SM, "The Orations after the Pentecost Vigil in the 2008 Reprint of the 'Missale Romanum,'" EL 124 (2010) 354–82.

the Apostles of the great occurrence on Pentecost day is taken as the first reading." This is altogether to be expected. The gospel reading, continues the introduction in no. 102, "is a remembrance of Jesus bestowing his Spirit on the disciples on the evening of Easter day." The passage is John 20:19-23, an ingenious choice because it juxtaposes the two great outpourings of the Spirit, different though they be in their effects.[9] In this way Pentecost is linked to Easter, the conferral of the Spirit to the resurrection. The Lectionary offers as optional gospels John 15:26-27; 16:12-15 for Year B and John 14:15-16, 23b-26 for Year C. Their use is not advisable. They relate not bestowals of the Spirit but promises of Jesus to do so and, being spoken at the Last Supper, fail to connect the Pentecost event with the resurrection.

Of the second New Testament reading the introduction to the Lectionary, no. 102, says, "The texts from the Apostle Paul bring out the effect of the action of the Spirit in the life of the Church." The preferred reading is 1 Corinthians 12:3b-7, 12-13. Paul's declaration that "there are varieties of gifts but the same Spirit" harmonizes well with what the first reading describes the Spirit imparting to the apostles at Pentecost. And his observation that many people, radically different from each other—Jews and Greeks, slaves and free—were made one through baptism "in the one Spirit" recalls the astonishment of the crowd at Pentecost hearing a multitude of diverse peoples under the impulse of the Spirit united in praising the wonderful work of God.

The Lectionary allows as an optional second reading in Year B Galatians 5:16-25, which is about the opposition between the works of the flesh and the fruit of the Spirit. This one is not nearly as felicitous as 1 Corinthians 12:3b-7, 12-13 in Year A. Besides not mentioning baptism, it does not evoke much about the extraordinary happening on Pentecost reported in Acts. On the other hand, the Lectionary's permission to use Romans 8:8-17 as the second reading in Year C is excellent. Less an echo of the Pentecost story in the first reading, it is a wonderful prelude to the conferral of the Spirit on the evening of the resurrection in the gospel because it affirms that the Spirit of the Father is the agent of the resurrection—Christ's as well as ours. "If the Spirit of him who

---

[9] "The Pentecost of Acts and the risen One's first giving of the Spirit are evidently not the same reality" (Dillon-Fitzmyer, JBC 45:17). For example, the bestowal of the Spirit in John 20:22 does not provoke extraordinary phenomena or lead to missionary activity.

raised Jesus from the dead dwells in you," Paul says, "he who raised Christ from the dead will give life to your mortal bodies also through his Spirit that dwells in you." The trinitarian dimension of the resurrection and of Christian existence again comes to the fore.

The next verses about the Spirit being "a Spirit of adoption" lead easily to faith and baptism, which make us "children of God" and "joint heirs with Christ." From this flows the moral imperative of being witnesses who "suffer with him so that we may also be glorified with him." All things considered, of the three possible second readings this one may be the best.

The Missal of Paul VI replaces the presidential prayers of RM 1962, two of which were duplicates of the Saturday morning Mass, with formulas from ancient sources shaped by reflection on the promise and gift of the Spirit in John and Acts, thereby producing greater correspondence between the readings and the orations as well as between what the feast celebrates and what the church seeks in prayer. The collect is the second oration in the Mass of Pentecost in the Old Gelasian (GeV 638). Recognizing that in the event commemorated God sanctifies the "whole Church in every people and nation," the prayer asks him to

> pour out . . . the gifts of the Holy Spirit
> across the face of the earth
> and, with the divine grace that was at work
> when the Gospel was first proclaimed,
> fill now once more the hearts of believers.

Again we encounter the word "hearts," found so frequently in the prayers and other texts of the preconciliar Missal. This oration, however, asks not for internal purification or illumination but that the "hearts of believers" be filled with the same Spirit that propelled the apostles to proclaim everywhere what God did through Jesus and to witness to it by their lives. It asks, in other words, that the original effusion of the Spirit be actualized in the faithful of this time and place.

The prayer over the gifts, from the Pentecost Mass in the Sacramentary of Bergamo (B 772), asks that the Holy Spirit "reveal to us more abundantly / the hidden mystery of this sacrifice / and graciously lead us into all truth." This petition is founded on two promises Christ made about the Holy Spirit at the Last Supper: that the Spirit would teach us everything (John 14:26) and guide us into all truth (John

16:13). The content of the prayer after Communion is entirely ecclesial. Recalling that God lavishes "heavenly gifts" upon the church, it asks him to safeguard the grace given. Then, looking to the eschatological future, it prays that

> the gift of the Holy Spirit poured out upon her
> may retain all its force
> and that this spiritual food
> may gain her abundance of eternal redemption.

The reference to eternal redemption is taken from V 491 and inserted into the framework of a seventh-century Mozarabic prayer (LMS 793).

Anthony Ward summarizes by saying that the formulary for the Pentecost Sunday Mass "is completely renewed with respect to the preconciliar Missal, whose texts had gravitated over the centuries to being above all a votive Mass of the Holy Spirit, very fine, but shorn of a clear reference to the event of Pentecost and its relation to the paschal mystery which in liturgical terms the day's celebration served to conclude. To remedy this, recourse was had to prestigious ancient texts for Pentecost in the *Gelasianum vetus*, the ancient Ambrosian tradition and that of the Hispanic-Mozarabic liturgy."[10]

---

[10] Ward, "Ascension and Pentecost," 243.

General Conclusion

A. QUALITY OF READINGS, PREFACES, AND PRAYERS

Biblical readings in the current Lectionary are drawn from every book of both the Old and the New Testament. Distributed over a three-year cycle on Sundays and a two-year cycle on weekdays and arranged according to principles clearly enunciated in a general introduction, they are far more abundant and systematically organized than those in any previous lectionary or missal, Roman or non-Roman, ancient or modern. Without doubt the 1969 Order of Readings for Mass, revised in 1981, is the masterpiece of the reform of the eucharistic liturgy following the Second Vatican Council.

Astonishing growth in the repertoire of prefaces since the council is another wonderful achievement. The 1962 Missal has a mere fifteen prefaces. The Missal of Pius V in 1570 has but ten. No feast or season has more than one. Advent, many feasts, and special occasions such as weddings, ordinations, and dedications of churches have none. Some are used only once a year; others are repeated every day for entire seasons. By way of contrast, the third typical edition of the Missal of Paul VI contains some ninety prefaces, not counting the four variable beginnings of the Eucharistic Prayer for Various Needs and the unchanging prefaces of Eucharistic Prayer IV and the two eucharistic prayers for reconciliation. The index groups them under five headings: liturgical times, feasts and mysteries of the Lord, feasts of saints, ritual Masses, and various celebrations. Under the first heading ten liturgical times are distinguished, each having between two and nine prefaces.

Though focused on a specific event or aspect of salvation history, as is characteristic of the Roman tradition, each strives to include or at least allude to the whole of that history whenever possible. Taken together, the prefaces amount to a vast expansion of motives for giving thanks to the Lord around the eucharistic table, the large majority of which were hitherto not articulated. Filled with images and phrases taken directly from Sacred Scripture, but part of the eucharistic prayer itself and not a prelude to it, they show how proclamation of the Word culminates in celebration of the sacrament.

The quality of other presidential prayers is also significantly enhanced in the reformed Missal, and the addition of weekday Masses for the Advent, Christmas, and Easter seasons has greatly increased their number. With generic prayers eliminated and doublets drastically reduced, collects almost always reflect the content of the feast or season for which they are intended, and other prayers—those over the offerings, after Communion, and over the people—frequently do the same. With very few exceptions, replacements are drawn from the Old Gelasian Sacramentary or occasionally an Ambrosian or Mozarabic source and represent an astounding reappropriation of the euchological wealth of earlier centuries to augment the admittedly diminished deposit handed down in the Sacramentary of Pope Hadrian.

B. CENTRALITY OF THE PASCHAL MYSTERY

The readings, prefaces, and presidential prayers alone suffice to show the superiority of the Missal of Paul VI over its predecessor, of the ordinary form over the extraordinary form. Much more fundamental, however, is the emergence of the paschal mystery as the dominant theological category, imparting depth, coherence, and direction to the entire period of Lent, Triduum, and Easter Time. This explains the structure of the readings in the Lectionary as well as the choice and content of the new prefaces and prayers in the Missal, and it is another reason for the superiority of the ordinary form over the extraordinary one.

Since the 1969 Universal Norms on the Liturgical Year and the Calendar, Easter Sunday no longer follows the Triduum, as it does in the extraordinary form, but is part of it. Nor is it alone *Pascha*. Friday of the Passion is also paschal in character. The opening prayer on that day in the reformed Missal declares that Christ, "by the shedding of his Blood, / established the Paschal Mystery." In the ordinary form, then, *Pascha* is the entire Triduum: a paschal Triduum, all three days of which celebrate the passion of the Lord as his passage to fullness of life with the Father beyond the reach of death. This is the apex of the liturgical year. From it Lent and Easter Time derive their identity.

For forty days, at least in principle, Lent prepares for *Pascha*. For fifty days, understood to be but one, a single great Sunday, Easter Time prolongs it. Lent begins cleanly on Ash Wednesday with no Septuagesima preceding it. Easter ends cleanly on Pentecost with no octave following it. On the first day of Lent, when blessing the faithful marked with ashes, the priest prays that they may "come with minds made pure / to celebrate the Paschal Mystery." And at the vigil Mass on the last day of Easter he acknowledges that God "willed the

Paschal Mystery / to be encompassed as a sign in fifty days." The paschal mystery even links the palm procession on the Sunday before Easter with the reading of the passion at the Mass on that day, for the priest explains that "it was to accomplish this mystery" that Christ "entered his own city of Jerusalem."

Clearly, then, the paschal mystery is what binds together the readings, prayers, and prefaces of Lent, Triduum, and Easter Time in the postconciliar books. The 1962 Missal has no such overarching vision. It has no Triduum distinct from Holy Week, which is still Lent, and its Easter is Easter *week*—the Sundays between it and Pentecost being Sundays after Easter.

C. REINTEGRATION OF RITES OF INITIATION

Another reason for the superiority of the ordinary form over the extraordinary form is celebration of the various stages of initiation rites for adults throughout Lent, on Holy Saturday morning, at the Paschal Vigil, and during Easter Time. This is because the paschal mystery reaches completion only in the Father's outpouring of the Holy Spirit to actualize sacramentally the death and resurrection of Christ, thereby giving birth to the church and nourishing it. The current preface of Pentecost Sunday, not in RM 1962, expresses this when, giving thanks to the Father, it says,

> bringing your Paschal Mystery to completion,
> you bestowed the Holy Spirit today
> on those you made your adopted children
> by uniting them to your Only Begotten Son.
> This same Spirit, as the Church came to birth,
> brought together the many languages of the earth
> in profession of the one faith.

In keeping with the various liturgical books of the ordinary form, candidates who, after an extended period of preliminary formation, are judged ready for baptism at the vigil are officially chosen, and their names are enrolled on the First Sunday of Lent. Henceforth, they are no longer catechumens but the elect. They undergo scrutinies and exorcisms on the Third, Fourth, and Fifth Sundays of Lent. On these Sundays the gospels of Year A are read: the Samaritan woman, the man born blind, and the raising of Lazarus—episodes that are the basis of proper prefaces for each of these days. The Creed is presented to them during the third week and the Lord's Prayer during the fifth week.

Depending on circumstances, they may be invited to participate in preparatory rites on Holy Saturday morning. At the Paschal Vigil they are baptized, confirmed, and receive Holy Communion for the first time after being told that the Eucharist is "the climax of their initiation and the center of the whole Christian life."[1] Postbaptismal catechesis or mystagogy follows at Masses on the Sundays of Easter Time, on which, again, the readings are those of Year A. These celebrations are obviously an integral part of the Missal and Lectionary of Paul VI. The reason they are not in the 1962 *Missale Romanum* is that the Rite of Christian Initiation of Adults appeared for the first time in Latin only in 1966, four years after the publication of that Missal. Commitment to the extraordinary form, therefore, means foregoing the incalculable wealth of the RCIA, another masterpiece of the postconciliar reform.

D. FROM THE BIRTH OF CHRIST TO HIS BAPTISM

"After the annual celebration of the Paschal Mystery," states no. 32 of the Universal Norms, "the Church has no more ancient custom than celebrating the memorial of the Nativity of the Lord and of his first manifestations." Mass formularies of the Nativity and Epiphany of the Lord, like those of most other solemnities, are very similar in the two missals under comparison. But because of more readings, improvements in the prayers, and two new prefaces of the Nativity, the ordinary form is clearly superior. It also provides proper Masses for December 29–31 as well as for the weekdays from January 2 until the Baptism of the Lord, thus eliminating the repetitions in RM 1962 and offering a large collection of hitherto unknown prayers, mostly from the *Rotulus* of Ravenna and hence doctrinally profound. The reformed Missal also restores the ancient Roman tradition of dedicating January 1 to the divine motherhood of Mary, of which only traces remain in the collect and post-Communion of the 1962 Missal.

The most striking originality of the ordinary form, however, is celebration on the Sunday following January 6 of the Baptism of the Lord as a feast with proper readings, prayers, preface, and chants. Never before in the history of the Roman Rite had this event, marking the inauguration of Jesus' public ministry, received such recognition. But with the adoption of the three-year Sunday Lectionary, it was only natural to include with all requisite solemnity the episode with which

---

[1] RM 2011, Easter Vigil, rubric 64.

the body of the three Synoptic Gospels begins. In 1960 a calendar reform accorded it a commemoration on January 13, but Mass texts remained those of what was until then the octave of Epiphany. So do they remain in the extraordinary form.

E. THE ADVENT OF THE LORD IN HUMILITY AND IN GLORY

With the addition of weekday Masses the number of prayers and readings in the postconciliar Advent has expanded dramatically. The Lectionary includes a broad range of passages from Isaiah and other prophets, accounts of the preaching and witness of John the Baptist, and, especially from December 17 to 24, gospel narratives leading up to the birth of Jesus—virtually the entire corpus of biblical texts, remote and proximate, pertinent to the incarnation. Collects from the *Rotulus* of Ravenna in the latter part of the season provide ever-fresh expressions of wonder at the union of divinity and humanity in the person of Christ. A double thematic weaves through other prayers: recollection of the Lord's coming in humility to accomplish the plan of salvation and expectation of his coming in glory to reward with eternal life those who await him. The same two themes are in the first of the two new prefaces, meant to be used from the first Sunday to December 16. The second preface, meant for the last eight days, voices anticipated joy at celebrating the Nativity.

The readings, prefaces, and prayers in the ordinary form admirably express what the Universal Norms, no. 39, wants the season to be "a time of preparation for the Solemnities of Christmas, in which the First Coming of the Son of God to humanity is remembered, and likewise a time when, by remembrance of this, minds and hearts are led to look forward to Christ's Second Coming at the end of time." These texts surpass by far the Advent of the extraordinary form that contains Masses for just the four Sundays, three Ember Days, and morning of December 24, has no proper preface, and aims only at preparing for Christmas.

In short, the third typical edition of the Roman Missal of Paul VI and its companion, the Lectionary, are treasures of inestimable value. Together with the Rite of Christian Initiation of Adults, they represent the very best of the liturgical reforms generated by the Second Vatican Council. One of the most urgent pastoral challenges facing the church today is to raise the *ars celebrandi* of the ordinary form to the same level of excellence as these books.

Index

Communion, 159n6, 165–66, 190–
94, 195–96, 202n58
fast, 13, 78–79, 84, 85, 201
intercessory prayers, 174, 183–85,
190, 205
Good Shepherd, 256–57, 258, 262, 264,
267–68, 269

Hadrianum. See Sacramentary of Pope
Hadrian
Haec dies, 243, 247, 251, 259
Hanc igitur, 161, 214–15, 232, 243, 247,
250–51, 259–60, 291, 292, 294
Hellriegel, Martin, 103n1
Hesbert, René-Jean, 20, 21
High Priest, 147, 151, 169, 179, 194,
278, 287, 288–89
Holy Name of Jesus. *See* naming of
Jesus
Holy Thursday, 78, 144
Reservation, 159, 164–66, 174, 195
Thursday of Holy Week, 143, 149,
157, 129–54, 167
Thursday of the Lord's Supper,
79, 85, 89, 129, 130, 131, 139,
158–73, 177, 201, 213
Holy Saturday, 78, 84, 104, 156, 174,
196–231, 232, 234, 241, 249, 258,
275, 291, 303–4
Holy Week, xix, 77, 78, 86n20, 88–90,
101, 103–54, 155–58, 167, 172, 177,
183, 197–98, 231–32, 233, 291, 303

Ignatius of Antioch, 4, 5n10
Improperia. See Reproaches
in albis, 241, 242, 243, 246, 248,
249n17, 250, 254, 257, 258, 259
initiation, 93, 102, 151, 216, 227, 279,
294; *see also* Rite of Christian Initiation of Adults *and* sacraments
of initiation

Jackson, Pamela, 17n51, 93n34, 155n1

Jeffery, Peter, 163n10
Jerome, 7, 187
John the Baptist, 18, 19, 23, 24, 27, 28,
29, 35, 40, 41, 48, 53, 71, 72, 74,
228, 276, 282, 305
John Cassian, 8, 48
Johnson, Cuthbert, 30n68, 33n74,
39n81, 51n10, 56n18, 73, 74n43,
86n43, 86n21, 93n35, 118n27,
127n33, 141n59
Johnson, Maxwell E., 10–11n35,
44nn1–2, 63nn27–29, 64n31,
71n41, 79n5, 84nn15–16, 87–88,
100n43, 176n19, 239n1
Jounel, Pierre, 1n2, 12–13, 46n6, 77n1,
80, 84n18, 90n30, 105n6, 142,
242–43, 246, 255
Jungmann, Joseph A., 91n33, 191n45
Justin Martyr, 5–6

Kyrie, 19, 78, 122, 200, 210, 211, 214,
222, 233

lamb, 126, 157, 168, 173, 176, 177, 192
Lamb (Jesus), 157, 162, 168, 176, 181,
195, 219, 221, 228, 229–30, 231,
233, 269, 276–78
Lamb of God (of liturgy), 74
Lateran Missal, 12n41, 16n49
Lent, xix, xx, 11, 12, 14, 15, 21, 77–102,
129–30, 152–53, 155–58, 167, 170,
194, 198, 200–201, 205, 211, 213,
217n81, 243, 250, 291, 302–3
Leo the Great, 13, 56, 64, 78, 83–84, 89,
107, 273, 282, 284–86, 287, 289
Leven, Benjamin, 185n30
Löw, Josef, 103n2
Lucernarium, 201, 202–4, 217–21, 231

mandatum. See footwashing
Martimort, A. G., 132n44
Mary, mother of God, 6, 8, 22, 25, 28,
29, 33, 37, 38, 46, 47, 49, 50, 54,
58–62, 63, 64, 65, 190, 272, 297, 304

paschal
Vigil, 13, 78, 101, 103, 129, 145, 156,
196–231, 234–35, 236, 239, 242,
244, 246, 253–54, 261, 272, 273,
275, 277, 297, 303–4
mystery, x, 8, 43, 82n12, 93, 94, 95,
96, 114, 115, 116, 117, 128, 129,
135, 140n57, 141, 156, 157, 162,
176, 193, 194, 208, 215, 216,
233, 235, 240, 247, 253, 258,
272, 278, 296, 300, 302–3
fast, 77, 78, 84, 150, 202, 227
candle, 200, 203, 204, 210, 211, 212,
217–21, 224, 226, 231
Paschalis Sollemnitatis, 85–86, 116,
119, 129, 148n71, 150, 165, 190,
201n57, 203, 206, 214n77, 279, 297
passion, 104, 106, 107, 114, 115, 123,
124, 125, 127, 157–58, 162–63,
172, 174, 175, 176, 180, 192–94,
195, 196, 216–17, 219, 220, 221,
224, 226, 228, 230, 232, 233–34,
237, 263, 264, 267, 268, 302–3
passio, 157, 167, 217, 219, 222, 224,
228, 233, 236
Sunday, 88, 105, 155
Passiontide, 88–90, 113, 124, 200
according to Saint Matthew, 68,
107, 113, 123, 125, 126, 127, 160
according to Saint Mark, 123, 126,
127, 160
according to Saint Luke, 123, 126,
127, 160
according to Saint John, 120, 123,
126, 173, 174, 180, 194
Passover, 24, 97–98, 99, 119–20, 126,
127, 157, 161–62, 167–68, 169,
173, 176, 177, 179, 192, 194, 202,
209, 214, 217, 219, 220, 228–29,
264, 276, 292
Paulinus of Nola, 186
penance, 16, 77–78, 81, 88, 93, 96, 98,
100, 101, 130

Pentecost, xx, 6, 12–13, 14, 15, 16, 24,
72, 239–41, 247–48, 252, 255, 256,
257–58, 259, 261, 263, 268, 270–
72, 274–75, 279, 281–82, 291–300,
302–3
Philocalian Calendar. *See* Chronograph of 354
Pontifical of the Roman Curia, 191
Pope Benedict XVI, ix, xx, 162, 168,
169, 178n22, 185, 229–30
Pope John Paul II, ix, 162
post clausum Paschae, 240, 247, 254, 258
Pseudo-Alcuin, 187
Puniet, Pierre de, 131

Quartodecimans, *quartodecima*, 176,
202
Quinquagesima, 77–78, 80, 84, 242

Ratzinger, Joseph, 54n14
reform of Holy Week, 128, 197–98,
231, 291
renewal of baptismal promises, 200,
209, 213, 214, 216, 236
renewal of priestly promises, 142,
144, 146–47, 148–50, 152, 153–54
repository, 158, 165–66, 172, 174, 192
Reproaches, 187, 189
resurrection, 4–5, 24, 32–33, 48, 49,
73, 75, 97, 104, 107, 109, 116, 117,
119, 124, 141, 155–58, 160, 162n8,
167, 168, 174–75, 176, 177, 193–94,
195–96, 196–231, 231–37, 239–40,
242, 244, 248, 249, 252–53, 254,
255–56, 259–61, 266–67, 272, 273,
274, 275, 283, 285, 286, 292, 293,
296, 298–99, 303
Righetti, Mario, 46, 88, 90n29, 105n5,
247n13
Rite of Christian Initiation of Adults
(RCIA), 93, 99–101, 102, 151n75,
209, 211, 212nn69–71, 213, 215,
248, 261, 265, 278, 303–4, 305